# HEROES A
## TWELFTH-CEl

MW01258986

Nikephoros Bryennios's history of the Byzantine Empire in the 1070s is a story of civil war and aristocratic rebellion in the midst of the Turkish conquest of Anatolia. Commonly remembered as the passive and unambitious husband of princess Anna Komnene (author of the *Alexiad*), Bryennios is revealed as a skilled author whose history draws on cultural memories of classical Roman honor and proper masculinity to evaluate the politicians of the 1070s and, by implication, exhort his twelfth-century contemporaries to honorable behavior. Bryennios's story valorizes the memory of his grandfather and other honorable, but failed, generals of the eleventh century while subtly portraying the victorious Alexios Komnenos as un-Roman. This reading of the *Material for History* sheds new light on twelfth-century Byzantine culture and politics, especially the contested accession of John Komnenos, the relationship between Bryennios's history and the *Alexiad,* and the function of cultural memories of Roman honor in Byzantium.

LEONORA NEVILLE holds the John W. and Jeanne M. Rowe Professorship in Byzantine History at the University of Wisconsin-Madison, and is the author of *Authority in Byzantine Provincial Society: 950–1100* (2004).

# HEROES AND ROMANS IN TWELFTH-CENTURY BYZANTIUM

## The Material for History *of Nikephoros Bryennios*

LEONORA NEVILLE

CAMBRIDGE UNIVERSITY PRESS

# CAMBRIDGE
## UNIVERSITY PRESS

University Printing House, Cambridge CB2 8BS, United Kingdom

Cambridge University Press is part of the University of Cambridge.

It furthers the University's mission by disseminating knowledge in the pursuit of education, learning and research at the highest international levels of excellence.

www.cambridge.org
Information on this title: www.cambridge.org/9781316628935

© Leonora Neville 2012

First published 2012
First paperback edition 2016

*A catalogue record for this publication is available from the British Library*

*Library of Congress Cataloguing in Publication data*
Neville, Leonora Alice, 1970–
Heroes and Romans in twelfth-century Byzantium : the Material for history of Nikephoros Bryennios / Leonora Neville.
pages   cm
Includes bibliographical references.
ISBN 978 1 107 00945 5
1. Bryennius, Nicephorus, ca. 1062–1137. Historiarum libri quattuor.
2. Comneni dynasty, 1081–1185.   3. Byzantine Empire – History – 1025–1081.
4. Byzantine Empire – History – Alexius I Comnenus, 1081–1118.   I. Title.
DF600.N49   2012
949.5'02 – dc23        2012012596

ISBN 978-1-107-00945-5 Hardback
ISBN 978-1-316-62893-5 Paperback

# Contents

# *Tables*

# Acknowledgments

The task of understanding Nikephoros Bryennios's history has drawn me into new areas of scholarly specialization. The gracious generosity of friends has made this far more fun than daunting. Catherine Chin provided delightful orientation and guidance in gender theory. Sarah Ferrario helped me navigate the deep waters of classical studies and ancient historiography. Sarah has read more Nikephoros than probably any other card-carrying classicist. This book is much better because of her insights and I am deeply grateful for her interest. Philip Rousseau's invitation to help with the seminar of the Center for the Study of Early Christianity at The Catholic University of America, and his invariably insightful contributions on those occasions, provided an ongoing education on methodologies for approaching ancient and medieval texts. They are treasured friends and teachers.

Nikephoros Bryennios makes for good conversation, and I have had the pleasure of discussing this project with many friends, old and new. I presented parts of this project at various fora at The Catholic University of America where I benefited from discussions with Bill Klingshirn, Kate Jansen, Janet Timbie, Sidney Griffith, Therese-Anne Druart, Lourdes Alvarez, Frank Mantello, Tom Tentler, Leslie Wookcock Tentler, Jim Riley, Jerry Muller, Jennifer Davis, Caroline Sherman, Laura Mayhall, and John Petruccione. Elizabeth Fisher commented at a colloquium on an early chapter.

This is a far better book because of the thoughtful and incisive comments of the anonymous readers for Cambridge University Press. At a later stage Anthony Kaldellis graciously read and commented on a complete draft. Kate Bush, Marin Cerchez, Dana Robinson, Irina Tamarkina and Laura Wangerin were exemplary research assistants, editors, and talking partners. Marin Cerchez compiled Appendix One. Sections of chapter 3 appeared in *Byzantine and Modern Greek Studies*, carefully edited by Ruth Macrides. A part of chapter 12 appeared in *The Byzantine World* edited by Paul Stephenson. Thanks to all for your engagement with this project and saving me from errors. Those that remain are mine alone. Nancy Ševčenko advised me on possible cover images and Sharon Gerstel graciously shared her photo from Agioi Anargyroi in Kastoria.

The final stages of writing were supported by the John and Jeanne Rowe chair of Byzantine History at the University of Wisconsin Madison. Mr. and Mrs. Rowe's understanding of the value of scholarship in the humanities and the benefits of humanities education for reflective citizenship is a welcome light in an uncertain world. They have my deep gratitude.

When I first began to work on Nikephoros Bryennios's history one of the many factors recommending the project was that it seemed like something I could work on from home while tending my newborn son. One wonders whether the subject matter has had any influence on Anselm's particularly keen interest in play sword-fighting. By the time I realized I needed to write a chapter on Anna Komnene, my daughter Evangeline Joy had arrived and was old enough to ask if my book had any princesses in it. This book is dedicated to them in gratitude for their interest, patience, and delightful presence. As ever, many thanks are due to Stephen for his unwavering support.

# *Note on citations*

Citations of classical sources follow the standard system of abbreviations in the *Oxford Classical Dictionary*. I have cited Byzantine sources according to section divisions that have been used by the *Thesaurus Linguae Graecae*. Often this is a page number in a particular edition. In some cases it is a book and chapter in the medieval text. The *TLG* seems to present the best chance Byzantinists have to develop a uniform system of citing our sources because the internet is more widely available than print editions of the texts. In the case of Nikephoros Bryennios, the references are to the section and line numbers used in the *TLG*, not to the page numbers of Gautier's edition. Appendix 1 shows the correspondences between *TLG* and Gautier's line numbering, enabling those with access to either edition to find the relevant passages. Citations to Attaleiates use the page numbers of the Bonn edition (used by the *TLG*), which are noted in the margins of the 2002 Madrid edition. Greek names are transliterated following the usage of the *Oxford Dictionary of Byzantium*. For the transliteration of Turkish names I have tried to use the form most readily found in current scholarship.

# Main characters and genealogical tables

**Eastern Roman Emperors**

1057–1059 Isaac Komnenos
1059–1067 Constantine X Doukas
1067     Eudokia (Constantine's widow)
1068–1071 Romanos Diogenes (Eudokia's second husband)
1071–1078 Michael VII Doukas (Eudokia's son)

1078–1081 Nikephoros III Botaneiates

1081–1118 Alexios I Komnenos
1118–1143 John Komnenos
1143–1180 Manuel Komnenos

**Revolts/Counter Emperors (Select)**

Romanos Diogenes October 1071–August 1072
Roussel de Bailleul 1072–1073 or 1073–1074
John Doukas (with Roussel) 1073 or 1074
Nikephoros Bryennios November 1077–late spring 1078
Nikephoros Botaneiates October 1077–early spring 1078
Nikephoros Basilakes summer 1078
Konstantios Doukas (Michael VII's brother) spring 1079
Nikephoros Melissenos fall 1080–April 1081
Alexios Komnenos February–April 1081

Komnenos Family (simplified, emperors are in **bold**)

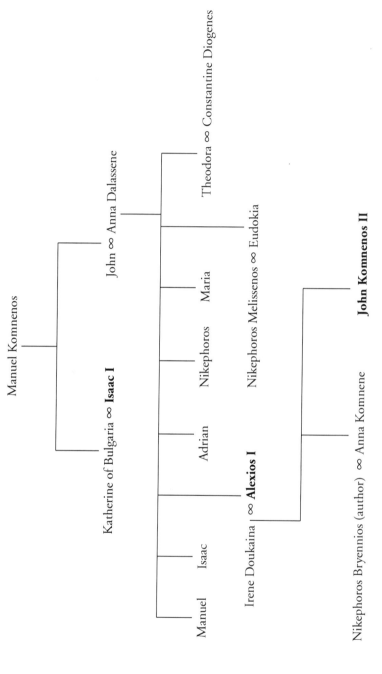

Manuel Komnenos

John ∞ Anna Dalassene

Katherine of Bulgaria ∞ **Isaac I**

Manuel

Isaac

Adrian

Nikephoros

Maria

Theodora ∞ Constantine Diogenes

Irene Doukaina ∞ **Alexios I**

Nikephoros Melissenos ∞ Eudokia

Nikephoros Bryennios (author) ∞ Anna Komnene

**John Komnenos II**

Doukas Family (simplified, emperors are in **bold**)

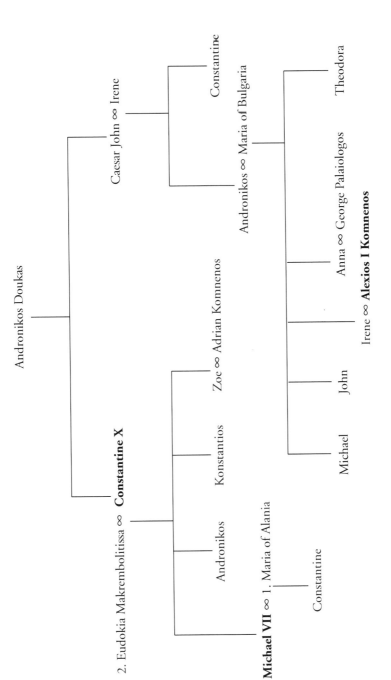

# *Note on Nikephoros and Bryennios*

Two gentlemen named Nikephoros Bryennios figure dominantly in this book. One led an unsuccessful bid to become emperor in 1077. His revolt is described in detail in the history written by his grandson and namesake. For the sake of clarity in the following I have tried to call the twelfth-century author "Nikephoros" and the eleventh-century usurper "Bryennios" or "Nikephoros Bryennios the Elder." This is my usage and not that of our source material.

# *Introduction*

The *Material for History* written by the Caesar Nikephoros Bryennios in the early twelfth century is a story of men and arms. The history is a remarkably sympathetic reading of a devastating decade in Byzantine history, 1070–1080. While Nikephoros maintains a sense of horror at the Empire's disastrous political situation, his history has remarkably few villains and a great many heroes. The laudatory characterization of nearly all the leading politicians is all the more remarkable in that Nikephoros is telling stories about men who fought each other. The most sympathetic and heroic characters in the history are three political enemies: Romanos Diogenes, John Doukas, and Nikephoros Bryennios the Elder. These men fought destructively and at times viciously. John unwillingly became a monk and Romanos and Bryennios were blinded. Romanos's blinding led to his death.

That Roman generals who were engaged in fighting other Romans while the Empire was being conquered by Turks, Pechenegs, and Normans can all emerge as heroes in Nikephoros Bryennios's history indicates that Nikephoros was a masterful rhetorician whose history is far more than a plain description of events. Such a text deserves a systematic reading as a work of literature as well as history. The present study is grounded in the conviction that all Byzantine historical texts need to be studied in their own right as coherent compositions before scholars can begin either constructing stories about the past or developing an accurate view of Byzantine culture and society. Byzantine historical texts are still too often mined for information deemed pertinent for the reconstruction of events rather than treated as coherent and complex texts. We need to understand the role that the history played in twelfth-century culture and politics before we can accept or reject its evidence about eleventh-century battles or society. My initial premise that Nikephoros's history is a well-constructed text and worthy of detailed analysis has not been disappointed. Neither has my suspicion that Nikephoros's narrative choices speak to his twelfth-century political and cultural situation in ways that should give pause to modern historians hunting for facts about the eleventh century. Here I have tried to illuminate some of Nikephoros's authorial choices and cultural attitudes, so far as they can be ascertained through the study of his history, to provide some preliminary guidance to this text and, hopefully, to bring readers to a greater appreciation of its literary and historical virtues.

Nikephoros's characterizations frequently call on classical Roman ideals of masculine virtue. A primary conclusion of the current work is that Nikephoros's sense of virtue and honor can be understood as a response to what he perceived as traditional Roman values. While scholars have identified renewed interest in classical Rome as one current in court thought in the twelfth century, Nikephoros's history has not been considered as part of this trend.[1] Nikephoros is here presented as a major proponent of classical Roman virtue and a central character in the growing engagement with Roman history in twelfth-century Constantinople.

When the text is read in light of classical Roman ideas of masculine virtue, new meanings emerge. Most significantly, the work supports a critique of Emperor Alexios Komnenos, the author's father-in-law. Alexios Komnenos is the most complex character in the book. Alexios is never a straightforward hero and some episodes admit of a highly critical reading. Like many Byzantine texts, Nikephoros's history seems designed to speak with double meanings much of the time.[2]

Nikephoros's history has long been seen as representing a shift in Byzantine culture from a more Christian, quietist ethic to a more military, 'aristocratic,' and valorous sensibility.[3] The seemingly more militaristic

---

[1] Paul Magdalino, "Aspects of Twelfth-Century Byzantine Kaiserkritik," *Speculum* 58, 2 (1983): 343–44; Ruth Macrides and Paul Magdalino, "The Fourth Kingdom and the Rhetoric of Hellenism," in *The Perception of the Past in Twelfth-Century Europe*, ed. Paul Magdalino (London: The Hambledon Press, 1992), 117–56.

[2] Panagiotis Roilos, *Aphoteroglossia: A Poetics of the Twelfth-Century Medieval Greek Novel* (Washington, DC: Center for Hellenic Studies, 2005), 20–24; Anthony Kaldellis, *Hellenism in Byzantium: The Transformations of Greek Identity and the Reception of the Classical Tradition* (Cambridge University Press, 2007), 237. The Byzantines were participating in an ancient tradition of veiled criticism: F. Ahl, "The Art of Safe Criticism in Greece and Rome," *American Journal of Philology* 105, 2 (1984): 174–208.

[3] Alexander Kazhdan and Annabel Jane Wharton, *Change in Byzantine Culture in the Eleventh and Twelfth Centuries* (Berkeley: University of California Press, 1985), 106; Kaldellis, *Hellenism*, 242; Antonio Carile, "La Hyli historias del cesare Niceforo Briennio," *Aevum* 43, 1–2 (1969): 56–87. On the 'aristocratization' of Byzantine culture in the twelfth century see: Alexander Kazhdan and Simon Franklin, *Studies on Byzantine Literature of the Eleventh and Twelfth Centuries* (Cambridge University Press, 1984), 59–60; Alexander Kazhdan, "Aristocracy and the Imperial Ideal," in *The Byzantine Aristocracy, IX–XIII Centuries*, ed. Michael Angold (Oxford: British Archaeological Reports, 1984), 43–57; George Ostrogorsky, "Observations on the Aristocracy in Byzantium," *Dumbarton Oaks Papers* 25 (1971): 1–32; Alexander Kazhdan and Giles Constable, *People and Power in Byzantium:*

and aristocratic culture of the twelfth century, with its greater emphasis on personal loyalty and martial honor, can give the superficial impression of being more 'medieval' than its predecessor. Nikephoros himself has been characterized as "a great seigneur," which draws an implicit parallel with conceptualizations of western medieval chivalric culture.[4] In some contexts the twelfth-century cultural change has been seen as a decline from the cultural traditions of the Byzantine Empire. In Ostrogorski's classic narrative, the influence of the "military aristocracy" was deeply connected with the lamentable "feudalization" of Byzantine society. Ostrogorski decried "feudalization" because he saw it as bringing economic and political decentralization.[5] While theories of Byzantine "feudalization" have become passé, the shift toward the values of the twelfth-century "military aristocracy" remains part of our understanding of twelfth-century Byzantine culture.

Rather than the implicit westernization of Ostrogorski's story however, the shift toward military culture is here seen as a response to the development and cultivation of cultural memories of classical Rome. Nikephoros's emphasis on personal military virtue can be understood as a return to traditional Roman cultural values and ideas of proper masculinity. While the emphasis on military glory bears a surface similarity to western knightly ideals, the details of Nikephoros's stories show that he was drawing on classical exempla. Nikephoros was not creating a new medieval sense of manly virtue, but recalling what he perceived to be classical Roman attitudes.

Within the field of Byzantine studies the interactions of the medieval Romans with their classical past generally have been discussed in terms of

*An Introduction to Modern Byzantine Studies* (Washington, DC: Dumbarton Oaks, 1982), 111–13; Paul Magdalino, *The Empire of Manuel I Komnenos, 1143–1180* (Cambridge University Press, 1993), 413–88; Paul Magdalino, "Byzantine Snobbery," in *The Byzantine Aristocracy, IX to XIII Centuries*, ed. Michael Angold (Oxford: British Archaeological Reports, 1984), 58–78; Paul Magdalino, "Honour among Romaioi: The Framework of Social Values in the World of Digenes Akrites and Kekaumenos," *Byzantine and Modern Greek Studies* 13 (1989): 183–218.

4 Kazhdan and Wharton, *Change*, 106.
5 "The age of the Comneni saw an intensification of the feudalizing process and those very feudal elements in the provinces, against which the tenth-century Emperors had battled with such insistence, were to become the mainstay of the new state. Alexios gave preference to those powerful and social factors which had persisted in spite of the opposition of the middle Byzantine state, and it was on these that he built his political and military organization. Therein lies the secret of his success as well as its limitations." George Ostrogorsky, *History of the Byzantine State* (New Brunswick: Rutgers University Press, 1969), 374; see also Ostrogorsky, *Pour l'histoire de la féodalité byzantine*, trans. Henri Grégoire (Brussels Éditions de l'Institut de philologie et d'histoire orientales et slaves, 1954). Kazhdan maintained the implicit connection between the 'aristocratization' of culture and the decline of the state: Kazhdan and Constable, *People and Power*, 15; Alexander Kazhdan, "State, Feudal and Private Economy in Byzantium," *Dumbarton Oaks Papers* 47 (1993): 83–100.

"renaissance" or "revival."[6] Intentionally or not, the biological metaphor of rebirth implies a period of death or decay. It also reifies culture into a somatic entity capable of birth and death. The logic of the growth, death, and new-birth model of history thus necessarily puts undue emphasis on issues of cultural continuity and disjuncture. Any perception of shifts in Byzantines' valuations of their past becomes embroiled in debate over continuity of culture and mechanics of change. The biological metaphor also carries an inherent valuation dividing history into "good," vital times and "bad" dead times.

Concepts of cultural memory provide a more flexible means of discussing the shifting relationships with the past seen throughout Byzantine history. Beyond the three-generation span of personally communicated memory, societies create cultural memory through the interplay of available textual and physical remnants of the past, the cultural memory of their elders and the context of their current society.[7] Texts, monuments, objects and stories from the past are the materials from which cultural memory evolves in response to the ever-changing environment and challenges each generation faces. The choices one generation makes about what in the past is valuable or dangerous can affect what texts and artifacts are preserved or destroyed for the future and can markedly alter their presentation and contexts. But the particular valuations and meanings one era bestows upon the detritus of history do not necessarily pass normatively into the future.

In this way Byzantine history is not the story of the repeated birth and death of a reified antiquity, but of different generations constructing their cultural memory differently. In perceiving as valuable and selecting for emphasis certain values and traits of the classical past, Nikephoros was participating in the ongoing process of creating cultural memory. The mass of textual and physical antiquities in Constantinople and throughout the Empire presented constant points of reference and demanded interpretation. The resonance that stories of old Romans who fought, struggled, and

---

[6] See for example: Steven Runciman, *The Last Byzantine Renaissance* (Cambridge University Press, 1970); Warren T. Treadgold, *Renaissances before the Renaissance: Cultural Revivals of Late Antiquity and the Middle Ages* (Stanford University Press, 1984); David Talbot Rice, *The Twelfth Century Renaissance in Byzantine Art* (University of Hull Publications, 1965).

[7] Jan Assmann, *Religion and Cultural Memory: Ten Studies*, trans. Rodney Livingstone (Stanford University Press, 2006), 1–30; Patrick J. Geary, *Phantoms of Remembrance: Memory and Oblivion at the End of the First Millennium* (Princeton University Press, 1994); Gerd Althoff, Johannes Fried, and Patrick J. Geary, *Medieval Concepts of the Past: Ritual, Memory, Historiography* (Washington, DC: Cambridge University Press, 2002); Paul Connerton, *How Societies Remember* (Cambridge University Press, 1989).

died for the glory of the Empire had for Nikephoros needs to be seen in light of the particular military defeats the Empire suffered in his childhood. In other eras the touchstones for the creation of cultural memory were Christian martyrs, rather than the Horatii. This shift is not a matter of anything dying and being reborn but a change in perceptions of what in the past had true meaning for the present; of what in the past held power for the identity, moral direction, and orientation of the present. The study of Byzantine cultural history is frequently the study of changes in medieval Roman constructions of their cultural memory and varieties within those changes.

The conception of classical Roman history at stake in this book is the one Nikephoros developed from the monuments, texts, landscape and cultural memories that surrounded him. This differs most obviously from contemporary textbook conceptions of Rome in having its textual basis in Greek but not Latin sources and in perceiving Plutarch, Polybius, Dionysius of Halicarnassus and Cassius Dio as all fully Roman rather than as Greeks variously negotiating Roman rule. The process by which Greeks came to adopt Roman identity was sufficiently thorough and distant to have left no trace on medieval Roman perceptions of the past.[8] More importantly, Greek assimilation to Rome had no meaning for Nikephoros; therefore he was blind to it in the texts he read as it played no role in his memory of Roman history.

Further, while contemporary scholars may consider Polybius and Plutarch to represent different cultural periods within Roman history, it appears that from the perspective of the twelfth century Nikephoros used their texts, among others, to develop a unified memory of old Roman traditional morality. Just as Plutarch made characters from widely different centuries serve as exemplars judged according to one moral system,[9] Nikephoros appears to have brought his reading of diverse periods in Roman history into a cohesive vision of Roman ancestral traditions. Nikephoros's textual sources did not mention the *mos maiorum* because that term is Latin. The Greek histories of Rome, however, did convey the sense that upholding the customs of the ancestors was a core Roman virtue and presented various visions of what those traditions were. Throughout this text I use terms such as "traditional Roman values" and "classical

---

[8] Kaldellis, *Hellenism*, 42–119. Medieval Romans did have a fine sense of historical change; the Greek assimilation to Rome simply appears to have been unimportant for them. Anthony Kaldellis, "Historicism in Byzantine Thought and Literature," *Dumbarton Oaks Papers* 61 (2007): 1–24.

[9] Rowland Smith, "The Construction of the Past in the Roman Empire," in *A Companion to the Roman Empire*, ed. David S. Potter (Oxford: Blackwell, 2006), 431.

Roman virtues" to refer to Nikephoros's perception of the *mos maiorum*. Nikephoros shared the experience of creating his own personal conception of what the *mos maiorum* was with every other Roman for whom Roman traditional morality held meaning. Aeneas, Romulus, and Horatio were ancient models for Cato and Seneca as much as for Nikephoros. Romans of widely different eras engaged in the process of learning traditional Roman virtues through their cultivation and education, broadly conceived. Nikephoros may have read Dionysius's "Roman Antiquities" rather than Livy, but they all were creating a cultural memory of Roman values on the basis of texts, monuments, stories and the memories of their elders.

This book has three parts, the first and last dealing with the twelfth-century period of composition and the middle with the close reading of Nikephoros's history. The first chapter presents our extant evidence about Nikephoros and largely deconstructs the standard narrative of the 'attempted coup' in 1118 of Anna Komnene in Nikephoros's name that derives from the later histories of John Zonaras and Niketas Choniates. The chapter then presents multiple possible scenarios for Nikephoros's allegiances and for the context of composition. By destabilizing his standard biography, this chapter frees the literary analysis in Part II from being determined by presuppositions about authorial intentions. The rest of Part I sets up a framework for understanding the functions of early twelfth-century court history, audiences, and the possible sources at Nikephoros's disposal.

The core literary analysis of Nikephoros's history in Part II endeavors to illuminate some of its many possible meanings. It opens with a discussion of Nikephoros's explanation of the causes of Roman decline. Chapter 6 describes his overt case for Alexios's right to accede to the rule of the Empire. Some of Nikephoros's views regarding Roman identity are discussed in Chapter 7. Chapter 8 explores the moral patterns behind Nikephoros's descriptions of the many military encounters in the history. Chapters 9 and 10 deal with Nikephoros's deployment of familial politics and his sense of religion. The remaining chapters of Part II treat individual characters in the history and endeavor to bring the previous discussions of Nikephoros's system of values to bear on understanding those portraits.

The deep reading in Part II makes the text far more telling as a source of information about Nikephoros when it is brought to bear on the discussion of Nikephoros's attitudes and politics in Part III. The first chapter of Part III explores how the reading of Nikephoros's history presented in

Part II may modify our understanding of the events surrounding John Komnenos's succession and the possible political contexts for the composition of the text. Nikephoros's relationship with his wife Anna Komnene and the various relationships between their histories form the middle chapter of Part III. The final chapter turns to a discussion of what Nikephoros's appeal to classical Roman exemplars meant for his twelfth-century Constantinopolitan culture.

### THE MANUSCRIPT

The only manuscript of Nikephoros's history is no longer extant. The manuscript had been acquired by the French legal scholar Jacques Cujaus (d. 1590). He gave it to Pierre du Faur de Saint-Jorri (d. 1600), the first president of the Parliament of Toulouse, who had wanted to edit the *Alexiad*. It is unclear what happened to the manuscript after Saint-Jorri's death. When in the mid seventeenth century the Jesuit scholar Pierre Poussines undertook the editing of the *Alexiad* for the Paris Corpus, he knew that Saint-Jorri's manuscript, which he called "Tolosanus," was of great importance. An acquaintance of Poussines's was able to borrow the manuscript from its owner for a few days. Upon inspecting the manuscript Poussines found that it contained, in addition to the complete text of the fifteen books of the *Alexiad*, another long work of history. From its content, Poussines supposed that it was the history written by Nikephoros Bryennios that Anna described in the *Alexiad*. Poussines interpreted a text at the beginning of Nikephoros's history as a prologue. It has since been understood that it is a separate work, briefly describing the dynastic reasons for the Komnenian coup of 1081.[10]

Poussines worked quickly with the help of his colleague Claudius Maltrait to transcribe the text before he needed to return the manuscript. Sometime later the manuscript came into the possession of Guillaume Puget who gave it to Poussines's Jesuit community. Poussines then worked to correct his transcription but before he completed his task Puget asked to borrow the text back temporarily. Puget died while the manuscript was in his possession; his heirs denied that he had intended to give it permanently to the Jesuits and refused to let Poussines study it further.

---

[10] Johannes Seger, *Nikephoros Bryennios: Eine philologische-historische Untersuchung*, Byzantinische historiker des zehnten und elften Jahrhunderts 1 (Munich: Verlag der J. Lindauerschen Buchhandlung, 1888), 83–106; Franz Hermann Tinnefeld, *Kategorien der Kaiserkritik in der byzantinischen Historiographie* (Munich: W. Fink, 1971), 151–52.

In the middle of the eighteenth century the manuscript was mentioned as having been part of the Jesuit library in Toulouse. Most of that collection seems to have been hidden by the Jesuits before the library was taken over by the French government in 1764 and added to the royal library of Toulouse. The manuscript was not among those added to the royal library. All published editions are based on the transcription made by Pierre Poussines and published in the Paris Corpus in 1661.[11] Meineke removed many of Poussines's conjectural emendations of the text in the Bonn edition of 1836. Paul Gautier thoroughly studied Nikephoros's use of other historians, primarily John Skylitzes and Michael Psellos, and corrected Nikephoros's text wherever he had a basis for comparison.

Since the publication of Gautier's edition in 1975, a new fragment of book 1 of Nikephoros's history has come to light in a fifteenth-century manuscript containing works by Pachymeres.[12] A section of the manuscript collects various passages from Pachymeres dealing with the origins of the Turks. The heading in the manuscript is "From the first volume (tome) of the history of the Caesar Bryennios, about the Turks." Nikephoros included large portions of John Skylitzes's description of early Turkish history into his text. The fragment is then mostly Skylitzes as utilized by Nikephoros. A comparison of the text of Skylitzes in the Marcianus manuscript with that of Poussines's transcription and other manuscripts of Skylitzes shows that the Marcianus text contains fewer errors. In one of the five chapters included in the fragment, Nikephoros reworked Skylitzes's text more thoroughly, changing the order of sentences and rewriting passages. This segment of Nikephoros's writing allows for a comparison with the text transcribed by Poussines. While the absence of any third standard makes it difficult to determine absolutely which reading is closer to Nikephoros's original, the comparison of the Skylitzes passages indicates that the Marcianus manuscript is far superior.[13] In addition the discovery of the fragment in the Marcianus manuscript provides significant confirmation that Poussines's transcription was not an invention.

[11] Seger, *Bryennios*, 107–09; Paul Gautier, ed. *Nicephore Bryennios Histoire; introduction, texte, traduction et notes* (Brussels: Byzantion, 1975), 33–40; Albert Failler, "Le texte de l'histoire de Nicéphore Bryennios à la lumière d'un nouveau fragment," *Revue des études byzantines* 47 (1989): 239–50.
[12] In Marcianus gr. 509, a manuscript of Bessarion copied in the third quarter of the fifteenth century. The fragment was catalogued in 1740 by A. Zanetti and A Bongiovani "excerpta quaedam ex historiis jam edits Georgii Pachymerae & Bryennii Caesaris." In the new catalogue of manuscripts in the Marcian library it is attributed to Manuel Bryennios. Failler found it by chance in working on Pachymeres. Failler, "Le texte," 240.
[13] Failler, "Le texte," 242.

Despite Poussines's stated desire to look at the manuscript again, it seems likely that his transcription included the whole of the text Nikephoros wrote. Anna describes her husband's history as unfinished. The loss of the manuscript means that matters of punctuation and possible variant readings are simply speculative.

PART I

*Contexts*

# CHAPTER I

# Twelfth-century politics and the House of Komnenos

Nikephoros's early twelfth-century history looks back on a period of intense civil war and political calamity in the 1070s. The Seljuk Turks entered practically unimpeded into Roman imperial territory following their defeat and capture of Emperor Romanos Diogenes at the famous battle of Manzikert in 1071. The disaster at Manzikert often overshadows the Norman capture of Bari, also in 1071, ending centuries of Byzantine rule in southern Italy.[1] Pechenegs raided as far south as Thrace and the Slavic provinces in the Balkans revolted.[2] Troubles with wild currency devaluation and a decrepit taxation system impeded imperial financing.[3] Not since the Arab conquests of the seventh century had so many things gone wrong for the Empire. But while the seventh century had the highly capable Heraclius, the eleventh-century Empire was ruled by Michael VII who was so incompetent that no one – from his most trusted relatives to his bitter enemies – thought he could govern without someone at his side doing the real work. During this chaotic period the ruling elite was consumed by a series of civil wars for control of the Empire that hindered any coherent opposition to the Seljuk or Norman advances. Fueled at least partially by Michael's incompetence, there were ten civil wars fought between 1070 and 1081.[4]

[1] The political fallout from Romanos's capture was more disabling for the Byzantines than the actual battle: Jean-Claude Cheynet, "Manzikert, un désastre militaire?," *Byzantion* 50, 2 (1980): 412–38; Catherine Holmes, "Political-historical Survey: C 800–1204," in *The Oxford Handbook of Byzantine Studies*, ed. Elizabeth Jeffreys, John Haldon, and Robin Cormack (Oxford University Press, 2008), 273; Carole Hillenbrand, *Turkish Myth and Muslim Symbol: The Battle of Manzikert* (Edinburgh University Press, 2007).

[2] Paul Stephenson, "Byzantine Policy Towards Paristrion in the Mid-Eleventh Century: Another Interpretation," *Byzantine and Modern Greek Studies* 23 (1999): 43–63; Stephenson, *Byzantium's Balkan Frontier: A Political Study of the Northern Balkans, 900–1204* (Cambridge University Press, 2000), 98–100, 41–44.

[3] Angeliki Laiou and Cécile Morrisson, *The Byzantine Economy* (Cambridge University Press, 2007), 90–165; Cécile Morrisson, "Byzantine Money: Its Production and Circulation," in *The Economic History of Byzantium from the Seventh through the Fifteenth Century*, ed. Angeliki Laiou (Washington, DC: Dumbarton Oaks, 2002), 909–66. On the taxation system see Leonora Neville, *Authority in Byzantine Provincial Society, 950–1100* (Cambridge University Press, 2004), 47–65.

[4] Using Treadgold's definition of a civil war as "an armed conflict in which a significant number of Byzantine soldiers fought on both sides with a significant number of casualties." Warren Treadgold,

The era of civil war was put to an end when Alexios Komnenos seized the throne in a violent coup in 1081. Alexios managed to stay in control for thirty-seven years and passed on stable rule to his son, John. Nikephoros uses the story of Alexios Komnenos's rise to power as a narrative core for his history of the civil wars of the 1070s. The political situation of the Empire during Nikephoros's mature years in the early twelfth century was markedly different from that of the chaotic period his history describes. In the early twelfth century the Empire was ruled by two energetic, reforming, warrior emperors: Alexios Komnenos and his son John. There were revolts against Alexios and John, but far fewer than had been the norm in the later eleventh century, and only one of these may be considered a full-scale civil war.[5] The reigns of Alexios and John were characterized by significant gains in the recovery of Byzantine power in the east and strengthening Byzantine control in the west, as well as by internal political stability. Alexios's and John's reigns were times of political steadiness, expansion, and strong rule.

Alexios presented himself as a reformer. He demonstrated a willingness to act radically in the face of old problems, a tendency he showed by instituting a monetary reform through issuing new coinage; extensively reforming the taxation systems of the Empire and pressing great monasteries to make appropriate fiscal contributions, cashiering age-old systems of government service, imperial titulature and salaries; as well as in bullying intellectuals and burning heretics.[6] No doubt some were riled by his vigorous pursuit of reform.[7]

Alexios came to power with the help of an extraordinary alliance of aristocratic households. Once firmly in power Alexios systematically reduced the authority of the families that helped bring him to office. Most of his

---

"Byzantium, the Reluctant Warrior," in *Noble Ideals and Bloody Realities: Warfare in the Middle Ages*, ed. Niall Christie and Maya Yazigi (Leiden: Brill, 2006), 224–32; Jean-Claude Cheynet, "La politique militaire byzantine de Basile II á Alexis Comnene," *Zbornik Radova Vizantolosko Instituta* 30 (1991): 61–73.

[5] Treadgold considers Michael of Amastris's revolt as fitting his definition. Treadgold, "Byzantium, the Reluctant Warrior," 232. Cheynet regards this as a more limited event: Cheynet, *Pouvoir et contestations à Byzance (963–1210)* (Paris: Publications de la Sorbonne, 1990), 102.

[6] Margaret Mullett and Dion Smythe, eds., *Alexios I Komnenos* (Belfast Byzantine Enterprises, 1996). Reform: Paul Magdalino, "Justice and Finance in the Byzantine State, Ninth to Twelfth Centuries," in *Law and Society in Byzantium, Ninth–Twelfth Centuries*, ed. Angeliki Laiou and Dieter Simon (Washington, DC: Dumbarton Oaks, 1994), 93–116; Paul Magdalino, "Innovations in Government," in *Alexios I Komnenos*, ed. Mullett and Smythe, 146–66. Taxation: Neville, *Authority*, 63–65. Heretics: Kaldellis, *Hellenism*, 228–33; Dion Smythe, "Alexios I and the Heretics: the Account of Anna Komnene's *Alexiad*," in *Alexios I Komnenos*, ed. Mullett and Smyth, 232–59. Alexios' reign saw further development in the urban landscape of Constantinople: Paul Magdalino, "Medieval Constantinople," in *Studies on the History and Topography of Byzantine Constantinople* (Aldershot: Ashgate, 2007), 76–95.

[7] Magdalino, "Aspects of Twelfth-Century Byzantine Kaiserkritik," 335–39.

military energy was spent on vigorous campaigns in the Balkan frontier. Alexios's re-conquests in Asia were limited largely to coastal areas, leaving the highlands of Anatolia in the hands of the Turks. Alexios's ability to grant his chosen followers estates in newly conquered territory in the Balkans to replace those lost in the east gave him an unprecedented power over the aristocracy. While the imperial elite undoubtedly benefited in some ways from the cessation of civil war and the stability which Alexios's reign brought, those whose wealth had come from eastern estates were permanently displaced and increasingly dependent on the largesse of the ruling Komnenos family to maintain their elite status.[8] This spike in the power of the emperor vis-à-vis the aristocracy created a new social situation for the aristocracy than had existed in the previous several centuries.

## NIKEPHOROS THE AUTHOR

In the mid eleventh century the Bryennios family rose to be among the greatest aristocratic houses in the Empire. They had been known as an influential military family since the ninth century, based primarily in Thrace and particularly in Adrianople. Nikephoros Bryennios the Elder was *magistros* and *dux* of the West under Romanos Diogenes and commanded the left flank in the battle of Manzikert. He was appointed *dux* of Dyrrachion by Michael VII.[9]

Bryennios was proclaimed emperor by his troops in Traianopoulos in November of 1077. The following spring Nikephoros Botaneiates, who had rebelled in eastern Anatolia, was welcomed into Constantinople and crowned emperor. Immediately upon his accession, Botaneiates sent Alexios Komnenos to fight Bryennios's insurrection. Alexios was victorious in the conflict, capturing Bryennios who was then blinded. The elimination of Bryennios's rebellion was a key step in paving the way for Alexios's own successful bid for the throne in 1081. Although their rebellion had failed, the Bryennios family was not destroyed, either by Botaneiates or Alexios. Their property was restored and the blinded Bryennios the Elder lived until at least 1095.[10]

---

[8] Cheynet, *Pouvoir*, 359–77, 413–16; Peter Frankopan, "Kinship and the Distribution of Power in Komnenian Byzantium," *English Historical Review* 122, 495 (2007): 1–34; Frankopan, "Challenges to Imperial Authority in Byzantium: Revolts on Crete and Cyprus at the End of the 11th century," *Byzantion* 74, 2 (2004): 382–402.

[9] Diether Roderich Reinsch, "O Nikephoros Vryennios – Enas Makedonas Syngrapheas," in *2. Diethnes Symposio Vyzantinē Makedonia, dikaio, theologia, philologia* (Thessaloniki: Hetaireia Makedonikōn Spoudōn, 2003), 169–78; Cheynet, *Pouvoir*, 66, 68, 83, 220; Antonio Carile, "Il cesare Niceforo Briennio," *Aevum* 42 (1968): 429–54.

[10] Cheynet, *Pouvoir*, 99; Carile, "Niceforo Briennio," 432–36.

When Alexios's daughter Anna Komnene was born in 1083, Alexios betrothed her to Constantine Doukas, the son of Michael VII, strengthening the Komnenos claim to power by making Alexios the protector of the previous ruling dynasty. After young Constantine's death in 1094, Alexios moved to consolidate his authority by marrying Anna to the grandson of his former enemy, Nikephoros Bryennios the Younger. While some scholars have argued that the younger Nikephoros Bryennios was the son of the usurper, the preponderance of evidence indicates that Nikephoros was his grandson.[11] Nikephoros was given the title Caesar and married Anna in around 1097. In 1108 Nikephoros received one of the new Komnenian court titles, *panhypersebastos*. According to the *Alexiad*, Alexios gave Nikephoros command in a fight with the troops of Godfrey of Bouillon outside the walls of Constantinople in 1097.[12] He continued to serve Alexios and campaigned with John. Nikephoros died in 1136/7.[13]

The key political event of Nikephoros's life to have entered the historical record was the dispute regarding the succession to imperial power of John Komnenos, Nikephoros's brother-in-law. Discontent with Alexios's mode of autocratic government, and especially his subordination of the other grand aristocratic families of the eleventh century, has been interpreted as fueling an attempt to have Nikephoros succeed Alexios rather than his son John. The standard story is that Alexios's wife Irene Doukaina and her daughter Anna plotted to have Anna and Nikephoros succeed to the throne instead of John. Nikephoros became the natural focal-point of the attempted rebellion because of the imperial ambitions of his family, but he allowed the plot to fail through his refusal to participate.[14] The event is commonly seen as the last gasp of the leading aristocratic families of the

---

[11] Reinsch resolved the question of whether Nikephoros was the son or grandson of Nikephoros Bryennios the rebel by making use of additional information in George Tornikes' funeral oration for Anna; Diether Roderich Reinsch, "Der Historiker Nikephoros Bryennios, Enkel und nicht Sohn des Usurpators," *Byzantinische Zeitschrift* 83 (1990); Antonio Carile, "Il problema della identificazione del cesare Niceforo Briennio," *Aevum* 38 (1964): 74–83.

[12] Anna Komnene, *Annae Comnenae Alexias*, edited by Diether R. Reinsch and Athanasios Kambylis, (Berlin and New York: Walter de Gruyter, 2001): 10.9.6; Jonathan Harris, *Byzantium and the Crusades* (London: Hambledon and London, 2003), 56.

[13] Carile, "Niceforo Briennio," 442–45; Elizabeth Jeffreys, "Nikephoros Bryennios Reconsidered," in *The Empire in Crisis (?) Byzantium in the Eleventh Century, Diethnē symposia, 11* (Athens: Institouto Vyzantinon Ereunon, 2003), 201–14; Reinsch, "Der Historiker Nikephoros Bryennios," 423–24.

[14] Carile, "Niceforo Briennio," 445–54; Élisabeth Malamut, *Alexis Ier Comnène* (Paris: Ellipses, 2007), 445–482; Paul Magdalino, "The Pen of the Aunt: Echoes of the Mid-Twelfth Century in the Alexiad," in *Anna Komnene and her Times*, ed. Thalia Gouma-Peterson (New York: Garland Publishing, 2000), 17–18; Barbara Hill, "Actions Speak Louder than Words: Anna Komnene's Attempted Usurpation," in *Anna Komnene and Her Times*, ed. Thalia Gouma-Peterson (New York: Garland Publishing, 2000), 47–49; Lynda Garland, *Byzantine Empresses: Women and Power in Byzantium AD 527–1204* (London: Routledge, 1999), 197–98.

eleventh century, the Doukai and the Bryennioi, who had been pushed aside as Alexios gained power.

While this interpretation is entirely plausible, it is worth pausing to remember how much of this story is a matter of modern analysis. Scholars have identified possible causes of discontent and associated them with information about the revolt. Our medieval sources describe the revolt in terms of the personalities and personal relationships of various members of the imperial family, rather than the more general social or political problems that are the usual subject of modern explanations. Because the revolt is a central act in the modern reconstruction of Nikephoros's biography, it is worth reviewing what we actually know about the events. The only sources that speak about the succession dispute explicitly are the histories of John Zonaras, written in the middle of the twelfth century, and that of Niketas Choniates, written in the early thirteenth century. A brief notice of the dispute occurs in an anonymous Syriac chronicle written in Edessa around 1240.[15] Zonaras's chronicle covers history from the Creation to the death of Alexios in 1118 and is largely hostile to Alexios.[16] Choniates's history begins with the stories of strife surrounding the death of Alexios and ends in the early thirteenth century after the Latin conquest of Constantinople. The *Alexiad*, a biography of Alexios written by Anna Komnene in the middle of the twelfth century, makes no mention of an attempted usurpation against her brother, although her portrait of John is not flattering. A funeral oration for Anna by George Tornikes alludes vaguely to tensions surrounding the death of Alexios but argues strongly for Anna's proper conduct.[17]

In both Zonaras and Choniates the actions of the women in the imperial family serve, at least in part, to create a gendered critique of the imperial men.[18] The narratives of Zonaras and Choniates either question or entirely undermine the masculinity of Alexios, John, and Nikephoros. Medieval Roman authors seem to share in the classical Roman cultural logic that

---

[15] *Anonymi Auctoris Chronicon ad A. C. 1234 Pertinens*, ed. Albert Abouna (Louvain: Corpus Scriptorum Christianorum Orientalium, 1974), vii, 63.

[16] Magdalino, "Aspects of Twelfth-Century Byzantine Kaiserkritik," 328–34.

[17] *George et Demetrios Tornikes. Lettres et discours*, ed. Jean Darrouzes (Paris: Editions du Centre national de la recherche scientifique, 1970), 267–69.

[18] On the study of gender as a means of revealing some of the functions of women in Greek texts see: David M. Halperin, "Why is Diotima a Woman?," in *One hundred Years of Homosexuality and Other Essays on Greek Love* (London: Routledge, 1990), 113–51; Elizabeth Clark, "Ideology, History, and the Construction of 'Woman' in Late Ancient Christianity," *Journal of Early Christian Studies* 2 (1994): 155–84; Elizabeth Clark, "The Lady Vanishes: Dilemmas of a Feminist Historian after the 'Linguistic Turn'," *Church History* 67 (1998): 1–31; Kate Cooper, "Insinuations of Womanly Influence: an Aspect of the Christianisation of the Roman Aristocracy," *Journal of Roman Studies* 82 (1992): 150–64. Similar methodologies may be fruitfully applied to medieval Greek texts.

equated virtue with maleness so that an attack on one impugned the other.[19] The criticism implicit in both histories becomes clearer when we pay attention to how the actions of the imperial family invert the Roman ideals of proper familial relations between men and women. The function of Irene and Anna in these critical narratives should inform our reading of the evidence for their participation in the revolt.

Zonaras's story casts Irene and her son John as the major antagonists. Zonaras introduces the topic of Irene's excessive influence at court with a discussion of the marital relations between Alexios and Irene. As a young man Alexios was not particularly devoted to her and only had sex with her out of a sense of duty until "the passing of time blunted the fire-throwing arrows of *Eros*."[20] He then became inordinately fond of Irene and she shared in the administration. As Alexios's health declined the empress became increasingly powerful and held power over her son John. This situation was intolerable for John, who was not only a full-grown man, but already had been a husband for some time and was a father of children.[21] John came to fear for his life as well as his succession and went around secretly asking friends and relatives to renew the oaths they had already taken that they would accept no other ruler after Alexios's death.[22] The men were eager to reassert their loyalty to John.[23] Irene had John followed by spies and tried to cut off access to him, but he continued to draw supporters anyway.[24]

Here Zonaras's story implicitly criticizes Alexios first for having affairs as a young man and then for over-indulgence of his wife as an old man.

---

[19] On Roman masculinity see Mathew Kuefler, *The Manly Eunuch: Masculinity, Gender Ambiguity, and Christian Ideology in Late Antiquity* (University of Chicago Press, 2001), 19–31; Myles Anthony McDonnell, *Roman Manliness: Virtus and the Roman Republic* (Cambridge University Press, 2006). On Byzantine conceptions of gender see Charles Barber, "Homo Byzantinus?," in *Women, Men and Eunuchs: Gender in Byzantium*, ed. Liz James (London: Routledge, 1997), 185–99; Kathryn M. Ringrose, *The Perfect Servant: Eunuchs and the Social Construction of Gender in Byzantium* (University of Chicago Press, 2003); Martha Vinson, "Gender and Politics in the Post-Iconoclastic Period: The *Lives* of Antony the Younger, The Empress Theodora, and the Patriarch Ignatios," *Byzantion* 68 (1998): 469–515; Dion Smythe, "Gender," in *Palgrave Advances in Byzantine History*, ed. Jonathan Harris (New York: Palgrave, 2005), 157–65.

[20] Zonaras, *Ioannis Zonarae epitomae historiarum libri xviii*, edited by M. Pinder and T. Büttner-Wobst, 3 vols. (Bonn: Weber, 1841–97): 747.2–9. πρὸς δὲ τὴν κοινωνὸν τοῦ βίου ὁ βασιλεὺς οὗτος οὔτ' ἀποστρόφως εἶχε τὸ πρότερον οὔτε λίαν ἐκείνῃ προσέκειτο, ἀφροδισίων δ' ἡττώμενος οὐ πάνυ τὰ ἐς εὐνὴν ἐτύγχανε δίκαιος, ὅθεν καὶ βέλεσιν ἡ Αὐγούστα ζηλοτυπίας ἐβέβλητο. ἐπεὶ δ' ὁ χρόνος προήκων τῷ αὐτοκράτορι τὰ πυρφόρα βέλη τοῦ ἔρωτος ἤμβλυνε, τότε πρὸς τὴν Αὐγούσταν τρέψας τὸν ἔρωτα ὅλος ἦν τῆς πρὸς ἐκείνην στοργῆς καὶ ἤθελεν εἶναι σχεδὸν αὐτῆς ἀδιάσπαστος.

[21] Zonaras 747.9–748.3 τῷ δὲ τὸ σκέμμα οὐκ ἀνεκτὸν ἐς ἄνδρας ἤδη τελοῦντι καὶ γυναικὶ πρὸ πολλοῦ συναφθέντι . . . καὶ παίδων γεγονότι πατρί.

[22] Zonaras 748.4–10.    [23] Zonaras 748.11–12.    [24] Zonaras 748.12–17.

The incontinent young Alexios fails to exhibit the virtue of self-control, *sophrosyne*, considered particularly vital for an emperor.[25] The overly affectionate elderly Alexios exhibits a different form of weakness in allowing himself to be ruled by his wife. In not striving to nurture and support her son, Irene is portrayed as derelict in the most basic duties of a mother. By denying John's status as an adult man and actively fighting against him, Irene inverts the natural order of an ideal family.[26]

Zonaras further relates that as the emperor's health continued to decline "the empress was extremely powerful and much authority belonged to her son-in-law Caesar Bryennios."[27] Nikephoros was entrusted with making proclamations and giving justice. Zonaras describes Nikephoros as a man "inclined to knowledge" whose wife:

held her ground in intellectual pursuits, speaking accurate Attic and having a keen mind for complex concepts. She added to her natural intelligence through study. She was engrossed by books and profound conversations with learned men.[28]

Everything was going well for the Caesar, who was universally praised. This situation cast John, "the emperor's son and emperor," into despondency and anguish, which he bore with endurance.[29]

Zonaras admits doubts about what actually happened when Alexios died. He presents several versions of Alexios's deathbed scene, inviting his audience to choose between competing stories. All of these, however, describe the succession struggles as exclusively between Irene and John. Nikephoros's prominence in palace administration prior to Alexios's death is presented as a corollary to Irene's control of the government. Neither Anna nor Nikephoros figured at all in the drama surrounding Alexios's death, although Anna and her sisters were all present at Alexios's death. Zonaras says that after he was firmly in control of the Great Palace, John

---

[25] Helen North, *Sophrosyne: Self-Knowledge and Restraint in Classical Antiquity* (Ithaca: Cornell University Press, 1966); Barbara Hill, "The Ideal Komnenian Woman," *Byzantinische Forschungen* 23 (1996): 14; Kazhdan, "Aristocracy and the Imperial Ideal," 42–57; Kuefler, *Manly Eunuch*, 77–96.

[26] Roman mothers were expected to support their son's careers without being overly ambitious: Suzanne Dixon, *The Roman Mother* (London: Croom Helm, 1988), 175–6, 202–03; Susan Treggiari, "Women in the Time of Augustus," in *The Cambridge Companion to the Age of Augustus*, ed. Karl Galinsky (Cambridge University Press, 2005), 143–47. On care for family as a chief virtue of women in twelfth-century panegyrics see: Hill, "The Ideal Komnenian Woman," 8.

[27] Zonaras 754.

[28] Zonaras 754.10–755.16 ἦν γὰρ καὶ λόγοις προσκείμενος ὁ ἀνήρ, καὶ ἡ σύνοικος δέ οἱ οὐδὲν ἧττον, εἰ μὴ καὶ μᾶλλον ἐκείνου, τῆς ἐν λόγοις παιδείας ἀντείχετο καὶ τὴν γλῶτταν εἶχεν ἀκριβῶς ἀττικίζουσαν καὶ τὸν νοῦν πρὸς ὕψος θεωρημάτων ὀξύτατον. ταῦτα δ' αὐτῇ προσεγένετο φύσεως ὀξύτητι καὶ σπουδῇ· προσετετήκει γὰρ ταῖς βίβλοις καὶ λογίοις ἀνδράσι καὶ οὐ παρέργως ὡμίλει αὐτοῖς.

[29] Zonaras 754.16–755.2.

considered what he should do about his mother and sisters and Nikephoros because he suspected them of wanting to plot against him.[30] Zonaras does not specify what John decided to do and turns instead to further description of Alexios's end and an assessment of his reign.

Choniates, although writing over half a century after Zonaras, presents himself as having more information about the attempted coup. Zonaras's competing versions of Alexios's death are replaced by one seamless narrative. The characters are more fully drawn, but they are drawn as stock types. Choniates uses the story of the succession dispute to create an image of an unharmonious and unnatural imperial family in which all the familial and gender roles are inverted. Setting the beginning of his history in the context of Alexios's disfunctional household contributes to Choniates's larger agenda of explaining the fall of Constantinople in 1204 in terms of Komnenian failings.[31] The opening of Choniates's history invites a comparison with the opening of Xenophon's *Anabasis,* in which a king and queen fight over which of their two *sons* ought to succeed.[32] In Choniates's telling, the Komnenos dynasty was perverse and unsound from its foundation.

Choniates opens with a shrewish Irene badgering Alexios about his son John's faults. Choniates's exquisite use of *double-entendre* allows him to have Irene complain simultaneously about John's moral weaknesses of rashness, luxuriousness, and lack of virtue and his bodily weaknesses of diarrhea, feebleness from recurring twisting of his bowels, and general ill-health.[33] In response to Irene's nagging, Alexios manages to maintain his composure some of the time, which crucially means that he lost his temper some of the time.[34] Choniates recreates one of Alexios's tirades in which he points out not only the logical reasons for John's succession but also the bloody nature of his acquisition of power:

[30] Zonaras 764.1–5.
[31] On the larger agenda see Alicia Simpson, "Before and After 1204: The Versions of Niketas Choniates' 'Historia'," *Dumbarton Oaks Papers* 60 (2006): 189–221; Alicia Simpson, "Studies on the Composition of Niketas Choniates' *Historia*" (Ph.D., King's College London, 2004), 178–200.
[32] Anthony Kaldellis, "Paradox, Reversal and the Meaning of History," in *Niketas Choniates: A Historian and a Writer*, ed. Alicia Simpson and Stephanos Efthymiadis (Geneva: La Pomme d'Or, 2009), 78–79.
[33] Choniates, *Nicetae Choniatae Historia*, ed. Jan Louis van Dieten (Berlin and New York: Walter de Gruyter, 1975): Choniates, *John* 5.7–9 . . . προπετῆ τοῦτον ἀποκαλοῦσα καὶ ὑγρὸν τὸν βίον παλίνστροφόν τε τὸ ἦθος καὶ μηδαμῆ μηδὲν ὑγιές . . . On στρόφος used in contexts of incipient defecation see Jeffrey Henderson, *The Maculate Muse: Obscene Language in Attic Comedy* (Oxford University Press, 1991), 197.
[34] Choniates, *John* 4.24–6.11.

Oh woman, sharer of my bed and Empire, will you not stop admonishing me
on behalf of your daughter, undertaking to destroy praiseworthy harmony and
order as if you had been struck mad? Put it down to good fortune. Or rather
let's now study and observe together who of all of those taking up the scepters of
Rome until now who had a son appropriate for rule overlooked him and selected
instead his son-in-law? Even if this did happen at some point, oh woman, we
should not follow the rarity as law. The whole of Rome would laugh out loud at
me and conclude that I had lost my senses if I, who seized the Empire, not in a
praiseworthy manner, but with the blood of compatriots and ways departing from
Christian laws, when I need to find an heir for it, would banish the one from my
loins and welcome in the one from Macedonia.[35]

Here Alexios condemns himself for usurpation and his wife for insanity.
Irene's lack of support for her own son again is an unnatural action that
disrupts the proper harmony and order of the household. When Irene
ignored Alexios's arguments and persisted in pestering him, he would
pretend to think about it "since he was a dissembling man beyond all
others."[36] Within the cultural logic of Choniates's text, the idea of disputing
the succession of the reigning emperor's healthy adult male heir is absurd
and irrational. In addition to criticizing Irene for persisting with a bad
idea, Choniates disparages both Irene and Alexios for their inversion of
proper marital roles. Alexios lacked the authority to get his wife to stop
arguing with him while Irene did not respect her husband's judgment.
Alexios appears weak and conniving while Irene appears shrewish.

Choniates provides a single continuous narrative of Alexios's death.
John's struggle to secure power is the narrative center. Choniates provides
a story about a second moment of contention within the first year of
John's reign. John's relatives formed a plot in favor of Nikephoros. The
plan was to strike against the emperor murderously in the night when
John was encamped outside the city. The guards had been bribed and
the conspirators would have struck "had not the customary dullness and

---

[35] Choniates, *John* 5–6. ὦ γύναι, κοινωνέ μοι λέχους καὶ βασιλείας, οὐ τὰ πρὸς χάριν παύσῃ τῆς
σῆς ὑποτιθεμένη μοι θυγατρός, ἁρμονίαν τε καὶ τάξιν ἐπιχειροῦσα λύειν ἐπαινετήν, ὡς εἴπερ
θεοβλαβείας μετέσχηκας; βάλ' ἐς τύχην ἀγαθήν· ἢ μᾶλλον δεῦρο κοινῇ συνδιασκεψώμεθα καὶ
γνωσόμεθα, τίς ἐξ ἁπάντων τῶν πρώην τὰ Ῥωμαίων σκῆπτρα παρειληφότων, υἱὸν ἔχων
ἁρμόδιον εἰς ἀρχήν, τοῦτον μὲν παρεβλέψατο, γαμβρὸν δὲ ἀνθείλετο. εἰ δέ ποτε καὶ τοιόνδε τι
ξυμβέβηκεν, οὐ νόμον, ὦ γύναι, τὸ σπάνιον ἡγησόμεθα. ἐπ' ἐμοὶ δὲ καὶ μάλα καπυρὸν γελάσειε
τὸ Πανρώμαιον, καὶ τῶν φρενῶν κριθείην ἀποπεσών, εἰ τὴν βασιλείαν οὐκ ἐπαινετῶς εἰλη-
φώς, ἀλλ' αἵμασιν ὁμογενῶν καὶ μεθόδοις Χριστιανῶν ἀφισταμέναις θεσμῶν, δεῆσαν ταύτης
ἀφεικέναι διάδοχον, τὸν μὲν ἐξ ὀσφύος ἀποπεμψαίμην, τὸν δὲ Μακεδόνα εἰσοικισαίμην. All
translations are my own unless otherwise stated.
[36] Choniates, *John* 6.10.

languidness stopped [Nikephoros] Bryennios from taking in hand the attempt on the Empire and compelled him to remain in place, forgetting his agreements, and extinguishing the hot desire of the conspirators."[37] Choniates relates that the conspirators were only temporarily deprived of their property and that Anna and John were reconciled.[38] Choniates includes a gratuitously sexual appraisal of Anna's disappointment:

It is said that the Kaisarina Anna was so disgusted with her husband's frivolity that she considered herself as suffering something terrible and blamed nature most of all. Nature was placed under a grave indictment on the grounds that Anna's genitals were spread wide and hollowed whereas Bryennios had the long member and was balled.[39]

The term translated as "frivolity" also refers to passive anal penetration while "nature" is a euphemism for female genitals.[40] With Choniates's pornographic depiction of Anna's frustration with her womanhood, his use of gender inversion to disparage the Komnenoi becomes patent. Nikephoros becomes a weakling in this narrative through his marriage to an ambitious woman as much as through his failure to attack John. The analytic goal of Choniates's history was to explain what went wrong with the Roman Empire that led to the Latin conquest. By portraying Alexios's court as a locus of gender inversion and unnatural power relations, Choniates undermined the good standing and reputation of those who founded the dynasty. In Choniates's narrative, the story of John's accession is sordid and full of perverse characters: men who let women rule them, women who want to rule, women who egg their husbands on to murder. The whole

---

[37] Choniates, *John* 10.16–22: τάχα δ᾽ ἂν καὶ νυκτὸς ἐπέθεντο μεθ᾽ ὅπλων τῶν φονουργῶν αὐλιζομένῳ τῷ βασιλεῖ κατὰ τὸ μικρὸν ἄποθεν τῶν χερσαίων πυλῶν ἱππήλατον Φιλοπάτιον, δώροις προδιαφθείραντες ἁδροῖς τὸν ἐπὶ τῶν εἰσόδων τῆς πόλεως, εἰ μὴ τὸ εἰωθὸς ὑπόνωθρον καὶ χαλαρὸν πρὸς βασιλείας ἐπίθεσιν τῆς ἐγχειρήσεως ἔπαυσε τὸν Βρυέννιον, αὐτόν τε μένειν κατὰ χώραν παραβιάσαν τῶν ξυνθηκῶν λαθόμενον, καὶ κατασβέσαν τὸ θερμὸν τῶν συνελθόντων φρόνημα·

[38] Choniates, *John* 11.27–28.

[39] Choniates, *John* 10.22–25: ὅτε καὶ λέγεται τὴν καισάρισσαν Ἄνναν πρὸς τὸ χαῦνον τοῦ ταύτης ἀνδρὸς δυσχεραίνουσαν ὡς πάσχουσαν δεινὰ διαπρίεσθαι καὶ τῇ φύσει τὰ πολλὰ ἐπιμέμφεσθαι, ὑπ᾽ αἰτίαν τιθεῖσαν οὐχὶ μικρὰν ὡς αὐτῇ μὲν διασχοῦσαν τὸ ἄρθρον καὶ ἐγκοιλάνασαν, τῷ δὲ Βρυεννίῳ τὸ μόριον ἀποτείνασαν καὶ σφαιρώσασαν.

I thank Anthony Kaldellis for calling my attention to the error in Magoulias's translation. Magoulias's mistranslation has entered the literature: Malamut, *Alexis Ier Comnène*, 446; Dion Smythe, "Middle Byzantine Family Values and Anna Komnene's *Alexiad*," in *Byzantine Women: Varieties of Experience 800–1200*, ed. Lynda Garland (Aldershot: Ashgate, 2006), 127. Quandahl and Jarratt discuss the text of Magoulias's translation while acknowledging that it does not reflect Choniates's meaning: Ellen Quandahl and Susan C. Jarratt, "'To Recall Him ... Will be a Subject of Lamentation': Anna Comnena as Rhetorical Historiographer," *Rhetorica* 26, 3 (2008): 308.

[40] χαῦνον: Henderson, *Maculate Muse*, 211, φύσις: John J. Winkler, *The Constraints of Desire: The Anthropology of Sex and Gender in Ancient Greece* (New York: Routledge, 1990), 217–20.

story is rife with sexualized vocabulary. It makes for a gripping and fitting opening chapter for his story of the Empire's decline. Because the story fits his thirteenth-century purposes so well, however, we must be cautious in accepting it as evidence for the events of 1118.

The account of the anonymous Edessan chronicler is more violent and spare than either Zonaras or Choniates. The anonymous casts Irene as supporting her son-in-law over John, leading to enmity between the two men. The main event of the story is John's assault on the walls of the palace and subsequent violent plunder of the imperial treasure. The anonymous says that once in power John exiled his brother-in-law and sent his mother to a monastery.[41] Anna is not mentioned.

Anna Komnene's *Alexiad* does not mention any attempted coup but makes a strong case for Anna and her mother and sisters behaving appropriately at the time of her father's death and casts John's actions to secure the succession as power-hungry and lacking in filial sentiment. The *Alexiad* systematically builds in emotional intensity throughout Book XV moving toward Alexios's death.[42] In Anna's history Alexios is surrounded by his wife and three daughters who minister to him with increasing grief. Anna's account shows Anna and Irene acting in their proper gender roles and has John improperly concerned with politics at the hour of his father's death. Nikephoros plays no role whatsoever in Anna's version of the succession story. Anna employed the same standard ideas of proper gender roles as Choniates, but used them to opposite effect.

Overall, modern historians have preferred to synthesize Zonaras and Choniates while ignoring Anna – her eye-witness notwithstanding. Standard modern accounts of the event hold that Irene and Anna together were the active impetus for the coup which failed because of Nikephoros's loss of nerve. The women were then forced into monastic retirement. Choniates's story is heavily represented in this synthesis. Choniates is the only source that implicates Anna in the coup, when he describes her frustration as a means of disparaging Nikephoros. Nikephoros similarly appears as failing to pursue power only in Choniates's story. In the others he does not figure. Zonaras has Irene as the instigator and Anna, who is never named, only figures as the wife of Nikephoros.

The standard view combines those elements from Zonaras's and Choniates's histories that appeal to modern sensibilities. Modern historians

---

[41] *Anonymi Auctoris Chronicon ad A.C. 1234 Pertinens*, 63.
[42] Margaret Mullett, "Alexios I Komnenos and Imperial Renewal," in *New Constantines: The Rhythm of Imperial Renewal in Byzantium, 4th–13th Centuries*, ed. Paul Magdalino (Aldershot: Ashgate, 1994), 264.

conceive of this as 'Anna's coup' because they are interested in women's authority and attracted to Anna's mystique as a great medieval woman writer. In valorizing the perceived efforts of Anna and Irene to take power, modern historians have given the texts a meaning that runs opposite to what appears to have been the authors' intent. Cultural changes in ideals of womanhood have complicated our reading of these histories. On the other hand, cultural continuities regarding negative associations with passive men persist into the modern era with sufficient force that Nikephoros is now generally regarded as a wimpy intellectual because he chose not to murder his brother-in-law.

It is likely that there was some internal palatial dissension at the time of Alexios's death. Tornikes's funeral oration indicates that some people regarded Anna and John as rivals but strongly insists upon her proper behavior. There is no reason to think the stories in Zonaras and Choniates had no basis in at least rumor and gossip. The attempts against John cannot have been particularly threatening, however, because they apparently had no significant consequences for the participants. Zonaras does not say what John decided to do about Irene, Anna, and Nikephoros once he had become emperor. Choniates says that property was temporarily seized but that Anna and John were soon reconciled. Irene retired to the convent she founded sometime after her husband's death, but we do not have reason to associate her retirement with John's displeasure. Anna may have joined her mother in monastic retirement only after Nikephoros's death.[43] Anna was tonsured shortly before she died.[44] Nikephoros remained at court and ended his life while in military service.

Whether Nikephoros wrote his history before or after John's accession must remain a subject of speculation. We do not know how much of it he left unfinished or even how much of what he did write we have. The narrative breaks off unfinished in 1080. Since it seems that Nikephoros was born sometime in the late 1070s or early 1080s, it is unlikely that he began to write much before around 1100. Jeffreys plausibly speculates that a period of "enforced leisure" after Anna and Irene's unsuccessful coup in Nikephoros's name could have provided the opportunity for Nikephoros to engage in serious literary activity and possibly write his history.[45] We

---

[43] The idea of Anna's immediate retirement comes from her description of her internal exile in the *Alexiad* at 14.7.6. Anna's self-proclaimed isolation is contradicted to some extent by her ongoing lively intellectual work. Robert Browning, "An Unpublished Funeral Oration on Anna Comnena," *Proceedings of the Cambridge Philological Society* 8 (1962): 4–12.

[44] Demetrios I. Polemis, *The Doukai: a Contribution to Byzantine Prosopography* (London: Athlone, 1968), 70–74, Basile Skoulatos, *Les personnages byzantins de l'Alexiade: analyse prosopographique et synthèse* (Louvain: Bureau du recueil College Erasme, 1980), 119–24.

[45] Jeffreys, "Nikephoros Bryennios Reconsidered," 211–13.

have however no call to think he was so deeply busy with other work that he could not have written this history at other times as well. The history as we have it is hardly monumental. I have known too many good historians to leave half-finished books on their desks for decades at a time to think that the unfinished nature of the text means that Nikephoros had pen in hand in the last months of his life.

Nikephoros's historical writing was described by his wife, Anna Komnene, in the prologue to her history of her father's reign, the *Alexiad*.[46] She wrote that her mother, Irene, had commissioned Nikephoros to compose a history of Alexios's reign and that Nikephoros was able to complete the first part of the work, from the reign of Romanos Diogenes through that of Nikephoros Botaneiates. In the preface to the *Material for History* Nikephoros addresses a wise woman who had commissioned a history of Alexios, presumably Irene Doukaina.[47] While there is no conclusive proof that the text we know as the *Material for History* is the history said to have been written by Nikephoros Bryennios, it matches Anna's description well enough to proceed on that assumption.

To gain any traction on the dating of the text, we need to reflect on the political messages in the history and speculate about possible contexts of composition. Since working out the meanings of the text is the subject of the core of the present book, the discussion of possible political contexts in Part III is more satisfying. Here the task is to lay out the various possible scenarios for the political context. One key result of the close reading of the text with immediate significance for the political context of composition is the understanding that Nikephoros's history contains veiled criticism of Alexios and marked valorization of Bryennios the Elder. While the argument for the negative reading of Alexios will unfold over the core section of the present book, in thinking about possible political contexts of composition we need to address its fundamental plausibility.[48]

Alexios Komnenos was the logical person to blame for the blinding of Nikephoros's grandfather, Bryennios the Elder, a fact unlikely to have been forgotten by Bryennios's descendants. There is very little reason to doubt that if Alexios had failed to defeat Bryennios's rebellion, Nikephoros would have become emperor. In addition to dealing the Bryennios family one dramatic and devastating blow in 1080, Alexios effectively reduced

---

[46] Komnene, P.3.

[47] P.II.1–3, On Irene's literary patronage see Margaret Mullett, "Aristocracy and Patronage in the Literary Circles of Comnenian Constantinople," in *The Byzantine Aristocracy: IX–XIII Centuries*, ed. Michael Angold (Oxford: British Archeological Reports, 1984), 175–76.

[48] Reinsch outlines evidence for Nikephoros's loyalty to his grandfather: Reinsch, "O Nikephoros Vryennios," 173–76.

the power and influence of the other aristocratic families throughout his reign. Nikephoros would have had more than one possible reason to dislike Alexios. Although he was a fairly high-ranking courtier and the husband of the princess, Nikephoros very reasonably can be supposed to have been politically disappointed.

Anna Komnene's highly laudatory depiction of her father in the *Alexiad* may give rise to a natural presupposition that her husband liked Alexios too. Anna wrote about her great affection for her husband in moving terms. She may well have been entirely sincere. Affection of a wife for her husband was a mark of good character however and it is equally possible that Anna said she loved her husband because that was the emotional relationship most flattering for a good woman. That it is at least possible for loving couples to disagree significantly on matters of politics is proven by common experience. There is no reason *a priori* to assume that Anna and Nikephoros had the same evaluation of Alexios's character and success. As will be shown in subsequent chapters, the *Alexiad* and the *Material for History* can be seen as engaging in a critical dialogue regarding Alexios's character.

The evidence for an abortive coup after the death of Alexios, such as it is, indicates resistance to John. Given the solid material reasons for growing resentment among the old aristocracy at the increasing centralization of power and authority in the hands of the Komnenos family over the course of Alexios's reign, it is reasonable to expect some courtiers would have disliked Alexios. Several conspiracies were revealed during Alexios's reign, the most dangerous of which aimed to replace Alexios with a descendant of the eleventh-century aristocracy.[49] That a negative portrait of Alexios could have circulated in Constantinople should not be surprising.

Interpretations of possible contexts for the composition of a critical portrait of an emperor depend in turn on judgments of how dangerous such criticism was, for either the author or the emperor. The criticism of Alexios in Nikephoros's history is veiled, but thinly. The criticism is never overt, but hardly so esoteric or deeply subtle to be truly hidden. I doubt anyone would have expected that John could have listened to the history and been too naïve to catch the negative underlay. More likely keeping the criticism veiled allowed it to be more polite, or at least not so insulting as to require a response.

Much, but not all, of the negativity depends on hearing the story told with a conception of classical Roman ideals of masculinity and honor

---

[49] The most politically threatening revolts were probably those of Gregory Gabras, Nikephoros Diogenes, and Michael Anemas. Cheynet, *Pouvoir*, 90–103.

in mind. Therefore various audience members may have perceived it as more or less critical depending on the degree of their engagement with classical culture. Assessment of the degree of openness and intensity of the criticism then depends to some extent on a judgment regarding the depth of education at court. In the later twelfth-century court, where references to Plutarch and other classical authors in court rhetorical performances were routine, the value system that codes Alexios as dishonorable and un-Roman would have been widely known. If Nikephoros's criticism was fairly esoteric in 1110, it might have seemed quite obvious by 1200. Even in the early twelfth century enough people at court had heard enough Roman history to be sure that Nikephoros's history would not have passed as purely laudatory. Some strands of criticism, such as that which aligns Alexios's behavior with that of the Turks, required no classical education.

Several possible basic scenarios for the context of composition then present themselves. One possibility is that the history was written when Alexios was alive and that it formed part of Nikephoros's bid for power in Alexios's last months. In this case the criticism of Alexios would work with the lionization of Bryennios the Elder to make a case for Nikephoros's superior qualifications for rule. This scenario would present Nikephoros as more active in the pursuit of power than he appears in the standard narrative.

The second half of Nikephoros's history is more biting in its criticism than the first half, which contains more cloying overt praise of Alexios. This observation led Seger to suggest that the first half was written when Alexios was alive and the second after his death.[50] A third possibility is that the first half was written shortly after John's accession, perhaps as an effort to reassure John that Nikephoros would support the Komnenos regime, but that as time went on and both John and Nikephoros became more secure in their relationship, Nikephoros felt free to be more critical. This case would have Nikephoros writing slowly, or in fits and starts, over a long period of time.

A fourth possibility is that it was written well after John's accession at a time when any attempted coup could be considered safely in the past. The criticism of Alexios and the valorization of the Bryennios family at such a point may have been emotionally satisfying but would have carried little political bite. It is possible that Nikephoros wrote more critically in later chapters because John's response to early chapters indicated that there would be no recriminations to doing so. In this scenario John did not

[50] Seger, *Bryennios*, 32–33.

need to worry about criticism of his father because such talk was of no
political importance. It is of course possible that John did not mind, or
even enjoyed, hearing his father criticized.

There are certainly other plausible scenarios as well, but they all likely fall
somewhere in the range from an early highly politically significant context
near the end of Alexios's reign to an almost purely academic context in the
middle of John's reign. This range of options is offered to the reader as an
aid in contextualizing the analysis which follows and will be revisited in
Part III.

# CHAPTER 2

# Writing history in twelfth-century Constantinople

That a close member of the imperial family engaged in writing history is less surprising for the twelfth-century Byzantine court than it would be for many others. History in the eleventh and twelfth centuries was not written by cloistered academics, but by high-ranking imperial officials, judges, and courtiers.[1] Psellos served as a close advisor and high-ranking official for a number of emperors.[2] Michael Attaleiates, a high-ranking imperial judge, wrote a history covering the period 1034–1079/80.[3] The chronicler John Skylitzes was also a judge and an important figure within the upper levels of the Komnenian court.[4] John Zonaras held the high titles of *megas droungarios tes viglas* and *protasekretis* in the court of Alexios Komnenos before entering monastic retirement. As close members of the ruling dynasty, Nikephoros Bryennios and Anna Komnene were clearly the most highly ranking historians of the twelfth century, but their literary activities were not anomalous.

Live performance of literary compositions was an increasingly significant aspect of court life in the twelfth century.[5] This context of aristocratic patronage of orally performed literature is remarkably similar to that for

---

[1] Psellos, Attaleiates, Skylitzes, Zonaras and Choniates all served as judges for some or most of their careers and had considerable legal interests and training. Angeliki Laiou, "Imperial Marriages and Their Critics in the Eleventh Century: The Case of Skylitzes," *Dumbarton Oaks Papers* 46 (1992): 166–7; Angeliki Laiou, "Law, Justice, and the Byzantine Historians: Ninth to Twelfth Centuries," in *Law and Society in Byzantium: Ninth–Twelfth Centuries*, ed. Angeliki Laiou and Dieter Simon (Washington, DC: Dumbarton Oaks, 1994), 173; Catherine Holmes, *Basil II and the Governance of Empire (976–1025)* (Oxford University Press, 2005), 89.

[2] Anthony Kaldellis, ed. *Mothers and Sons, Fathers and Daughters: The Byzantine Family of Michael Psellos* (University of Notre Dame Press, 2006), 3–10.

[3] Dimitri Krallis, "History as Politics in Eleventh-Century Byzantium" (Ph.D., University of Michigan, 2006), 32–83.

[4] *Jean Skylitzès, Empereurs de Constantinople*, trans. Bernard Flusin and Jean-Claude Cheynet, *Réalités byzantines*, 8 (Paris: Lethielleux, 2003): v–vi.; Holmes, *Basil II*, 89.

[5] Magdalino, *Manuel*, 339–53; Mullett, "Aristocracy and Patronage," 173–201; Roderick Beaton, *The Medieval Greek Romance*, 2nd edn. (London: Routledge, 1996), 16–17, 225; Kaldellis, *Hellenism*, 235–37.

classical Roman oratory.[6] It seems reasonable to think that histories were written for oral performance, as were most kinds of literary production in medieval Constantinople.[7] Performances are said to have taken place in the *theatron*. 'Theater' has been defined not with reference to a particular place, but as an instance of "the performance of a text to an audience."[8] Any occasion and place that brought together a potential audience with the performance of a text became a site of theater. This context is necessary for an appreciation of the aesthetics of the Byzantine rhetorical compositions which were written for occasions such as weddings, funerals, arrivals and assorted celebrations.[9] Letters, which were always read aloud, also fit into this category of texts composed for oral delivery. The texts modern scholars read are "the dry bones of an experience from which all sense of drama and occasion have now gone."[10] Silently reading a Byzantine text of this era gives as little an idea of the Byzantine experience as "reading the score of a symphony compares to the experience of its actual sound."[11]

Twelfth-century "theater" was performed for the pleasure of the presiding patron before an audience of people also attendant on the leading figure. Emperors, empresses, patriarchs, and magnates are all known to have been the sponsors and recipients of theatrical performances, which generally took place in the throne rooms or reception halls of their houses.[12] Writers had the reactions of their audience in mind.[13] Male rhetoricians regularly performed for audiences that included women. Empress Irene Doukaina, who commissioned Nikephoros's history, is known as the patroness of a *theatron*.[14] This imperial commission, along with the evidence for the tradition of oral performance at court, makes it entirely reasonable to think that Nikephoros's history was performed aloud before members of

[6] Rex Winsbury, *The Roman Book: Books, Publishing and Performance in Classical Rome* (London: Duckworth, 2009), 125; J. P. Sullivan, *Literature and Politics in the Age of Nero* (Ithaca: Cornell University Press, 1985); Christina S. Kraus, "Forging a National Identity: Prose Literature Down to the Time of Augustus," in *Literature in the Greek and Roman Worlds*, ed. Oliver Taplin (Oxford University Press, 2000), 315–27. Performance has also attracted the attention of scholars of medieval Europe: Evelyn Birge Vitz, Nancy Freeman Regalado, and Marilyn Lawrence, *Performing Medieval Narrative* (Cambridge: D.S. Brewer, 2005).
[7] Mullett, "Aristocracy and Patronage," 180; Beaton, *The Medieval Greek Romance*, 16–17; Brian Croke, "Uncovering Byzantium's Historiographical Audience," in *History as Literature in Byzantium*, ed. Ruth Macrides (Aldershot: Ashgate, 2010), 42–50.
[8] Magdalino, *Manuel*, 336.
[9] A possibility that Anna Komnene incorporated a memory of a contemporary folk story into her history suggests the parameters for what was heard at court may have been larger than is generally assumed. Roderick Beaton, "Byzantine Historiography and Modern Greek Oral Poetry: The Case of Rapsomatis," *Byzantine and Modern Greek Studies* 10 (1986): 41–50.
[10] Magdalino, *Manuel*, 353.    [11] Kaldellis, *Hellenism*, 237.
[12] Magdalino, *Manuel*, 339–52.    [13] Mullett, "Aristocracy and Patronage," 175.
[14] P.11.1–3; Komnene 1.3; Mullett, "Aristocracy and Patronage," 175–6; Polemis, *The Doukai*, 72–73.

the ruling class, if not also at the imperial court itself. Nikephoros's history is made up of fairly short stories woven together into a larger narrative. Several of the smaller narrative units could be read as an evening's entertainment without overly burdening an audience.

Nikephoros's interactions with his audience would have been particularly interesting because he was telling stories about the parents and grandparents of key figures in his audience. Many, if not all, of the basic stories would have been well known to most of the people in the audience. The entertainment and pleasure of hearing the history would not have come from learning new things about the past, but from hearing familiar, significant, family stories stirringly narrated in the form of a grand classical history. Nikephoros's history includes the story of how, with the help of his tutor, one of Nikephoros's contemporaries and fellow courtiers, the *sebastos* and *protostrator* Michael Doukas, had escaped daringly from a Norman fortress where he was being held hostage as a child. The event was historically insignificant, but it made a wonderful story and there is no doubt that Michael, his family, and companions enjoyed hearing it well told. Such an audience would be highly attuned to the particularities of characterization and the nuances Nikephoros chose for each episode. They likely were waiting to hear how their own family members came off in one scene or another. Needless to say, Nikephoros's task was all the more difficult because he was telling the history of a period in which the progenitors of his audience had been both fighting each other and losing wars against invaders.

Such an audience also undoubtedly included people that Nikephoros would not have wanted to offend. For Byzantine as well as classical writers, criticism of those in power was accomplished through figured speech and the use of textual allusion to suggest meanings left unsaid.[15] Byzantine texts routinely admitted of several simultaneous meanings. The skill of writing a text that could be understood in multiple ways was a standard part of Byzantine rhetorical education.[16] The role of such ambivalence has been increasingly appreciated in the study of Byzantine literature. Roilos

---

[15] Ahl, "Safe Criticism," 174–208; Thomas Conley, "Byzantine Teaching on Figures and Tropes: An Introduction," *Rhetorica* 4 (1986): 353–74; Jeffrey Walker, "These Things I Have Not Betrayed: Michael Psellos' Encomium of His Mother as a Defense of Rhetoric," *Rhetorica* 22 (2004): 49–101. For some examples of the techniques see: Charles Pazdernik, "Xenophon's *Hellenica* in Procopius' *Wars*: Pharnabazus and Belisarius," *Greek, Roman and Byzantine Studies* 46, 2 (2006): 175–206; Anthony Kaldellis, *Procopius of Caesarea: Tyranny, History, and Philosophy at the End of Antiquity* (Philadelphia: University of Pennsylvania Press, 2004).

[16] Kaldellis, *Hellenism*, 237; George L. Kustas, *Studies in Byzantine Rhetoric* (Thessalonike: Patriarchikon Hidryma Paterikon, 1973), 95–100, 183–99.

successfully applies the indigenous term *"amphoteroglossia"* or "double-tonguedness" to describe the ambivalence in twelfth-century literature.[17] Some writers wove hidden meanings into their texts that could only be understood by certain members of their audience. Some Byzantine writers used irony to speak with double meanings.[18] Embedding multiple meanings in a text was a means of intellectual play as well as a means of criticizing without exposing oneself to censure.[19] The significant result of this research for our purposes is that we should not be surprised if Nikephoros's text seems to express multiple, apparently inconsistent, viewpoints. The lessons Nikephoros drew for his audience could be interpreted and applied in a variety of ways. Our goal is to tease out as many possible meanings as we can.

In style and content, Nikephoros's history participated fully in the Greek tradition of narrative history writing. The twelfth century was a remarkably fruitful and creative era of Byzantine literature.[20] Several extremely fine works of history were produced in this era that participated in long-established traditions of classical historical writing. Nikephoros's work fits clearly into the tradition of detailed narrative history writing for which Thucydides and Polybius were key models.[21] Nearly all Byzantine history

[17] Roilos, *Amphoteroglossia*, 1–24; Roilos, "The Sacred and the Profane: Re-enacting Ritual in the Medieval Greek Novel," in *Greek Ritual Poetics*, ed. Dimitrios Yatromanolakis and Panagiotis Roilos (Cambridge, Mass.: Harvard University Press, 2004), 210.

[18] Jakov Ljubarskij, "The Byzantine Irony – the Case of Michael Psellos," in *In Buzantio Kai Koinonia Mneme Nikou Oikonomide*, ed. A Avramea, A Laiou, and E Chrysos (2003), 349–60; Jakov Ljubarskij, "Byzantine Irony: The Example of Niketas Choniates," in *In To Byzantio Orimo Gia Allages: Epilogos, Euaisthesies Kai Tropoi Ekphrases Apo Ton Endakato Ston Dekaton Pempto Aiona*, ed. Christine Angelidi (Athens: Institute for Byzantine Research, 2004), 287–98; Dimitri Krallis, "Attaleiates as a Reader of Psellos," in *Reading Michael Psellos*, ed. Charles Barber and David Jenkins (Leiden: Brill, 2006), 189–90.

[19] Ahl, "Safe Criticism," 174–208.

[20] On historiography see Macrides and Magdalino, "Fourth Kingdom," 117–56. On twelfth-century writing in general: Paolo Odorico and Panagiotis A. Agapitos, eds., *Pour une "nouvelle" histoire de la littérature byzantine: problèmes, méthodes, approches, propositions* (Paris: Centre d'études byzantines, néo-helléniques et sud-est européennes, 2002); Elizabeth Jeffreys, *Rhetoric in Byzantium* (Aldershot: Ashgate, 2003); Catherine Holmes and Judith Waring, *Literacy, Education and Manuscript Transmission in Byzantium and Beyond* (Leiden: Brill, 2002); Herbert Hunger, *Schreiben und Lesen in Byzanz: die byzantinische Buchkultur* (Munich: C.H. Beck, 1989).

[21] Procopius, Agathias, Leo the Deacon, and Michael Attaleiates, for example, also participated in this narrative tradition of historical writing. The division between historians and chroniclers has been de-emphasized: Hans-Georg Beck, "Die byzantinische 'Mönchschronik'," in *Ideen und Realitäten in Byzanz* (London: 1972), 188–97; Jakov Ljubarskij, "New Trends in the Study of Byzantine Historiography," *Dumbarton Oaks Papers* 47 (1993): 131–38. Yet distinctions may still be fruitfully drawn between the aesthetic requirements of chronicles and histories: Lia Raffaella Cresci, "Ποικιλια nei proemi storiografici bizantini" *Byzantion* 72, 2 (2004): 330–47. Judging from the manuscript tradition, one of the most popular histories ever composed was Constantine Manasses's truly genre-blending verse chronicle which told the story from Adam to the accession of Alexios Komnenos in

texts open with an introduction in which the author echoes Herodotus's statement that the purpose of writing history is to prevent the passage of time from obliterating the memory of the past, and professes his or her desire to write a history that is genuinely truthful.[22] Truth was displayed through the composition of persuasive rhetoric. Good historical narrative needed to be persuasive, meaning that the audience had to be convinced through the force of the presentation that the author's claims were true.[23] Nikephoros had to present his version of the past in such a way that his audience would be persuaded he had gotten it right.

Kazhdan's impression that Nikephoros's history took the form of a romance has been widely repeated, but not explored in detail.[24] The idea is that Nikephoros's story is like a romance in that impediments are placed to the marriage of Alexios and Irene. The union however is not a central structural element in Nikephoros's plot and the ceremony itself is not mentioned. Unlike romances, no bond of affection or desire is ever expressed between Alexios and Irene. Their marriage is mentioned as a political event strengthening a bond between two factions.[25] Rather than the core of a romance, the notice of a leading general's marriage arrangements is one of

---

fifteen-syllable political verse: Ingela Nilsson, "Discovering Literariness in the Past: Literature vs. History in the *Synopsis Chronike* of Konstantinos Manasses," in *L'écriture de la mémoire: la littérarité de l'historiographie*, ed. Paolo Odorico, Panagiotis A. Agapitos, and Martin Hinterberger (Paris: Centre d'études byzantines, néo-helléniques et sud-est européennes, 2006), 15–31; Ingela Nilsson, "Narrating Images in Byzantine Literature: The Ekphraseis of Konstantinos Manasses," *Jahrbuch der Österreichischen Byzantinistik* 55 (2005): 121–46; Roger Scott, "The Classical Tradition in Byzantine Historiography," in *Byzantium and the Classical Tradition*, ed. Margaret Mullett and Roger Scott (Birmingham: Centre for Byzantine Ottoman and Modern Greek Studies, 1981), 61–74.

[22] Byzantine historians agree in claiming that the distinguishing feature of history is that it should be *true*. It was common to criticize previous historians for being biased flatterers who distorted the truth because of their personal prejudices. Iordanis Grigoriadis, "A Study of the Prooimion of Zonaras' Chronicle in Relation to other 12th-century Prooimia," *Byzantinische Zeitschrift* 91, 2 (1998): 327–44; Holmes, *Basil II*, 121–25.

[23] A. J. Woodman, *Rhetoric in Classical Historiography: Four Studies* (Portland: Areopagitica Press, 1988); Colin Macleod, *Collected Essays* (Oxford: Clarendon Press, 1983), 68–87; M.J. Wheeldon, "'True Stories': The Reception of Historiography in Antiquity," in *History as Text: the Writing of Ancient History*, ed. Averil Cameron (Chapel Hill: The University of North Carolina Press, 1989), 33–63; Margaret Mullett, "Novelisation in Byzantium: Narrative after the Revival of Fiction," in *Byzantine Narrative: Papers in Honour of Roger Scott*, ed. J Burke, *et al.* (Melbourne: Australian Association for Byzantine Studies, 2006), 7–8.

[24] For example: Jan Olof Rosenqvist, *Die byzantinische Literatur: vom 6. Jahrhundert bis zum Fall Konstantinopels 1453* (Berlin: Walter de Gruyter, 2007), 125–26. The idea entered common discourse through Kazhdan's entry on Nikephoros Bryennios in the *ODB*: Alexander Kazhdan, ed. *The Oxford Dictionary of Byzantium* (New York: Oxford University Press, 1991), vol. II, 331.

[25] The Doukas and Komnenos families were already kin through marriage, in Nikephoros's view, because Michael VII and Isaac, Alexios's brother, had both married Georgian noblewomen who were cousins, 2.1.6–13.

many elements that place Nikephoros's history in continuity with classical Roman histories.

Nikephoros's stories about the eleventh century were undoubtedly aimed to speak to currents of thought and debate among his contemporary audience. The performance of a history of the civil wars of their ancestors necessarily contributed to the formation of identities and allegiances of the twelfth-century courtiers themselves. When nations are understood as "imagined communities" then, as Beaton has emphasized, "a prime site where that 'imagining' takes place must be that community's literature."[26] Performances of texts at court participated in the creation of the communal perception of the court's identity and cultural memory.

The performance of history could go beyond creating and enacting the contemporary culture and cultural memory of the audience to an attempt to modify and correct contemporary behavior through the moralizing presentation of models for emulation. Greek and Roman historians commonly wrote about the past in order to affect the behavior of their contemporaries and were explicit in their claims that history should provide examples for future action.[27] Byzantine historical texts were designed to present models of proper and foolish behavior for imitation and derision.[28] The tendency to focus on the "teachable moments" of history may have been accentuated in the medieval reception of the classical corpus. Part of the preponderance of moralizing passages in the surviving portions of Polybius may well be due to the interest of the tenth-century excerpters in precisely those moral lessons drawn from the examples of the past and their disinterest in the details of all the intervening events.[29] When the audience included influential members of the ruling class, political commentary in the form of stories about the past could be expected to have real impact on debates

---

[26] Roderick Beaton, "Antique Nation? 'Hellenes' on the Eve of Greek Independence and in Twelfth-Century Byzantium," *Byzantine and Modern Greek Studies* 31, 1 (2007): 78, discussing Benedict Anderson, *Imagined Communities: Reflections on the Origin and Spread of Nationalism*, rev. edn. (London: Verso, 1991).

[27] Jane D. Chaplin, *Livy's Exemplary History* (Oxford University Press, 2000); Smith, "The Construction of the Past," 411–38; A. M. Eckstein, *Moral Vision in the Histories of Polybius* (Berkeley: University of California Press, 1995), 16–27; F. W. Walbank, *Polybius* (Berkeley: University of California Press, 1972), 58–65; Frances Pownall, *Lessons from the Past: The Moral Use of History in Fourth-Century Prose* (Ann Arbor: University of Michigan Press, 2004), 176–82.

[28] On the development of this characteristic see Athanasios Markopoulos, "Byzantine History Writing at the End of the First Millennium," in *Byzantium in the Year 1000*, ed. Paul Magdalino (Leiden: Brill, 2003), 186.

[29] On the role of Byzantine selectivity in the survival of Polybius see J. M. Moore, *The Manuscript Tradition of Polybius* (Cambridge University Press, 1965); Nigel G. Wilson, *Scholars of Byzantium* (Baltimore: Johns Hopkins University Press, 1983), 140–45.

about current policies. They necessarily had a role in informing the behavior of the audience. Contemporary political criticism and apology logically are core concerns in Nikephoros's history.

Romanizing historians like Attaleiates and Bryennios could instruct their contemporaries through the use of classical exempla. Eleventh- and twelfth-century Byzantine historians were able to call on a common understanding and appreciation of classical Roman behavioral ideals among their audience. Writers of twelfth-century encomia were able to use heroes of republican and early imperial Rome as comparative exemplars.[30] These writers shared a finely tuned appreciation of the antiquity of their Empire and a sense of how cultures and societies, including their own, changed over time.[31] Historians could appeal to ideals of properly gendered behavior, and memories of how great Romans of the past had acted, in order to comment on the behavior of the historical actors whose deeds they were narrating. For both writers and audience, particular situations would call to mind dramatic events of the past. The historian's rhetorical positioning of the current event in relation to the remembered past could craft the response of the audience to recent history.

For Nikephoros, as for many of his contemporaries, one of the key issues for discussion was the political collapse in the eleventh century. Through the first quarter of the twelfth century a key part of the intellectual and cultural agenda of Constantinople was dealing with the displacement and upheaval caused by the loss of most of the Empire's eastern territories. Emotional and intellectual responses to the loss of the east found expression in literature.[32] Nikephoros's history is likewise an attempt to deal with the ramifications of eleventh-century political failure.

Interest in Roman history increased markedly in the later eleventh and twelfth centuries.[33] Nikephoros is conceptually part of the eleventh-century interest in Roman classicism, along with Attaleiates and Psellos, far more than part of the twelfth-century engagement with Hellenism. The strengthening of a "Hellenic" identity was at least in part a response to the political and cultural challenge of western Europe from the later twelfth century

---

[30] Lia Raffaella Cresci, "Exempla storici greci negli encomi e nella storiografia bizantini del XII secolo," *Rhetorica: A Journal of the History of Rhetoric* 22, 2 (2004): 120.

[31] Kaldellis, "Historicism."

[32] Roderick Beaton, "Cappadocians at Court: Digenes and Timarion," in *Alexios I Komnenos*, ed. Margaret Mullett and Dion Smythe (Belfast Byzantine Enterprises, 1996), 329–38.

[33] On the revival of Roman history see Athanasios Markopoulos, "Roman Antiquarianism: Aspects of the Roman Past in the Middle Byzantine Period (9th–11th Centuries)," in *Proceedings of the 21st International Congress of Byzantine Studies*, ed. Elizabeth Jeffreys and F. Haarer (Aldershot: Ashgate, 2006), 277–97; Magdalino, "Aspects of Twelfth-Century Byzantine Kaiserkritik," 343.

onward and was a new addition to the fundamental Roman identity of the
Byzantines.[34]

Keen interest in classical Roman history is seen in several late eleventh-
and twelfth-century histories. John Xiphilinos made an abridgement of the
Roman history of Cassius Dio, working on a commission from Michael
VII Doukas.[35] Xiphilinos reorganized Dio's annalistic history into a bio-
graphical form with one book for each emperor. Xiphilinos's re-working
displays a conception of history as the deeds of emperors. Its core goal is
to provide examples of past emperors for the purpose of educating current
rulers.

The emphasis on individual rulers in Xiphilinos's history matches that of
Michael Psellos's *Historia Syntomos,* a brief textbook history of the Roman
Empire from its foundation. Psellos started by describing the events of each
king's reign. He describes key achievements of six sets of consuls but then
jumped over the rest of republican history because:

> As to the history of the consuls who were chosen yearly . . . I have decided to omit
> the rest, because it is determined by that specific form of government and thus
> lacks the continuity of personal leadership; but I shall occupy myself for you with
> the further history and start from the rule of Caesar Julius, in order that you may
> either imitate the good deeds of the emperors, or criticize and despise the bad
> ones.[36]

Rulers who were only in power for a year could not serve as an organi-
zational principle for Psellos. Since his goal was to educate the current
emperor, he omitted history that could not easily be treated as a series
of exempla. The rest of the *Historia Syntomos* fulfills Psellos's promise to
provide educational models.

Michael Attaleiates also drew heavily on Roman history for the moral
framework of his history. Although dedicated to the emperor Nikephoros
Botaneiates (1079–1081) and ostensibly praising him, Attaleiates' history
contains a strong argument in defense of Emperor Romanos Diogenes
and criticizing Botaneiates. Attaleiates achieved this double meaning by
embedding allusions to events of classical Roman history, especially as
described by Polybius. Attaleiates patterned his relationship with Romanos

[34] Kaldellis, *Hellenism,* 317–88; Paul Magdalino, "Hellenism and Nationalism in Byzantium," in *Tradition and Transformation in Byzantium* (Aldershot: Ashgate, 1992), 1–29. For an illuminating
comparison of Hellenism in the twelfth and nineteenth centuries see Beaton, "Antique Nation?,"
76–95.
[35] His work covers Dio Books 36–80, except Books 70 and 71 which had already been lost. Fergus
Millar, *A Study of Cassius Dio* (Oxford: Clarendon Press, 1964), 2.
[36] Psellos, *Historia* 15.

on Polybius's relationship with his patron Scipio.[37] Those familiar with classical Roman history would understand Attaleiates's defense of Diogenes completely.

In the mid-twelfth century the courtier and historian Zonaras wrote a history of the world from creation to 1118, giving unprecedented attention to republican Rome.[38] For the period from Aeneas to 146 BCE, Zonaras followed Cassius Dio so closely that modern reconstructions of Dio's text rely on Zonaras. Thereafter Plutarch's lives become one of Zonaras's major sources, as well as later books of Dio for the classical period of Roman history.[39]

Given this vogue for classical Roman history, it is not surprising that Nikephoros drew heavily on the cultural norms of classical Roman historians. Scholars of classical Rome have long noted that ancient Greek history was received by the Romans as a relatively chronologically unmarked whole. Plutarch applied the "same set of ethical criteria" equally to the Greeks and Roman subjects of his parallel lives.[40] A similar flattening of the past is perceptible in the medieval Byzantine reception of antiquity.[41] Events from ancient Greek history were well known to twelfth-century writers. Yet, in the usage of the encomiasts, references to classical Greek and Roman antiquity become de-contextualized as the individuals referenced stand for generalized characteristics.[42] Some Byzantine writers came close to our homogeneous "Graeco-Roman antiquity."[43] This flattening of history into models of behavior makes it easier for us to see Nikephoros Bryennios drawing on behavior types than to place him in dialogue with a specific era of ancient history. Nikephoros often appeals to general attitudes that are recognizably 'classical' but cannot be made much more specific. Yet in regard to the key issue of military virtue, Nikephoros seems to appeal to a particularly Roman sense that valor is best displayed through virtuous conduct in the face of defeat.[44] The valorization of honorable defeat is not

---

[37] Krallis, "History as Politics", 102–26.    [38] Macrides and Magdalino, "Fourth Kingdom," 127–31.

[39] Zonaras did not have the text of Dio for the period between 146 and 44 BCE. For the period from the death of Julius Caesar until Nerva he used Plutarch and Dio with some Eusebius, Josephus, and Appian: Millar, 3; Ernest Cary, "Introduction," in *Cassius Dio's Roman History*, Loeb Classical Library (Cambridge, Mass.: Harvard University Press, 1914), 20.

[40] Smith, "The Construction of the Past," 431.

[41] Michael Glykas provides a wonderful example of this in his twelfth-century universal history in which the reign of the Persian king Artaxerxes is identified as the era of "Sophocles, Heraclitus, Anaxagoras, Pythagoras, Thucydides, Euripides, Herodotus, Empedocles, Diogenes, Hippocrates, Plato and Aristotle." The following two paragraphs move from Alexander the Great to the revolt of the Maccabees. Glykas, 376.14–21

[42] Cresci, "Exempla storici greci," 115–45.    [43] Kaldellis, *Hellenism*, 301.    [44] See chapter 8 below.

a Homeric value and constitutes a major indication that Nikephoros chose a specifically Roman rather than Greek orientation for his history.

The challenges and successes of Nikephoros's history are put into high relief when the full contexts of composition are appreciated. This text was written to be presented to a live audience, consisting largely of the descendants of the combatants described in the history. Those descendants were politically engaged in responding to the failure of their grandparents' generation to effectively fight the Empire's enemies. The appeal to classical Roman history in Nikephoros's history reminds the court both of the noble heritage of the Empire, and in so far as Nikephoros alludes to dark moments in Roman history, puts the eleventh-century problems in the context of a deeply aged and ultimately successful Empire. Nikephoros's Roman modeling exhorts his audience to positive behaviors and reminds them of their continuity with the ancient Empire. The particular political meanings that will be brought out in the following chapters can be appreciated within the context of a court trying to come to terms with current tensions and the lingering effects of past disappointments.

# CHAPTER 3

# *Nikephoros's reading*

The *Material for History* is the work of a well-educated individual. Working out exactly what Nikephoros had read, and in what form, however, is a necessarily speculative enterprise. Nikephoros's interactions with classical literature range from direct quotations and clear allusions to more vague echoes and shared cultural logic. The set of texts Nikephoros chose to quote and echo in his history should not be confused with the set of texts he had read. That Nikephoros quotes little or no theological literature reflects his choices about how to position his history within his culture and does not indicate that he had read no theology. He may also have read far more classical Greek literature and history than we can attest through his choice of quotations. In this text, at least, Nikephoros engaged most directly with histories of the Roman Empire written in Greek. Whatever else his education included, Nikephoros appears to have read deeply in classical Roman history.

If Nikephoros read theological literature, it did not make an impact on his writing. Aside from a reference to a psalm – which was likely proverbial – all of Nikephoros's scriptural allusions are confined to one paragraph describing the false charges of treason made against Anna Dalassene.[1] In this passage the biblical allusions form a standard denunciation of false witnesses and judicial corruption. A discussion of divine Providence and Envy possibly alludes to one of Gregory of Nazianzus's poems.[2] The almost total absence of scriptural and patristic references is a significant departure from much of Byzantine writing. The relative absence of Christian literature in itself constitutes an imitation of classical historiographic style.

Nikephoros shows signs of considerable familiarity with ancient Greek literature and history and wove Homeric lines into his descriptions. He was compelled to write his history by a Herculean force; using a Homeric

---

[1] A proverbial psalm: 3.4.1–5; Anna's trial 1.22.
[2] Martin Hinterberger, "*Phthonos* als treibende Kraft in Prodromos, Manasses und Bryennios," *Medioevo Greco* 11, 1 (2011): 19; Gregory of Nazianzus, *Carmina moralia* 1.2.32, *PG* 37.926.

tag.[3] Michael Boutoumites was "a small man but mighty, as Homer says."[4]
Nikephoros compares Alexios chasing Basilakes to Achilles chasing Hector:
"in front a good man fled, behind a mightier followed."[5] He said that it
would take "another Iliad" to tell the story of his grandfather properly.[6]
Alexios exhorts his followers that they need to choose either "a good life
or a good death, as the saying goes."[7] It is unclear whether Nikephoros
recognized that the "saying" is a quote from Sophocles's *Ajax*.[8] He claimed
only to be providing materials for others to write into a history because he
did not have the strength of Thucydides or the eloquence of Demosthenes.[9]
Nikephoros apologized for not knowing the classical name of a particular
river. He described its location and gave its common local name.[10] The
Spartan general Brasidas is invoked to praise a warrior.[11]

Nikephoros's conception of classical Greek history appears to have been
negative. When Nikephoros wanted to criticize one of Michael VII's min-
isters, he said the man was worse than Pericles.[12] The Athenian states-
man was remembered for having stirred up endless trouble rather than
for having been a great leader. Apparently Pericles, or perhaps the entire
democratic system of classical Athens, was regarded negatively in twelfth-
century Constantinople. Nikephoros also uses Alexander the Great as a
negative model. When Alexios Komnenos heard that a force of Turks
was foraging in the vicinity of Heraclea where he was staying, he was
moved to take up arms immediately. Nikephoros contrasts Alexios stirred
to arms by the Turks with Alexander the Great stirred to arms by Timotheos's flute.[13] In an oration on kingship Dio Chrysostom explained
how Timotheos adapted his playing to Alexander's character with the result
that:

Alexander at once bounded to his feet and ran for his arms like one possessed, such
was the exaltation produced in him by the tones of the music and the rhythmic
beat of the rendering. The reason why he was so affected was not so much the
power of the music as the temperament of the king, which was high-strung and
passionate.[14]

The story is told twice in the tenth-century lexicon known as the *Suda*.[15]
Jumping to arms at the sound of a flute was considered sufficiently bad
behavior that Nikephoros could expect his audience to have a negative

---

[3] P.II.II quoting *Il.* 2.658.    [4] 2.27.6–7; *Il.* 5.801.    [5] 4.26.11–13; *Il.* 22.158.    [6] 4.15.9.
[7] 2.10.12–13.    [8] Soph. *Aj.* 479–80.    [9] P.II.17–18.    [10] 4.5.2–5.    [11] 2.13.8.
[12] 2.1.19–20.    [13] 2.27.2–3.    [14] Dio Chrys. *Or.* 1.1–3, trans. Cohoon (Harvard, 1932).
[15] *Suidae lexicon*, ed. A. Adler (Leipzig: Teubner, 1931–35) omicron 573, tau 1122.

view of Alexander. Nikephoros's negative reading is taken up by several later writers.[16]

That the content of ancient Greek history did not provide alluring models to Nikephoros does not mean that he did not read deeply in ancient Greek literature. The opening sentence of Nikephoros's first book, which introduces the two sons of Manuel Komnenos, recalls the opening of Xenophon's *Anabasis,* which introduces the two sons of Darius. Much of the military vocabulary of camping and marching is reminiscent of Xenophon, although certainly not unique to him. Nikephoros's descriptions of single combats have a Homeric ring and one could plausibly argue that Bryennios the Elder's final battle constituted an *aristeia,* a display of finest military virtue in the manner of a Homeric hero.[17]

While Xenophon may have been a key stylistic model, Nikephoros's primary touchstones seem to have been histories of the Roman Empire written in Greek. For Nikephoros, as for classical Roman historians, Greek literature provided powerful paradigms to be deployed in the service of expressing a Roman cultural identity and memory. In his quotations, vocabulary, and, most importantly, behavioral modeling, Nikephoros drew on authors such as Dionysius of Halicarnassus, Plutarch, Polybius, and Procopius. These writers, all of whom he would have considered to have been writing the imperial history of Rome, provide the models for correct and incorrect behavior that underlay some of Nikephoros's narrative constructions. Nikephoros's history indicates considerable familiarity and engagement with Greek historians of the Roman world.

Nikephoros incorporated a verbatim passage of Polybius's history of the Roman Empire into the fourth book of his history. After describing how Alexios triumphed unexpectedly over the rebellion of Basilakes, Nikephoros meditates:

The things done by him show that it is necessary not to trust too much in fortune, especially in success, and what Euripides said well – "one good resolution is victorious over many hands" – seems to have been given confirmation though his deeds. For it was one man, one judgment, who brought down in a short time the most clever of the Roman generals covered in glory and the myriad crowd of soldiers and he led to better things and restored to confidence a whole polity that

---

[16] Anna Komnene makes the same point as Nikephoros saying that, unlike Alexander, Alexios did not need Timotheos's "orthian mode" to spring to action. Komnene 9.5.1; Euthymios Tornikes and Michael Choniates use the story in similar ways. Tornikes, *Oration* 1.2 line 12 in Darrouzès, *Tornikès. Lettres*; Niketas Choniates, *Oration* 18.317 in *Nicetae Choniatae Orationes et Epistulae.*

[17] The insights of this paragraph are those of Dr. Sarah Ferrario to whom I am deeply grateful for many conversations about Nikephoros and ancient Greek literature.

was unmistakably ruined, and raised up the spirits of the army of the emperor which had sunk to the lowest depths of despair.[18]

This passage incorporates many phrases from Polybius 1.35:

Above all, the disaster of Marcus [Regulus] gives the clearest possible warning that no one should feel too confident of the favors of Fortune, especially in success. Here we see one, who a short time before refused all pity or consideration to the fallen, brought incontinently to beg them for his own life. Again what Euripides said well – "one good resolution is victorious over many hands" – seems to have been given confirmation though his deeds. For it was one man, one judgment, that defeated the numbers which were believed to be invincible and able to accomplish anything; and restored to confidence a whole polity that was unmistakably and utterly ruined, and the spirits of its army which had sunk to the lowest depths of despair.[19]

It is likely that the textual correspondence would have been even closer had the scholars transcribing Nikephoros's text recognized the parallel.[20] Nikephoros here quoted Polybius quoting a line of Euripides. The excerpt was included in several classical compendia of fragments of ancient texts.[21] The entire four-line fragment is quoted completely also in the life of Homer attributed to Plutarch and Johannes Stobaeus's anthology, where it is labeled as from Euripides's *Antiope*.[22] The particular line used by Polybius and Nikephoros was also quoted by several other classical and medieval authors.[23] Polybius was thus not alone in privileging this phrase.

[18] 4.28.1–9: ἔδειξεν οὖν καὶ τὰ παρ' ἐκείνου πραχθέντα ὡς χρὴ μὴ πάνυ τι πιστεύειν τῇ τύχῃ καὶ μάλιστα ἐν ταῖς εὐπραγίαις καὶ μὴν καὶ τὸ παρ' Εὐριπίδη καλῶς εἰρῆσθαι δοκῶ ὡς 'ἓν σοφὸν βούλευμα τὰς πολλὰς χέρας νικᾷ, <ὃ> τότε δι' αὐτῶν τῶν ἐκείνου ἔργων τὴν πίστιν εἴληφεν. εἷς γὰρ ἄνθρωπος καὶ μία γνώμη τοὺς δεινοτάτους τῶν στρατηγῶν Ῥωμαίων εἰς μέγα κλέος ἀρθέντας καὶ τὰ μυριόλεκτα πλήθη τῶν στρατευμάτων ἐν βραχεῖ καθεῖλε καιρῷ, τὸ δὲ προφανῶς πεπτωκὸς πολίτευμα καὶ τὰς ἀπειρηκυίας ψυχὰς τῶν ὑπὸ τὸν βασιλέα δυνάμεων ἐπὶ τὸ κρεῖττον ἤγαγε καὶ ἀνύψωσε.

[19] Polybius 1.35.2–5: καὶ γὰρ τὸ διαπιστεῖν τῇ τύχῃ, καὶ μάλιστα κατὰ τὰς εὐπραγίας, ἐναργέστατον ἐφάνη πᾶσιν τότε διὰ τῶν Μάρκου συμπτωμάτων· ὁ γὰρ μικρῷ πρότερον οὐ διδοὺς ἔλεον οὐδὲ συγγνώμην τοῖς πταίουσιν παρὰ πόδας αὐτὸς ἤγετο δεησόμενος τούτων περὶ τῆς ἑαυτοῦ σωτηρίας. καὶ μὴν τὸ παρ' Εὐριπίδη πάλαι καλῶς εἰρῆσθαι δοκοῦν ὡς ἓν σοφὸν βούλευμα τὰς πολλὰς χεῖρας νικᾷ τότε δι' αὐτῶν τῶν ἔργων ἔλαβε τὴν πίστιν. εἷς γὰρ ἄνθρωπος καὶ μία γνώμη τὰ μὲν ἀήττητα πλήθη καὶ πραγματικὰ δοκοῦντ' εἶναι καθεῖλεν, τὸ δὲ προφανῶς πεπτωκὸς ἄρδην πολίτευμα καὶ τὰς ἀπηλγηκυίας ψυχὰς τῶν δυνάμεων ἐπὶ τὸ κρεῖττον ἤγαγεν. Translation adapted from that of Evelyn S. Shuckburgh, *The Histories of Polybius* (Bloomington: Indiana University Press, 1962).

[20] I suspect that Bryennios's τὰς ἀπειρηκυίας ψυχάς ought to match Polybius's τὰς ἀπηλγηκυίας ψυχάς, and have translated accordingly.

[21] Eur., *Frag. Ant.* 19.3–4.    [22] [Plut.] *de Hom.* 2.1950–54; Stob. *Flor.* 4.13.3.4.

[23] Philo *CW De specialibus legibus*, 4.47; Plut. *An seni.* 790A.4; Them. *Or.* 191a, 207s; Gal. *Adhortatio ad artes addiscendas* 13.35; Sex. Emp. *Math.*1.279; Theodoret *Ep.*37; Eustathios of Thessaloniki, *Oration* 16.267, in *Eustathii Thessalonicensis opera minora (magnam partem inedita)*, edited by Peter Wirth

As it seems to be a proverbial phrase it should not be taken as evidence that Nikephoros read much Euripides. Modern readers of Nikephoros have taken the passage as the use of a Euripidean proverb but it should rather be seen as indicating close familiarity with Polybius.[24]

Plutarch is not quoted directly at any point in the *Material for History*. Yet there are a few hints that Nikephoros was familiar with Plutarch's corpus. The de-contextualized use by twelfth-century encomiasts of characters from classical antiquity suggests that Plutarch was commonly read.[25] Another clue comes in a comparison Nikephoros made between the Alan mercenary Arabates and the Spartan general Brasidas:

An arrow struck him in the right hand. But he pulled that arrow out and warded off the barbarian with it, just like Brasidas of old.[26]

Brasidas was one of the leading Spartan generals in the first decade of the Peloponnesian war. Both Brasidas and Cleon died in the Spartan victory in the battle of Amphipolis in 422 BCE. Although numerous ancient historians preserve information about Brasidas, this particular story is preserved only in Plutarch's collection of sayings of the Spartans:

In a battle he was wounded by a spear which pierced his shield, and, pulling the weapon out of the wound, with this very spear he slew the foe. Asked how he got his wound, he said, "when my shield turned traitor."[27]

Many of the sayings Plutarch collected eventually found their way into his parallel lives. This story however seems only to have been known from this source.

A second indication that Nikephoros may have read Plutarch comes in another moderately obscure reference to Roman history. When describing how Alexios first entered into military service Nikephoros wrote:

(Berlin: De Gruyter, 1999); Niketas Choniates, *Oration* 18.321, in *Nicetae Choniatae Orationes et Epistulae*, ed. Jan Louis van Dieten (Berlin and New York: Walter de Gruyter, 1973); Leo of Synada, in *The Correspondence of Leo, Metropolitan of Synada and Syncellus*, ed. Martha Pollard Vinson (Washington, DC: Dumbarton Oaks, 1985), letter 2.

[24] This section of Polybius survives both in the manuscript tradition of the first five books of Polybius's history and in the Constantinian Excerpts volume on "De Sententiis." Constantine Porphyrogenitus, "De Sententiis," in *Excerpta historica iussu Imp. Constantini Porphyrogeniti confecta*, ed. Ursulus Philippus Boissevain (Berlin: Weidman, 1903), 109.19.

[25] Cresci, "Exempla storici greci," 130. On Plutarch in the *Alexiad* see Margaret Mullett and Roger Scott, eds., *Byzantium and the Classical Tradition* (Birmingham: Centre for Byzantine Studies University of Birmingham, 1981), 71–72.

[26] 2.13.7–9: ἀφεὶς δέ τις βέλος βάλλει τούτου τὴν δεξιάν· ὁ δ' ἐκεῖθεν τὸ βέλος ἑλκύσας αὐτῷ τούτῳ τὸν βάρβαρον, καθάπερ ὁ Βρασίδας πάλαι, ἠμύνατο.

[27] Plut. *Apophthegmata Laconica* 219c.10; ἐν δέ τινι μάχῃ διὰ τῆς ἀσπίδος ἀκοντισθεὶς καὶ τὸ δόρυ τοῦ τραύματος ἐξελκύσας αὐτῷ τούτῳ τὸν πολέμιον ἀπέκτεινε καὶ πῶς ἐτρώθη ἐρωτηθεὶς 'προδούσης με' ἔφη 'τῆς ἀσπίδος.'

Alexios then appeared as the great hope of the Romans, later becoming the great help to the Romans, not yet wearing a full-blooming beard, but displaying military virtues even before the age at which the Roman historians say Scipio accompanied Aemilius while campaigning against Perseus of Macedonia.[28]

According to Plutarch's life, Aemilius divorced his first wife, Papiria, after she had borne him two sons. When he remarried he placed Papiria's sons in two illustrious Roman families and they took the names of those families. Aemilius's sister Cornelia and her husband, the son of Scipio Africanus the Elder, adopted the younger of Aemilius's sons who grew up to be Publius Cornelius Scipio Aemilianus Africanus the Younger.[29] The detail that Scipio Aemilianus campaigned with his father against Perseus of Macedonia is today only preserved in Greek in Plutarch's life of Aemilius Paulus. The story was also in Livy, and so may have been in a section of Polybius now lost.[30] This section may have been available to Nikephoros either in a lost manuscript tradition of Polybius or as part of a now lost volume of the Constantinian Excerpts. It is highly likely that Nikephoros had more Polybius than we do. Yet we know that he had access to Plutarch, who was fairly popular.[31] It seems reasonable that he read both.

Although there are no direct quotations, there is at least one matter of vocabulary and content indicating that Nikephoros read the *Roman Antiquities* of Dionysius of Halicarnassus. One of Nikephoros's favorite phrases for describing a brave and daring man, "brave of hand," is fairly unusual. The classical author who used it most often, in the same manner as Nikephoros, is Dionysius of Halicarnassus.[32] The phrase remains relatively rare until it makes a few appearances in Theophanes Continuatus.[33] It was used by Psellos and it becomes more common in the twelfth century.[34] Although this became a reasonably common turn of phrase in the twelfth century, Nikephoros's appears to follow Dionysius in using it particularly of heroic warriors who are about to lose battles despite fighting bravely. For example Dionysius applies it to the Sabine Mettius Curtius who led a brilliant yet doomed rally against Romulus.[35] It is the emphasis on bravery

---

[28] 2.3.14–19.

[29] Aemilius's older son was adopted by Fabius Maximus and became Quintus Fabius Maximus Aemilianus. Plut. *Aem.* 5.5.

[30] Livy 44.44.2–3.      [31] Cresci, "Exempla storici greci," 130.

[32] Dion. Hal. *Ant.Rom.* 2.42.2, 3.13.2.3, 3.16.3.2, 10.16.7.9, 11.48.2.1, 12.4.4.1. On Dionysius see Emilio Gabba, *Dionysius and The History of Archaic Rome* (Berkeley: University of California Press, 1991); Matthew Fox, *Roman Historical Myths: The Regal Period in Augustan Literature* (Oxford: Clarendon Press, 1996), 49–95.

[33] Theophanes Continuatus, *Chronogr.* 255.12, 270.5, 273.10, 313.2.

[34] Psellos, *Chronographia*, 6.10.6, 7.45.12. Some examples: Skylitzes, *Basil I* 4.52. Anna Komnene 1.8.4.9, 1.10.4.3, Zonaras vol. 3, 410.19.

[35] Dion. Hal. *Ant.Rom.* 2.42.2.

in the face of incipient defeat that recalls Dionysius.[36] This is hardly solid proof that Nikephoros read Dionysius, but perhaps indicates that we should add Dionysius to the list of works that Nikephoros probably had read.

Cassius Dio's history of Rome was well known to Nikephoros's contemporaries, and was extensively excerpted by Zonaras. Zonaras used Appian as one of his sources.[37] Although Nikephoros has no verifiable debts to Dio or Appian, the other indications of his interest in Roman history suggest that he may have read at least some of both. Certainly an argument to the contrary would be difficult to establish.

In addition to reading ancient history, Nikephoros appears to have been a keen student of eleventh-century histories. His debts to Psellos and Skylitzes are clear from extensive quotations of their works. Nikephoros does not appear to quote Attaleiates, but as Attaleiates's history covers the same period of eleventh-century history, it is safe to assume that Nikephoros knew it well and used it at least as a source of information.[38] Attaleiates has significant interests in classical Roman history and he refers to some of the same famous figures of Roman history as Nikephoros.[39]

Individual quotations and allusions are less significant in determining how Nikephoros chose to situate his history within the tradition of Greek historiography than the cultural logic underlying his portrayal of characters and events. The issues of his intertextual dialogue with classical authors will be revisited throughout this work. It is in Nikephoros's representation of the heroes and villains of eleventh-century history that he most displays kinship with classical Roman conceptions of honor and virtue.

---

[36] On Nikephoros's valorization of defeat see chapter 8.

[37] Millar, *Cassius Dio*, 3; Cary, "Introduction," 20.

[38] On the similarities and divergences in the narratives of Attaleiates, Nikephoros and Skylitzes see Seger, *Bryennios*, 40–58.

[39] In discussing Botaneiates's ancestry, Attaleiates discusses the Fabii, Scipio Africanus, and Aemilius Paulus. Attaleiates, 217–220; Krallis, "History as Politics," 102–26.

CHAPTER 4

# *Sources for the* Material for History

Nikephoros's early twelfth-century court audience would have been familiar both with the basic course of the events described – no mystery who
becomes emperor after Botaneiates – and with various previously exist-
ing narratives of those events. The appearance and modification of other
histories in Nikephoros's text is then not mere copying, but part of a deliberate conversation about how the events surrounding the foundation of the
current dynasty should be understood.[1] To comprehend the intertextual
play at work and the meanings ascribed to eleventh-century politics in
Nikephoros's narrative, it is vital to understand as much as possible about
the texts he used in his composition.

Nikephoros's historical narrative incorporates and redeploys several late-
eleventh century histories. The passages Nikephoros incorporated from
Skylitzes and from Psellos have long been known and are marked in Gautier's edition.[2] In addition to those citations noted by Gautier, Nikephoros
quoted Psellos's description of John Doukas in his initial depiction of
Alexios Komnenos.[3]

Nikephoros relied heavily on Psellos for his story of the reign of Romanos
Diogenes.[4] When Nikephoros used the material from Psellos's history
of Romanos, he generally was quite faithful, but made slight changes
to cast blame in different directions. Nikephoros modifies Psellos's text

---

[1] Nilsson reminds us that among Byzantine historians "The intense recycling of sources is not a weakness, but a prominent part of the creative and political principles of writing chronography." Ingela
Nilsson, "To Narrate the Events of the Past: on Byzantine Historians and Historians on Byzantium,"
in *Byzantine Narrative*, ed. John Burke (Melbourne: Australian Association for Byzantine Studies,
2006), 51.

[2] Seger, *Bryennios*, 40–58. 1.5 follows Psellos, *Chronographia* 7 (*Constantine Doukas*) 3. Sections 1.7–1.10
follow Skylitzes, *Constantine Monomachos* 9–10, ed. Thurn 442–47. A few lines of 1.13–14 follow
Psellos, *Chronographia* 7 (*Eudokia & Romanos*) 18–19. Substantial portions of 1.17–25 follow Psellos,
*Chronographia* 7 (*Eudokia & Romanos*) 22–43. The first chapter of Book 2 contains a line from
Skylitzes continuatus 155.

[3] Nikephoros: 1.6.20–29; Psellos, *Chronographia* 7 (*Michael*) 16.1–7.

[4] Carile, "La Hyli historias," 56–87; Seger, *Bryennios*, 40–57.

to exonerate Caesar John Doukas and his children, shifting blame onto Michael VII and his advisors, presumably Psellos. Nikephoros occasionally added lines that emphasized the role of Caesar John Doukas or put John's actions in a better light.[5] Nikephoros departs from Psellos to explain that John came to Constantinople to join in the deliberations about what to do after Romanos's defeat at Manzikert.[6] Psellos insists strongly on Michael's ignorance of the orders to blind Romanos.[7] Nikephoros abandons Psellos on this point and asserts rather that Andronikos Doukas protested the order to have Romanos blinded and wrote to his father the Caesar to intercede on Romanos's behalf. The efforts of Andronikos and John to save Romanos came to nothing, in Nikephoros's account, because of "those around the Emperor."[8]

Nikephoros also modified Psellos's story in continuing to call Romanos 'emperor' after the battle of Manzikert. Romanos continues to be called emperor as Andronikos Doukas campaigns against him, in contrast to Psellos.[9] Nikephoros added Romanos's title to Psellos's story with the result that there are two emperors fighting each other.[10] These slight variations in wording and viewpoint suggest that Nikephoros wanted to create a more positive impression of both Romanos Diogenes and John Doukas than that which emerges from Psellos's description.

Nikephoros used substantial sections of Skylitzes (or Skylitzes's source) for the description of the origins of the Turks. Nikephoros's changes to Skylitzes's text are minor, but crucially change the meaning. To his source's account of the dissolution of the Abbasid caliphate, Nikephoros adds that this was a matter of civil war.[11] His modifications to the story of how the Seljuks conquered the empire of Mahmud al-Ghazna all serve to condemn the use of mercenaries. These slight modifications allow the digression on Seljuk history to serve a vital function as a morality tale pointing out the problems facing the Roman Empire.[12]

In addition to these known sources, some clear changes in texture and viewpoint indicate that Nikephoros used two additional sources that are now lost to us. The final section of Nikephoros's work appears to have been told from the perspective of George Palaiologos, whom Anna Komnene names as one of her sources as well. The last seven chapters of Nikephoros's history are told from George's point of view and he is remembered as the protagonist. George makes his appearance in chapter 33 of book 4, just after

[5] Carile, "La Hyli historias," 67–68.     [6] 1.18.12–14, 1.18.24–25.
[7] Psellos, *Chronographia* 7 (*Eudokia & Romanos*) 37.     [8] 1.25.27–32.     [9] 1.23.27; 1.25.11.
[10] 1.21.1; 1.23. Compare Psellos, *Chronographia* 7 (*Eudokia & Romanos*) 32.1–3.
[11] 1.7.20.     [12] See below pp. 65–67.

Alexios has been ordered by Botaneiates to yield the command of his army to the protovestiarios John, a eunuch long in Botaneiates's service. John's task was to bring down the rebellion of Nikephoros Melissenos. Alexios had refused the commission because, since Melissenos was his kinsman by marriage, any failure would be taken as treason. George Palaiologos and his cousin Kourtikes accompanied John on this expedition, giving him sound military advice at every turn which he ignored, bringing disaster. The depiction of John is scathing and mocking, drawing on standard negative stereotypes about eunuchs' instability and ambition.[13]

The biting personal criticism of John is uncharacteristically acerbic for the text. The first joke about John is in chapter 32 when Alexios gives his army to John. In farewell Alexios began to perform a horse exercise for the troops. A surprised John galloped after him, and "immediately everyone roared with laughter and mocked him saying the usual 'klou klou' for eunuchs."[14] While we do not know anything more about the "usual" joke for eunuchs, it is clear that the narrator expected the audience to think a eunuch on horseback was funny. This scene is in keeping with the rest of the mocking of John in chapters 33–40, and I therefore see this episode as part of material narrated by George Palaiologos.

Stylistically, the chapters of this story about the eunuch John are significantly shorter than Nikephoros's usual style. They are only 10–15 lines long. George's narrative calls infantry 'hoplites,' a term only occurring one other time in the history.[15] A shift in narrative tone is clear and it is possible, although not necessary, that George's stories existed in written form. Anna Komnene wrote that she *heard* George Palaiologos telling stories and so our assumption perhaps should be that his memoirs were not written.[16] On the other hand, since the common way to apprehend a text was by hearing it performed, the Greek verb for hearing was not uncommonly used for reading.[17] As authors were often the first performers of their texts, it is also possible that Anna heard George perform a memoir he had written. Both Anna and Nikephoros could have had access to a text written from George's perspective that they had heard him recite. The history ends abruptly in the middle of George's story about how John betrayed him in Constantinople after George had saved his life in battle.

---

[13]  4.31.24.    [14]  4.32.12–15.
[15]  4.37.7; 4.38.3; 4.38.6; the other occurence is in the preparations to fight Basilakes at 4.21.6.
[16]  Komnene 14.7.5.
[17]  Dirk M. Schenkeveld, "Prose Usages of Ἀκούειν 'To Read'," *The Classical Quarterly* 42, 1 (1992): 128–41.

Regardless of whether George's stories were written down or remembered from an oral performance or informal story-telling, they form a coherent block of narrative, with a uniform outlook, focalized by George. As such, George's material can be fairly easily recognized.[18]

A more complex case involves sections of the history that seem to derive from a history of the deeds of John Doukas. Caesar John Doukas, the brother of Emperor Constantine X Doukas, emerges as one of the major heroes of the history. It is possible that Nikephoros learned all of the stories about John that occur in his history from John's descendants who were his companions at court. There are stylistic and narrative shifts in the text where John is the subject, however, that are not explained by simple access to positive information about John Doukas. Several episodes in Nikephoros's history are narrated from John's vantage point. In some cases he is the central figure in the episode, and so it is unremarkable that he is at the center of the narrative focus. Other events are narrated from John's perspective even though he was a marginal actor in them. As well as differences in narrative structure, the sections on John contain a somewhat different vocabulary and some syntactical oddities. These stylistic shifts suggest that Nikephoros drew on a narrative source which told the history of the 1070s through the personal perspective of John Doukas.[19]

The supposition that Nikephoros employed a text about John now lost to us runs parallel to work on other Byzantine historians that has made significant progress in recognizing and understanding the impact of no-longer-extant sources on the composition of those texts.[20] Given how many

---

[18] George seems to be the primary source for sections 4.33–4.40.

[19] The sections of Nikephoros's history that I believe are based at least in part on a history about John Doukas are: 2.14–2.18, describing John's campaign against Roussel de Bailleul and Roussel's revolt in John's name; 3.6, John's efforts to arrange a marriage alliance with Alexios Komnenos; 3.18 describing the efforts of Botaneiates's agents to win John's support for his revolt; and 3.25 describing John's role in the wedding of Botaneiates and Maria of Alania. A few other lines may be reasonably suspected to derive from this source: parts of 1.23 about Andronikos Doukas; 1.25.27–33 on Andronikos's efforts to prevent the blinding of Romanos; and possibly parts of 2.1–3 on John Doukas.

[20] Holmes, *Basil II*, 99–119, 25–52. Catherine Holmes, "The Rhetorical Structures of Skylitzes' Synopsis Historion," in *Rhetoric in Byzantium*, ed. Elizabeth Jeffreys (Aldershot: Ashgate, 2003), 187–200. Shepard has suggested the existence of a pamphlet lauding Maniaces and denouncing his enemies and a laudatory biography of Katakalon Kekaumenos: Jonathan Shepard, "Byzantium's Last Sicilian Expedition: Scylitzes' Testimony," *Rivista di studi bizantini e neoellenici* 14–16, 24–26 (1977–79): 156, Jonathan Shepard, "A Suspected Source of Scylitzes' *Synopsis* Historion: The Great Catacalon Cecaumenus," *Byzantine and Modern Greek Studies* 16 (1992): 54. Work of Sjuzjumov and Kazhdan on identifying an anti-Phokas source and a pro-Phokas family chronicle used by Skylitzes and Leo the Deacon has become generally accepted: Jakov Ljubarskij, "Nikephoros Phokas in Byzantine Historical Writings. Trace of the Secular Biography in Byzantium," *Byzantinoslavica* 54, 2 (1993): 252–53; Tinnefeld, *Kategorien der Kaiserkritik*, 108–10; Alice-Mary Talbot and Denis Sullivan, *The History of Leo the Deacon: Byzantine Military Expansion in the Tenth Century*, (Washington, DC: Dumbarton Oaks, 2005), 14–15; *Jean Skylitzès*, xiii–xvi.

Byzantine texts have disappeared without a trace it is entirely reasonable to expect that our surviving sources frequently drew on materials no longer extant.

Shifts in focalization form one of the main clues that Nikephoros drew on a text about John Doukas. The entire narrative of John Doukas's effort to bring down the rebellion of Roussel de Bailleul is told from John's personal point of view. This narrative puts the best possible light on John's actions, making it clear that John would have made a good emperor and at the same time insisting on his essential innocence of treason. Since John was a main character throughout this story he forms a natural focalizer for the narrative. The politically apologetic portrayal of John, the attention to his personal reactions, and the high level of precise and circumstantial detail suggest that Nikephoros had access to a thorough account of John's adventure.

This account of the battle of Zompos, in which Roussel defeated John, is far more detailed than those surviving in other histories.[21] John is portrayed as having offered the best attack possible against Roussel and only having been defeated because of the disloyalty of his barbarian mercenaries. In the other versions it is simply another defeat. John is captured in the course of the battle and his son Andronikos is severely wounded. Roussel released Andronikos upon receiving his two young sons as hostages. A dramatic story about the escape of one of these hostages, Michael Doukas, is told with great detail and considerable excitement. After the narrative of the battle and its aftermath, the scene turns to Constantinople, where Michael commissions John's son Constantine to continue the fight. Constantine's sudden and unexpected death is described jarringly as the summit of the Caesar's misfortunes, although John was not present in Constantinople.[22] John was still with Roussel in Asia. Why is Constantine's death called the summit of *John's* problems when so many people closer to hand had reason to mourn his passing? Constantine's wife and children were aggrieved and the emperor Michael had just chosen him to lead a vital offensive. That their grief is passed over in favor of describing the impact of the news on John suggests that at some point the entire story was told from John's point of view. John was the only mourner mentioned because this narrative is essentially about John.

The story of Roussel's attack on Constantinople and elevation of John as his ostensible candidate for imperial power continues to be told from John's point of view. Altogether John comes across remarkably well in this

---

[21] Attaleiates 185–86; Skylitzes continuatus 158; Zonaras 710.      [22] 2.17.13–14.

account of his adventures with Roussel. He appears steady, heroic, and he engages the reader's sympathy; all despite leading an utterly disastrous military campaign and marching on the capital with a foreign rebel army. This narrative does not present him as an ineffective general and disloyal courtier but as a victim of a series of extravagant misfortunes.

John is a central character in the story of his adventures with Roussel. As such it is not surprising that he figures prominently in that story. He also figures prominently, however, in other episodes in which he was not the natural focal point. The description of the creation of the marriage alliance between Alexios Komnenos and John's granddaughter is framed by John's narrative and emotional perspective, although the key actors in the passage are Andronikos and his wife, Maria of Bulgaria. The opening of this chapter indicates that it will be about the response of John Doukas to the approaching death of his son Andronikos. This expectation is not fulfilled as Andronikos and his wife take up the action: "The Caesar, seeing his son dying and his young children in need, strove, it seems, to introduce a defender to Andronikos's house, and Andronikos prodded the Caesar to do this along with his wife, the most beautiful of all women, for whom inner beauty shone as brightly as external beauty and fame of family and the adornment of virtues and the decorum of good manners sparkled."[23] The transition from John's thoughts to the description of his daughter-in-law is awkward and unusually unclear for Nikephoros. It is perhaps not going too far to see in this an abbreviation of a longer original. A few other points suggest that this chapter has been reworked from another narrative. At one point Irene is called "the aforesaid Irene" when she has in fact not been mentioned by name.[24] Andronikos's wife, Maria, is never mentioned by name, despite being described at length and having one of the most active women's roles in this story of men's deeds. The chapter ends with the promise to describe the marriage of Alexios and Irene after the main thread of the story has been taken up. This promise is not kept and the marriage is mentioned later only in passing. These are perhaps hints of cuts in the original text.

There are a number of things in this narrative that suggest intimacy with the Doukas's household. John's daughter-in-law, Maria of Bulgaria,

---

[23] 3.6.1–7: ὁ δὲ καῖσαρ τὴν πρὸς θάνατον φερόμενον ὁρῶν τὸν υἱὸν καὶ τοὺς παῖδας αὐτοῦ κομιδῇ νέους, ἔσπευδεν ὡς ἔοικεν ἐπίκουρον τῇ οἰκίᾳ ἐκείνου εἰσαγαγεῖν, ἐκείνου τε πρὸς τοῦτο αὐτὸν παραθήγοντος καὶ τῆς καλλίστης πασῶν γυναικῶν αὐτοῦ ὁμευνέτιδος, ἧς τῷ ἔξωθεν κάλλει τὸ ἐντὸς ξυνεξέλαμπε κάλλος καὶ τῇ περιφανείᾳ τοῦ γένους αἱ τῶν ἀρετῶν ἀγλαΐαι καὶ ἡ τῶν ἠθῶν κοσμιότης συνήστραπτε. I am grateful to Ruth Macrides for correcting my reading of this passage.
[24] 3.6.18.

is praised lavishly. This in itself stands out in Nikephoros's history, in which female characters are rarely mentioned, let alone described in any detail. While the chapter opens with John's view of the situation, Maria is the principal agent in the chapter. After her character is introduced, she is described as having urged her husband to "bring some defender for his children" into their household.[25] She suggested a match between her daughter, Irene, and Alexios Komnenos. John approved and Andronikos was so happy he "all but forgot his illness."[26] John suggested the idea to Alexios when he was visiting. Alexios was delighted but needed his mother's consent. This response immediately threw the entire household into "agony" because Maria "roused the servants and domestics."[27] Maria, "the wisest of women," did not relent "nor did she give sleep to her eyes, or drowsiness to her eyelids, nor did she spare money until the best young woman was betrothed to the best of young men."[28] The description of the household in distress because Maria was running the servants ragged is a rare view of the domestic matters of a great household and speaks to the personal nature of this section of Nikephoros's narrative.

John next appears in the course of Botaneiates's rebellion where the narrative includes a detailed scene in which John refuses to join Botaneiates against Michael VII. In the course of this scene John makes a speech to Botaneiates's agent, Barys, that convinces him to switch sides and join with John in supporting Michael VII against Botaneiates. The content of John's speech has been cut. The lacuna may be the fault of the text's copyist, but the amount of material that seems to have been left out suggests that perhaps the text was awkwardly abbreviated. Nikephoros, whose history contains an overt argument for the legitimacy of the Komnenian dynasty, may not have wanted to include a speech supporting Michael VII Doukas's claim to the throne. Such an argument however, would be entirely appropriate in a history about John Doukas.

Besides being a very favorable account of the Caesar's actions, this scene displays a greater intimacy with the details of the encounter than is typical for Nikephoros's description of Botaneiates's rebellion. Other conspirators are described generically as having corresponded secretly with Botaneiates and plotting to arm the city's rabble and release prisoners. Aside from Barys, only one, Aimilianos the Patriarch of Antioch, is named.[29] Their

---

[25] 3.6.12.    [26] 3.6.22.

[27] 3.6.29–31: ἐν ἀγῶσιν οὖν εὐθὺς ἅπας ὁ οἶκος τοῦ καίσαρος, τῆς καλλίστης πασῶν γυναικῶν διεγειράσης ἅπαν τὸ θεραπευτικὸν καὶ οἰκίδιον.

[28] 3.6.38–41: τοσούτων τοίνυν ὄντων τῶν ἐμποδίων, οὐκ ἀνῆκεν ἡ συνετωτάτη πασῶν γυναικῶν, οὐδ᾽ ἔδωκεν ὕπνον τοῖς ὀφθαλμοῖς οὐδὲ νυσταγμὸν τοῖς βλεφάροις, οὐδὲ χρημάτων ἐφείσατο, ἔστ᾽ ἂν τῷ καλλίστῳ τῶν νεανιῶν τὴν καλλίστην ἐμνηστεύσατο.

[29] 3.18.12.

actions are not described with the same care for the specificity of time and place as the scene with the Caesar.

The story of Botaneiates's marriage with Maria of Alania is another example of an event narrated from the viewpoint of John Doukas, even though he is only one of several active characters. Once Botaneiates was established in Constantinople as emperor, John urged him to marry Maria of Alania. This marriage would have helped the Doukas cause by supporting the inheritance rights of Maria's son Constantine Doukas. The other candidate for Botaneiates's hand was Eudokia Makrembolitissa. The marriage to Eudokia was presumably less welcome to John because she had previously undercut the Doukas family by marrying Romanos Diogenes. At the moment of the marriage, the priest performing the ceremony had an attack of conscience and hesitated to proceed because Botaneiates and Maria both had living spouses. Michael Doukas, John's grandson, slipped out and found another priest:

Since it was the will of the Caesar, as the narrative will show clearly below, Botaneiates, having been persuaded, chose to lead her [to marriage]. Calling [Maria] forth, the Caesar led her into the palace. Then, when they were prepared for the marriage and the emperor and empress were already standing before the doors of the temple as a bridal pair, at that point [the priest] who was about to perform the marriage came to himself and was afraid of being deposed because she also had the emperor Doukas as a husband and Botaneiates's partner from his second marriage was still living. Collecting himself, and knowing how much evil he would bring by blessing both adultery and trigamy, [the priest] then delayed his progress from the altar. Seeing this and guessing at the thought troubling the priest, [the Caesar] was in agony lest the Patriarch, hearing about this, would dissolve the completed marriage and afterward turn towards Eudokia. Not wanting to explain what he wanted because of those standing around, looking intently at his grandson Michael Doukas, he wished to indicate the secret by a glance. The young man, seeing the delay of the priest and the Caesar's gaze upon him, quickly understood what was necessary and immediately got another priest ready to complete the marriage. [Michael] kept him unseen for the time being, and then approaching the altar, he summoned the priest who was declining the marriage. [The priest] asked why he was called. Grabbing his vestment [Michael] quietly removed him from there and brought in the other one, who performed the marriage ceremony. From then on the Caesar had freedom of access to the empress.[30]

[30] 3.25.7–31: ἐπεὶ δὲ τῷ θελήματι τοῦ καίσαρος, ὡς ὁ λόγος σαφέστερον ἐν ὑστέρῳ δηλώσει, καταπειθὴς γεγονὼς ὁ Βοτανειάτης ἀγαγέσθαι ταύτην προείλετο, μετακαλεσάμενος αὐτὴν ὁ καῖσαρ εἰς τὰ βασίλεια εἰσάγει κἄπειτα τῶν πρὸς τὴν μνηστείαν ἑτοιμασθέντων καὶ πρὸ τῶν πυλῶν τοῦ τεμένους τοῦ τε βασιλέως καὶ τῆς βασιλίδος νυμφίων ἤδη ἱσταμένων, ἐπεὶ ὁ μέλλων τὴν μνηστείαν τελέσαι ἑαυτοῦ γεγονὼς καὶ πτοηθεὶς τὴν καθαίρεσιν διὰ τὸ τόν τε βασιλέα [καὶ] Δούκα καὶ σύνευνον αὐτῆς καὶ ἣν εἶχεν ὁ Βοτανειάτης ἐκ δευτέρου συνοικεσίου ὁμευνέτιν ἔτι τῷ βίῳ περιεῖναι, συναγαγὼν ἑαυτὸν καὶ γνοὺς ὅπη κακοῦ φέρεται μοιχείαν ἅμα

The meaning of the text here is far less clear than usual for Nikephoros. The first fourteen lines translated above form one extremely long sentence containing a great many masculine first-person singular participles and verbs. The subject of these participles shifts from Botaneiates, to John, to the scrupulous priest and back to John in a manner that is not transparent. After the thoughts of the priest are described, the subject of the masculine participles shifts to someone observing the priest. Who was in agony at seeing the hesitation of the priest? One would expect the subject to be Botaneiates because it was his wedding. Only four lines later is the new subject revealed as having a grandson Michael Doukas and two lines after that he is definitely identified as the Caesar.

The key to understanding the passage is the realization that the story is told through the perspective of John Doukas, even though he is mostly a passive participant in the situation. The narrative does give information about the thinking of the hesitant priest and young Michael, but John serves as the primary narrative perspective. The narrative dwells on John's agony at the delay and his desire for young Michael to do something. Michael, however, figured out what was needed on his own and may have been only slightly encouraged by his grandfather. While John's counsel may have been important in convincing Botaneiates and Maria to marry, he was not a central figure in the marriage. John's role in the episode does not justify it being told from his viewpoint. Of all the episodes in Nikephoros's history dealing with John Doukas, this is the one in which the meaning of the text is most elucidated by supposing that Nikephoros worked with a first-person narrative by John Doukas. If we imagine that the passage was originally narrated by John in the first person, the number of third-person actors in the sentence would be reduced significantly. This passage may have lost a great deal of clarity because Nikephoros reworked his source into a third-person narrative. As with the other passages examined, this story displays an intimate knowledge of the details of events in which the Caesar John participated and observed.

καὶ τριγαμίαν εὐλογῶν, ἀνεβάλλετο τέως τὴν ἐκ τοῦ βήματος πρόοδον, τοῦτο θεασάμενος καὶ στοχασάμενος τοῦ ὀχλοῦντος τὸν ἱερέα λογισμοῦ ἐν ἀγωνίᾳ ἦν μὴ τὴν τελουμένην μνηστείαν λύσει ὁ πατριάρχης ἐνωτισθεὶς περὶ τούτου καὶ αὖθις πρὸς τὴν Εὐδοκίαν ἀπονεύσει· φράσαι δὲ τὸ βουλητὸν διὰ τοὺς περιεστῶτας μὴ θέλων, πρὸς τὸν ἔκγονον αὐτοῦ Μιχαὴλ τὸν Δούκα ἐνατενίσας διὰ τοῦ βλέμματος τὸ ἀπόρρητον ἐπισημήνασθαι ἤθελεν. ὁ δὲ νεανίας οὗτος τὴν ἀναβολὴν τοῦ ἱερέως ὁρῶν καὶ τὸ εἰς ἑαυτὸν βλέμμα τοῦ καίσαρος γοργῶς συνῆκε τὸ δέον καὶ εὐθὺς ἕτερον ἱερέα ἑτοιμάσας τὸν τὴν μνηστείαν τελέσοντα τέως εἶχεν ἀφανῆ, αὐτὸς δὲ τῷ θυσιαστηρίῳ πλησιάσας προσκαλεῖται τὸν παραιτούμενον τὴν μνηστείαν ἱερέα. ὁ δὲ ἐπυνθάνετο τί ἂν εἴη δι᾽ ὃ προσκαλοῖτο καὶ ὃς τῶν ἀμφίων αὐτοῦ ἀψάμενος μεθίστησι τοῦτον ἐκεῖθεν ἠρέμα, ἀντεισάγει δὲ τὸν ἕτερον, ὃς καὶ τὴν ἱερολογίαν ἐτέλεσεν· ἐντεῦθεν ὁ καῖσαρ τὴν πρὸς βασιλίδα παρρησίαν ἔσχηκεν.

If young Michael Doukas had done his job well, few people would have known that the marriage service was concluded by a different priest than the one who started it. It is therefore not surprising that other surviving histories do not include an account of this episode. The story of John's role in securing the marriage of Botaneiates to Maria of Alania also portrays John as politically important. By this account John was a highly significant power-broker in Constantinople, even after his family had been entirely driven from imperial power. In the precision of its detail, knowledge of essentially private events, and flattering depiction of John, this passage is similar to the others discussing the actions of John Doukas.

These sections focalized by John are also distinguished from the rest of Nikephoros's history by differences in vocabulary and style. There are some lexical differences between the chapters of book 2 dealing with John and Roussel's adventures and the rest of Nikephoros's history. In Chapters 14–18, describing John's campaign against Roussel, the ethnic label given to Franks is "Kelt." John's forces included a cohort of mercenaries under the command of "the Kelt Papas," who joined Roussel in the course of combat.[31] Roussel's army is referred to as Keltic.[32] Outside of these five chapters, Franks are called "Franks." On several occasions before and after these chapters Roussel himself and his associates are called Franks.[33] The term "Franks" is used of various groups of mercenaries from southern Italy.[34] While "Kelt" was more classicizing than "Frank," the terms were somewhat interchangeable and it is certainly possible that the same author would have used both. There is a pattern here, however, with the sections devoted to the history of John Doukas using Kelt and the rest of the text using Frank. The pattern is easily explained by supposing that Kelt was the term of choice for the writer of the Doukas text and Nikephoros, who normally chose "Frank," simply accepted that usage when he was following that source.

In the description of the battle of Zompos the names of ancient regions are preferred to those of contemporary military units.[35] John's army includes phalanxes of Phrygians, Lykaonians, and Asians, under the command of Nikephoros Botaneiates.[36] It appears that Botaneiates's "Phrygians" and "Lykaonians" were the same troops that were known as the Chomatenoi.[37] This portion of the text is following the standard practice of substituting

---

[31] 2.14.36; 37; 44.    [32] 2.16.1.    [33] 1.24.12; 1.24.15; 2.4.1; 2.24.26.
[34] 3.3; 4.4.10; 4.6.11; 4.7.18; 4.10.12; 4.14.4; 4.24.13.    [35] 2.14.    [36] 2.14.40–44.
[37] Gautier, *Histoire*, 169n8; Hélène Ahrweiler, "Choma-Aggelokastron," *Revue des études byzantines* 24 (1966): 279; Hélène Ahrweiler, "Recherches sur l'administration de l'empire byzantin aux IX–XI siècles," *Bulletin de correspondance hellénique* 84 (1966): 34–36.

archaizing proper names for roughly equivalent medieval realities. This practice is not followed elsewhere in the text. When in book 4 Alexios commands the Chomatenoi for Botaneiates, they are called Chomatenoi.[38] This reinforces the impression that Nikephoros used a text that described the battle of Zompos in a more archaizing style than that he chose to maintain in later books.

The preference for ancient proper names is matched by a slightly more classicizing military vocabulary. A comparison of the description of the battle of Zompos with other battles described in depth in book 4 reveals a marginal preference for ancient epic military vocabulary in book 2 and more standard medieval military vocabulary in book 4. The most noticeable instance is the choice of smiting verbs. In the narrative of the battle of Zompos the preferred verb for striking a blow is *ballo*. In the detailed battle descriptions of book 4, the smiting verb of choice is *paio*.[39] *Paio* is rare in classical Attic prose but becomes increasingly common in medieval Greek.[40] Again, the words are essentially synonymous, but the variation may indicate a source that had a more archaizing style.

The sections dealing with John Doukas differ in their narrative structures as well as vocabulary. The continual references to John Doukas help give dramatic power to Nikephoros's narrative. The reader's sympathy is easily engaged in following the career of one well-drawn individual rather than a political party. If this was due to a deliberate literary strategy on the part of Nikephoros, however, we would expect to see the same treatment for the story's other great hero, Nikephoros Bryennios the Elder. Bryennios the Elder receives highly favorable treatment in the narrative, but it is not of the same nature as the treatment of John. The description of Nikephoros Bryennios the Elder, while detailed, lacks the psychological intimacy of the portrayal of John. The motives for Bryennios's actions are explained but the reader is not invited to witness his inner deliberations or emotions. He is presented as an idealized general; calm, heroic, concerned for his people but not fraught with John's uncertainty or practical difficulties.

The narrative structure of the story about Bryennios the Elder is different from that about John Doukas. Whereas John's story is told in blocks of text focusing on John, Bryennios the Elder's story is interwoven with

---

[38] 4.4.8; 4.7.19; 4.9.2.

[39] *Ballo* appears four times in book 2 chapter 15; once in book 1 chapter 17, and once in book 4 chapter 34. *Paio* appears not at all in books 1–3, but twelve times in book 4.

[40] Henry George Liddell *et al.*, *A Greek–English Lexicon*, rev. edn. (Oxford: Clarendon Press, 1968), 1289. The assessment of the increasing use of *paio* in the medieval period is based on a search of the *TLG* web version in May 2006.

that of Botaneiates's and Alexios's opposition. In book 4 the narrative focus moves quickly between Bryennios and Alexios. The juxtaposition of scenes points up the contrast between Bryennios's steady heroism and Alexios's no-holds-barred machinations. Especially in book 4 when Alexios is charged by Botaneiates with ending Bryennios's rebellion, the actions and choices of the two generals are implicitly compared as the narrative focus moves continuously from one camp to the other. These differences in methodology for creating heroic portraits of John Doukas and Nikephoros Bryennios the Elder add to the impression that this is a composite text.

At minimum, Nikephoros had access to detailed information about John Doukas and his family. Nikephoros was married to John Doukas's great-granddaughter and stories about John would have been discussed among his descendants who were Nikephoros's contemporaries and companions at court. John's nephew Michael Doukas was active at the court of Alexios Komnenos, holding the rank of *sebastos* and the office *protostrator* and participating in significant military campaigns.[41] He could have told Nikephoros directly about his adventures escaping from Roussel and getting a back-up priest for Botaneiates's wedding. Other details about the Doukas household, such as Maria of Bulgaria's dealings with her servants, similarly would have been shared with Nikephoros because through his marriage he was part of that household.

The differences in vocabulary in the sections dealing predominantly with John, and the changes in narrative viewpoint, however, suggest that the author was not just including elements of orally preserved stories, but was incorporating portions of a written text about John. These stylistic arguments are not definitive, but, especially in light of the way the author freely included portions of Psellos's and Skylitzes's histories, they all lead to the supposition that Nikephoros also used a text about John Doukas that no longer survives. One wonders whether Anna Komnene had access to this text when she wrote her description of John's participation in the revolt of the Komnenoi, which is also told predominantly from John's point of view.[42]

While we can only speculate about the form of the Doukas text, two factors may point to John Doukas's personal authorship: first, John is known to have had significant literary interests, and second, politicians of this era wrote histories. Regardless of the relative importance of John's political career, he seems to have been engaged in the literary culture of late eleventh-century Constantinople. We owe to John's antiquarian interests

---

[41] Polemis, *The Doukai*, 63–66.          [42] Komnene 2.6.

the survival of *De administrando imperio,* which was copied by a member of John's household.[43] John himself wrote several letters to Psellos, who praised John's interest in learning.[44] Of Michael Psellos's surviving letters, more were written to John than to any other named recipient.[45] John reportedly made his letters from Psellos into a book,[46] a fact which may well account for the preponderance of his correspondence in the surviving corpus of Psellos's letters. This evidence for his appreciation of old books and well-written letters suggests that John enjoyed classicizing highbrow literary culture. John thus seems to have been the sort of person who, if he were to write about Franks, would call them Kelts. John probably would have liked the more archaizing description of the battle of Zompos in Nikephoros's history, whether he wrote it or not. It seems that John would have had both the interest and the ability to write a historical memoir. Alternatively the text also may well have been part of a funeral encomium for John, or part of a history about the Doukas family.

Our ability to identify sections of Nikephoros's history as based on the histories of Psellos, Skylitzes, or a text about John Doukas, does not mean that we should excerpt those sections to find the "real" Nikephoros. Rather such identification allows us to begin the process of understanding the meanings they acquired through the context and logic of Nikephoros's history. The use of this pro-Doukas text indicates that one of Nikephoros's goals was to make John Doukas look good. John is one of several men in Nikephoros's history that come off as heroic despite presiding over, and arguably contributing to, the political collapse of the Empire.

When the whole of Nikephoros's history is studied for its consistent patterns and rhetorical strategies, it appears that the sections from Psellos and Skylitzes, George Palaiologos's stories, and the Doukas text complement those patterns. Nikephoros bends them into his argument.[47] A change

---

[43] Gyula Moravcsik, ed. *De administrando imperio. Constantine VII Porphyrogenitus* (Washington, DC: Dumbarton Oaks, 1967), 16, 32–33.

[44] Michael Psellos, in *Scripta minora,* ed. E. Kurtz and F. Drexl (Milan, "Società editrice vita e pensiero," 1936–41), vol. II, 276–8.

[45] Paul Moore, *Iter Psellianum: a Detailed Listing of Manuscript Sources for All works Attributed to Michael Psellos, Including a Comprehensive Bibliography* (Toronto: Pontifical Institute of Mediaeval Studies, 2005), 580–86.

[46] Psellos in De operatione daemonum, ed. Jean François Boissonade (Nürnberg, 1838. Reprint Amsterdam, A.M. Hakkert, 1964), 176.

[47] One possible exception to Nikephoros's consistency may be the inclusion of the line about Anna Dalassene's "ancient enmity" toward John Doukas and the Doukas family, occurring in the discussion of Alexios's engagement, told from the viewpoint of John Doukas: 3.6. None of this enmity is apparent in the earlier passage discussing the alliance Anna formed with the Doukai, when Michael VI and Isaac became kin-by-marriage by marrying Alan cousins. This union is portrayed as part of the reconciliation of the Komnenoi and the Doukai after Diogenes's death and Anna's recall from

of a few words in Skylitzes's explanation of the entry of the Turks into the Middle East changes the original text with significant meaning for Nikephoros's narrative.[48] Nikephoros's changes to Psellos's text work to make it more sympathetic to Romanos and John Doukas. The moral patterns that motivated the descriptions of warfare are consistent across the history even when it draws on different sources. Although Nikephoros drew significantly from other historical texts, his own history is internally consistent and coherent.

exile: 2.1. In book 2 Nikephoros tells a fairly rosy story of reunion in which any resentment Anna may have felt is omitted from the narrative. Personal enmity on Anna's part may surface in the discussion in book 3 because that passage originated in the text about John Doukas. The appeal to a personal grudge is in keeping with the emphasis on inner emotions and subjective details characteristic of the text about John Doukas.

[48] See below pp. 65–67.

# PART II

*Readings in the* Material for History

CHAPTER 5

# *Problems of the Empire: civil war and mercenaries*

Nikephoros tells the story of one of the most disastrous periods in the military history of the Roman Empire, and he never lets his readers forget just how dire the situation was. Nikephoros's elegiac descriptions of the political state of the Empire form an essential backdrop to his depiction of the generals and politicians struggling to govern well. The stark assessment of the bleak military outlook for the Empire in the 1070s becomes a central key allowing Nikephoros to present many of the men in charge of affairs in this time of disaster reasonably positively. Things were so bad that even good generals were losing.

While the story opens with the history of the Komnenos family in the late tenth century, the narrative quickly moves toward the eleventh-century Turkish invasions, Romanos's loss at Manzikert, and the subsequent outbreak of civil war. By the opening of book 2 the Empire is described as in the process of complete collapse. The Empire was already in "decline" when Romanos's attempt at restoration failed, and when Romanos fell, he brought down the Empire with him.[1] Michael ruled in dire times in which the Turks "pillaged and ravaged the entire east" at the same time that the "Scythians" rebelled and "overran Thrace and Macedonia, so that nearly all Asia and Europe were plundered by these two enemies."[2] After discussing the eastern campaigns in book 2, Nikephoros opened book 3 by swiftly enumerating the collapse of Roman authority in the Balkans. In the west the "Scythians" continued invasions of Thrace and Macedonia. The Slavs "rebelled against servitude to the Romans," and attacked and pillaged

---

[1] 2.1.1–4: ὁ μὲν δὴ βασιλεὺς Ῥωμανὸς ὁ Διογένης προθυμηθεὶς τὰ Ῥωμαίων ὑψῶσαι ἀρξάμενα ἤδη κλίνειν οὐκ εὐφυῶς οὐδ᾽ ἐπιστημόνως τὰ τῆς ὑψώσεως μεταχειρισάμενος αὐτός τε κατεβέβλητο καὶ τὰ Ῥωμαίων ἑαυτῷ συγκατέβαλε πράγματα·

[2] 2.3.2–8: ὁ δὲ βασιλεὺς Μιχαήλ, συγκλειομένων αὐτῷ τῶν πραγμάτων ἤδη κατά τε τὴν ἔω καὶ τὴν ἑσπέραν – οἵ τε γὰρ Τοῦρκοι τὰ κατὰ τὸν Διογένην πυθόμενοι καὶ τὰς πρὸς Ῥωμαίους δι᾽ ἐκεῖνον γενομένας ξυμβάσεις τε καὶ σπονδὰς διαλύσαντες τὴν ἑῴαν πᾶσαν ἐδῄουντο καὶ ἐληΐζοντο, οἵ τε μὴν Σκύθαι πρὸς τούτοις συστασιάσαντες Θρᾴκην τε καὶ Μακεδονίαν κατέτρεχον, ὡς πορθεῖσθαι μικροῦ δεῖν ἅπασαν τὴν Ἀσίαν καὶ τὴν Εὐρώπην ὑπ᾽ ἀμφοῖν τοῖν ἐχθροῖν.

Bulgaria.[3] The cities of Skopje, Naissos, and Sirmium were plundered and the regions along the Sava and Danube rivers were attacked. The Croats and Dukljans also rebelled throughout Illyricum.[4] The Illyrian provinces were further threatened by the "race of the Franks, who having conquered Italy and Sicily, were plotting hostilities against the Romans."[5]

Aside from these generalized descriptions of threats to the Empire, Nikephoros includes vignettes and details in his story that more poignantly drive home the dire situation of the Empire in Asia. Alexios's visit to his grandfather's house in Paphlagonia which had been abandoned because of Turkish raids, receives brief yet affecting treatment:

When he was near Kastamon, [Alexios] desired to see his grandfather's house. Asking everyone to go on, he turned off the road with a few men. Going inside and seeing it deserted of inhabitants, he was filled with tears and groans, remembering his ancestors.[6]

His entourage dragged him away from the scene only steps ahead of a Turkish trap.[7] Nikephoros does not say why the house was abandoned, or even if it had belonged to Manuel Komnenos or Alexios Charon. Nikephoros's audience would have known the answers to these basic questions. The most reasonable supposition is that it was abandoned because of the raids of the Turks. Nikephoros's story that Alexios had difficulty rejoining his party because of Turks raiding in the immediate vicinity of his grandfather's house shows how far imperial control had lapsed in even the inner regions of the Empire. The entire episode would have driven home the dire nature of the situation. On another occasion a peasant near Nikomedeia saw a raiding party of several hundred Turks and assumed they were working for Alexios and Isaac, who were dining nearby with a friend.

---

[3] 3.1.22–24.

[4] 3.1.21–27: τῶν τε Σκυθῶν Θρᾴκην τε καὶ Μακεδονίαν κατατρεχόντων, τοῦ τε Σθλαβίνων ἔθνους τῆς δουλείας Ῥωμαίων ἀφηνιάσαντος καὶ τὴν Βουλγάρων δῃοῦντός τε καὶ ληϊζομένου· Σκοῦποί τε καὶ Ναϊσὸς ἐπορθοῦντο καὶ αὐτὸ δὴ τὸ Σίρμιον καὶ τὰ περὶ τὸν Σαβίαν ποταμὸν χωρία καὶ αἱ Παρίστριοι πόλεις αἱ μέχρι Βυδίνης κακῶς διετίθεντο· ἐκεῖθεν δ᾽ αὖθις Χωροβάτοι καὶ Διοκλεῖς ἀποστάντες ἅπαν τὸ Ἰλλυρικὸν κακῶς διετίθουν. On these events see Florin Curta, *Southeastern Europe in the Middle Ages* 500–1250 (Cambridge University Press, 2006), 298–310; Stephenson, *Byzantium's Balkan Frontier*, 141–44.

[5] 3.3.8–10: . . . καὶ τὸ Φράγγων ἔθνος κατακυριεῦσαν τῆς Ἰταλίας καὶ Σικελίας δεινὰ κατὰ Ῥωμαίων ἐμελέτων.

[6] 2.26.2–6: περὶ δὲ τὴν Κασταμόνα γενόμενος ἐπεθύμησε τὴν τοῦ πάππου οἰκίαν ἰδεῖν. παρακαλεσάμενος οὖν ἀπιέναι πάντας αὐτὸς μετ᾽ ὀλίγων ἀπένευσε τῆς ὁδοῦ· ἐντὸς δὲ ταύτης γενόμενος καὶ ἔρημον ταύτην τῶν οἰκούντων ἰδὼν δακρύων ἐπληροῦτο καὶ στεναγμῶν, ἐν μνήμῃ γενόμενος τῶν αὐτοῦ γεννητόρων·

[7] 2.26.7–9: βίᾳ δ᾽ ἐκεῖθεν ἀποσπασθεὶς πρὸς τῶν ἐπομένων ἀπῄει, ὅτε μικροῦ δεῖν ἐνηδρεύθη παρὰ τῶν Τούρκων, εἰ μὴ ταχέως αὐτὸν οἱ περὶ αὐτὸν ἀποσπάσαντες συνέμιξαν τοῖς λοιποῖς.

The peasant offered to show the Turks the way to the party, inadvertently bringing on a desperate fight.[8] It is a problem when reliance on foreign troops is such that invaders are assumed to be part of the army. With these stories Nikephoros creates a sense of desperation about the state of the Empire that drives the narrative forward.

Nikephoros provides no overt discourse on the reasons for Roman military decline, which helps him avoid pinning blame on particular individuals. At the same time, he is clear that poor human choices are ultimately responsible for Roman failures. Nikephoros embeds into his narrative an argument that two central factors in Roman decline were an over-reliance on mercenaries and civil war. These themes are first introduced in a digression on Turkish history and then followed through the remainder of the text.

Just as Nikephoros pivots from a narrative about the origins of the Komnenos family to his main tale of the decline of the empire, he inserts his only "digression" regarding the origins of Turks. In this story the Abbasid and Ghaznavid states are elided into a single empire that suffers first from civil war and then from losing control of its Turkish mercenary force. While the overt function of the digression is to let the audience know how the Turks and Romans came to be at war, no similar digressions are included regarding Scythians or other imperial enemies. A second indication that the purpose of the passage is more than merely informational is that Nikephoros modeled this section closely on Skylitzes (or Skylitzes's source), but made modifications that adjust the meaning to suit the story's function in his text. Skylitzes's narrative is perfectly functional to explain how the Romans and Turks came to fight, but it does not advance Nikephoros's argument for the causes of imperial decline.

The discussion of how the Turks entered Persia in the midst of a civil war and then destroyed the Persian Empire is a mirror to the sad tale of Roman history to come. Instead of overtly criticizing any of the eleventh-century Roman politicians, Nikephoros tells the story of the fall of another Empire which forms a morality tale about two key problems: civil war and the use of mercenaries. Within Nikephoros's history, the narrative of the origins of the Turks serves not only to give background information about an enemy of the Empire, but also as a morality tale about the dissolution of a great Empire through civil war and unwise use of mercenaries.

Nikephoros adjusts Skylitzes's account to place greater emphasis on the destructive nature of political infighting. Skylitzes describes the breakup

[8] 2.9.13–18.

of the Abbasid Caliphate as a matter of gradual dissolution followed by disagreements between neighbors.[9] Nikephoros presents it as a matter of civil war, *emphylios polemos*.[10] Nikephoros relates that whereas once the descendants of Hagar had ruled "not only Persia and Media and Babylonia and Assyria, but also Egypt and Libya and not small parts of Europe; then they of Hagar rebelling against each other they divided the great Empire into many parts, one striking another, so the nation entered civil wars."[11] Nikephoros thus chose to put greater emphasis on internal causes of destruction than his source did.

Other aspects of this narrative highlight problems inherent in calling on the help of foreign "allies." In both Skylitzes's and Nikephoros's versions Mahmud, the ruler of Persia, sent emissaries to the Turks asking for allies in order to further his personal desire to conquer India.[12] Skylitzes explains that the ruler of the Turks accepted the call for an alliance with Persia because he planned to use it as a way to take possession of the fortified passage over the Araxes river. Nikephoros omits this reasoning, which shifts all of the responsibility for the entrance of the Turks to Mahmud's ambition. In both accounts Mahmud's refusal to allow the Turks to return home after one campaign led them to revolt and encamp in the desert. Mahmud's attempts to end their rebellion failed and ended up destroying all his military power. After Mahmud fell in battle against the Turkish leader Tughril-beg, the latter was declared king of Persia. Tughril-beg immediately removed the guards from the bridge over the Araxes. Skylitzes says that this allowed the Turks to enter Persia *en masse*, while Nikephoros says that Tughril-beg deliberately called them to come over. The entrance of the Turks into Persia allowed Tughril-beg to conquer all the Persians and Saracens.[13]

---

[9] Skylitzes, *Constantine Monomachos* 9.7–12: τῆς δὲ τῶν Περσῶν ἀρχῆς εἰς Σαρακηνοὺς διαλυθείσης, καὶ τῆς τῶν Σαρακηνῶν ἐπικρατείας μὴ μόνον Περσίδος καὶ Μηδίας καὶ Βαβυλῶνος καὶ Ἀσσυρίων κυριευούσης, ἤδη δὲ καὶ Αἰγύπτου καὶ Λιβύης καὶ μέρους οὐκ ὀλίγου τῆς Εὐρώπης, ἐπείπερ ἔτυχον ἐν διαφόροις καιροῖς ἀλλήλων καταστασιάσαντες καὶ ἡ μία καὶ μεγίστη αὕτη ἀρχὴ εἰς πολλὰ διῃρέθη μέρη, καὶ ἄλλον μὲν ἀρχηγὸν εἶχεν ἡ Ἰσπανία, ἄλλον δὲ ἡ Λιβύη, ἄλλον δὲ ἡ Αἴγυπτος, ἄλλον δὲ ἡ Βαβυλών, ἕτερον δὲ ἡ Περσίς, καὶ πρὸς ἀλλήλους μὲν οὐχ ὡμονόουν, μᾶλλον μὲν οὖν καὶ προσεπολέμουν οἱ γειτονοῦντες.

[10] 1.7.2.

[11] 1.7.13–21: τῆς γοῦν Περσῶν ἀρχῆς εἰς τοὺς τῆς Ἄγαρ διαλυθείσης καὶ τῆς μὲν Σαρακηνῶν ἐπικρατείας μὴ μόνον Περσίδος καὶ Μηδίας καὶ Βαβυλῶνος καὶ Ἀσσυρίων κυριευούσης, ἀλλ' ἤδη καὶ Αἰγύπτου καὶ Λιβύης καὶ μέρους οὐκ ἐλαχίστου τῆς Εὐρώπης, ἐπείπερ ἀλλήλων καταστασιάσαντες οἱ ἐξ Ἄγαρ τὴν μεγίστην ἀρχὴν εἰς πολλὰς ἐμερίσαντο, ἄλλος ἄλλης κατάρχων, καὶ εἰς ἐμφυλίους πολέμους τὸ ἔθνος ἐχώρησεν.

[12] The *Mouchoumet* mentioned by Skylitzes and Nikephoros has been associated with Mahmud al-Ghazni. Gautier, *Histoire*, 90n1.

[13] 1.7–9; Skylitzes, *Constantine Monomachos* 9–10. Nikephoros makes an addition to Skylitzes's account to mention that Mahmud fell in battle, not by an arrow or spear, but through the fall of his own horse. It is a detail that calls attention to the fate and military actions of the individual commander.

The two mistakes of the Muslims, civil war and reckless use of foreign allies, are repeated by the Romans in Nikephoros's subsequent history. The destruction of the Persian Empire served as a warning against this behavior for the Romans. Nikephoros's changes to Skylitzes's text are slight, but crucial. They help the digression on the Turks become an example of figured speech in which the audience is invited to draw the conclusion that the problems of Mahmud's empire are the causes of their own decline. That the argument required the audience to draw the obvious connection made it more emphatic than an overt statement.[14] Conclusions that audience members make for themselves have greater power than assertions they are asked to believe.

The concept of civil war presented in the history of the Turks is taken up elsewhere in Nikephoros's text. Civil war provided Nikephoros with an alternative to the highly negative political discourse of rebellion and revolt. The standard pattern in Byzantine political discourse was to consider one man the legitimate emperor and all rivals rebels. Nikephoros does not adopt this political theory but tells stories of several rulers in relatively equal contestation. Nikephoros alters Psellos's narrative here to continue to refer to Diogenes as emperor after the battle of Manzikert. Nikephoros added Romanos's title to Psellos's story with the result that there are two emperors fighting each other.[15] Although Andronikos is sent out with an army to capture Romanos Diogenes after his defeat at Manzikert, Romanos is not called a tyrant or a rebel. Romanos continues to be called emperor as Andronikos Doukas campaigns against him, again in contrast to Psellos.[16] When Anna Dalassene was accused of conspiring with Romanos, Michael and John Doukas are called "those ruling."[17] Michael is consistently called the "ruler" rather than the "emperor" throughout the description of the revolt of Bryennios.[18] Botaneiates gained the support of influential people in Constantinople who were disgruntled with "the ruler and the Logothete."[19] Michael remains merely the "ruler" throughout the narrative of Botaneiates's coup.[20] During the revolt of Botaneiates against Michael VII, Michael's brother Konstantios Doukas is called the brother of the "ruler."[21] Michael is again called the "emperor" when his entry into monastic life is described.[22]

---

It plays up the irony of the accidental death. Also rather than riding back and forth "disorderly" as in Skylitzes, Mahmud was properly acting to exhort his troops when his horse slipped and killed him. 1.9.14–17.
[14] On emphasis and figured speech see Ahl, "Safe Criticism," 174–208.    [15] 1.21.1; 1.23.1; 1.23.27.
[16] 1.23.27; 1.25.11.    [17] 1.22.38–39 Michael is also called the emperor in the same story.
[18] ὁ κρατῶν, 3.11.9; 3.13.1; 3.13.15.    [19] 3.16.7.    [20] 3.18.5; 3.19–3.21.15.
[21] 3.6.34.    [22] 3.24.1.

Botaneiates is called both "emperor" and "ruler" in this narrative, but not indiscriminately.[23] When Alexios went to meet Botaneiates with Konstantios Doukas before Botaneiates's entry into Constantinople, he addressed Botaneiates as "emperor."[24] Later, after defeating Bryennios the Elder, Alexios sent Bryennios's red bejeweled imperial slippers to "the ruler" Botaneiates.[25] Botaneiates grips the imperial scepter,[26] but he is not often directly called "emperor."

While he demotes Botaneiates to "ruler," Nikephoros comes close to naming his grandfather emperor in the description of his revolt. The author does not refer to Nikephoros Bryennios as a tyrant, but as "the one aspiring to rule"[27] This is a fairly unusual usage which aligns Bryennios closely with the imperial office, at least lexically, and may imply that Bryennios was the one *being* an emperor even if Botaneiates formally had the title. Bryennios is also called the "ruler" when, dressed in imperial garments, he received the envoys from Botaneiates.[28] Although the people of Traianoupolis had wanted to keep faith with the "rulers" they became the first city to proclaim Bryennios "emperor of the Romans."[29] Once proclaimed, Bryennios sent an envoy to Constantinople to make a treaty with the "ruler."[30]

When Alexios and Bryennios have their final battle, both John Bryennios, Bryennios's brother, and Alexios Komnenos have the title *domestikos ton scholon*. In Nikephoros's description of Bryennios battle-order his brother is called "the *kouropalates* John, who had been appointed *domestikos ton scholon*."[31] Since that was the title Alexios had been given by Botaneiates, mentioning the title had the effect of emphasizing that both parties were fighting for legitimacy. In Anna's account of the battle the *domestikos ton scholon* is always and exclusively Alexios.[32]

This deliberate ambiguity in the terminology of rule sets the Empire in a true state of contestation. These wars were not simple cases of revolts against emperors. Bryennios calls his rebellion a "civil war."[33] After he defeated Bryennios, Alexios was disappointed that he was not rewarded by Botaneiates because he had defeated not a tyranny, but rather a great Empire.[34]

---

[23] Emperor 4.2.39; ruler 4.3.1. He may be called emperor in section 4.2 because it is in the same sentence that Bryennios is called ruler and it would be confusing to have two rulers in the same sentence.

[24] 3.22.12; 3.23.2.    [25] 4.16.2–3.    [26] 3.25.1–2.

[27] 4.5.7–10: καὶ γὰρ ἔμελλε μετ' ὀλίγων μάχεσθαι πρὸς πολλοὺς στρατηγούς τε ἅμα γενναίους καὶ πολυπειροτάτους, ὧν καθάπερ ἀστέρων ἥλιος ἐξῆρχεν ὁ βασιλειῶν. 4.13.12: ὁ δὲ τοῦ βασιλειῶντος υἱὸς ἐν τῷ διώκειν πόρρω γενόμενος.

[28] 4.2.34.    [29] 3.9.2; 3.10.2.    [30] 3.10.16.    [31] 4.6.9–10; John as *domestikos ton scholon* : 4.12.5–6.

[32] Komnene 1.4.4; 1.5.8; 1.6.1.    [33] 4.3.13: καὶ τὸν πόλεμον καταλῦσαι ἐμφύλιον.    [34] 4.16.17.

By any account, the ineffectiveness and incompetence of the Byzantine government in the 1060s and 1070s was compounded by the nearly continuous rebellions of various generals. Given the undeniable damage caused by the revolts, Nikephoros had a delicate task in presenting the history of his grandfather, the rebel. Byzantine political discourse had nothing but opprobrium for an unsuccessful rebel. Rebels destroyed peace and acted out of vanity. They were also guilty of blasphemy in disputing the authority of God's chosen emperor. In accepting successful rebels as just agents of God, Byzantine political ideology encouraged many to revolt, but failure was proof of divine disfavor.[35] As the grandson of an unsuccessful rebel, Nikephoros would have been motivated to find an alternative vocabulary to that of rebellion.

Casting the conflicts of the 1070s as civil wars not only absolved the contenders of the crime of revolt, but may have aggrandized the conflicts through implicit comparison with grand political conflicts leading up to the establishment of the Roman Principate. Caesar, Pompey, Anthony, and Octavian contended as relative equals and, from the perspective of the twelfth century, all were grand characters. Their names are not invoked within Nikephoros's history and only his choice to employ the discourse of civil war brings them to mind. But at least for some members of Nikephoros's audience, casting the bloody politics of the 1070s as civil war may have prompted them to remember the civil wars of the late Republic, and that comparison would have been relatively flattering.

While the discourse of civil war may have been preferable to the discourse of rebellion, it was still bad. Nikephoros's fairly strenuous efforts to portray the politics of the 1070s as civil war rather than rebellion may have excused his grandfather from the worst of political sins, but Roman political infighting remained a key cause of Roman decline. By whatever name, the habit of Romans fighting Romans while the Empire was being invaded on all sides is blamed for leading toward the dissolution of the Empire. In Nikephoros's telling, civil war was one of the main reasons for Roman failure.

Turks, Franks, and Scythians were all hired to help fight alongside the Roman army in this period in which the Roman Empire was facing invasions of Turks, Franks, and Scythians. Some historians have argued that mercenaries were perceived as more loyal than the native military and held certain administrative advantages.[36] Although much of the time these

---

[35] Treadgold, "Byzantium, the Reluctant Warrior," 209–34; Cheynet, *Pouvoir*, 177–84.
[36] Jonathan Shepard, "The Uses of the Franks in Eleventh-Century Byzantium," *Anglo-Norman Studies* 15 (1993): 275–305; Magdalino, *Manuel*, 147, 231–33.

mercenaries and allies were reliable, they also caused significant problems
for the Romans trying to use them. Nikephoros's history acknowledges
these problems.

A number of episodes reveal a clear discomfort with the use of mercenaries. One of Romanos's great mistakes leading to the battle of Manzikert
was to be over bold because he was leading many "allies."[37] Romanos put
his trust in the arrival of Persian allies to defend him against the forces of
Andronikos Doukas.[38] That foreign mercenaries were perceived by many
as problematic is seen in the story of John Bryennios's failed siege of
Constantinople during his brother's rebellion. When John laid siege to
Constantinople his army included a large force of Scythians who were "not
foreigners and mercenaries, but had long ago entered into the empire of
the Romans voluntarily."[39] It was important for Nikephoros to note that
these "Scythians" had ceased to be foreigners by virtue of having joined the
Roman polity long ago. The implication is that attacking the capital with
an army of foreign allies would have been considered bad behavior. The
Bryennios revolt lost the support of the citizens of Constantinople when
some of John's troops set fire to a number of the suburban palaces.[40]

One obvious problem with mercenaries is that they only fight for money.
The escape of Alexios and Isaac Komnenos from the unexpected Turkish
attack near the town Dekte is attributed in part to the heroism of two Alan
mercenaries, Arabates and Chaskares.[41] Arabates served Isaac for wages
as Chaskares served Alexios, presumably as private bodyguards. Initially
they hung back from the fighting because their odds looked bad. Arabates
argued that it would be a disgrace to the Alan race if they lost. They were
motivated to fight by their pride in the "Alan race" – not their wages.
Apparently the situation of being heavily outnumbered – supposedly 20
against 200 – had rendered their contract void. Their wages were not worth
that sort of fight. This is a significant acknowledgment that mercenaries
need more motivation than money in desperate situations. This is the fight
that started because a peasant mistook a Turkish raiding party for a group
of mercenaries and gave them directions to the house where the Komnenoi
were staying.

Later the emperor Michael sent Nikephoros Palaiologos to hire an army
of Alan mercenaries with which to fight the rebellion of Roussel. He
recruited an army of 6,000, but they left and went home again when

---

[37] 1.13.26.     [38] 1.25.1–4; 9–10.
[39] 3.11.6–7: οὐ τῶν ξένων καὶ μισθοφόρων, ἀλλὰ τῶν πρὸ πολλοῦ αὐτομολησάντων ὑπὸ τὴν
βασιλείαν Ῥωμαίων.
[40] 3.12.8–13.     [41] 2.12.17–32.

he could not pay them.[42] Palaiologos's inability to raise an army allowed Roussel to establish himself as the local ruler.

Another problem with mercenaries and foreign allies is that they occasionally switch sides. Frankish mercenaries switch sides in the midst of battle on two occasions in Bryennios's history. Both times they are described as unwilling to fight against their perceived ethnic kin. John Doukas marched against Roussel with a contingent of "Keltic" mercenaries under the command of Papas.[43] The "mercenaries" began to speak with the "enemies" and soon Papas took his contingent to join Roussel against John.[44] Alexios had a contingent of "Franks from Italy" with him in his fight against Bryennios.[45] Bryennios also had a Frankish contingent that was said to have been brought from Sicily by the general Maniakes, who had revolted in the middle of the eleventh century.[46] In the course of the battle all of Alexios's Franks joined with Bryennios's Franks.[47] This ethnic solidarity is not seen in Turks or Scythians. Franks alone refused to fight each other.

Sometimes allies changed sides because they saw a better opportunity for their own prosperity. This seems to have been the case with Bryennios's Scythian allies at the battle of Kalavryai.[48] Bryennios's Scythians fought vigorously and effectively against Alexios for the first part of the battle but then broke off their attack to pillage Bryennios's baggage train. This disruption was one of the key factors in Bryennios's defeat.

Paid allies help within the context of their own political agenda. Michael VII hired the Turkish general Artuq to fight against Roussel and John Doukas.[49] After capturing Roussel, Artuq allowed Roussel's wife to ransom him, and Roussel continued his rebellion.[50] Artuq defeated the enemy he was set against, but he did not follow through in a way that was politically advantageous for his employer.

The employment of foreign allies was most dangerous and destructive when those allies were themselves in the process of conquering parts of the Empire; as was the case with the Franks, Scythians, and Turks. Although in most campaigns these allies did fight reliably for the generals who hired them, Nikephoros's audience would have been keenly aware of their destructive force and, with respect to Asia, their ultimate conquest of the Empire. Nikephoros makes this point most overtly in the story of Roussel's principality, perhaps because in this case the Romans were victorious.

---

[42] 2.19.5–14.  [43] 2.14.36–37.  [44] 2.14.44–48.  [45] 4.4.10.

[46] 4.6.11. On Maniakes see Shepard, "Byzantium's last Sicilian Expedition," 149–59. Either the contingent had continued to recruit new members, or they were old men by 1078, or the detail that they were Maniakes's troups was a flattering elaboration.

[47] 4.10.11–14.  [48] 4.6–9.  [49] 2.17.29–33.  [50] 2.18.24–29; 2.19.2–5.

Roussel was considered to have led not a desertion or foreign attack, but a rebellion, *apostasia*. Roussel led a contingent of Franks who had entered Roman service under the leadership of Crispin. Andronikos Doukas hired Crispin to help him bring down Romanos Diogenes after the battle of Manzikert.[51] Crispin is said to have taken the commission in part out of personal hatred for Romanos, the causes of which are unknown. After Crispin died, Roussel took over the leadership of his contingent. When Michael dispatched Isaac Komnenos to combat the Turks, Roussel accompanied him, but looked for a pretext for rebellion.[52] Roussel's rebellion was sparked by an incident in which Isaac meted out a punishment against one of Roussel's men. The Frank had "done injustice" to an inhabitant who then complained to Isaac. When Isaac tried to have an "equal measure" of "injustice" done to the Frank, Roussel took the offense as opportunity for rebellion.[53] Roussel may well have been planning to revolt anyway. Yet the story points out several problems with the discipline of foreign military contingents.

The ultimate destructive power of Roussel's rebellion was limited by the number of Franks who had crossed the Adriatic. Scythian and Turkish allies were less limited. John Bryennios and Nikephoros Bryennios the Elder fought against Scythians both before and after they fought with them as allies. When John Bryennios needed to raise his siege of Constantinople, he used the invasion of some Scythians across the Danube as a pretext to leave.[54] John established an alliance with the Scythians he defeated by exchanging prisoners and taking oaths.[55]

As the situation of the Empire deteriorates over the course of Nikephoros's narrative, the implicit criticism of hiring the Empire's enemies to fight internal conflicts grows. The Turks who were hired by Michael VII to fight Botaneiates ended up joining with Botaneiates and fighting for him against Michael. Michael and Nikephoritzes had sent envoys to the Turks and hired Suleiman, the son of Qutlumush to fight against Botaneiates.[56] These Turks were then suborned by Chrysoskoulos, who was working for Botaneiates.[57] By the time Botaneiates took power nearly all of Asia was controlled by the Turks.[58]

When Botaneiates commissioned Alexios to put down the rebellion of Nikephoros Bryennios, Alexios made an alliance with two Turkish leaders, Suleiman and Mansur, because "he had no army of his own."[59] These are the same Turks who had been hired by Michael VII to fight Botaneiates.

---

[51] 1.24.12–16.    [52] 2.4.2–5.    [53] 2.4.5–11.    [54] 3.14.4–9.    [55] 3.14.11–14.
[56] 3.16.9–13.    [57] 3.16.32–35.    [58] 4.1.23.    [59] 4.2.10–15.

Since, according to Nikephoros, Botaneiates had destroyed the fiscal system of the Empire and all of Asia was being ruled by Turks and nearly all the west was being ruled by Bryennios, with what revenue did Botaneiates plan to pay Suleiman and Mansur? Presumably they were persuaded on the hope of personal gain rather than steady payment. Botaneiates must have arranged their transportation to Europe. The criticism of this policy is implicit in the narrative.

Nikephoros Melissenos was supported in his rebellion by Turkish allies. By this point however, the Turks had become too well established in Anatolia for Melissenos to have any ability to control them. Nikephoros the author presents Melissenos's rebellion as a cover for the final Turkish conquest of Anatolia. Melissenos,

drawing the Turkish rulers and the Turkish forces to himself, went around the cities of Asia wearing red slippers. The citizens handed themselves and their cities over to him as Emperor of the Romans. And he unwillingly handed them over to the Turks. In this way all the cities of Asia and Phrygia and Galatia quickly came to be ruled by the Turks.[60]

Nikephoros's history breaks off unfinished in the midst of describing the disastrous campaign of eunuch John undertaken against Turks who were ostensibly fighting for Nikephoros Melissenos.[61]

Diodorus Siculus's statement that despite the rational advantages of using mercenary forces, their employment was not Roman custom was included in Constantine VII's excerpts.[62] Regardless of whether Nikephoros read Diodorus's assessment, he knew enough classical history to know that ancient Romans rarely hired mercenaries, in contrast to the Carthaginians and Hellenistic kingdoms.[63] As noted above, Nikephoros does not overtly censure Roman generals for hiring Turkish soldiers to fight other Roman generals. Such criticism, however, is deeply embedded in his narrative. That a raiding party was assumed to be in government service, that a Roman civil war caused the Turks to be transported to Europe, and that Melissenos's revolt became a thin cover for a Turkish conquest, all manifest the dangers of relying on foreign military forces. Nikephoros's history cannot be read as an apology for the use of foreign forces in domestic civil wars. The history shows uneasiness with the use of mercenaries and regrets that local troops are not available to do most of the fighting.

---

[60] 4.31.4–10.    [61] 4.34–40.    [62] Diod. Sic. 29.6.1; Const. Porph. *De Sententiis* 362.
[63] J. E. Lendon, "War and Society." In *The Cambridge History of Greek and Roman Warfare*, ed. Philip A. G. Sabin, Hans Van Wees, and Michael Whitby (Cambridge University Press, 2007), 508.

The two problems of civil war and dangerously uncontrollable merce-naries created, in Nikephoros's vision, the political and military situation that allowed the Roman Empire to experience rapid decline in the 1070s. Nikephoros's theory allows ultimate responsibility to lie with the decisions of the Roman politicians and generals. Roman losses are in no way con-nected with divine wrath. Nor do the Romans lose because any of their external enemies are militarily superior to Roman armies. Neither Turks, Scythians, or Franks are shown as better fighters than a well-managed Roman army. Bad management of the Roman state allowed for specific failures leading to both civil war and the over-reliance on mercenaries. While Nikephoros works deliberately to exonerate his grandfather and sev-eral other key political leaders, his political theory ascribes considerable agency to the decisions of the Roman political and military leadership.

CHAPTER 6

# *The rise of Alexios*

Throughout his history Nikephoros argues overtly and systematically that imperial power rightly resides with Alexios Komnenos. All indications of criticism of Alexios in the text need to be set in the context of the overt argument for Alexios's rule. Given that no one in Nikephoros's audience would have forgotten that Alexios came to power through a violent coup that resulted in considerable looting and destruction of Constantinople, such an argument for his legitimacy was necessary. It was too easy to consider Alexios as an illegitimate usurper for a history written at his family's court to do other than argue explicitly for Alexios's claim to the throne. The political argument on the surface of Nikephoros's narrative needs to be understood as a prelude for deeper analysis.

Nikephoros constructs the case for Alexios by continuously placing members of the Komnenos family within or near the imperial household. Throughout the text he associates the Komnenoi with whoever is ruling the Empire. This is done through adoption and spiritual kinship when marriage or other connections are not available for emphasis. By privileging all connections between the Komnenoi and the imperial throne Nikephoros makes familial relationships a prominent part of his history. The systematic association of Alexios with imperial rule would have the political effect of bolstering Komnenian claims to legitimacy.

Nikephoros establishes his narrative as the story of the Komnenos family in the first sentence of book 1:

The famous Manuel of the Komnenos family served as ambassador during the negotiations and treaties between Basil, who held the imperial scepters, and Bardas Skleros, who was a rebel for many years and subdued not a small part of the east. Manuel tried to rejoin the severed members of the Roman Empire to wholeness and indeed brought them together very intelligently and vigorously. This Manuel had two children; the older was called Isaac and the younger John.[1]

---

[1] 1.1.1–8: Μανουὴλ ἐκείνου τοῦ πάνυ, ὃς ἐς Κομνηνοὺς ἀναφέρων τὸ γένος, τῶν μεταξὺ συμβάσεων καὶ σπονδῶν τοῦ τε τηνικαῦτα τὰ Ῥωμαίων σκῆπτρα ἰθύνοντος Βασιλείου καὶ Βάρδα

This remarkable sentence starts Nikephoros's narrative, not with the emperor, but with Manuel who, as the negotiator of the truce, is cast as a kingmaker. Basil II is not introduced as a mighty or effective emperor, but as one clinging to power and enduring the attacks of Bardas Skleros. In the late eleventh century, to recall Basil's reign as a time of turmoil rather than strength announces this as a history of aristocratic rivalries. The mention of Skleros's revolt may have served to remind the audience that political trouble was known under great emperors of the past as well as its contemporaries.

Still in the first chapter, Manuel Komnenos entrusted his children Isaac and John to the Emperor Basil.[2] Nikephoros used the term commonly applied to cases of adoption.[3] Basil was in charge of arranging the marriages for the two boys.[4] This may have been a consequence of their membership in Basil's household. They did not live in the palace, however, but in the Stoudios monastery. Nikephoros explained that they lived in the monastery on the outskirts of the city so that they could learn virtue by imitating the best men and be able to leave the city easily for hunting trips and military exercises.[5] While the boys undoubtedly enjoyed these benefits, Nikephoros was explaining why they were not actually at the palace if they were considered Basil's children. They lived in a prominent local monastery like any number of orphaned aristocrats.

The reign of Alexios's uncle, Isaac Komnenos (1057–1059), is passed over quickly, so as to skirt his embarrassing deposition. Yet other details about Isaac's family continue to place the Komnenoi close to the throne. It is possible that Nikephoros inflated the social status of Katherine, Isaac's wife, by claiming that she was the daughter of the Bulgarian Khan Samuel.[6] One of the manuscripts of Skylitzes adds the detail that Katherine was Samuel's niece and the daughter of Ivan Vladislav.[7] Constantine Doukas is described as continuing to honor Isaac and his family, particularly his wife and daughter and brother John, even after Isaac had become a monk.[8] This detail keeps the Komnenoi close to the seat of power. They remained familiars of the emperor.

---

ἐκείνου τοῦ Σκληροῦ, τοῦ ἐπὶ πολλοῖς ἔτεσι τυραννήσαντος καὶ τὴν ἑῴαν μικροῦ δεῖν ἅπασαν καταστρέψαντος, ἀποδέδεικτο πρέσβυς, τὰ διερρωγότα μέλη τῆς Ῥωμαίων ἡγεμονίας συνάψαι πειραθεὶς πρὸς ὁλότητα καὶ μέντοι ἔτι καὶ συνάψας ἐπιστημόνως λίαν καὶ νεανικῶς, Μανουὴλ οὖν τούτου γίνονται παῖδες δύο, ὧν ὁ μὲν πρεσβύτερος Ἰσαάκιος, ὁ δὲ νεώτερος Ἰωάννης ἐκέκλητο.

[2] Attaleiates similarly claims that Basil II took a special interest in Nikephoros Botaneiates's father. Attal. 233–34.

[3] παρατίθημι, 1.1.11 and 13.    [4] 1.2.6–9.    [5] 1.1.23–26.    [6] 1.2.8.

[7] This manuscript, U, contains interpolations displaying a particular interest in Bulgarian history. *Jean Skylitzès*, xxii and 404n30.

[8] 1.5.24–28.

After Isaac's abdication, Nikephoros keeps the focus of the narrative on the Komnenoi by moving quickly over the reign of Constantine Doukas to describe the family of Isaac's brother John.[9] Nikephoros presents Anna Dalassene, John's wife, as taking over the leadership of the Komnenos family and marrying her children in ways that worked to connect her family to leading political families of the empire.[10] Anna married her daughter Theodora to Constantine Diogenes, the son of the emperor Romanos Diogenes. This Constantine was the son of Romanos's first wife and was formally excluded from the succession in favor of Eudokia's children, Michael and Constantine Doukas. Nikephoros clarified that Theodora's marriage to Constantine was celebrated while Romanos was the reigning emperor. This match would closely associate the Komnenoi with the emperor. As the brothers of the emperor's daughter-in-law, Alexios and his brothers would have had a claim on access to the palace household. Romanos also made Manuel, the oldest brother, his "kinsman" and appointed him *protostrator*.[11] Romanos may have benefited by associating an important formerly imperial family with himself as a counterweight to the Doukai, on whom he was dependent and who feared any encroachment on the authority of Constantine Doukas's children.

In the midst of the maneuvering surrounding the ouster of Romanos and the establishment of Constantine Doukas's son as emperor Michael VII, the Doukai exiled Anna on suspicion of helping Romanos. Nikephoros presents the accusations of treasonous correspondence as products of malicious slander, although the supposition that Anna sided with Romanos is entirely reasonable.[12] Once the Doukai had returned firmly to power however, Nikephoros explains that Anna quickly was recalled and able to arrange a further connection with the Doukai through the marriage of her son Isaac. At the time that Michael VII married Maria of Alania, Isaac married Maria's cousin Irene. By marrying two cousins, Isaac and Michael became "kin by marriage."[13] The reasonably successful military careers of Isaac and Alexios ensured that they would remain significant individuals at court.

[9] 1.6.1–5.
[10] Two of the daughters were married while John was still alive: Maria to Michael Taronites and Eudokia to Nikephoros Melissenos. Nikephoros mentioned that Nikephoros Melissenos was related through his father to the Bourtzes family. This family held great power in Antioch in the tenth and eleventh centuries. Cheynet, *Pouvoir*, 219, 25–7.
[11] 1.7.1–3: ἄρτι δὲ καὶ τοῦ Διογένους Ῥωμανοῦ τῶν τῆς βασιλείας οἰάκων ἐπειλημμένου, πρῶτος τῶν ἀδελφῶν Μανουὴλ ᾠκείωτο τῷ βασιλεῖ καὶ πρωτοστράτωρ πρὸς αὐτοῦ ἀποδέδεικτο.
[12] The episode is more fully discussed at pp. 151–52.
[13] 2.1.8–9: διὰ κήδους αὐτοὺς ἑαυτῷ οἰκειοῦται· On the family of Maria see Lynda Garland and Stephen Rapp, "Mary 'of Alania': Woman and Empress Between Two Worlds," in *Byzantine Women: Varieties of Experience 800–1200*, ed. Lynda Garland (Aldershot: Ashgate, 2006), 95–108.

After several disastrous years of Michael's rule, the Doukas family was interested in a much tighter connection with the Komnenoi. Nikephoros relates that Caesar John, his son Andronikos, and especially the latter's wife Maria, wished to tie Alexios more firmly to the Doukas house by marrying him to Irene, Andronikos and Maria's daughter. Michael VII's younger brother Konstantios wanted Alexios to marry his younger sister Zoe. After Alexios's coup, Zoe married Alexios's younger brother Adrian. Anna Dalassene is said to have opposed Alexios's union with the Doukas family on the grounds of "ancient enmity" toward John and the Doukas family.[14]

Although he had not yet married into the Doukas family, Alexios is portrayed as one of Michael VII's key advisors during Botaneiates's rebellion.[15] When it became clear that Michael would have to abdicate, Alexios was again at his side helping with the decisions. He demanded that Michael write down his wish to abdicate and, armed with this document, Alexios went immediately to Botaneiates to argue for clemency for Michael's younger brother Konstantios.[16] Alexios's actions as an advocate for a *porphyrogennetos* placed him in the role of a familiar of the ruling family.

After the success of Botaneiates's coup against Michael VII, Botaneiates retained Alexios as one of the leading officers of the Empire and was soon named *domestikos ton scholon*.[17] Botaneiates was sufficiently elderly for his accession to be a prelude to further succession politics. His first task as emperor was to defeat the rebellion of Nikephoros Bryennios, which had begun the previous year. During John Bryennios's siege of Constantinople, Botaneiates gave Alexios command of the city's defenses. Alexios's marriage to Irene Doukaina was completed at that time.[18] Botaneiates also elevated Alexios's brother Isaac to the high rank of Sebastos and gave him a room in the palace.[19]

Botaneiates tried to legitimate his rule by marrying Michael VII's widow, Maria of Alania.[20] Alexios then added another major connection between himself and other imperial families when he was adopted by Maria.[21] Their association is described in terms usually used for spiritual adoption.[22] His adoption gave him ready access to the palace and a cover for regular private communication with his "mother." As the fictive son of the empress Alexios had joined the imperial household. While it is entirely unclear how

---

[14] 3.6.33.    [15] 3.19.10–13.
[16] Vlada Stanković, "Nikephoros Bryennios, Anna Komnene and Konstantios Doukas: A Story about different Perspectives," *Byzantinische Zeitschrift* 100, 1 (2007): 170–72.
[17] 4.2.8–9.    [18] 3.13.1–3; 16–19.    [19] 4.29.2–10.    [20] 3.25.    [21] 4.2.9.
[22] Claudia Rapp, "Ritual Brotherhood in Byzantium," *Traditio* 52 (1997): 285–326.

widely their relationship was known, at least among the elite contenders for imperial power, Alexios had brought himself a step closer to being part of the imperial family.

Alexios's association with Maria can be seen as strengthening his alliance with the Doukas family. John Doukas took the lead in supporting Maria of Alania in arranging her marriage to the new emperor Nikephoros Botaneiates. Once her first husband Michael had resigned, the Doukas family rallied behind Maria's son Constantine and worked to preserve his status as the heir to the throne. By adopting Alexios, Maria tied him to her interests and secured his help in working to protect Constantine. This brought his interests further into line with those of the Doukas family. In becoming Maria's "son," Alexios became Constantine's big brother. Alexios thus became part of the Doukas clan in two ways: his marriage to Irene and his adoption by Maria.

All of these connections between Alexios Komnenos and the imperial throne form a strong association between Alexios and imperial rule. Nikephoros lays the groundwork for making Alexios appear as the natural choice for emperor through constantly associating him with the imperial household. This narrative of Alexios's rise to power creates an ostensible argument for Komnenian legitimacy.

# CHAPTER 7

# Romans and their enemies

In Nikephoros's eyes no extra words were needed to explain who the Romans were or what defined a Roman. His story describes the efforts of loyal Romans to support and defend the Roman Empire while struggling through political contention over who would best manage the affairs of the Romans. The Romans in his story interact, however, with people of different languages, religions, ethnic and political affiliations, some of whom are sometimes called barbarians. Some ideas about Roman identity implicit in Nikephoros's history can be teased out of his depiction of interactions with these non-Romans.

The Roman Empire seems to have been defined for Nikephoros by those noble men and women who were in charge of sustaining it. Nikephoros talks more about the Romans than the Roman Empire. While he occasionally mentions the Empire, *arche* (usually when he is following Psellos),[1] most often the state is denoted periphrastically as the "matters of the Romans"[2] or the "common matters."[3] Sometimes Nikephoros refers to the rule of the Romans[4] or the polity of the Romans.[5] The nautical metaphor of the emperor taking up the rudder of Empire is used a few times.[6] Emperors also grasp the scepters of Empire.[7] This preference for periphrastic designations for the Empire leaves Nikephoros talking about the Romans themselves.

Nikephoros provides a hint about who constituted the key stake-holders in the Roman Empire when he complained about Nikephoros Botaneiates's debasement of imperial titles. Botaneiates's excessive generosity undermined the strength of the state by giving titles to "everyone who asked" rather than to only "the best people or the military or those descended from the senate, or those deserving some benevolence."[8] Most of the characters Nikephoros depicts positively in his history would fall into one of the

---

[1] 1.4.25; 3.4.26–29; 4.17.2–3. Nikephoros preserves Psellos's use of *arche* in book one.
[2] P.11.4; 2.1.4; 2.16.7–8; 2.25.9.   [3] 1.4.9; 1.4.13; 1.4.31,1.5.9; 1.18.26–27; 2.1.14.
[4] P.11.3–4; 1.1.6.   [5] 4.1.9; 4.17.2–3.   [6] 1.7.1; 1.5.13.
[7] 1.1.2–3; 1.6.14; 2.17.26; 3.21.13; 3.25.1; 4.1.2.   [8] 4.1.13–16.

categories here described as deserving of gifts of honor. These are the people whose fortunes seem to correspond to those of Rome. They are deeply and personally involved in "the common matters."

Nikephoros's Roman heroes interact frequently and systematically with non-Romans. Further insight into how Nikephoros conceived of the Romans can be gained by examining the treatment of the many kinds of non-Romans who take part in his story. Nikephoros does not use the term "barbarian" in the classical sense of "anyone who does not speak Greek."[9] It appears from Nikephoros's usage that "barbarian" is a relational term rather than an absolute category. Neither language, nor religion nor ethnic affiliation defines a barbarian. Rather, barbarianism in this text is a bad attitude toward the Romans. Non-Romans are generally called by their ethnic names: Franks, Turks, Alans, "Scythians," etc. They all have the potential to be barbarians if they fight against the Romans.

The Turks are barbarians some of the time. Alexios wanted to join Romanos Diogenes on his campaign against the "barbarians," the Turks.[10] The Turks who held young Isaac Komnenos captive were barbarians.[11] The Turks were also barbarians when they attacked Alexios and Isaac at Dekte.[12] The Turks who finally captured Nikephoros Bryennios were barbarians.[13]

While the Turks are barbarians in these contexts, they appear in plenty of other situations in which they are not called barbarians.[14] Nikephoros's digression on the history of the Turks does not refer to barbarians but rather to Persians, Saracens, Arabs and Turks.[15] Romanos Diogenes sent Alexios's older brother Manuel Komnenos to fight against the Turks led by Chrysoskoulos.[16] Manuel became famous for convincing Chrysoskoulos to desert to the Roman Empire. After Manuel had brought him to Constantinople and both were honored by the emperor, Chrysoskoulos went with Manuel the following spring to campaign against other Turks.[17] We are told that Chrysoskoulos was so upset at the death of Manuel Komnenos that he wanted to die himself. Apparently Manuel and Chrysoskoulos were friends. Much later Chrysoskoulos appears again in the employ of Nikephoros Botaneiates.

The Turks are called barbarians when young Alexios pleaded with Romanos Diogenes to be able to stay and fight them.[18] In the next scene,

[9] On medieval usage see Gill Page, *Being Byzantine: Greek Identity Before the Ottomans* (Cambridge University Press, 2008), 42–46.
[10] 1.12.35.   [11] 2.8.18.   [12] 2.11–13.   [13] 4.14.1.
[14] For example: 1.7; 2.17.29–34; 2.26.7–9; 2.27; 3.16; 4.1.21–26; 4.2.10–15; 4.4.7–11; 4.31; 4.34.
[15] 1.7–10; he adds the detail that the Turks are raised on milk to Skylitzes's description. 1.7.11.
[16] 1.11.1–5.   [17] 1.11.16–12.6.   [18] 1.12.34–37.

when it came time for Romanos and his generals to discuss the plan of attack, they are fighting Turks and "enemies."[19] The entire campaign of Manzikert was undertaken against Turks, rather than barbarians.[20] The Turks dissolve their treaties with the Romans once Romanos was blinded.[21] Isaac Komnenos was appointed *domestikos ton scholon* of the east and sent off to fight against the Turks.[22] Alexios ransomed Isaac from his Turkish captors.[23] It was Turks who attacked Isaac and Alexios at Dekte, although in the midst of the fighting they are called barbarians and Turks alternately.[24]

On the whole, the Turks are Turks far more often than they are barbarians. The act of allowing them to have their own contemporary name accords them a significant presence and status. They are not assimilated into the category of an ancient people long since conquered by the Romans. They have a contemporary reality that is not collapsed into self-flattering conceptions of unbridgeable gulfs between Romans and barbarians. Bryennios's usage differs from the common Byzantine practice of relegating enemies to false ancient categories.[25]

Turks are not differentiated by any peculiar cultural characteristics. Arrangements and treaties are made with individual, named, Turkish leaders. Artuq is introduced as "a clever general."[26] The arguments that convince Turkish generals to fight on the side of the Romans are presented as entirely reasonable. Manuel convinced Chrysoskoulos that the Romans could protect him from the enmity of his kinsman, the Sultan.[27] Tutakh is persuaded by Alexios's analysis of the political situation and promise of payment.[28] Artuq accepts payment for his services.[29] The Turks are not some random force of nature but rather rational leaders acting in their own best interests. The story of how the Turks came to border on the Romans and why they were at war presents an explanation based on political calculation and clever generalship – not any deep-seated cultural, religious, or national reasons. Bryennios omitted Skylitzes' statement that the Turks were racially Huns.[30] There is no hint of a fight between Christianity and Islam playing a motivating role for any of the characters in this history. Rational men are competing for power and resources; civilizations are not clashing.

Like the Turks, Franks are "barbarians" from time to time but are most often referred to by their ethnonym. In the sections of the history

---

[19] 1.13–17.    [20] 1.13–17.    [21] 2.3.3–6.    [22] 2.3–6.    [23] 2.8.1–15.

[24] Turks: 2.9.11; 2.11.14; 2.12.7; 2.13.3. Barbarians 2.9.24; 2.11.7; 2.11.12; 2.12.19; 2.13.8–13.

[25] For the subordination involved in calling Bulgarians Mysians see Paul Stephenson, "Conceptions of Otherness After 1018," in *Strangers to Themselves: The Byzantine Outsider*, ed. Dion Smythe (Aldershot: Ashgate, 2000), 256.

[26] 2.17.33.    [27] 1.11.18–29.    [28] 2.21–22.7.    [29] 2.17.29–33.

[30] Skylitzes, *Constantine Monomachos* 9.3–4.

deriving from the text about John Doukas, the Franks are occasionally "Kelts" and usually "barbarians" throughout the story about John Doukas's failed attempt to end Roussel's rebellion.[31] In Romanos Diogenes's final fight against Andronikos Doukas, he appealed to Crispin to help him. Here Nikephoros calls Crispin a barbarian and describes how Andronikos flattered him into joining his side.[32]

Roussel's status as a barbarian depends on the situation. Roussel is called a barbarian in the description of Alexios's campaign of harassment against Roussel's fortresses.[33] Throughout his fight with Roussel, Alexios is called by his title, the *Stratopedarch*. When Tutakh arrives on the scene with a host of Turks, Roussel is called by his name and Tutakh's ambassador becomes the "barbarian."[34] Alexios succeeded in convincing the "barbarian" Tutakh to fight with him against Roussel, on the promise of payment.[35] When Tutakh captures Roussel, Alexios asks the citizens of Amaseia for money to pay Tutakh saying that they should be glad "the barbarian," i.e. Roussel, has been captured.[36] There is only one barbarian in the story at any given moment.

One reading would be that the Turks are somehow more barbaric than Franks and so Roussel stops being a barbarian whenever Tutakh enters the narrative to make room for the "barbarian." Yet this reading is not upheld by the rest of the depiction of the Turks discussed above. Rather it seems that Roussel is the barbarian whenever it is important to emphasize the threat he poses to Rome and to undercut his claims to good rule. Alexios faced serious opposition in getting money out of the Amaseians as a strong party in the town preferred Roussel's rule to that of the ineffective imperial government. When Roussel was posing as a credible ruler, it became important to designate him as a "barbarian."

As soon as Roussel was safely under Alexios's control, he ceased to be a barbarian. Alexios convinced the people of Amaseia to pay the fee for the capture of Roussel by pretending to have him blinded. On the way back to Constantinople, Alexios stopped at the house of his cousin, Theodore Dokeianos, with Roussel apparently blinded. Theodore was "filled with sadness" and immediately reproached Alexios for blinding a "noble man who was able to help the Roman Empire."[37] Once they were inside together in private, Alexios took off the bandages and revealed the trick. Theodore and Roussel immediately embraced. Theodore:

was amazed at the surprise and filled with joy and hugging the famous Alexios, kissed his lips and cheeks and his beautiful eyes. He shouted loudly that the spirit

---

[31] 2.14–18. See above p. 55.   [32] 1.25.5–8.   [33] 2.20.19–21.1.   [34] 2.21.21.
[35] 2.22.1–7.   [36] 2.22.23; 2.23.16.   [37] 2.25.8–9.

of the young man was worthy of his ancestors and he applauded the performance and marveled at the acting.[38]

This burst of joy and the initial outrage provide significant evidence of the mutual respect afforded to good foreign commanders. Even though Roussel's insurrection had consumed considerable imperial military resources for several years, the cultural expectation was that mutilating him would have been outrageous behavior.

Theodore's complaint did not focus on the cruelty of blinding, but on the maiming of a man he expected to be fighting together with again in the future. Once Roussel was in prison in Constantinople, Alexios took good care of him, furnishing all his necessities out of his own house and "calming the anger of the emperor against him."[39] Theodore's expectation that Roussel would fight for the Romans again was borne out when Roussel was allowed out of prison and set to work with Alexios in defending Michael VII against Nikephoros Bryennios's rebellion.[40] Alexios called Roussel a barbarian in making his case to the Amaseians that they should not support him, but in his cousin's house and at Constantinople he treated Roussel as an honorable man. This respectful treatment makes sense in a cultural and political context in which men would be fighting against each other in one year and together in another.

"Scythians" are never called barbarians, although one could quite reasonably say that barbarism was inherent in the title "Scythian." It would be pleonastic to say that a Scythian was a barbarian. "Scythians" are described both as invaders and as rebels against Roman authority. The defining characteristic of the "Scythians" seems to be geographic: they attack the northern rather than western provinces. On more than one occasion the "Scythians" were described as overrunning Thrace and Macedonia.[41] The "Scythians" are the concern of generals fighting in the European provinces.[42] No individual Scythian leaders are named and they are not ascribed with any political motivations. There is a distinct lack of interest in Scythian personalities. With the help of other histories, the "Scythians" of Nikephoros's history have been identified in modern scholarship

---

[38] 2.25.21–25: ὁ δὲ τῷ αἰφνιδίῳ κατεπέπληκτο καὶ πλήρης χαρμονῆς ἐγεγόνει καὶ τὸν κλεινὸν περιπλακεὶς Ἀλέξιον κατεφίλει χείλη καὶ παρειὰς καὶ τοὺς χαρίεντας ὀφθαλμοὺς καὶ μέγα ἐβόα ἄξιον εἶναι τῶν προαγόντων τοῦ νέου τὸ φρόνημα καὶ τὸ δρᾶμα ἐπήνει καὶ τὴν σκηνὴν ἐθαύμαζε.

[39] 2.28.8–9.    [40] 3.26.    [41] 2.3.6–7; 3.1.21–22.

[42] John Bryennios was disappointed at how Michael treated him after he had returned from a campaign against the Scythians: 3.4.16. Botaneiates had his ambassadors praise Nikephoros Bryennios's father for having won many trophies over the Scythians: 4.3.3. After defeating Bryennios and Basilakes, Alexios fought against invading Scythians: 4.30.

as Pechenegs and Uzes.[43] These people are usually described as "turkic." More precisely, the Pechenegs were "semi-nomadic Turkic-speaking people from the Eurasian steppe" while the Uzes were "a branch of the Oghuz confederation of Turkic-speaking peoples."[44] The material similarities between the Scythian allies and the Turkish enemies caused confusion during the battle of Manzikert.[45] That Nikephoros distinguishes clearly between "Scythians" and Turks indicates that similarities in language and culture were not fundamental to Nikephoros's definitions of communities. He saw these groups as distinct because they had different geopolitical roles.

Alans are also never barbarians. In an effort to exhort his men to fight against a surprise Turkish attack, however, the Alan mercenary Arabates insulted them "barbarically."[46] This may mean that he insulted them in his native tongue, or that he was acting somehow like a barbarian. After his bout of barbaric insults, Arabates goes on to fight brilliantly against the "barbarians," i.e. the Turks. Arabates is compared to the Spartan general Brasidas, who died at the battle of Amphipolis in 422 BCE. Heroism is not confined to Greeks or Romans. Michael VII Doukas and Alexios's brother Isaac married two Alan cousins.[47]

While Nikephoros uses these names for different groups – Alans, "Scythians," Turks, and Franks – he betrays little of what defined these categories in his mind. Religious differences are rarely discussed. It is impossible to judge from Nikephoros's account whether the "Scythians" are Muslim, Christian, or Pagan. That no mention is made of the religion of a major group of adversaries speaks to how little religious affiliation mattered to Bryennios. With one exception, the Turks are never designated by their religion. In that exception, Bryennios is putting words into the mouth of one of his most repugnant characters.[48] Alexios is credited with not killing those of Roussel's troops he captured because they were Christian, but nothing indicates that killing Muslim captives would have been normal.[49] No mention is made of anyone killing any captives and yesterday's enemies

---

[43] The Uzes allied with Romanos during the Manzikert campaign. Bryennios's usual enemies on the Balkan frontier were Pechenegs. John Haldon, *The Byzantine Wars* (Stroud: Tempus, 2001), 116, 127–33.

[44] Jonathan Shepard, ed. *The Cambridge History of the Byzantine Empire, c. 500–1492* (Cambridge University Press, 2008), 899, 904.

[45] Haldon, *Wars,* 121.     [46] 2.13.1.     [47] 2.1.9–13.

[48] The craven eunuch John, appointed by Botaneiates to replace Alexios, led his army into a disastrous situation against the advice of George Palaiologos, who is the hero of this episode. In the midst of the terrible defeat George had foretold, the eunuch loses his nerve and begs George to save him from the hands of the "Hagarenes." 4.37.11.

[49] 2.20.29–30.

are tomorrow's allies far too often to admit of rampant brutality toward captured fighters. This is warfare without a deep sense of enmity.

Nikephoros betrays little interest in what languages anyone spoke, often leaving it entirely unclear how conversations took place. "Latin" is only used once, to refer to the particular military device of the "Latin phalanx" cavalry charge rather than to a language.[50]

"Barbarian" therefore does not stand for a set category, and the enemies of the Empire are not necessarily barbarians. These enemies are enemies solely by virtue of their attacks on the Empire, not their religion, language, or perceived ethnicity. Leaders of all the foreign enemies are treated as reasonable generals who could become valuable allies, provided they renounced their opposition to the Roman Empire.[51] Nikephoros's text contains strikingly little ethnic typecasting. The Romans play in a world inhabited by reasonable military competitors rather than inherently inferior enemies.

Nikephoros's disapproval of the excessive use of mercenaries, discussed in chapter 5, does not appear motivated by an ethnic animus. The Turks themselves are not the problem and no ethnic strife seems to be in play. The Turks are the most dependable of all the foreign allies. The Franks are not portrayed poorly, even though they do the majority of the side-switching. Franks and Turks are all sensible actors subject to the same basic political and ethical motivations as the Romans. Their only fault lay in their lack of loyalty to the Roman Empire. Competing political goals and lack of loyalty to Rome, rather than any ethnic disdain, created Nikephoros's unease with mercenaries. The problems with mercenaries do not stem from their ethnicity, but lie with their unreliability. This lack of ethnic animosity goes some way to explain why the Byzantines used mercenaries so much. They had some classical precedents for the use of mercenaries, exigencies that called for extra help, and an expectation that foreigners were reasonable and would be helpful if properly motivated.

It follows that Nikephoros's vision of Roman identity was primarily political. Roman-ness for Nikephoros was not defined so much by religion or language as by perceptions of shared history and a common commitment to the imperial state. Nikephoros and his companions were Romans because they upheld the Roman Empire. Roman identity was not undermined by a lack of loyalty to any particular emperor, because commitment to the empire endured despite plenty of examples of ineffective or corrupt emperors. In that the categories of religion and language do not appear to

---

[50] 2.18.20.

[51] Nikephoros's Roman identity appears more self-confident than attitudes adduced about the later twelfth century. See Page, *Being Byzantine*, 67–71.

feed into Nikephoros's Roman identity, his text does not support major lines of twentieth-century scholarly discourse regarding "Byzantine" identity. Most modern discussions of "Byzantine" identity have taken religion, language, and political affiliations as the major categories of group identity. Language has been dominant in modern Greek nationalist discourse and its affiliates, which need the Byzantines' self-perception as Romans to be a false consciousness masking an essential and eternal Greek-ness.[52] The discourse of Hellenic continuity from Pericles to Papandreou requires the medieval identification as Romans to be a shallow false-consciousness. Religion has loomed large in scholarly analysis of Byzantine identity because Orthodoxy is central for the separation of the Roman Empire from the medieval "Byzantine" Empire.[53] Modern Orthodox societies that see the "Byzantine" empire as the fount of religious truth and the teacher of true culture read religion at the core of Byzantine identity.

On the other hand, Nikephoros's apparent engagement with an identity grounded in shared political community fits well with more recent efforts to understand medieval "Byzantine" identity. Recent analyses have emphasized that medieval Roman identity constituted a communal group feeling that was more than a set of religious and linguistic affiliations. Roman identity can be seen as a form of "ethnicity," defined as "a faith on the part of the members of the group that they are in some sense the same, and that this sameness is rooted in a racial kinship stretching into the past."[54] It is also reasonable to consider the medieval Romans as a nation, to which people of diverse ethnic origins could be completely assimilated in time.[55] Both of these views present identity as a matter of belief on the part of adherents, which is a crucial step in acknowledging that the people who had been ancient Greeks and would become modern Greeks were also, for a time, Romans.[56]

A cultural memory of a common Roman history seems to have been central to Roman identity for Nikephoros. Nikephoros's description of the Romans as those who fight for the Roman Empire is consistent with

---

[52] For a standard reading of Byzantium as a mix of Greek and Christian civilizations see Speros Vryonis, Jr., "Byzantine Civilization: a World Civilization," in *Byzantium: A World Civilization*, ed. Angeliki Laiou and Henry Maguire (Washington, DC: Dumbarton Oaks, 1992), 19–35.

[53] On this tendency see Kaldellis, *Hellenism*, 100–11 and Averil Cameron, "Byzantium and the Limits of Orthodoxy," *Proceedings of the British Academy* 154 (2007): 129–38, in a moment of agreement.

[54] Page, *Being Byzantine*, 11, 46–52.

[55] Kaldellis, *Hellenism*, 42–119.

[56] See also Beaton, "Antique Nation?," 76–95; Magdalino, "Hellenism and Nationalism in Byzantium," 1–29; Evangelos Chrysos, "Romans and Foreigners," in *Fifty Years of Prosopography: The Later Roman Empire, Byzantium and Beyond*, ed. Averil Cameron (Oxford: The British Academy: Oxford University Press, 2003), 119–36.

describing medieval Romans as either an ethnicity or a nationality in so far as both are created largely out of beliefs about the past. Perceptions of common history create cultural memory which can provide at least as much social glue as a common religion or language.[57] The proper maintenance of Roman morality and Roman historical traditions was thus a paramount concern because these traditions formed the basis of medieval Roman identity. The political and ethical traditions of the Romans bound Nikephoros's Romans together and provided the basis for their patriotism.

---

[57] J. Assmann, *Religion and Cultural Memory*; Jan Assmann, "Communicative and Cultural Memory," in *A Companion to Cultural Memory Studies*, ed. Astrid Erll and Ansgar Nünning (Berlin: De Gruyter, 2010), 109–18; Anne Whitehead, *Memory* (London: Routledge, 2009).

# CHAPTER 8

# *Military virtue*

There is a great deal of fighting in Nikephoros's history, and upon close inspection, it falls into remarkably stable moral patterns. Whenever men struggle in Nikephoros's narrative, they struggle bravely. When the outcomes of these contests are assessed, it turns out that whenever men struggle bravely, they are losing. Yet the rhetoric of the text works remarkably well to create positive impressions of these brave losing men.

Nikephoros contributes to the impression that he was telling a story of great men by rather bluntly saying so. Whenever he introduces a new Roman character to his narrative, Nikephoros typically offers a few words of description and assessment of the man's character. The Roman military men in the story receive overwhelmingly positive evaluations that frequently emphasize their courageous nobility and physical bravery. The succession of brave Romans in the story helps keep the focus on their good character despite the losses they suffer.

Nikephoros uses some terms for civilian virtues and others for military virtues in his initial character descriptions.[1] The key attribute of a military man is to be brave or noble, *gennaios*. While *gennaios* can refer to genetic nobility, in Nikephoros's usage it seems to have more to do with bravery and proper action than affinities of blood. This noble bravery is best when it is personal and physical. Nikephoros's interest in personal bravery is seen in his fondness for the phrase "brave of hand," *ten cheira gennaios*, in his introductions, usually in conjunction with another character trait. The phrase puts an emphasis on good character shown through physical actions. It indicates that bravery is defined by Nikephoros, not so much as a moral or intellectual strength as a willingness to endure bodily danger.

As the mettle of the characters is tested, Nikephoros qualifies their responses, commenting on men's characters in the course of their actions. Through this commentary Nikephoros's numerous descriptions of military

---

[1] Detailed argumentation for the claims of this paragraph is contained in Appendix Two.

Table 1: *Fighting done by "struggling"* ἀγωνίζομαι, ἀγών

| Character | manner | opponent | outcome | passage |
|---|---|---|---|---|
| Manuel Komnenos | γενναίως ἀγωνισάμενος | Chrysoskoulos | capture | 1.11.11 |
| Nikephoros Bryennios | ἡρωϊκῶς δ' ἀγωνισάμενος | Turks at Manzikert | defeat | 1.15.24 |
| Diogenes vs. Constantine Doukas | ἑκατέρων γενναίως ἀγωνιζομένων | Diogenes vs. Constantine Doukas | mutual losses | 1.21.22 |
| Isaac Komnenos | ὁ δὲ γενναίως τε ἀγωνίζεται | Turks at Caesarea | capture | 2.5.4 |
| Alexios's Guards | γενναίως ξὺν ἐκείνῳ ἀγωνισάμενοι | Turks | defeat | 2.5.17 |
| Isaac Komnenos | γενναίως ἀγωνισάμενος | Turks at Antioch | capture | 2.29.22 |
| Alexios Komnenos | γενναίως τε ἠγωνίζετο | John Bryennios | defeat | 4.8.11 |
| Nikephoros Bryennios | λαμπρῶς ἀγωνισάμενοι | Turks | capture | 4.12.16 |
| Nikephoros Bryennios | τοὺς γενναίους ἀγῶνας | Alexios | capture | 4.15.14 |
| George Palaiologos | γενναίως δ' ἀγωνιζόμενος | Turks | defeat | 4.38.8 |

engagements become a form of moral theater. Consistent moral patterns are found at the level of both individual responses to battle and of larger strategy. The first striking pattern, seen on the individual level, is that bravery is manifested through struggle and adversity. Nearly all brave, *gennaios*, action takes place in the context of fighting that is characterized as struggling or contending, *agonizomai*. In fact every time men struggle, that contention is done "bravely."[2] The verb in question, *agonizomai,* means to contend for a prize, and is applied to athletic contests and legal trials as well as military fighting. It emphasizes that the battle is a contest as well as a fight. The association of struggling with bravery is complemented by another correlation between such courageous struggling and defeat. Whenever brave men struggle and contend with nobility and courage, they are also losing the actual fight.

Nikephoros's association between a brave contest and ultimate defeat is as consistent as it is striking. Table 1 details the military engagements in

---

[2] γενναίως ἀγωνίσασθαι 2.12.31; 2.5.4; 2.5.17; 1.11.11; 2.29.22; 2.10.7; 4.38.8; 1.21.22; 4.8.11.

which a participant is described as fighting using some form of the verb
*agonizomai* or the noun *agon*.

On two occasions characters exhort each other to undertake such struggles bravely.[3] While most men who contended in the face of defeat did
so bravely, Bryennios was defeated despite struggling "heroically" and
"brilliantly."[4] His first heroic loss was against the ambushing Turks of
Alp Arslan the day before the battle of Manzikert.[5] Bryennios, with his
son and brother, "struggled brilliantly" before he was captured by Alexios's
Turks.[6] Bryennios's entire campaign against Alexios is called a "wrestling
match and noble struggle."[7]

Nikephoros's narrative also includes fights conducted with proper bravery that fit the pattern of the noble defeat, without including a form of the
"*gennaios agonizomai*" phrase. John Doukas's defeat at the river Zompos
is an example of a defeat meted out despite a tremendous effort on the
part of John and his son Andronikos.[8] Their fight has the same emotional
characteristics of a vigorous fight leading to a loss as Nikephoros's other
brave struggles. The absence of Nikephoros's preferred terminology can be
attributed to Nikephoros's choice to preserve the texture of his source on
John Doukas. The ability of a true struggle to manifest bravery, and the
association of that courageous contention with ultimate defeat, form an
emotional logic that Nikephoros deploys throughout his narrative.

A second strong pattern running throughout the military material in
Nikephoros's history is a contrast between the valorization of straightforward fighting in well-ordered battle formation and actual victories given
to those who fight by trickery and stratagems. Leading an army forward
in good battle-order is described as honorable action and those leaders are
praised as noble. A systematic catalogue of the military engagements reveals
that this sort of "honorable" Roman fighting usually leads to defeat. The
well-ordered attacks are nearly always defeated. The defeats are served up
by enemies who do not draw up their own forces in order to match the
Romans, but rather fight through ambushes, feigned retreats and traps. The
strongest contrast is made between a wily, devious, and successful Alexios
Komnenos and an upfront, honorable, tragically defeated Bryennios.

In many of the military engagements in his history,[9] Nikephoros provides
details that allow the methods of the protagonist or antagonist to be

[3] Alexios exhorted his fellows to "struggle bravely" to break out of the house at Dekte rather than be
taken captive: 2.10.7. One of Isaac Komnenos's Alan guards exhorted his companion to join "struggle
bravely" to help Isaac and Alexios in the same fight: 2.12.31.
[4] 1.15.24; 4.12.16.    [5] 1.15.24–25: ἡρωϊκῶς δ' ἀγωνισάμενος.
[6] 4.12.16: αὐτοὶ δὲ λαμπρῶς ἀγωνισάμενοι.    [7] 4.15.13–14.
[8] 2.14–15.    [9] Roughly 64 percent.

characterized as either devious or straightforward. A prepared attack with a formally drawn up army is a straightforward tactic that presents a clear challenge intended to elicit an engagement from the enemy. Any attack using trickery, surprise, or that is designed to catch the enemy off guard, or gain an unfair advantage is considered devious. Table 2 lists those engagements in which the actions of a party can be so characterized, sorted by mode of fighting and whether that mode led to success or defeat.[10] There is room for debate about what should be considered a discrete military event and, in some cases, whether the mode of the protagonist can be determined clearly. Yet the overall pattern shows that devious generals enjoyed greater success. Generals using devious tactics were victorious sixteen times and defeated three times; two of those three defeats were at the hands of equally devious opponents. Generals using straightforward tactics were victorious eight times and defeated twenty times.

Bryennios and his brother John always fought in a straightforward manner. With the exception of the battle of Manzikert, they were victorious against foreign enemies but lost to other Romans disputing their rebellion. Alexios fought deviously in seven of the eight engagements he led. Alexios's only straightforward attack was his first adolescent military command in which ten of the fifteen men accompanying him were killed or captured.[11]

In the first phases of the complex battle of Kalovrye between Alexios and Nikephoros Bryennios, Bryennios and his brother John were initially successful in leading two straight-on charges against Alexios. In one of these encounters Alexios was trying to execute an ambush. Alexios tried several different ruses during the rest of the battle, which he ultimately went on to win with the help of Turkish allies. The phases of this battle account for two of the successful straight-on engagements, as well as Alexios's only temporary defeat when he was fighting deviously. If the whole of the battle of Kalovrye were taken as one victory for Alexios, fighting deviously, then the patterns in Table 2 would be even more stark.

Turks fight using ambushes and feigned retreats twice as often as they attack head on. Franks always fought using straightforward tactics, with the exception of suborning the loyalty of fellow Franks hired to fight against them. While the Turks "attack" and give a good fight some of the time, they are never described as lining up in formal battle-order.

[10] Engagements in which the mode of both the protagonist and antagonist can be assessed are listed separately. Passages based on other texts are indicated in the table with a superscript after the citation: P Psellos; s Skylitzes; d Doukas.

[11] 2.5.10–19.

Table 2: *Military engagements*

| Text | Engagement | Mode | Outcome |
|---|---|---|---|
| 4.8 | Alexios ambushes John Bryennios at Kalovrye | Devious | Defeat |
| 4.19 | Basilakes attacks Alexios's camp at night | Devious | Defeat |
| 3.16 | Suleiman guards roads against Botaneiates | Devious | Defeat |
| 1.8[s] | Tughril-beg attacks Mahmud's generals at night | Devious | Success |
| 1.21.15[p] | Constantine Doukas forces Romanos out of Amaseia by skirmishing | Devious | Success |
| 2.18[d] | Artuq attacks Roussel, using terrain to prevent the use of the "Latin Phalanx" | Devious | Success |
| 2.14–15[d] | Roussel battles John Doukas, suborning John's Norman mercenaries | Devious | Success |
| 2.20 | Alexios leads harassment campaign against Roussel | Devious | Success |
| 2.24 | Alexios captures the fortresses held by Roussel by repeatedly attacking foragers | Devious | Success |
| 2.27 | Alexios frightens off raiding Turks | Devious | Success |
| 3.13 | Alexios makes a sudden sortie against John's foraging soldiers during siege | Devious | Success |
| 4.10–13 | Alexios's Turkish allies ambush Bryennios at Kalovrye | Devious | Success |
| 4.19 | Alexios lures Basilakes into a trap set for his night attack | Devious | Success |
| 1.14 | Turks under Alp Arslan draw Basilakes into an attack, then ambush him | Devious | Success |
| 1.15 | Turks under Alp Arslan draw Bryennios into an attack, then ambush him | Devious | Success |
| 1.17 | Turks retreat, then encircle Romanos | Devious | Success |
| 3.16 | Botaneiates evades the army of Suleiman | Devious | Success |
| 1.11 | Chrysoskoulos ambushes Manuel | Devious | Success |
| 4.9.5 | Bryennios's Scythians break off their attack to pillage Bryennios's camp | Devious | Success |
| 1.8[s] | Mahmud's generals defend against Tughril-beg | Straight | Defeat |
| 1.24[p] | Chatatourios battles Andronikos Doukas | Straight | Defeat |
| 1.21[p] | Romanos battles Constantine Doukas | Straight | Defeat |
| 2.14–15[d] | John Doukas battles Roussel | Straight | Defeat |
| 2.18[d] | Roussel defends against Artuq | Straight | Defeat |
| 1.14 | Basilakes is lured into attacking Turks | Straight | Defeat |
| 2.5 | Isaac Komnenos battles Turks | Straight | Defeat |
| 2.29.18 | Isaac Komnenos battles Turks | Straight | Defeat |
| 4.33–39 | John the Eunuch attacks Nicaea | Straight | Defeat |
| 1.9 | Mahmud battles Tughril-beg | Straight | Defeat |
| 1.11 | Manuel Komnenos attacks Turks; caught in an ambush after feigned retreat | Straight | Defeat |
| 1.15 | Bryennios is ambushed by Turks | Straight | Defeat |
| 4.10–13 | Bryennios is drawn into ambushes and captured at Kalovrye | Straight | Defeat |

*(cont.)*

Table 2: (*cont.*)

| Text | Engagement | Mode | Outcome |
|------|-----------|------|---------|
| 2.19 | Nikephoros Palaiologos is attacked by Roussel | Straight | Defeat |
| 2.24 | Normans are defeated by Alexios | Straight | Defeat |
| 1.17 | Romanos tries to engage a battle against Alp Arslan | Straight | Defeat |
| 2.20. | Roussel defends against Alexios | Straight | Defeat |
| 1.21.20 | Romanos battles Constantine Doukas | Straight | Defeat |
| 2.5.11 | Alexios attacks Turks at Caesarea | Straight | Defeat |
| 1.24$^P$ | Andronikos Doukas attacks Chatatourios | Straight | Success |
| 1.21.20$^P$ | Constantine Doukas battles Romanos | Straight | Success |
| 3.3 | Bryennios battles the Dukljans and Croats | Straight | Success |
| 3.3.28 | Bryennios attacks pirates | Straight | Success |
| 4.8 | John Bryennios fights off Alexios's ambush at Kalovrye | Straight | Success |
| 4.9 | Bryennios's Scythians attack Alexios's left at Kalovrye | Straight | Success |
| 1.9$^s$ | Tughril-beg battles Mahmud | Straight | Success |
| 4.33–39 | Turks surround the besieging forces at Nicaea | Straight | Success |

The key to understanding the moral valuations behind Nikephoros's descriptions of military action is to read them against classical Roman ideas about the value of a straight fight and the dishonor involved in devious fighting. When considered from the viewpoint of individual honor, the success or failure of an enterprise was less significant than the manner of fighting. Romans often prized right action far above victory.[12] Virtue was a matter of aggressive courage.[13] Efficacy, as measured by preservation of life, was not part of classical Roman evaluation of success. Military tricks denied participants the opportunity for a noble struggle that would display their courage and nobility. A case from logic and utility could always be made for a stratagem that provided victory without the casualties and suffering of a pitched battle, but an undeniable current of distaste for military trickery runs through classical Roman culture. The moment of struggle has been identified as a defining moment in classical Roman life. The point of struggle could be a "'moment of truth' the equivocal and ardent moment . . . when truth was not so much revealed as created, realized, *willed* in the most intense and visceral way, the truth of one's being, the truth of being."[14] The emotional core of many stories about

---

[12] In regard to Polybius in particular see Eckstein, *Moral Vision*, 20–27.
[13] McDonnell, *Roman Manliness*, 71.
[14] Carlin A. Barton, *Roman Honor: The Fire in the Bones* (Berkeley: University of California Press, 2001), 31–33.

classical Roman military honor is a willingness to face grave danger head on. Polybius advocated personal bravery in battle as an essential quality of an aristocratic man.[15] Soldiers created reputations for courage by competing to distinguish themselves in charging into the center of the enemy forces.[16]

The necessity for young men in the Roman Republic of proving and displaying *virtus* through agonistic combat was so strong that it may have influenced the deployment of troops in battle. In an exception to their general willingness to embrace new military techniques quickly, the Romans fought with the manipular legion formation for over 200 years from the fourth through first centuries BCE. In this formation young men, *velites*, swarmed in front of the ranks formed by the maniples where they had the opportunity to engage in single combats and deeds of exceptional valor.[17] Aristocratic young men whose wealth allowed them to serve in the cavalry were known to dismount and join with the *velites* in order to display their valor. Behind the *velites* the soldiers in the manipular array were ordered by age with the younger men in front so that they could have the opportunity to prove their manhood. The cultural imperative of proving *virtus* thus directly affected Roman tactics.[18] Republican Romans continued to deploy in the manipular legion, despite losses attributable to that formation, because it "was a way of fighting embedded in the martial culture of the Romans."[19]

In the republican era, desire for the opportunity to display virtue through agonistic combat caused discontent with strategies that avoided straight-on fighting. Roman republican generals who employed trickery faced charges of cowardice. Fabius Maximus, who led a campaign of harassment against Hannibal rather than engage him immediately in battle was considered a coward and faced outright disobedience from his officers.[20] Those who led armies to ruin through excessive aggression, like Terentius Varro at Cannae, received no opprobrium.[21] While some republican generals keenly appreciated refined strategies, many Roman soldiers and generals believed the general's job was "to lead his army straight at the foe and to fight as soon as possible."[22]

---

[15] Eckstein, *Moral Vision*, 28–55.

[16] J. E. Lendon, *Empire of Honour: The Art of Government in the Roman World* (Oxford University Press, 1997), 244, 59.

[17] Lendon, "War and Society," 512–14; J. E. Lendon, *Soldiers & Ghosts: A History of Battle in Classical Antiquity* (New Haven: Yale University Press, 2005), 178–91.

[18] Lendon, *Soldiers & Ghosts*, 186–90.   [19] Lendon, "War and Society," 514.

[20] Polyb. 3.90.6; 3.94.8–10; 3.103.2.   [21] Lendon, *Soldiers & Ghosts*, 207.

[22] Lendon, *Soldiers & Ghosts*, 210–11.

Roman understandings of honor that highly prized honesty and face-to-face exchanges contributed to the perception that trickery and stratagems were contrary to *virtus*. Facing another man and looking him in the eye was considered to be an act of honor within the classical Roman construction of virtue, even in non-military contexts.[23] Striking an enemy in the head was an act of valor.[24] Deliberate, face-to-face combat thus brought greater honor than fighting by other tactics. Set battles required that men on both sides choose to engage. The contest is then one of skill, strength, spirit, endurance and other cultivated masculine qualities. In a set fight the better man wins. Devious fighting – fake retreats, ambushes, skirmishes – do not provide even contests. On the contrary, such tactics are designed to prevent opponents from leveraging their full strength. In addition to disrupting the level playing field, military stratagems involved deceit, which was fundamentally base. The dishonesty requisite for the execution of a stratagem could debase the honor of an aristocrat.[25]

Polybius describes the Romans as retaining a sense of honor in combat which had been lost by the Greeks of his day:

Some slight traces, however, of the ancient principles of warfare survive among the Romans. For they make declaration of war, they very seldom use ambuscades, and they fight hand-to-hand at close quarters.[26]

Polybius contrasts both the deviousness of his contemporaneous Greeks and the Roman lingering appreciation for honesty in combat to the more perfect morality of the "ancients" who were so concerned that battle be an even hand-to-hand contest that they banned missiles thrown from a distance and gave their enemies notice of when and where they intended to meet for battle.[27] Despite being an ardent supporter of one of Rome's most artful generals, Scipio Africanus, Polybius here upholds a valorization of straightforward fighting at the expense of manipulation. By describing the Romans as maintaining the ancient principles of honor in straightforward contests, Polybius contributes to a vision of Roman military culture as deeply concerned with proper modes of contestation, despite telling a history in which Romans fought by a great variety of techniques.

Romans of the imperial era fostered an intense nostalgia for the honor and devotion of the early Romans who fought – and were often defeated – in

---

[23] Barton, *Roman Honor*, 56–58.
[24] A. Pelzer Wagener, "Aiming Weapons at the Face – A Sign of Valor," *Classical Philology* 24, 3 (1929): 297–99.
[25] Eckstein, *Moral Vision*, 84–117.    [26] Polyb. 13.3.7.    [27] Polyb. 8.3.3–4.

the service of the early Roman state. An honorable death was remembered as far better than an inglorious victory. This emotional logic brought Roman military culture to the striking conclusion that honor was best displayed through defeat.[28] Military trickery may lead to victory, but warfare without an arena for contest ran contrary to Roman military ethos. The decline in honor among the Roman aristocracy of the imperial era came not only from their subordination to the emperor, but from the removal of true tests in which their virtue might be refined. While victory is an obvious good, it deprives participants of the opportunity to make the most noble sacrifice of life for the sake of honor.

Straight-on aggressive courage and struggle in the face of defeat thus became part of the self-presentation of classical Roman virtue, however often the Romans in fact used military stratagems and did whatever was necessary to gain empire. The belief that Romans prized properly agonistic contests and fought with a self-sacrificial code of military honor, or had done so in their great old days, remained apparent to those who read the Greek historians of Rome, even at a distance of twelve centuries. This conception of the Roman system of honor and virtue explains Nikephoros's close connection between a noble struggle, a good contest, and defeat. The implication of Nikephoros's composition is that the men he describes as losing only after a good fight participated in the ennobling behavior that led to Rome's greatness. Nikephoros describes men as struggling nobly when he valorizes them in the face of defeat. More than giving the men of his grandparents' generation an "A for effort," Nikephoros's text appears to associate them with some of the greatest cultural heroes of Rome.

The detailed description of the battle of Manzikert in book 1 sets up the dichotomy between fighting in ordered ranks and fighting by tricks that runs throughout Nikephoros's history. Order is praised overtly and is associated with Roman traditions, yet fighting through deception is shown in the course of events to be far more effective. Considerations of honor played a significant role in motivating Romanos Diogenes to advance his army eastward to meet Alp Arslan.[29] Once Romanos's army was camped outside of Manzikert, one of Romanos's generals, Basilakes, was tricked by Alp Arslan's skirmishers into leading a disorganized rush of an attack out from the main army's fortification. The Turks pretended to flee and then wheeled around on the Romans once they were outside their camp and out of reach of help. Nikephoros strongly condemns ill-prepared boldness

[28] Barton, *Roman Honor*, 42–56.  [29] 1.13. See below pp. 131–32.

in this story, but it is a clear case of bravery defeated through deception.[30] Bryennios then led out a well-ordered and disciplined force to attempt to rescue Basilakes. The Turks suddenly ambushed Bryennios's men and defeated them after a heroic fight. Bryennios managed to withdraw his troops and return to the main camp.[31]

In the following main day of fighting, the Turks denied Romanos the opportunity for a tight engagement. The Sultan did not lead his army in person, but delegated the task to a eunuch, Taranges.[32] Taranges drew Romanos out of the encampment and toward him by refusing to fight "either by phalanx or by ambush."[33] While Romanos set out his forces in an elaborate classical battle formation, the Seljuk leader "divided his army into many groups and made many traps and set up ambushes and ordered them to go around the Roman ranks and use archery from everywhere."[34] By retreating before the advancing Romans all day long, Taranges nullified the advantages of the tight formation of Romanos's well-disciplined army, which became caught in the traps and ambushes and was resoundingly defeated, leading to Romanos's capture.

Nikephoros's narrative strongly implies that had Romanos been able to engage the Turks in a close fight, he would have defeated them. Nikephoros uses the wrestling metaphor of "coming to grips" to describe the hand-to-hand combat that the Turks denied the Romans.[35] This phrase is used in other cases where a weaker party refuses to engage in head-on combat.[36] The Turks had not fought fairly. By pretending to attack and then pretending to retreat, they had run the Romans ragged without ever giving them a real fight. The tragedy of the defeat at Manzikert was that there had been no opportunity for a good *agon*.

The portrait is tragic in that the Romans were defeated without a good struggle. It also means that, in a sense, the Romans were never *defeated*. They were not put to a contest, tried, and proven inferior in battle. They were tricked, manipulated, and brought to ruin, but not brought down by a superior enemy in a fair fight. Nikephoros thus nullified the damage

[30] 1.14.26–43: Nikephoros presented Basilakes as disorganized and undisciplined in his attack which created the need for Bryennios to march out to rescue him. Other historians say that Bryennios was the general to be captured after an unsuccessful attack and that Basilakes rescued him. Attaleiates 154–55; Skylitzes continuatus 145–46.

[31] 1.15.    [32] 1.17.1–6.    [33] 1.17.2: οὐ κατὰ φάλαγγας οὐδὲ κατὰ λόχους.

[34] 1.17.6–9.    [35] 1.17.3: εἰς χεῖρας ἐλθεῖν.

[36] The Frank Crispin charged out before Andronikos Doukas's army had come to grips with Romanos's forces: 1.24.14–15; the servants and guests at Dekte were not apparently able to come to grips with the Turks: 2.9.23; Alexios's army put that of Basilakes to flight before they came to grips: 4.25.10. In these episodes the avoidance of tight fighting allows the weaker party to escape.

done to Roman honor by the greatest military disaster in memory. The veterans of Manzikert remained heroic despite their loss.

Other generals found themselves equally frustrated by Turkish tactics. Roussel lost his fight against Artuq, who had been hired by Michael VII's minister Nikephoritzes to defeat him, because Artuq attacked by means of skirmishes and ambushes and prevented the Franks from charging in their usual "Latin phalanx."[37] Several of those who lost in the midst of noble struggles did so against such deceptive tactics.[38]

The Turkish generals are not the only ones who fought by means of deception. Such ruses are most often attributed to Alexios. The task of reducing Roussel's rebellion fell to Alexios who was appointed *Stratopedarch* and sent out from Constantinople without "money from the emperor for the costs of the war or a battle-worthy army."[39] Arriving at Amaseia, Alexios took command of the remaining Alan mercenaries, numbering about 150. But he did not lead them out in battle against Roussel. Rather he set ambushes and attacked Roussel's men when they were out foraging. He frustrated Roussel's desire for a set battle and fought a campaign of harassment:

> Roussel, having a battle-worthy force, wanted the matter against him decided in one battle, but the *Stratopedarch*, poor in might, hastened to overcome the barbarian by stratagem. Whenever Roussel gathered his army, he feigned quietude, but after a few days he would go out secretly and set up traps not far from Roussel. Frequently he laid ambushes and captured those supplying the army with necessities.[40]

This campaign prevented Roussel from exerting his authority and the cities which had been tributary to him began to reject his rule.[41] After Roussel himself had been captured and handed over to Alexios by his Turkish ally Tutakh, Alexios continued to harass Roussel's followers by attacking their foraging parties until they also surrendered.[42]

During his return to Constantinople Alexios was told that some Turks were foraging outside of Heraclea. Alexios had no significant forces, but he drew up his men and those of his host into a formal order in a place where the Turks could see them. The Turks "seeing them from far off – the glint of the weapons and the good order of the ranks and the irresistibility

---

[37] 2.18.14–27.
[38] Manuel Komnenos was lured into a pursuit and ambushed: 1.11.9–16. Bryennios was ambushed by Turks the day before the battle of Manzikert: 1.15. Bryennios was captured after a heroic struggle against Alexios's Turkish allies who drew him into an ambush at the end of the battle of Kalovrye: 4.10–13.
[39] 2.20.6–7.  [40] 2.20.20–26.  [41] 2.21.2–6.  [42] 2.24.20–30.

of the attack – were not up to it and fled uncontrollably."[43] Alexios here drew up the available forces in formal battle array, but did not actually engage the enemy. Since we have been told that he did not have a "battle worthy" army at the time, he was bluffing. Had the Turks attacked anyway, they would have found themselves fighting a few dozen Alan mercenaries augmented with a private household's retainers.

During John Bryennios's siege of Constantinople, Alexios, who had been given command of the city defenses, did not lead a force out of the city to engage John's army. But when he saw some of John's men moving out of their camp for the sake of foraging, he made a quick sortie and succeeded in capturing some of them before racing back into the city.[44]

As soon as he was enthroned in Constantinople, Botaneiates appointed Alexios *domestikos ton scholon* and charged him with ending Bryennios's rebellion. As was the case with his fight against Roussel, Alexios faced a far superior enemy with few resources. Again the author emphasizes Alexios's need and ability to fight in a sly manner. When Alexios set up camp outside of Kalovrye:

> He did not dig a trench or erect a stockade. Indeed, he wanted to watch out for the approach of his enemies and, if possible, to steal victory because he was about to fight with a few against many noble and experienced generals, among whom the one acting as emperor rose as a sun among stars. Because of this and since his forces were lesser in number and power, the *domestikos ton scholon* wanted to oppose the enemy not only with daring but with study and shrewdness.[45]

Alexios tried a number of tricks in his uneven fight against Bryennios. He tried to gain an advantage in information by sending out spies.[46] He tried to keep his troops from learning about the magnitude of the mismatch by arranging them so that most of Bryennios's forces were hidden behind a hill.[47] He started the fight off with an attempt at a sudden ambush.[48] He contemplated running behind enemy lines to kill Bryennios himself.[49] Although he was talked out of that plan, he did succeed in capturing Bryennios's parade horse, which in turn allowed him to proclaim Bryennios's death plausibly.[50] The key to Alexios's victory in this case was not any of his strategies, but the last minute arrival of some new Turkish allies and the defection of Bryennios's Scythian allies.

[43] 2.27.7–10.   [44] 3.13.6–12.
[45] 4.5.6–13: οὔτε τάφρον ὤρυξεν, οὔτε ἐπήξατο χάρακα· ἐβούλετο γὰρ αὐτοῦ μὴν πολεμίων ἐφοδεύειν ἔφοδον καὶ τὴν νίκην κλέπτειν, εἰ οἷόν τε, καὶ γὰρ ἔμελλε μετ' ὀλίγων μάχεσθαι πρὸς πολλοὺς στρατηγούς τε ἅμα γενναίους καὶ πολυπειροτάτους, ὧν καθάπερ ἀστέρων ἥλιος ἐξῆρχεν ὁ βασιλειῶν. διὰ τοῦτο ἐβούλετο τῷ πλήθει καὶ ταῖς δυνάμεσιν ἐλαττούμενος ὁ δομέστικος τῶν Σχολῶν μὴ τόλμῃ μόνον, ἀλλὰ καὶ μελέτῃ καὶ ἀγχινοίᾳ καταστρατηγῆσαι τῶν πολεμίων·
[46] 4.5.13–14.   [47] 4.7.1–7.   [48] 4.8.1–8.   [49] 4.8.14–17.   [50] 4.9.10–18.

In other cases, Alexios's ruses work well. After capturing Bryennios, Alexios was sent to bring down the rebellion of Bryennios's ally Basilakes. The centerpiece of this story is a night battle. Alexios tricked Basilakes into attacking his camp at night and prepared by moving his forces out of his camp and hiding them in nearby woods. When Basilakes attacked the deserted camp, Alexios allowed them to become engaged in plundering. Only when Basilakes's troops had broken their ranks and become completely disorganized, did Alexios's forces charge out from their hiding place.[51]

The narrative set-up for this trick is somewhat confused. It appears that two different possible ways of introducing the ruse were combined or that Nikephoros started with one then changed course. One possible way to introduce the story would be for Alexios to send out spies and learn that Basilakes was planning a night attack. Another possible way to start the story would be for Alexios to send one of his own men, pretending to be a deserter, to lead Basilakes into the trap through misinformation. Nikephoros's actual narrative hints at both of these scenarios:

Since Alexios was shrewd and had enough experience from previous combats, he discerned the intention of the enemy, supposing that Basilakes would attack him by night, which indeed he did. That is why he made his preparations and sent out scouts everywhere. These were the actions of Alexios. Then, when one of those following Komnenos deserted to Basilakes and suggested that if he wanted to attack Alexios, he would betray him sleeping in his tent, without delay Basilakes ordered everyone to arm and immediately everyone was in arms.[52]

If Alexios knew ahead of time that Basilakes was going to attack by night, then he would not need to send out a false deserter to lure Basilakes into the night attack. If Basilakes indeed attacked on the suggestion of a genuine deserter, then it does not make a lot of sense to say that Alexios had discerned Basilakes's plan before then. The text may be corrupt or Nikephoros may have switched to a more dramatic introduction to the ruse without thoroughly harmonizing that story with what had gone before.

The significant point for our purposes is that Nikephoros was at pains to describe Alexios as operating through deception. The first story has Alexios catch wind of Basilakes's trick. The second gives Alexios a more

[51] 4.22–24.
[52] 4.19.1–8: καὶ γὰρ ἀγχίνους ὢν καὶ πεῖραν λαβὼν ἱκανὴν ἐξ ὧν ἔδρασε πρότερον, ἐθήρασε τὸν τοῦ πολεμίου σκοπόν, οἰόμενος ἐπιθέσθαι τούτῳ ἐκεῖνον νυκτός, ὃ δὴ καὶ γέγονε. ταύτῃ τοι καὶ προπαρεσκευάσατο καὶ σκοποὺς πανταχόθεν ἐξέπεμπεν· ἀλλ' οὗτος μὲν οὕτως· ὁ δὲ Βασιλάκης, τῶν ξυνόντων τῷ Κομνηνῷ αὐτομολήσαντός τινος πρὸς αὐτὸν καὶ φράσαντος ὡς, εἰ βούλοιτο ἐπιθέσθαι τούτῳ, παραδώσει τοῦτον αὐτὸς καθεύδοντα ἐπὶ τὴν σκηνήν, μηδὲν μελλήσας ἐκέλευσε πάντας ὁπλίζεσθαι καὶ εὐθὺς ἅπαντες ἦσαν ἐν ὅπλοις.

active role in manipulating Basilakes into his own trap. Alexios is shown as being in control of the situation whereas Basilakes is reactive. Nikephoros also depicted Alexios as willing to accept consequences that others would consider dishonorable in allowing his own camp to be plundered.

Alexios's brother Isaac was also capable of a good ruse. He was ordered by the emperor to remove the popular Patriarch of Antioch from that city and send him to Constantinople. Isaac tricked the Patriarch into leaving Antioch by pretending to the Patriarch that he was ill. The Patriarch invited Isaac to go to his country estate to recover. Then while he was receiving the Patriarch as a visitor in the country, Isaac got up, ostensibly to hunt a hare, and raced back to town and shut the gates.[53] Like his brother, Isaac was able to find a way to be successful even when he was at a political disadvantage. Also like his brother, the means of this victory was dishonesty.

Alexios's use of stratagems and deceptive fighting puts him at odds with the Roman valorization of straightforward fighting. Not only is deviousness contrary to Roman ethos, it is precisely the ethos of the Turks. Alexios most often fights like a Turk. This analysis of the moral patterns of fighting in Nikephoros's history reveals a strong undercurrent of criticism of Alexios. In a work that lionizes the Romans for their valor and bravery, Alexios is denigrated as both ignoble and un-Roman.

One might be tempted to object that Alexios's skirmishing and ambushing cannot be seen as ignoble because these tactics were a standard and significant element of the Byzantine military system of the eleventh and twelfth centuries. There is no doubt that Byzantine military officers were trained in laying ambushes and that stratagem formed a central theme in Byzantine military theory.[54] John and Isaac Komnenos are taught how to lay ambushes as part of their formal education.[55] A treatise on skirmishing is attributed to Nikephoros Phokas (963–969).[56] These tactics were in fact a significant element in the Byzantine military successes of the tenth and eleventh centuries.

The literary presentation of warfare, however, is a matter of cultural choice guided by moral interest. Nikephoros's choices in how to depict

[53] 2.28.
[54] Walter Kaegi, *Some Thoughts on Byzantine Military Strategy* (Brookline: The Hellenic Studies Lecture, 1983); Everett L. Wheeler, *Stratagem and the Vocabulary of Military Trickery* (Leiden: Brill, 1988), 12.
[55] 1.1.21.
[56] Gilbert Dagron and Haralambie Mihaescu, eds., *Le traité sur la guérilla (De velitatione) de l'empereur Nicéphore Phocas (963–969)* (Paris: Éditions du Centre national de la recherche scientifique, 1986); George T. Dennis, *Three Byzantine Military Treatises*, (Washington, DC: Dumbarton Oaks, 1985), 138–244.

events should be evaluated in the context of the classical tradition of history writing, which was not a simple mirror. Scholars interested in reconstructing the realities of classical and medieval warfare are well aware of the difficulties our textual sources pose in their selective presentation of those moments in which military action displays personal character. Historians wrote to preserve the memory of great deeds and allow those deeds to serve as guides for the present. In presenting the past as a set of *exempla*, classical historians presented a moral vision of military activity. A consequence of this selection of moments in history that best display character is a focus on agonistic warfare. Battles and single combats are disproportionately represented in histories and literature because they test men.[57] Other forms of combat are under-represented.

Nikephoros's choice to present Alexios as an advocate of military trickery therefore cannot be dismissed as simply reflecting contemporary military usage. If members of Nikephoros's audience had a sense of cultural memory that included classical Roman ideas of warfare as an arena for the display of moral character, in which true nobility is manifested by conduct during defeat, they would not regard Alexios as a hero. Nikephoros's portrayal of Alexios as trying to "steal victory" and persistently avoiding straight fights constitute an alignment of Alexios with ignoble and dishonorable behavior.

Devious fighting is easily denigrated in moral systems underpinned by standards of fairness, but it may also be valorized. If winning is more important than how the game is played, then Alexios is the hero because he could always scrape out a victory. In settings where mismatches of power make the playing field uneven, such as those faced by Br'er Rabbit or Robin Hood, the trickster is the hero.[58] Anything is fair for a small disadvantaged group fighting a mighty empire. Yet Nikephoros is writing from the perspective of the Roman Empire, the paradigmatic great state. In fighting like a scrappy underdog Alexios showed ingenuity and brought victory, but he was not fighting like a Roman.

---

[57] Simon Hornblower, "Warfare in Ancient Literature: The Paradox of War," in *The Cambridge History of Greek and Roman Warfare*, ed. Philip A. G. Sabin, Hans van Wees, and Michael Whitby (Cambridge University Press, 2007), 44; Eckstein, *Moral Vision*, 20–27.

[58] Wheeler reminds us that the "attitude of the writer toward the respective parties or a particular event determines whether a stratagem is praised as genius, defended as necessity, or condemned as a war crime," Wheeler, *Stratagem and the Vocabulary of Military Trickery*, 93.

CHAPTER 9

# Roman family politics

All men have mothers, and most men get married, but whether those relationships make it into the historical record is a matter of cultural choice. Descriptions of family relationships and networks are relatively lacking in detail in ninth- and tenth-century Byzantine histories because that information was not important to the cultural construction of politics of that era. Byzantine political culture of the ninth and tenth centuries organized power, at least ostensibly, through titles and offices more than through family networks. In contrast Nikephoros presents familial connections as essential for successful operation of the highest levels of imperial politics. Family relationships appear throughout the text as a means of conducting politics and exercising government.[1] Familial connections were very likely highly important for political success in earlier centuries as well, but Nikephoros's history shows a new interest in talking about them.

Nikephoros's emphasis on cooperation between family members and the reliance on family for political action are indicative of a clear change in Byzantine culture.[2] Rather than as an aspect of "feudalization" however, the increasing prominence of aristocratic households in the history can be seen as cultural patterning upon classical exempla. Because the politicians in Nikephoros's history work through family connections rather than government offices, the politics of his era can appear more "medieval" and less "imperial." Yet the essential contrast between a bureaucratic empire in which power was inscribed within offices and a feudal state with power resting on kinship networks is grounded in the study of medieval and early modern western European history. It is highly unlikely that such a dichotomy would have occurred to Nikephoros. When Plutarch and Polybius are recognized as key models for Nikephoros, then the emphasis on

---

[1] Seger, *Bryennios*, 30.
[2] Kazhdan and Constable, *People and Power*, 111–12; Kazhdan and Wharton, *Change*, 106; Kazhdan and Franklin, *Studies on Byzantine Literature*, 23–86; Carile, "La Hyli historias," 56–87; Kazhdan, "Aristocracy and the Imperial Ideal," 43–57.

family relationships can better be interpreted as imitation of accounts of classical Roman political practice. Nikephoros's presentation of aristocratic families contending for service to Rome is remarkably similar to republican Roman ideals of service to the state.[3] Nikephoros presents us with a medieval reading of Roman aristocratic practice.

Nikephoros presents the support of a vigorous extended family as necessary for political success. Michael VII did not know who to get to fight in the west since his uncle Caesar John Doukas had become a monk and John's children were unavailable through illness and death.[4] This absence of cousins and uncles was a reasonable cause of governmental problems. John Doukas, facing the deaths of his sons, similarly *had* to get a well-connected strong young man married into his family. This necessity pushed John to turn to his former rivals, the Komnenoi. Plutarch describes one of Aemilius Paulus's key qualifications for the consulship in 168 as his "many sons and sons-in-law and a great crowd of friends and kinsmen of great influence."[5] The model of family support for a political leader presented by Plutarch would be entirely consonant with the actions of the aristocratic families of the eleventh and twelfth centuries.

Nikephoros's images of family members working together for mutual political advancement have parallels with descriptions of republican Roman aristocratic practice. When Isaac Komnenos became emperor he appointed his brother John *kouropalates* and put him in charge of the western defenses.[6] Bryennios the Elder enjoyed the support of a vigorous family loyal to him.[7] One of Bryennios's first acts as a newly proclaimed emperor was to appoint his brother, John, *domestikos ton scholon* with the rank of *kouropalates*.[8] John campaigned in Thrace on behalf of his brother's revolt while Bryennios solidified his control of the western provinces. Numerous other examples show brothers and in-laws working together to further their common interests. The depictions of brothers and sons working together and caring for each other found in Nikephoros's history have multiple parallels in classical Roman histories. The story of Andronikos Doukas leaving relative safety to rush again into battle to save his father John is strongly reminiscent of the story of young Scipio Africanus charging

---

[3] Saller emphasizes the significance of household connections above kinship connections: Richard Saller, "Roman Kinship: Structure and Sentiment," in *The Roman Family in Italy: Status, Sentiment, Space*, ed. Beryl Rawson and Paul Weaver (Oxford: Clarendon Press, 1997), 31.
[4] 3.1.10–21.   [5] Plut. *Aem.* 10.2.   [6] 1.3.4–6.   [7] 3.4.
[8] 3.11.1–3. In his negotiations with Botaneiates, both ambassadors were relatives of the adversaries. Stravoromanos was chosen as an ambassador to Bryennios because he was Botaneiates's relative. Choirosphaktes was sent as the secondary ambassador because he was connected to Bryennios by marriage. 4.2.15–21, 39–42.

forward to rescue his father in the Battle of Ticinus against Hannibal.[9] Various members of the Scipio and Paulus families, to name two of many, helped promote each other's careers all while serving Rome. Scipio Africanus ran for an aedileship early because he was concerned his older brother Lucius would not win on his own.[10] Publius Cornelius Scipio acted in concert with his brother Gnaeus, just as the Carthaginians Hasdrubal and Hannibal worked together. The innate loyalty of both sets of brothers allowed them to conduct war against each other simultaneously in Spain and Italy with greater confidence.[11] Aemilius Paulus was pleased when his son volunteered for dangerous service while on campaign.[12] Nikephoros and his contemporaries could read Plutarch and Polybius with a keen appreciation for how the workings of their kin networks mimicked those of the great old Romans.

The marriages of Alexios's brothers and sisters are presented in Nikephoros's history as forging alliances with various families with the expectation that a marriage marked an accord of mutual support in political advancement and a cessation of possible hostilities. While there is no doubt that the marriages indeed served these functions, what they did is a separate matter from why and how they were described. In other eras the women necessarily involved in family networks were rarely included in the historical descriptions of politics. Nikephoros explained all of the Komnenos family arrangements in detail because it served his rhetorical purposes to include them. Two of Alexios's sisters were married while their father was still alive: Maria to Michael Taronites, and Eudokia to Nikephoros Melissenos.[13] The youngest daughter, Theodora, was married to Constantine, the son of Romanos Diogenes, after Romanos had become emperor.[14]

The interest Nikephoros expresses in marriage alliances and connections between various families mimics the practice of classical Roman histories. To take one example, Plutarch's *Life of Pompey* records in detail the attempts of various leading politicians to forge marriage connections with Pompey. The marriage of Julia, Caesar's daughter, to Pompey was a significant political event and her death was considered a catalyst of their civil war.[15] Similarly, the Triumvirate arrangement of Octavian, Antony, and Lepidus was sealed by the marriage of Octavian to Clodia,

[9] Polyb. 10.3.4–7.    [10] Polyb. 10.4.1–3.
[11] For one example among many: Publius Cornelius Scipio sends his brother to fight Hasdrubal in Spain while he fought Hannibal in Italy: Polyb. 3.49.4.
[12] Plut. *Aem.* 15.5.    [13] 1.6.9–12.    [14] 1.6.12–16.
[15] Plut. *Pomp.* 49.3.1–3, 53.1–7, 55.1, 70.4; Plut. *Caes.* 23.5–7.

the daughter of Antony's wife Fulvia.[16] When Octavian wanted to break this alliance he sent this wife back to Fulvia and dissolved the marriage kinship.[17] The alliance was reestablished after Fulvia's death by the marriage of Antony to Octavian's sister Octavia.[18] These examples could be easily multiplied.[19] Women were crucial in forging alliances between contending parties in republican Roman politics.[20] We see their roles clearly because Plutarch and Cassius Dio believed it was appropriate to describe Roman politics in terms of aristocratic family relationships. The visibility of aristocratic women in Nikephoros's history and the importance placed on marriage alliances may in part reflect Nikephoros's desire to tell his story in the style of a classical Roman history.

The fictive kinship mentioned in Nikephoros's history also has precedents in classical Roman history. Isaac and John Komnenos are described as entering Basil II's household upon the death of their father Manuel.[21] Romanos Diogenes strengthened the bond between his family and the Komnenoi, already established by the marriage of his son Constantine to Theodora Komnene, when the oldest of Anna's sons, Manuel, became part of the imperial household. As soon as Romanos had "seized the rudder of the Empire, the first of the brothers, Manuel, was made kinsman with the emperor."[22] This practice of the sons of one family joining in the household of another family mimics the practice of the Roman republican aristocracy. When Aemilius Paulus remarried, he placed the sons by his first marriage to Papiria with two other aristocratic families. Aemilius's oldest son was adopted by Fabius Maximus and became Quintus Fabius Maximus Aemilianus. The second son was adopted by Aemilius's sister Cornelia and her husband Cornelius Scipio. He took the name Publius Cornelius Scipio Aemilianus and earned the epithet Africanus the Younger.[23] While this case is not unique, it was perhaps particularly well known.

---

[16] Cass. Dio 46.54.3–4.    [17] Cass. Dio 48.6.    [18] Plut. *Ant.* 31.1–4; Cass. Dio 48.31.

[19] Suzanne Dixon, "The Marriage Alliance in the Roman Elite," *Journal of Family History* 10 (1985): 366.

[20] On the actions of women in classical Roman politics see Margaret L. Woodhull, "Matronly Patrons in the Early Roman Empire: The Case of Salvia Postuma," in *Women's Influence on Classical Civilization*, ed. Fiona McHardy and Eireann Marschal (London: Routledge, 2004), 77; Suzanne Dixon, "A Family Business: Women's Role in Patronage and Politics at Rome, 80–44 BC," *Classica et Medievalia* 34 (1983): 91–112; Suzanne Dixon "Polybius on Roman Women and Property," *American Journal of Philology* 106 (1985): 147–70.

[21] 1.1.

[22] 1.7.1–3: ἄρτι δὲ καὶ τοῦ Διογένους Ῥωμανοῦ τῶν τῆς βασιλείας οἰάκων ἐπειλημμένου, πρῶτος τῶν ἀδελφῶν Μανουὴλ ᾠκείωτο τῷ βασιλεῖ.

[23] Plut. *Aem.* 5.5.

The practice of an emperor adopting a leading general as his heir was established in the first century when Nerva adopted Trajan. The adoptive emperors provided an uncommonly stable government.[24] Diocletian attempted to revive a version of the adoptive principle in laying out the planned succession of Caesars to Augustae in the Tetrarchy. Diocletian's scheme did not function in the long term, but the use of the title Caesar to designate the Augustus's heir persisted. The title Caesar was used in the ninth through eleventh centuries to designate an heir to the emperor, especially in circumstances when the emperor did not have a son named as co-emperor. Michael VII intended to elevate one of his generals to the rank of Caesar because many of his relatives were dying and his uncle Caesar John Doukas had taken monastic vows after his failed rebellion.[25] Michael's plan of nominating a Caesar implied that the solution to the Empire's problems was to pass imperial rule to another powerful aristocratic family. Later Botaneiates tried to end Bryennios's rebellion by offering him both the title Caesar and to adopt Bryennios as his son. While the practice of promoting a Caesar to serve as the presumptive imperial heir had precedents in the more recent history of the ninth and tenth centuries, it also recalled the practice of the more famous emperors of antiquity.[26]

Nikephoros presents his heroes as emotionally concerned with the well-being of their families. Familial regard is an aspect of virtuous conduct. Bryennios is described as unwilling to put down his rebellion and accept Botaneiates's offer of the rank of Caesar because he wanted guarantees of amnesty for his followers.[27] This reason casts Bryennios as caring greatly for his family and supporters. In his final battle, Bryennios entrusted his right flank to his brother John, who is specified as being of the same blood.[28] A series of unexpected reversals leaves Bryennios fighting alone with his son and brother against an entire Turkish host. The three men of the same blood fought on alone against the Turks after they were abandoned by all other allies.[29] John Doukas's heroism similarly takes the form of tender concern for the members of his family. John mourned the death of his son Constantine and was motivated to arrange his granddaughter's marriage by the realization that his son Andronikos also was dying.[30] Andronikos Doukas's prolonged illness was caused by wounds he received when he rushed back

---

[24] Michael Peachin, "Rome the Superpower: 96–235," in *A Companion to the Roman Empire*, ed. David Potter (London: Blackwell, 2006), 144.
[25] 3.2.1–5.
[26] On adoption and ritual kinship in Byzantium see Ruth Macrides, "Kinship by Arrangement: The Case of Adoption," *Dumbarton Oaks Papers* 44 (1990): 109–18; Claudia Rapp, "Ritual Brotherhood."
[27] 4.3.14–25.    [28] 4.6.    [29] 4.12.    [30] 3.6.1–3.

into battle in order to save the life of his father.[31] A presumption of familial affection and honor lie behind the compliments that Botaneiates's envoy made to Bryennios regarding his father. The speech read by Botaneiates's ambassador opened with the compliment that Botaneiates remembered Bryennios's father as a great man and a worthy companion in arms.[32]

Women in Nikephoros's history are similarly portrayed as emotionally committed to the well-being of their families. The women appear to "follow the model of the Roman *matrona*" in taking great concern for a good marriage and their children.[33] Nikephoros brings women into his story of men's deeds when their responses to the difficulties of their families add pathos to the story. John Doukas's concern over the survival of his family after the impending death of his son Andronikos was shared by Andronikos's wife, Maria of Bulgaria. Maria urged her husband to "bring some defender for his children" into their household.[34] In Nikephoros's story it is Maria who suggested a match between her daughter, Irene, and Alexios Komnenos. Maria is described as working tirelessly to secure the match.[35] Alexios's mother Anna Dalassene is also shown as emotionally committed to her children. She grieved deeply at the death of her son Manuel.[36]

None of the phenomena described here are unique to either Roman or Byzantine political culture or practice. Many societies organize politics through families. One could point to marriage alliances and brothers helping each other in numerous other contexts. But while the practice of organizing politics through families may be common, it is not universal, and Byzantine political culture of the eighth and ninth centuries presents one of the great counter-examples of a society that organized power through title and office rather than through family.[37] Ninth-century emperors were known to sideline or eliminate relatives as potential competitors.[38] While aristocratic family networks were always a key part of the reality of politics, the presentation of families, complete with their women, as engines of political action represents a change in medieval Roman political culture. Nikephoros's presentation of family affection and cooperation therefore cannot be interpreted as "natural," and the specificity of the alignment with Roman cultural models is compelling.

The significant roles for family networks in Nikephoros's history sit comfortably alongside his use of formal imperial titles. Nikephoros's emphasis

---

[31] 2.15.14–32.   [32] 4.3.1–7.
[33] Constantine D. S. Paidas, "Issues of Social Gender in Nikephoros Bryennios' *Yle Istorion*," *Byzantinische Zeitschrift* 101, 2 (2008): 740.
[34] 3.6.12.   [35] 3.6. 38–41.   [36] 1.12.19–24.   [37] Neville, *Authority*, 14–38.
[38] Shaun Tougher, *The Reign of Leo VI (886–912): Politics and People* (Leiden, Brill, 1997), 31.

on family, when associated with the "aristocratization" of Byzantine culture, can be seen as a movement away from the apparently more meritocratic system of the ninth and tenth centuries, in which power was vested solely in imperial offices, toward a system in which power was held by virtue of kinship with the emperor.[39] Yet Nikephoros consistently refers to characters by their governmental titles. He may have disdained the petty titles that could be purchased, but military titles are central to his way of talking about history. The *kouropalates* Manuel Komnenos was appointed *strategos autokrator* of the eastern *tagmata*.[40] Andronikos Doukas was called the *protovestiarios*.[41] John is always the Caesar. Throughout his fight with Roussel, Alexios was *stratopedarch* and *strategos autokrator*. Nikephoros Bryennios was the *dux* of the West.[42] Andronikos Doukas is called the *domestikos ton scholon*.[43] *Magistros* Joseph Tarchaneiotes was *katarchon* of the *tagmata*.[44] Anna Dalassene is called by her title, *kouropalatissa*.[45] Nikephoros does not reject the tradition of formal imperial titulature. He rather uses it extensively within a narrative that also includes additional information about the family relationships and marriage policies of the major characters.

The idea that Nikephoros did not hold the honorary titles in high regard may stem from his explanations of the old title system. In describing the early careers of Manuel's children Isaac and John, Nikephoros relates that Basil II gave them senatorial titles, because it is "a custom for emperors of the Romans to appoint the children of the best men and of good heritage to their own service."[46] To what audience did this aspect of Byzantine culture need to be explained? The actual titles that they received are not mentioned. Similarly, Nikephoros explained that the *protostrator* was an important office always given to the best of those by the emperor.[47] It is highly unlikely that anyone in Nikephoros's circle would have needed his explanation that the granting of honorary titles was an old Roman custom. It is possible that these honors had been so devalued that the explanation reminded the audience that they had been high honors in the past. Alternatively these explanations of Roman governmental habits may be an imitation of Polybius's stylistic habit of offering asides instructing his Greek audience about Roman matters.[48] Perhaps Nikephoros's pointed

[39] Kazhdan and Wharton, *Change*, 56–73, 99–119.    [40] 1.7.4; 1.11.1–2.
[41] 3.6.21.    [42] 1.13.9–10; 1.15.2–3.    [43] 1.24.7–8.    [44] 1.13.9–10.    [45] 2.1.6.
[46] 1.2.2–4: ἔθος γὰρ τοῦτο βασιλεῦσι Ῥωμαίων τοὺς τῶν ἀρίστων ἀνδρῶν παῖδας καὶ τῶν εὖ γεγονότων τῇ σφῶν αὐτῶν ὑπηρεσίᾳ συγκαταλέγειν.
[47] 2.2.10–13: θάτερος δὲ τῶν τούτου υἱέων ὁ Κωνσταντῖνος ἔμεινε παρὰ τῷ βασιλεῖ· προεβέβλητο γὰρ πρὸς αὐτοῦ πρωτοστράτωρ, τουτὶ δὲ τὸ ὀφφίκιον μέγα ἦν ἀεὶ παρὰ βασιλεῦσι καὶ μεγίστοις ἐδίδοτο·
[48] One example among many: Polyb. 3.87.6–9.

explanations that emperors ought to give honors to the best people were meant to criticize the current emperor's choices.[49] By any reading Nikephoros's text seems to prize the custom of granting imperial titles.

In the late eleventh century Byzantine political culture appears to have changed from a more anonymous, formal system to one increasingly dominated by family connections.[50] To some extent this was a change in presentation rather than real function. There was manifestly less interest in family names and the details of family connections in eighth- and ninth-century histories, but family networks undoubtedly played some role in politics in those eras. Reading classical Roman history may have influenced Nikephoros to highlight family connections, and also familial emotions, in writing his history. In highlighting familial relationships more than previous histories, Nikephoros may have been contributing to the creation of a fresh presentation of how politics should look.

---

[49] This suggestion was made by Irina Tamarkina.     [50] Neville, *Authority*, 5–38.

CHAPTER 10

# *Religion and Providence*

Nikephoros's history is not overtly committed to any theological position and religion is not a major topic of discussion in his history. The history does not participate in fights to establish proper religion that dominate some other Byzantine histories. A joke about calling a warrior a 'God' indicates a change from the earlier Byzantine concerns with supporting Orthodox Christianity. While the cowardly eunuch John was being helped by George Palaiologos in the midst of battle, John called George "another God" and promised to adopt him and make him heir of all his possessions.[1] John is a comically arrogant, fearful, and ungrateful character. His absurdly timid behavior in the battle and overblown gratitude make everything he says ridiculous. So his statement that George was "another God" should be understood as more ridiculous than blasphemous; it indicates that polytheism was a matter for joking. In other eras Byzantine people did not have such a lighthearted and casual relationship with polytheism. By the twelfth century it seems that the era of contention between Christianity and traditional Roman religions was but dimly remembered.

Nikephoros's apparently light cultural engagement with Christianity deserves further investigation. Some aspects of his narrative draw on specifically Christian theological ideas. Nikephoros also presents a view of divine interaction in human affairs that is not incongruous with traditional pre-Christian Roman ideas. The solution to this apparent dissonance lies in an understanding that few religions present entirely comprehensive totalizing systems as options and few people take on all aspects of such a system. A disagreement between religions on one aspect of thought or practice does not necessarily set all of both systems in opposition. The following tries to tease out Nikephoros's sense of religion with a view toward understanding how he

---

[1] 4.38.15: ὁ δὲ μετρίως ἀνενεγκὼν ὡς τοῦ ὕδατος ἀπεγεύσατο, Θεόν τε αὐτὸν ἄλλον ἀπεκαλεῖτο καὶ υἱὸν τοῦ λοιποῦ, εἰ διασωθείη, ἐκ προαιρέσεως τοῦτον ποιήσασθαι ἐπηγγέλλετο, οὐ μέχρι δὲ λόγου τὰ τοῦ λόγου ἐβεβαίου, ἀλλ᾽ ὡς κληρονόμον τοῦτον καταστῆσαι ἐπὶ πᾶσι τοῖς αὐτοῦ καὶ τὰ ὑπὲρ αὐτοῦ ὥσπερ οἰκείου παιδὸς σπουδάσειν.

was able to negotiate differences between the Christianity of his characters and the traditional (polytheistic) religion of his textual, and moral, models.

Nikephoros's history is concerned predominately with war and politics, not religion. Some evidence however indicates a belief in Christian theological ideas of salvation and ultimate judgment after death or at the end of days. The primary indication of this comes in the story of Anna Dalassene's trial for treason. When accused of conspiring with Romanos against Michael VII, Anna Dalassene dramatically pulled an icon of Christ out of her robe and declared that he was her only judge.[2] Anna Dalassene's direct appeal to Christ as her only judge indicates that Nikephoros's audience would hold Christian ideas about ultimate judgment seriously. The drama and power of Anna's actions depend on the acceptance of Christ as the ultimate judge by the temporal judges she is endeavoring to intimidate. By pulling an icon of Christ out of her robe she unambiguously appeals to the specifically Christian idea of divine judgment after death. The story of Isaac's abdication and monastic retirement similarly draws on Christian ideas of the need for repentance and concern with immortal salvation. Intercessory prayer makes a brief appearance in the story of Alexios's return to Constantinople from Heraclea by sea. A sudden strong wind endangered the ship, but the Mother of God calmed the sea in response to Alexios's prayer.[3] These stories clearly indicate a basic Christian theological backdrop for Nikephoros's history.

Other expressions of Christian piety on the part of Nikephoros's generals are easily aligned, at least their literary presentation, with the pious actions of their classical antecedents. The piety of Nikephoros's heroes takes the form of going into (Christian) temples at appropriate moments to give thanks and ask for help. A visit to a temple in thanksgiving for victory was a standard part of the proper behavior of an ancient Roman general.[4] After his success in bringing down Roussel's rebellion, Alexios went to the church of the Theotokos at Heraclea to give thanks.[5] Bryennios's first act upon being proclaimed emperor in Adrianople was to go to the church of the Mother of God and offer thanks.[6] On the eve of his battle with Alexios, Bryennios spent the night praying in the church of the Mother of the Divine Word, while Alexios sent spies out in search of tactical advantage.[7]

[2] 1.22.27–33.   [3] 2.27.20–24.

[4] Valerie M. Warrior, *Roman Religion* (Cambridge University Press, 2006), 56–66. Roman triumphs ended at the temple of Jupiter on the Capitoline hill. Mary Beard, *The Roman Triumph* (Belknap Press, 2007), 82; Michael McCormick, *Eternal Victory: Triumphal Rulership in Late Antiquity, Byzantium, and the Early Medieval West* (Cambridge: Cambridge University Press, 1986), 12.

[5] 2.26.16–19.   [6] 3.10.9–11.   [7] 4.6.1–6.

In contrast to the heady emotional mysticism taught by Symeon the New Theologian, for example, these visits to holy sites appear to be more a matter of proper action in regard to divine things than a deep engagement with Christian redemption.[8] The generals are practicing Christianity in a traditional way, but in performing rituals designed to maintain divine favor, their actions create no jarring discord with the *pietas* of Nikephoros's classical Roman heroes.[9]

While the generals act in traditionally pious manners, the success or failure of their endeavors does not correlate to the degree of their piety. Their fortunes are not keyed to their moral actions. In explaining the success or failure of individual generals Nikephoros appeals to the idea that divine favor or disfavor had a decisive impact on human affairs. Nikephoros usually describes divine favor as *pronoia*, "Providence," although when quoting Polybius he preserves Polybius's use of *tyche* (*fortuna*). In Christian theological contexts, *pronoia* is associated with the divine Providence of the Christian God. Nikephoros's Providence, however, does not function in a "Christian" sense of favoring the morally virtuous while opposing the sinful. Providence is far more neutral and capricious, much like classical *tyche*.

Roman *fortuna* was sometimes appreciated as a divinity in her own right but more often seems to have expressed the "manifestation and fulfillment of the gods' will."[10] Polybius used *tyche* to translate *fortuna*[11] and reserved *pronoia* for describing the forethought of careful human generals and the mundane supplying of their soldiers' needs.[12] Plutarch follows Polybius's usage and contrasts random *tyche* with human virtue.[13] Dionysius of Halicarnassus, however, uses *pronoia* to speak of the divine providence which guarded Rome and in several instances makes *pronoia* an attribute of the

---

[8] *Symeon the New Theologian: The Discourses*, ed. C. J. De Catanzaro (Mahwah, NJ: Paulist Press, 1980).

[9] Interpretations of traditional Roman religion since the 1990s have emphasized that the public ritual actions of Roman politicans constituted a true religious practice that was not cynical or somehow deficient for being unconcerned with personal interior spirituality. Religious practices were seamlessly integrated into political and military actions. John North, "The Religion of Rome from Monarchy to Principate," in *Companion to Historiography*, ed. Michael Bentley (London: Routledge, 1997), 57–68; John North, "Rome," in *Ancient Religions*, ed. Sarah Iles Johnston (Cambridge: Belknap Press, 2007), 228; John Scheid, *An Introduction to Roman Religion*, trans. Janet Lloyd (Bloomington: Indiana University Press, 2003); Mary Beard, John A. North, and S. R. F. Price, *Religions of Rome*, 2 vols. (Cambridge University Press, 1998).

[10] Jason Davis, *Rome's Religious History: Livy, Tacitus and Ammianus on their Gods* (Cambridge University Press, 2004), 116–23, 121.

[11] For example, Polyb. 3.118.6; 1.58.1; 3.20.4; 10.37.4.

[12] For example Polyb. 1.57.1; 2.33.6; 3.60.7; 3.106.7; 3.115.11; 10.17.16; 11.6.6; Walbank, *Polybius*, 58–65.

[13] Plut. *De fort.* 99F10.

gods.[14] When Nikephoros has occasion to talk about human forethought, he describes it periphrastically, reserving *pronoia* for divine influence.[15]

Nikephoros appeals to *pronoia* whenever he wishes to describe a failure without assigning moral blame to the losing general. Whatever human strategic and tactical errors Romanos Diogenes made, his capture by the Sultan is attributed to Providence. Bryennios says that he does not know why divine Providence allowed for the capture of Romanos Diogenes.[16] The account gives plenty of scope for a discussion of the military errors he made. The problems that led Romanos to disaster were those of military judgment. So Nikephoros's decision to attribute his defeat to Providence rather than blame Romanos was a deliberate choice. The choice creates a narrative that is far more sympathetic to Romanos.

The failure of John Doukas's revolt against Michael VII is similarly attributed to divine will. After the renegade mercenary Roussel defeated and captured John, he proclaimed John emperor. John wrote to friends in the city and succeeded in gathering considerable support. Between John's supporters in Constantinople and Roussel's military power, their revolt was well positioned for success and "were it not for the manifestation of divine opposition, he would have easily gained possession of the imperial scepters."[17] Roussel and John were defeated by the Turkish prince Artuq, working at the request of Michael VII. John's story does not use the same terminology of Providence, *pronoia*, but follows the same logic of attributing the failure of a good enterprise to divine will.[18] Nikephoros's telling of the story allows John to maintain his standing as someone who could have been a good emperor, if only things had gone his way.

Nikephoros ultimately attributed the defeat of his grandfather's rebellion to Providence. Only divine favor could satisfactorily explain how Alexios was able to defeat Bryennios in their battle: "after this wrestling match and noble struggle and defeat, not through greater numbers but through perseverance, daring and military care, taking divine Providence as a helpmate who brings great enterprises to successful ends."[19] Alexios is credited

<hr/>

[14] Dion. Hal. *Ant. Rom.* 5.54.1: ἡ δ' ἐν παντὶ καιρῷ σώζουσα τὴν πόλιν καὶ μέχρι τῶν κατ' ἐμὲ χρόνων παραμένουσα θεία πρόνοια διεκάλυψεν αὐτῶν τὰ βουλεύματα.

   10.10.2: ἐπεὶ δὲ ἡ τοῦ δαιμονίου πρόνοια, ὑφ' ἧς ἀεὶ σωζόμεθα κοινῇ, καλῶς ποιοῦσα τὰ κεκρυμμένα βουλεύματα καὶ τὰς ἀνοσίους ἐπιχειρήσεις τῶν θεοῖς ἐχθρῶν εἰς φῶς ἄγει. 2.63.3; 3.5.1; 3.14.2; 3.16.2; 15.3.1; 20.5.2.

[15] ὑπαισθέσθαι τὸ μέλλον, "prescient regarding the future" 3.2.9.  [16] 1.17.28–30.

[17] 2.17.25–27: εἰ μὴ γοῦν τὸ θεῖον ἀντιπρᾶττον ἐφάνη, ῥαδίως ἂν τῶν βασιλείων σκήπτρων γέγονεν ἐγκρατής.

[18] The difference in vocabulary may be due to Nikephoros's use of the text about John Doukas in this passage. See chapter 4, pp. 55–56.

[19] 4.15.13–16.

with military virtues he undoubtedly had, but set against the epic hero Nikephoros drew of Bryennios, readers are left with little doubt that the role of Providence was essential. Several events of the battle as described by Nikephoros contribute to his overall thesis that Providence handed victory to Alexios. Alexios did not win by having the best troops or the best tactics. The unexpected decision of the Scythians to break off their pursuit of Alexios's fleeing forces and instead attack Bryennios's baggage train, Alexios's capture of Bryennios's parade horse, and most of all the fortuitous arrival of additional Turkish allies in the middle of the battle, were all unforeseen acts of Providence.[20]

Conversely, Nikephoros attributes the accomplishments of individuals who succeed beyond their apparent merits to the favor of divine Providence. In his resignation speech Michael VII said that he had been chosen by Providence to be emperor against his will, and that he would now gladly turn away from power.[21] Alexios's rise to prominence at every step of his career is the work of Providence. Alexios was "guarded by the right hand from above" during his first fight against the Turks.[22] Divine Providence wanted Alexios's virtues to be known and therefore Michael sent him to fight against Roussel.[23] Alexios told the citizens of Amaseia that Roussel was captured "by the will of God and our own effort."[24] The story of Alexios's prayers calming the sea functioned to show divine care for Alexios.[25] The works of Providence overcame the obstacles to the marriage of Alexios and Irene Doukaina.[26] Alexios was also favored when Providence brought down his enemies. Providence was Alexios's "helpmate" in defeating Nikephoros Bryennios.[27]

Nikephoros explains the rise of Botaneiates to power entirely in terms of divine Providence. Botaneiates himself claims that God had raised him to the throne.[28] Botaneiates's race to Nicaea is described as improbable and his acclamation there was a marvel. When Botaneiates's meager forces approached Nicaea, the garrison came out in front of the city in battle order. Botaneiates expected the garrison to attack and only continued to approach because he knew the Turks he had evaded were chasing him. Suddenly the garrison shouted acclamations of Botaneiates as emperor and allowed him to enter the city, "saved contrary to all expectation."[29] Nikephoros then draws an interesting lesson from Botaneiates's undeserved and unearned victory:

---

[20] See chapter 8, p. 100.   [21] 3.21.3–5.   [22] 2.5.13–14.
[23] 2.19.16–18.   [24] 2.22.22–23.   [25] 2.27.20–24.   [26] 3.6.46.
[27] 4.15.15–16.   [28] 4.3.5–6.   [29] 3.17.9.

Not more than three hundred men went to rebel with him. Yet walking through the midst of many traps and ambushes clearly set for them, they were preserved from harm by divine Providence. So God showed again how, with His leave, malice cannot prevail and without it, effort is vanity; and throngs of soldiers and ambushes and the best-arranged phalanxes are vanity, marvelous strategies are useless and plans are utterly impotent.[30]

God's will becomes the deciding factor in Botaneiates's acclamation. The "malice," *phthonos,* of Nikephoros's text underwent a significant semantic change from its classical meaning of "envy" to a more general ill fortune or malignant agency that is closely associated with the concept of the devil in medieval texts, even highly classicizing ones.[31] Divine Providence (and God) acts to disrupt the natural order by which good plans and well-organized armies ought to prevail. All of a general's skill and military might is worthless when opposed by divine Providence.

Nikephoros's appeal to Providence is thus somewhat fatalistic. Providence steps into his causal system when human virtues and vices, skills and incompetences do not function properly as explanations for success and failure. The fatalism of Nikephoros's concept of Providence explains the lack of disjuncture when Fortune, *tyche,* appears in the story. Nikephoros did not change the word *tyche* when he was quoting Polybius because he saw it as functionally synonymous with *pronoia. Pronoia* was a twelfth-century way of talking about those factors outside human control.

Nikephoros quotes Polybius when Alexios has brought down the revolt of Basilakes, contrary to expectation. Nikephoros reflects that Alexios's inexplicable success should serve as a warning about the capriciousness of Fortune:

---

[30] 3.17.9–16. This translations follows the emendations of Martin Hinterberger, who draws on a parallel with a couplet by Gregory of Nazianzus: θεοῦ διδόντος, οὐδὲν ἰσχύει φθόνος, | καὶ μὴ διδόντος, οὐδὲν ἰσχύει κόπος. *Carm.* 1.2.32, *PG* 37.926. Hinterberger also restores an οὐ Gautier had deleted to improve the sense of the text. Hinterberger, "*Phthonos* als treibende Kraft," 19. The amended text would read: ὁ γὰρ ξὺν αὐτῷ πρὸς ἀποστασίαν χωρήσαντες οὐ πλείους ἦσαν τριακοσίων ἀνδρῶν, οἵτινες ἅμα αὐτῷ διαβάντες μέσον παγίδων, πολλῶν δηλαδὴ τῶν ἐνεδρευόντων αὐτούς, ὑπὸ τῆς θείας προνοίας ἀσινεῖς διεσώθησαν, δεικνύοντος τοῦ θεοῦ κἀνταῦθα ὡς, ἐκείνου διδόντος, φθόνος <οὐ> κατισχύει καί, μὴ διδόντος, μάταιο<ι οἱ κόποι>, μάταια δὲ τῶν στρατευμάτων πλήθη καὶ λόχοι καὶ φάλαγγες ταττόμεναι ἄριστα, κενὰ δὲ δεινὰ στρατηγήματα καὶ βουλεύματα καὶ παντάπασιν ἄπρακτα.
[31] Hinterberger, "*Phthonos* als treibende Kraft," 1–24; Martin Hinterberger, "Envy and Nemesis in the *Vita Basili* and Leo the Deacon: Literary Mimesis or Something More?," in *History as Literature in Byzantium,* ed. Ruth Macrides (Farnham: Ashgate, 2010), 197–203; Martin Hinterberger, "Emotions in Byzantium," in *A Companion to Byzantium,* ed. Liz James (Malden: Wiley-Blackwell, 2010), 130–32. *Phthonos* can be particularly concerned with lust for personal advancement and power: Martin Hinterberger, "O phthonos, anthropine adunamia kai kineteria duname," in *To Vyzantio hōrimo gia allages: epiloges, euaisthēsies kai tropoi ekphrasēs apo ton hendekato ston dekato pempto aiōna,* ed. Christina Angelidē (Athens: Institouto Vyzantinōn Ereunōn, 2004), 310.

The things done by [Alexios] show that it is necessary not to trust too much in fortune, especially in success, and what Euripides said well – "one good resolution is victorious over many hands" – seems to have been given confirmation through his deeds. For it was one man, one judgment, who brought down in a short time the most clever of the Roman generals covered in glory and the myriad crowd of soldiers and he led to better things and restored to confidence a whole polity that was unmistakably ruined, and raised up the spirits of the army of the emperor which had sunk to the lowest depths of despair.[32]

This passage incorporates a quotation from Polybius's description of the first major Roman defeat in Africa by the forces from Carthage. The Roman general Regulus, seeing that the Carthaginians had been defeated at land and sea, wanted to take the credit for the capture of Carthage before Rome sent out new consuls. He asked the city to come to terms but then treated the ambassadors arrogantly and made such terrible demands that he increased their resolve to resist. The Spartan mercenary Xanthippos arrived at Carthage and said their defeats were not due to the strength of the Romans but to poor Carthaginian generalship. He was put in charge of the Carthaginian military and soundly defeated the Romans. Polybius then reflects:

This event conveys many useful lessons to a thoughtful observer. Above all, the disaster of Marcus [Regulus] gives the clearest possible warning that no one should feel too confident of the favors of Fortune, especially in success. Here we see one, who a short time before refused all pity or consideration to the fallen, brought incontinently to beg them for his own life. Again what Euripides said well – "one good resolution is victorious over many hands" – seems to have been given confirmation through his deeds. For it was one man, one judgment, that defeated the numbers which were believed to be invincible and able to accomplish anything; and restored to confidence a whole polity that was unmistakably and utterly ruined, and the spirits of its army which had sunk to the lowest depths of despair.[33]

Taken as a straightforward intertextual commentary, Nikephoros's use of Polybius likens Alexios to Xanthippos and Basilakes to Regulus. Alexios is credited with good generalship, like Xanthippos. The primary meaning of Polybius's passage is not to praise Xanthippos, however, but to warn against the fickleness of fortune. The warning for the successful men not to trust their good fortune would fall on all victorious generals, including Alexios. The allusion would have told those in Nikephoros's audience enjoying good favor not to count on it. Such an admonition to the triumphant also

---

[32] 4.28.1–9.
[33] Polyb. 1.35.1–5, adapted from the translation of Evelyn Shuckburgh, *The Histories of Polybius* (Bloomington: Indiana University Press, 1962).

would have served as a comfort to the less successful. In wanting to create a strong statement about the capriciousness of human affairs, Nikephoros recalled this passage from Polybius's history and incorporated it into his story. That Polybius spoke of Fortune rather than Providence does not seem to be significant. Both Providence and Fortune play the same role in Nikephoros's history of explaining the success of the undeserving and the failure of the virtuous.

This mixture of *pronoia* and *tyche* is not unique to Nikephoros. Providence and fortune coexist happily in Dionysius of Halicarnassus's history of ancient Rome. He seems to use them interchangeably. Psellos's textbook, the *Historia Syntomos,* also has both Providence and Fortune impacting upon human affairs. There the emperor Tacitus (275–276) was Fortune's toy and the conspirators trusted themselves to Fortune in climbing up to the palace to murder Nikephoros Phokas in 969.[34] Leo the Deacon's tenth-century history likewise appeals to both Fortune and Providence without drawing a sharp distinction between them.[35]

Nikephoros similarly uses Christian vocabulary of "the demon" to discuss divine disfavor, or what his ancient models would have called the anger of the gods. Isaac, Alexios's brother, was unable to calm the insurrections in Antioch because of the ancient enemy of Christians.[36] The author makes a reference to "the demon" who opposed harmony as the cause of the difficulty Nikephoros Bryennios had in his rebellion. The people of Constantinople were ready to welcome the army of John Bryennios when he arrived at the gates, and so the "demon" stirred up trouble.[37] The "demon" also caused Anna Dalassene to be slandered as conspiring with Diogenes.[38] Texts of this era written as part of dispute settlements blame the "demon" for causing problems in situations where any other assignation of blame would cause further disturbance. Community harmony was fostered by blaming an outside force for the conflict.[39] Nikephoros's usage functions to shift blame for human problems onto external divine forces. In Nikephoros's history divine Providence and the demon are like *tyche* in that they explain outcomes inconsistent with moral effort and human virtue. They are both invoked to explain lamentable, unalterable, events.

For both Botaneiates and Alexios, the attribution of their success to Providence implicitly denies that their victories were due to their own virtue and strength. In saying that Providence supported Botaneiates and

---

[34] Psellos, *Historia* 51.72–74; 105.60.
[35] Talbot and Sullivan, *Leo the Deacon*, introduction by Denis Sullivan, 16–19; Hinterberger, "Envy and Nemesis," 187–203.
[36] 2.29.3–4.     [37] 3.11.11–13.     [38] 1.22.16–19.     [39] Neville, *Authority*, 162.

Alexios, Nikephoros implicitly argues that his grandfather did not lose to them because of any failing of skill or virtue on his part. Nikephoros may have called the experience of Bryennios the Elder to mind when he lamented that without divine favor "throngs of soldiers and ambushes and the best-arranged phalanxes are vanity, marvelous strategies are useless and plans are utterly impotent."[40] At no point does Nikephoros hint that Bryennios lacked divine favor because he was a sinful man. Rather the workings of Providence are depicted as inscrutable, if not entirely unbound by human morality. In this, Nikephoros does not engage with a theology of retribution, in which God would punish the wicked and help the virtuous.

Nikephoros's history is not interested in theology or the ongoing Christianization of society. A good general's piety consists in going into churches at appropriate moments to give thanks and ask for help. One could accuse Nikephoros of theological inconsistency, or even blasphemy, in that a possible logical conclusion from his depiction of divine Providence as an amoral force is that God is amoral. But we have no evidence that Nikephoros had a particular interest in theology, let alone theological consistency. He probably never followed through to the logical conclusions of his conception of Providence, but rather saw divine favor as fundamentally inscrutable. Nikephoros appears to have advocated a religious practice of going to church before and after battle to seek divine favor that was combined with taking responsibility for making the utmost efforts for success (without expecting divine help) and accepting the verdict if fortune gave victory to another. This religious practice was remarkably similar to that of his classical exempla. Nikephoros's use of *pronoia* and *tyche* to explain the failure of virtuous men and the success of undeserving men may not be strictly correct theology, but it was roughly compatible with most aspects of Christian practice.

The Roman-ness of Nikephoros's religious expression may be a consequence of his efforts to write a thoroughly Roman history. Concern with salvation, Christian morality, and Trinitarian theology may have been far more common among the people whose history he is writing than appear from his story. Even if this were the case, the acceptability of his portrayal indicates that the defense of formal Christian theology was at most an optional matter of interest.

---

[40] 3.17.13–16.

# CHAPTER II

# Roman heroes

Nikephoros Bryennios the Elder emerges as the great tragic hero of Nikephoros's history. Bryennios's heroism is not inherent in any of his political actions. As the leader of a damaging and costly revolt in a time of deep crisis for the Empire, Bryennios could have gone down as one of the chief villains of Byzantine history. At a time when Seljuks were aggressively expanding and solidifying their control over large sections of Anatolia, Bryennios's rebellion prevented the resources of the Balkan provinces from being brought to bear on the fight against the Seljuks. Nikephoros's rhetorical and narrative skills, however, enabled him to create an entirely positive and deeply sympathetic portrait of his grandfather. The virtues that emerge in the detailed portrait of Bryennios are echoed in the depictions of the history's other tragic heroes, Romanos Diogenes and John Doukas. A common set of personal masculine virtues allows these three political enemies to be remembered as heroic, despite their military failures.

Nikephoros Bryennios the Elder is portrayed as a general in the old Roman style. After Michael VII appointed him *dux* of Bulgaria, Nikephoros Bryennios conducted his campaign against the Dukljans and Croats in Illyria in the manner of a classical Roman general. The people of Dyrrachion were said to have received Bryennios with joy. After gathering materials for war he established military camps.[1] Bryennios here constructed one of the few purpose-built military camps appearing in this history. The construction of proper military camps was part of classical Roman generalship.[2] Then Bryennios had the roads cleared and repaired so that he could advance his army without fearing difficult marches on their return.[3] Apparently he wanted to lessen the chances of facing an enemy ambush.

---

[1] 3.3.17.
[2] Philip A. G. Sabin, "Battle: Land Battles," in *The Cambridge History of Greek and Roman Warfare*, ed. Philip A. G. Sabin, Hans van Wees, and Michael Whitby (Cambridge University Press, 2007), 404.
[3] 3.3.19–22.

The concern with the logistical need for a good road also puts Bryennios squarely in the Roman military tradition.[4] Nikephoros cannot but have been aware of the classical Roman foundations of the network of roads that served his Empire. The ancient Via Egnatia and the "Military Road," which passed through Nikephoros's ancestral home city of Adrianople, remained the main highways across the Balkans in the twelfth century.[5] Beyond any specific associations between road building and Roman generalship, Bryennios's conduct displays concern with good order, *taxis.* Keeping an army in good order was an essential aspect of good Roman generalship.[6]

Once the way was clear, Bryennios's soldiers marched out with enthusiasm. He then engaged the enemy in a "mighty battle and was completely victorious."[7] Formal pitched battles are rare in Nikephoros's history. A decisive pitched battle is distinct from general fighting in having a cultural significance as an arena of contest.[8] Bryennios is here successful in the most valorous form of warfare, a direct military confrontation.

Once victorious, Bryennios "put all the cities under a truce with the Romans" and left a garrison in each.[9] The term "*hypospondous,*" "under treaty," was a common classical military term, but rare enough in the medieval period. Bryennios sent out scouts to locate the Italian pirates that were harassing Adriatic shipping and then sent triremes against them.[10] He sank and captured many of the pirate ships and "the entire fleet in Italy cowered and shortened sail."[11] In setting up formal camps, clearing roads, and fighting pitched battles – both on land and sea – Bryennios acts in a more classically Roman military style than the other generals in this history.

Bryennios's brilliant generalship only excited the envy of sycophants who slanderously told the emperor that Bryennios was planning an insurrection. The narrative of Bryennios's revolt is carefully constructed to exonerate him from the charge of disloyalty and conspiracy. Michael VII sent a spy to

---

[4] Jonathan P. Roth, "War," in *The Cambridge History of Greek and Roman Warfare*, ed. Philip A. G. Sabin, Hans van Wees, and Michael Whitby (Cambridge University Press, 2007), 383.

[5] Klaus Belke, "Communications: Roads and Bridges," in *The Oxford Handbook of Byzantine Studies*, ed. Elizabeth Jeffreys, John Haldon, and Robin Cormack (Oxford University Press, 2008), 295–98.

[6] For example in Dion. Hal. *Ant. Rom.* 5.44.     [7] 3.3.24–25.

[8] Everett L. Wheeler, "Battle: Land Battles," in *The Cambridge History of Greek and Roman Warfare*, ed. Philip A. G. Sabin, Hans van Wees, and Michael Whitby (Cambridge University Press, 2007), 188–89. See chapter 8 of this volume.

[9] 3.3.25–27. The phrase "under treaties" appears in a section of Cass. Dio, 62.23.2.3, that was included in the Constantinian excerpts (*De Legationibus* 421 line 33) and quoted in the *Suda*: alpha 3375.

[10] 3.3.28–33.

[11] 3.3.30–33. Pompey the Great also gained great fame through defeating pirates in the eastern Mediterranean. Plut. *Pomp.* 24–28; Cass. Dio 36.20–37.

Dyrrachion to see if Bryennios was loyal. Bryennios's hospitality was so good that the spy confessed his mission to Bryennios and told him that he was suspected of raising a rebellion. At this news Bryennios was "bitten in his soul and plunged into fear."[12] Yet he did not respond in anger but patiently considered what he should do. The depiction of a victorious general facing slander parallels the story of Belisarius.[13]

It is possible to depict Nikephoros Bryennios as calm, patient, and loyal because all the impetus for revolt is attributed to his brother, John Bryennios. John had returned to Constantinople after a successful campaign against the Scythians expecting to be paid and honored by the emperor. He was turned away empty handed, as was another successful general, Basilakes. The two men fell to griping about Michael's illiberality and sealed a pact to put John's brother on the throne.[14] While their grievances are portrayed as reasonable, this story exonerates Nikephoros Bryennios by making his brother the chief architect of the rebellion.

Even when told that the emperor suspected him of treason and that his brother had sworn oaths to start a rebellion in his name, Bryennios refrained from joining the revolt. Michael's *logothete,* Nikephoritzes, sent one of the imperial guard of "ax-wielding barbarians" to assassinate Bryennios.[15] He got drunk at an inn in Adrianople and let the story out. John Bryennios had him arrested and slit his nose.[16] John then sent word to his brother using the story as a further incitement to revolt. Bryennios was still not moved:

When the letters were brought to him in Dyrrachion, the man was very worried, not knowing what he would do. It seemed terrible to move toward rebellion and cause the greatest of evils. Further he did not think that it was characteristic of a good and wise and noble man to hand himself over to such obvious danger despising all other considerations. He remained wrestling with these thoughts for a long time, even though he was being roused constantly by the letters of his brother.[17]

The extended discussions of Bryennios's reluctance to rebel, and all the forces that drove him hesitantly to it, indicate that revolt was a great crime.

---

[12] 3.4.13.   [13] Hinterberger, "*Phthonos* als treibende Kraft," 19.   [14] 3.4.   [15] 3.5.3.
[16] 3.5.2–12. In arresting and meting out judicial-style punishments, John was acting like an agent of government.
[17] 3.5.12–18: διακομισθέντων οὖν πρὸς αὐτὸν τῶν γραμμάτων κατὰ τὸ Δυρράχιον, πλήρης ἦν ὁ ἀνὴρ φροντίδος, οὐκ ἔχων ὅ τι καὶ δράσειε· τό τε γὰρ πρὸς ἀποστασίαν χωρῆσαι δεινὸν ᾤετο καὶ μεγίστων κακῶν αἴτιον, τό τε ἑαυτὸν εἰς προὔπτον κίνδυνον παραδοῦναι πάντων καταφρονήσαντα οὐκ ἀνδρὸς ἔκρινεν ἀγαθοῦ εἶναι καὶ συνετοῦ καὶ γενναίου· τούτοις παλαίων τοῖς λογισμοῖς διέμεινε μέχρι πολλοῦ, καίτοι συχνῶς ὑπὸ ἐπιστολῶν ἐρεθιζόμενος ὑπὸ τοῦ ἀδελφοῦ.

To be both a hero and a rebel, Bryennios needed considerable goading. The long run-up of provocations that finally goad Bryennios into rebellion creates an apology for his disruption of peace.

John Bryennios moved forward with the revolt in Adrianople despite his brother's continued resistance.[18] When he was told that Michael VII had sent Basilakes to capture him and bring him bound to Constantinople, Bryennios still did not revolt, but thought it prudent to return to his home in Adrianople.[19] Michael's incompetence is displayed by trusting the capture of Bryennios to one of his revolt's primary conspirators. Along the way, Bryennios met with Basilakes at Thessaloniki and Basilakes eventually confirmed the oaths he had made to John to support Nikephoros Bryennios's rebellion. John then joined them with a large army from Adrianople and they camped together. While Bryennios built a camp and had food prepared for the forces, John pushed him to put on imperial insignia.[20] This rather muddled narrative shows the difficulty the author had in telling a story about the conquest of Thrace while maintaining Bryennios's innocence of treason.

When Bryennios declined to put on the insignia, John "persuaded everyone to try to force the man."[21] Bryennios still resisted and wanted to put off the official announcement of his revolt for a year.[22] Nikephoros the author then tells a fairly improbable story about how the siege of Traianoupolis started without Bryennios's knowledge.[23] The day after turning down his brother's request that he put on the imperial regalia, Bryennios happened to be campaigning near Traianoupolis. Nikephoros does not attempt to explain why Bryennios was campaigning if he was not in revolt. The people in the town closed the gates against him and took to the walls out of loyalty to the ruler. Then some of Bryennios's men went unbidden and unarmed to the city walls, to take in the view.[24] The defenders mocked them for their disloyalty and started throwing things at them. The violence soon escalated to a full-scale attack on the town. As his troops began to fight with the people of Traianoupolis, they "defile[d] their hands with the blood of brothers."[25] In the guise of taking control of the situation, Bryennios set guards around the city walls for the night, much as one would do in a siege. During the night Bryennios's son and his friends snuck onto

---

[18] 3.7.1–7.     [19] 3.8.1–6.

[20] 3.8.23–27: τότε μὲν οὖν στρατοπεδευσάμενοι ἀριστεῦσαι παρεσκευάζοντο, ἀλλὰ τῷ Βρυεννίῳ Ἰωάννῃ ἠρεμεῖν οὔτι δέον ἐδόκει οὐδ' ἀναβαλέσθαι τὸν καιρόν. ἐπιφερόμενος οὖν μεθ' ἑαυτοῦ τὰ τῆς βασιλείας παράσημα, ἠνάγκαζε τὸν ἀδελφὸν ταῦτα περιβαλέσθαι·

[21] 3.8.28–9: ἐκείνου δὲ ἀναδυομένου καὶ σκέψασθαι περὶ τούτου ζητοῦντος, αὐτὸς ἀνέπειθε πάντας, εἰ οἷόν τε, τὸν ἄνδρα βιάσασθαι.

[22] 3.8.29–31.     [23] 3.9.     [24] 3.9.4–5.     [25] 3.9.13.

the city walls, woke the surprised guards, and forced them to proclaim Bryennios as emperor.[26] The inhabitants, hearing the shouts of the guards from the walls, believed that the city had been captured and so joined in the proclamation of Bryennios.[27]

This story shows a serious lapse in Bryennios's usual strong control over his military forces. Rather than being fully in control of his well-ordered army, here Bryennios was not able to restrain his men or control even his own son's actions. The explanation for this failure is that failing to control high-spirited youngsters is far less bad than starting an insurrection and attacking fellow citizens.[28] Active rebellion and military action against a Roman city were considered such awful activities that they must have been done by people not under Bryennios's command. Throughout this highly apologetic account of the opening of his revolt, Bryennios never actively chose to rebel but was forced to it by Michael's incompetence and aggression against him.

Once his rebellion had been proclaimed Bryennios is again portrayed as fully in control of his army and acts, not only as a steady, thoughtful, Roman general, but also as an emperor. Nikephoros the author refers to Bryennios as the "one aspiring to being emperor," "*o basileion*," as well as the "ruler."[29] Bryennios's imperial nature is also displayed through his conduct. For example, when Botaneiates's ambassadors arrive to try to make terms with Bryennios they, "seeing the ranks and good order of the phalanx were amazed at the size of them and the good order and the greatness of the leader."[30] Bryennios went to greet them with his officers dismounted in a file behind him while he was seated on a white horse. He was not armed but dressed in imperial costume, "which seemed to adorn him more, being a man good to look at and most clever at speaking."[31]

Bryennios's essential worthiness for imperial rule is best displayed in his final battle against Alexios Komnenos. This episode, which was simultaneously the defeat of the Bryennios family and a highly significant triumph for the ruling Komnenos family, puts Nikephoros's rhetorical skills on display. Nikephoros tells the story in quickly alternating paragraphs about

---

[26] 3.9.19–34.   [27] 3.9.34–47.

[28] On the cultural need for Roman youth to be ferociously aggressive see Lendon, *Soldiers & Ghosts*, 188.

[29] *Basileion*: 4.5.10; *kraton*: 4.2.34. See chapter 5.

[30] 4.2.21–25: ἀπελθόντες οὖν ἐντυγχάνουσι τῷ Βρυεννίῳ περὶ τὴν Θεοδωρούπολιν τὴν φάλαγγα τάξαντι καὶ βάδην πορευομένῳ· ἔτι δὲ πόρρω ὄντες καὶ τὰς τάξεις θεώμενοι καὶ τὴν φάλαγγα κοσμίως συντεταγμένην ἐθαύμαζόν τε τὸ πλῆθος ὁμοῦ καὶ τὴν τάξιν καὶ τὸν ἄγοντα ἐμεγάλυνον.

[31] 4.2.31–33: ἵστατο δὲ οὐκ ἐν τοῖς ὅπλοις, ἀλλ' ἐν κόσμῳ βασιλικῷ, ὃν ἐδόκει μᾶλλον ἐκεῖνος κοσμεῖν, ἀνὴρ ὢν ἀγαθός τε τὸ εἶδος καὶ ὁμιλῆσαι δεινότατος.

Alexios and Bryennios. All of the contrasts between the two generals are highlighted by having the narrative focus cut back and forth between the two camps.

Once Botaneiates's negotiations to end Bryennios's rebellion had failed, Alexios was sent out to oppose him. Alexios camped in an old fortress, but did not put up a stockade or trench around his camp because he wanted "to steal victory, if possible."[32] Alexios needed to steal a victory because he knew he could not win it outright. On the eve of the battle, when Alexios was sending out spies, Bryennios spent the evening in a church. Although Alexios is described as eager to have scouts bring him information, it was actually Bryennios who learned the disposition of Alexios's forces because his scouts just happened to capture some of Alexios's Turkish allies while they were out foraging.[33] It reflects badly on Alexios that his Turkish allies fell into Bryennios's hands.[34] Following on the description of Bryennios's well-ordered army, it suggests that Alexios was not able to keep good order among his troops.

The next morning Bryennios drew up his large army in a formal battle formation. This description of the battle arrangement is a standard part of classical military historiography.[35] Bryennios's brother John commanded the right flank which included the contingent of Franks that had been recruited by George Maniakes.[36] They were paired with a large number of cavalry from Thessaly and many infantry of the *hetaireia*, so that there were no less than 5,000 men in the right flank of Bryennios's army. On the left Katakalon Tarchaneiotes led a second phalanx of 3,000 Thracians and Macedonians. Bryennios led the center in which "he had arranged all those from the leading men of Macedonia and Thrace and the elite cavalry of Thessaly."[37] The archers of the Scythian allies were placed to the left and in front of the main army by two stades. They were to encircle the enemy from behind and attack when signaled by a trumpet.

Alexios, learning about Bryennios's preparations, "hid his entire army in a ravine."[38] He wanted to keep Bryennios's army hidden from his own

[32] 4.5.6–8: ἐκεῖσε τοίνυν στρατοπεδεύσας, οὔτε τάφρον ὤρυξεν, οὔτε ἐπήξατο χάρακα· ἐβούλετο γὰρ αὐτοῦ μὴν πολεμίων ἐφοδεύειν ἔφοδον καὶ τὴν νίκην κλέπτειν, εἰ οἷόν τε, καὶ γὰρ ἔμελλε μετ' ὀλίγων μάχεσθαι πρὸς πολλοὺς στρατηγούς τε ἅμα γενναίους καὶ πολυπειροτάτους, ὧν καθάπερ ἀστέρων ἥλιος ἐξῆρχεν ὁ βασιλειῶν.
[33] 4.6.1–6.    [34] 4.6.3–6.
[35] Just a few examples of an extremely common narrative element: Plut. *Pomp.* 69.1–3. Dion. Hal. *Ant. Rom.* 5.22.2–23.
[36] 4.6.8–14. See note on p. 71.
[37] 4.6.18–20: τὸ δὲ μέσον τῆς φάλαγγος αὐτὸς ἐκεῖνος ὁ Βρυέννιος ἦγεν, ἐν ᾧ τό τε ἀρχοντικὸν ἐτάττετο ἅπαν καὶ Θρᾳκῶν τε καὶ Μακεδόνων καὶ τῆς ἵππου τῶν Θεσσαλῶν ὅσον ἐπίλεκτον.
[38] 4.7.2.

because he feared his forces would flee if they knew what they were facing. Alexios gave Constantine Katakalon command of the Chomatenoi and the Turks. Taking command of the contingent called the "Immortals" and the Franks, he prepared an ambush for Bryennios's right wing.[39]

Alexios sprang the ambush he had prepared but John Bryennios's troops brushed it off. John Bryennios's personal attack was so strong that he turned Alexios's division of Immortals to flight single-handedly.[40] Bryennios's Scythians attacked and defeated the Chomatenoi, but after defeating Bryennios's enemies, they then turned to attack Bryennios's own camp too. They plundered the camp and departed the field.[41] Alexios, facing defeat, contemplated a mad effort to rush behind Bryennios's lines and kill him personally. He was dissuaded by his guards, but in the confusion caused by the Scythian attack on Bryennios's camp, Alexios was able to capture Bryennios's parade horse. He proclaimed that it was proof that Bryennios had been killed and so managed to rally some of his fleeing troops.[42]

At this point Alexios happened upon other contingents of Turks whom he was able to persuade to join his side by showing them, from a small hill, the disorder in Bryennios's camp.[43] Their help was critical to the success of Alexios's counterattack. It seems that they had been sent to join Alexios by Botaneiates but had hung back thinking him unlikely to win. Their last-minute entry into the battle could not have been anticipated by Bryennios. Once they had joined Alexios, the Turkish officers planned out their attack.[44] In her version of this story Anna Komnene repeatedly gives Alexios credit for the plan for the second half of the battle of Kalovrye whereas Nikephoros attributes it to the Turks.[45]

These Turks divided their army into three groups; they used two to set ambushes and the third to chase Bryennios's army into them.[46] In the face of this unexpected attack, Bryennios's men "being clever men in war tried to arrange the phalanx in order and called their own soldiers to be good men."[47] Despite this good leadership they were routed. Nikephoros fought on with his brother and son for a long time, but eventually even he was captured.[48]

Alexios's desire to "steal victory," expressed before the battle, is seen in his actions throughout the battle. He tried to trick his men into fighting a superior force by hiding it from them. He tried to lure Bryennios's right wing into an ambush. He tried to kill Bryennios by sneaking behind his

[39] 4.7–8.    [40] 4.8.6–8.    [41] 4.9.1–7.    [42] 4.9.10–24.    [43] 4.10.1–8.
[44] 4.10.15–21.    [45] Komnene 1.6.2–4. See chapter 15 pp. 186–87 of this volume.
[46] 4.10–12.    [47] 4.11.9–10.    [48] 4.13.

lines. He tried to claim that Bryennios had fallen. Bryennios met each challenge by simply fighting well. The actions of unreliable allies and mercenaries were decisive in Bryennios's defeat.

The description of Bryennios's final fight before his capture highlights his own valor, exemplary personal courage, and skill in warfare. Nikephoros may be adding to the poignancy of the situation by emphasizing that Bryennios was eventually defeated by Turks rather than Romans. This is one of the few places Nikephoros engages in a blow-by-blow account of a fight and can plausibly be seen as following the Homeric model of an *aristeia,* in which the hero fights his best under divine inspiration.[49] Like any number of Roman authors of the classical period, Nikephoros enhanced the glory and intensity of his characterization by adopting elements of Homeric style. The scene is highly effective in portraying Bryennios as the real hero of the day. Crucially, Bryennios only stops fighting when he cannot attack an enemy who is hiding behind his back. After Bryennios had been unhorsed and separated from his son and all other supporters, he continued to defend himself courageously against numerous mounted Turks who surround him:

Then the Turks, seizing the opportunity, fell harder upon Bryennios. One of them, having drawn his sword against him, attacked more boldly. But Bryennios, turning around, struck him with his sword and cut off his hand and made it fall to the ground along with the enemy's blade. The rest tried to encircle him. But he was warding them off nobly. Charging then against those coming on in front of him, he was struck with a spear. While he was trying to cut through the spear, the first Turk whose hand had been cut off by him, having dismounted from his horse, came up behind Bryennios's back. He, whirling his sword, was not able to strike him, hidden as he was behind his back. The rest of the Turks, dismounted from their horses, were beseeching him not to choose death, but to yield to the circumstances. Until then his hand had not tired, nor had he given up striking and being struck.[50]

One of the most powerful "cultural features" of Roman war was "the habit of single combat and the associated moral quality of *virtus,* aggressive

[49] This case was made to me by Dr. Sarah Ferrario.
[50] 4.13.17–29: λαβόντες οὖν ἄδειαν οἱ Τοῦρκοι ἐπῇεσαν κατὰ τοῦ Βρυεννίου σφοδρότερον. εἷς οὖν αὐτῶν τὸ ξίφος σπασάμενος κατ᾽ ἐκείνου τολμηρότερον ἐξώρμησεν· ὁ δ᾽ ἐπιστραφεὶς παίει τοῦτον τῷ ξίφει καὶ τήν τε χεῖρα ἀπέτεμε καὶ κατὰ γῆς αὐτὴν πεσεῖν σὺν τῷ ἀκινάκῃ παρεσκεύασεν· οἱ δὲ λοιποὶ κυκλοῦν ἐπεχείρουν αὐτόν· ὁ δὲ γενναίως ἠμύνετο. ἐξορμήσας οὖν κατὰ τῶν ἔμπροσθεν ἐπιόντων πλήττεται δόρατι· ἀσχοληθέντος δ᾽ αὐτοῦ διακόψαι τὸ δόρυ, ὁ πρῶτος τὴν χεῖρα ὑπ᾽ αὐτοῦ ἐκτμηθεὶς Τοῦρκος τοῦ ἵππου καταπηδήσας ἐπιβαίνει τοῖς νώτοις τοῦ Βρυεννίου. ὁ δ᾽ ἐπιστρέφων τὸν ἀκινάκην οὐχ οἷός τε ἦν παίειν αὐτὸν τοῖς νώτοις τούτου κρυπτόμενον. ἀποβάντες οὖν οἱ λοιποὶ τῶν Τούρκων τῶν ἵππων ἱκέτευον μὴ θνήσκειν ἐθέλειν αὐτόν, ἀλλὰ πρὸς τὸ ξυμπεσὸν ἐνδιδόναι. ἕως μὲν οὖν αὐτῷ ἡ χεὶρ οὐ κεκοπίακεν, οὐκ ἐνέδωκε παίων τε καὶ παιόμενος·

courage."[51] Here Bryennios displays extreme *virtus* through perseverance in an uneven combat. So long as he could fight his enemies face-to-face, Bryennios prevailed, but he could not defeat an attack from behind. Roman contest culture placed tremendous emphasis on the honor and propriety of fighting face to face.[52] The descriptions of Bryennios's personal combat thus associate him with classical Roman military ideals.

When the defeated Bryennios was brought before Alexios, Nikephoros takes the opportunity to describe Bryennios's majestic greatness and contrast it with Alexios's youth:

When Bryennios was brought before Alexios, he marveled at the sight and size of the man, which were truly worthy of tyranny. He rejoiced in seeing what sort of general he had prevailed against: one who had a noble hand, a daring soul and a steadfast character.[53]

It is at first surprising that Nikephoros the Elder is described as worthy of tyranny, given the profoundly negative associations with tyranny in both antiquity and the middle ages.[54] Here, however, Nikephoros incorporates a line, "having the appearance worthy of a tyrant," attributed to Euripides' *Aiolos*, but that had a long life as part of Greek philosophical education.[55] The meaning of the phrase drifted from the philosophical tradition into historical discourse as a way to speak of the physical appearance appropriate for a ruler, without any apparent connotations of tyranny as such and without seeming to recognize a Euripidian origin of the phrase.[56] For

---

[51] Lendon, *Soldiers & Ghosts*, 312.  [52] Barton, *Roman Honor*, 31–130.

[53] 4.15.1–5: τὸν δὲ Βρυέννιον πρὸς τὸν Κομνηνὸν Ἀλέξιον ἀπαχθέντα ἰδών, ἐκεῖνος ἐθαύμασε τό τε εἶδος τοῦ ἀνδρὸς καὶ τὸ μέγεθος καὶ γὰρ ἦν ὄντως ἄξιον τυραννίδος· ἐγεγήθει δὲ ὁρῶν οἵου κατηγωνίσατο στρατηγοῦ, τὴν χεῖρα γενναίου καὶ τὴν ψυχὴν τολμηροῦ καὶ στάσιμον ἦθος ἔχοντος·

[54] Kaldellis, *Hellenism*, 242.

[55] *TGF* fr.15.2. The line was used in philosophical treatises to distinguish between the two meanings of *eidos*, "form, appearance" and "form, manner, kind:" *Porphyrii isagoge et in Aristotelis categorias commentarium*, ed. A. Busse (Berlin: Reimer, 1887), volume IV.1 page 4, line 1; *Eliae in Porphyrii isagogen et Aristotelis categorias commentaria*, ed. A. Busse (Berlin: Reimer, 1900), page 61 line 19. John of Damascus: "Capita philosophica," in *Die Schriften des Johannes von Damaskos*, ed. P. B. Kotter (Berlin: De Gruyter, 1969), section 10.6. *Doctrina patrum de incarnatione verbi*, ed. F Diekamp (Münster: Aschendorff, 1907), 258. Psellos: *Michaelis Pselli philosophica minora*, ed. John M. Duffy (Leipzig: Teubner, 1992), *Opusculum* 50 line 39 and *Opusculum* 51 line 37.

[56] Evagrius Scholasticus applies the Euripidian phrase to Emperor Tiberius II positively, speaking of Tiberius's bodily height. *The Ecclesiastical History of Evagrius with the Scholia*, ed. J. Bidez and L. Parmentier (London: Methuen, 1898; reprint, 1979), 209. Theophanes Continuatus and historians who follow him include the Euripidian line as the first line of a doggerel attributed to Michael III about a oarsman from the imperial barge that he says he ought to have made co-emperor instead of Basil I. *Theophanes continuatus* ed. Immanuel Bekker (Bonn: Weber, 1838), 208, 50; Skylitzes, *Michael* 3.23. Eleventh- and twelfth-century historians applied the phrase to men who are not yet ruling, but look as though they could do the job: Psellos, *Historia* 66.95–2; Zonaras 126, 614; Komnene P.4.1, 6.7.6.

medieval authors the phrase *eidos axion tyrannidos* referred to a good-looking man who had the physical appearance appropriate for a ruler. Nikephoros was wholly positive in saying that his grandfather had a "form worthy of tyranny." It was a highly complimentary way of saying that he looked like a man who ought to be emperor. Far from implicating Nikephoros the Elder in a rebellion, the phrase adds to the sense that he was the real ruler who was conquered.

Nikephoros expands on his description of his grandfather, asking that his audience not consider him to be engaging in self-aggrandizement:

> He had a heroic soul. Let no one suppose that I am bragging to say and write these things. One must know, however, that the righteous actions, graces, and splendors of the man defeat all words. Indeed if this story were not about something else, but wished to describe the deeds of Bryennios, a second *Iliad* would be needed. Then this man, who was masterful at making the right choice in a moment and at skillfully arranging phalanxes and fighting with enemies, was conquered by Alexios Komnenos (who was not yet bearing a full beard, but still budding and golden – for he was [lacuna]). Alexios won after this wrestling match and noble struggle and defeat, not through greater numbers but through perseverance, daring, and military care, taking divine Providence as a helpmate who brings great enterprises to successful ends.[57]

Here Nikephoros draws out the contrasts implicit throughout the story of the battle of Kalovrye. Bryennios, possessing magisterial skill and strength, was the hero worthy of an *Iliad*. Alexios had Providence as his helper. Again Providence appears to be capricious and functions to explain the defeat of the stronger party in the match. Alexios was disappointed with Botaneiates's relative lack of praise of his victory over Bryennios because he had defeated "not a tyranny, but rather a great Empire."[58] Having Alexios conquer an Empire rather than a tyranny was a way of making Bryennios an emperor. The responsibility for blinding Bryennios is given to Botaneiates's Bulgarian servant, Borilas.[59] Bryennios's blinding deprived

---

[57] 4.15.5–17. The manuscript had left a blank for Alexios's age to be filled in. ἡρωϊκὴν γὰρ ἔφερε τὴν ψυχὴν καὶ μή τις οἴοιτό με περιαυτολογοῦντα ταῦτα λέγειν καὶ γράφειν, ἀλλ' ἴστω πάντα λόγον νικώμενον τοῖς τἀνδρὸς κατορθώμασι καὶ ταῖς χάρισι καὶ ταῖς ἀγλαΐαις· εἰ γοῦν μὴ πρὸς ἄλλον σκοπὸν ὁ λόγος ἑώρα, ἀλλὰ τὰ ἐκείνου κατὰ μέρος διεξελθεῖν ἠβουλήθη, ἄλλης ἂν Ἰλιάδος ἐδέησε. τοῦτον οὖν τὸν ἄνδρα τὸν δεινὸν μὲν ἐν ἀπερισκέπτῳ χρόνῳ τὸ δέον εὑρεῖν, δεινὸν δὲ τάξαι φάλαγγα καὶ καταστρατηγῆσαι πολεμίων ὁ Κομνηνὸς Ἀλέξιος, μήπω τὸν ἴουλον φέρων ἀπαρτισθέντα, ἀλλ' ἔτι χλοάζοντα καὶ χρυσίζοντα – ἦν γὰρ ἐκεῖνος . . . –, μετὰ τὴν συμπλοκὴν ἐκείνην καὶ τοὺς γενναίους ἀγῶνας καὶ τὴν ἧτταν νενίκηκεν οὐ πλήθει δυνάμεως, ἀλλὰ καρτερίᾳ καὶ τόλμῃ καὶ μελέτῃ στρατηγικῇ, συνέριθον λαβὼν καὶ τὴν ἄνωθεν πρόνοιαν, δι' ἣν τὰ τέλη κατορθοῦντα τῶν ἐγχειρήσεων.

[58] 4.16.17: ὡς οὐ τυραννίδα, μᾶλλον δὲ βασιλείαν μεγίστην.    [59] 4.17.1–2.

the Roman state and Empire of a man who could only be replaced with the greatest difficulty.[60]

The portrait of Nikephoros Bryennios the Elder is strikingly positive, given the context of composition within the court of his conqueror. Nikephoros makes a sustained argument that Bryennios was worthy of imperial rule. Alexios's ultimate victory was not a matter of superior skill or character. Within this history, Bryennios was firmly in control of himself, moderate, brave and virtuous in every way. In terms of his morality and conduct, Bryennios the Elder was imperial.

Similar conceptions of steady Roman courage in the face of struggle work to redeem, at least partially, Romanos Diogenes. In general Romanos is depicted as sharing many character traits with Bryennios. The nobility and sacrificial honor displayed by both Romanos and Bryennios in the course of the battle of Manzikert works to make them appealing and heroic characters despite the magnitude of the military loss. When he was suddenly surrounded by a Turkish ambush on the first day of fighting, Bryennios exhorted his troops not to do anything "base and unworthy of the bravery of the Romans."[61] Bryennios received numerous wounds in the course of this heroic struggle against the Turks.[62] Romanos exhibited exemplarly generalship in maintaining order among his troops as they advanced for hours against the retreating Turks on the second day of the battle. In describing the agreement for Romanos's release from captivity, Nikephoros inserts into Psellos's narrative the exonerating statement that Romanos had signed no agreements with Alp Arslan that were unworthy of the Romans because he would rather die than betray his nobility.[63]

Romanos and Bryennios's personal heroism, however, does not obviate the difficulty that it would have been far better had they won. In order to disassociate Bryennios from the decisions that led to the defeat, Nikephoros includes a council scene at the start of the campaign in which Bryennios is credited with giving Romanos advice that is entirely inconsistent with the rest of his character, but that puts him in the position of arguing against the course of action that led to defeat. The debate centered on whether Romanos Diogenes should move his army to meet the Sultan in the east or await the advance of the Turks in their own territory. Joseph Tarchaneiotes and Bryennios advised the emperor to remain where he was, fortify all the surrounding cities, and burn the plains in order to deprive the enemies of necessities. If the emperor could not do this, then he should camp at

---

[60] 4.17.2–4.   [61] 1.15.13–17.   [62] 1.15.24.

[63] 1.19.11–13: . . . λαβὼν ἐνωμότους οὐκ ἀναξίας Ῥωμαίων – ἐβούλετο γὰρ ὁ βασιλεὺς μᾶλλον τεθνάναι ἢ ἀναξίας συμβιβάσεις ποιεῖσθαι τῆς ἑαυτοῦ γενναιότητος – .

Theodosioupolis and wait for the Sultan.[64] Romanos rejected this advice in favor of marching out in an effort to engage the Turks directly.

Bryennios's advice to evade a frontal assault by burning the Roman countryside is not consistent with the rest of the portrait of his character. In all other cases, Bryennios, like Romanos, fought with honor in formal frontal attacks. Bryennios's advice here is not an endorsement of utter ruthlessness as imperial policy but an attempt to disassociate Bryennios from the decisions that led to Romanos's failure. The primary purpose of this scene is to exonerate Bryennios from the charge that he was part of the problem that led to the Roman defeat at Manzikert. He plays the wise councillor whose advice should have been followed. Since the pitched battle turned out badly, Nikephoros portrayed his grandfather as having advocated something else.

Romanos, by pursuing the noble course of trying to involve the Turks in a properly agonistic battle, drove the Empire to ruin. Yet he fought bravely and tried to engage the Turks in a proper, straight-up fight. As was explored in chapter 8, Romanos was never defeated, although he lost, because the Turks never allowed him to engage in a real contest. In fighting bravely and losing with honor Romanos is valorized in the same way as Bryennios in the story of his fight against Alexios, and by appealing to the same set of cultural ideals of masculine warfare.

The third great hero of Nikephoros's history was John Doukas. The portrait of John differs stylistically from that of Bryennios and differences in tone can be attributed to Nikephoros's use of the text about John.[65] Despite the differences in style, however, the emotional core and logic of the portrait of John is consistent with the system of values used to valorize Bryennios and Diogenes.

Like Bryennios and Romanos, John is depicted as fighting courageously and heroically in a battle which he ultimately lost. Also like the defeats at Manzikert and Kalovrye, John's defeat at Zompos was not due to failures of Roman courage or generalship, but to an unfair advantage gained by his opponent. Although his commission is presented as a plot by Michael VII's minister Nikephoritzes to get John out of the way, once John was committed to the expedition, he took proper steps to assemble his army. John marched out into Bithynia and met Roussel's army at a bridge across the Sangarios River called Zompos. John drew up his forces into a classic Roman formation and personally commanded the center composed of "shield-bearing and axe-bearing barbarians" who were previously in the

---

[64] 1.13.9–14.     [65] See pp. 50–57.

palace guard.[66] A contingent of "Keltic mercenaries" led by a Kelt named Papas formed the right. The left was led by John's son, Andronikos Doukas, the *domestikos ton scholon*. The rear guard was commanded by the future emperor Nikephoros Botaneiates and composed of "the phalanx of the Phrygians and the Lykaonians, and also that of the Asians."[67]

John's frontal assault was frustrated by Roussel's efforts to entice a defection among John's mercenaries. When Roussel saw the arrangement of the Roman army he divided his own forces in two. Roussel advanced against John steadily with one half of his army, but he quickly sent the other to speak with John's Keltic mercenaries. Papas's troop promptly joined forces with Roussel and proceeded to help encircle John's force. When Botaneiates saw the defection of the Keltic mercenaries he withdrew his rear-guard from the field. This allowed the "barbarians" to easily complete the encirclement of John's contingent. John and his son Andronikos were then left fighting with a small number of forces while completely surrounded by the Kelts.

The story of John's final stand is full of heroic deeds of honor. John's troops were rallied by the sight of John calmly standing firm while they were being surrounded.[68] When John was eventually captured, his son Andronikos, who was safely out of the fighting, chose to "endanger his own salvation for his father" and returned to fight heroically in an effort to free his father.[69] Fighting so effectively that he seemed not "like a mortal man but immortal and immaterial," Andronikos was attacked by a great many enemies at once and finally fell to the ground with multiple wounds.[70] As the "barbarians" were trying to take off Andronikos's helmet and cut off his head, John broke free and ran forth to throw himself on "his noble child" and "thus saved the child from the danger at hand."[71]

The narrative emphasizes the filial relationship between John and Andronikos. While concern for his father turned Andronikos into a super-human warrior, that warrior is twice called a "child," *pais,* when John throws himself on his wounded body.[72] Both Doukai are described as fighting effectively and bravely in a situation made hopeless by the defection of the Kelts and the withdrawal of Botaneiates. When news of John and Andronikos's capture reached Constantinople, John's son Constantine was eager for vengeance. Constantine prepared to lead out an army against Roussel, displaying filial devotion and heroism. Only his sudden death

---

[66] 2.14.33–36.    [67] 2.14.36–41. On the more classicizing vocabulary of the Doukas text see pp. 55–56.
[68] 2.15.9–10.    [69] 2.15.17–18.
[70] 2.15.21: . . . οὐδὲ ἐῴκει ἀνδρί γε θνητῷ, ἀλλ' ἀθανάτῳ τε καὶ ἀσάρκῳ.
[71] 2.15.13–32.    [72] 2.15.30–31.

from illness prevented him from campaigning against Roussel.[73] The tenor of the story of the battle of Zompos is one of heroism, honor, and familial affection in the face of perfidious barbarians.

Like Bryennios, John participated in a revolt against Michael VII and, like Bryennios, John did so "unwillingly." After he had been captured by Roussel during the battle of Zompos, Roussel decided to proclaim John emperor as a pretext for marching against Constantinople. John is portrayed as initially being completely opposed to the idea, bound and in fetters. Once the project was underway, however, he gave it his full support, writing to supporters in Constantinople, who were delighted at the prospect of John becoming emperor. [74] John sent word secretly to "those in the city and drew the opinions of almost everyone to him. For the man was beloved by everyone, and he surpassed all contemporaries in adornment with all good things and good conduct."[75] Michael VII's *logothete* Nikephoritzes hired the Turkish prince Artuq to fight John and Roussel.[76] Artuq defeated Roussel's army by drawing him into terrain where they could not execute their "Latin phalanx." Roussel was ransomed by his wife and – after a delay – John was ransomed by Michael. Before returning to Constantinople, John renounced all attempts to make a bid for the throne by becoming a monk.[77]

Elsewhere John is shown as loyal to his nephew Michael. John was a key player in pushing Romanos and Eudokia out of power and establishing Michael's authority after the battle of Manzikert, although he quickly realized that Michael was "not suitably attentive for government" and began to "take up matters more nobly himself."[78] John spent time hunting on his estates in Bithynia when Romanos was in power and again when Nikephoritzes had alienated Michael from him. In both cases the hunting was a pretext for getting away from a ruler who suspected John of plotting, but in both cases the ruler's fears are dismissed as baseless.[79]

A stronger case for John's loyalty after the failure of his own rebellion is made in the story about Botaneiates's revolt. When Botaneiates was gathering his forces outside Constantinople, his adherents in the city brought a letter from him to John Doukas promising rewards and honors for John's

[73] 2.17.1–13.
[74] 2.17.14–22. In the other versions of Roussel's attack on Constantinople, John is described as a mere pawn in Roussel's effort to gain political advantage. Zonaras 710–11; Attaleiates 189–191; Skylitzes continuatus 159.
[75] 2.17.22–25.    [76] 2.17.27–33.    [77] 2.18.26–35.
[78] 2.1.13–14: ὁ δὲ καῖσαρ, ἐπεὶ τὸν ἀνεψιὸν εἶδεν οὐκ ἐπιτηδείως πρὸς τὴν τῶν κοινῶν ἀντίληψιν ἔχοντα, αὐτός τε γενναιότερον τῶν πραγμάτων ἀντελαμβάνετο.
[79] 1.18.18–21; 2.2.1–10.

support. Botaneiates's agent, Michael Barys, called on John in the church at Blachernai when the emperor Michael happened to be visiting him. Despite the presence of the emperor, Barys managed to speak with John privately in the late afternoon. He described the state of the rebellion and showed him Botaneiates's letter offering him highest honors.[80] John immediately interrupted Barys and declared that he would never betray his nephew and emperor. After a lacuna in the text, Barys goes to Nikephoritzes to warn Michael about the conspiracy.[81] Whatever John said clearly made Barys change his mind, switch sides, and inform Michael of the rebellion. Although Nikephoros probably omitted the content of John's speech in favor of Michael's legitimacy,[82] he included the scene displaying John's loyalty. In Nikephoros's hands the story of Botaneiates's attempt to suborn John speaks well of John's character as a loyal uncle, without making much of an argument for the legitimacy of Michael VII. John's continued loyalty to Michael VII despite the latter's incompetence, distrust, and declining fortunes, adds to John's heroism.

John's loyalty to Michael in the face of Botaneiates's revolt also works with his initial disapproval of Roussel's plans on his behalf to excuse him from the crime of rebellion. Both John and Bryennios are presented as having been pushed into revolts by others. John literally had his hands tied. The vigor with which both men pursued the revolts once underway naturally goes some way to calling out Nikephoros's rhetorical deception in arguing for their innocence of treason. Yet Nikephoros's concern with presenting them both as unwilling rebels reinforces the impression that loyalty to the Roman Empire was a key virtue for a politician.

In deliberate contrast to Bryennios and John, the portrayal of Nikephoros Botaneiates's revolt is markedly negative.[83] There is no invective against Botaneiates and he appears reasonable at all times. Yet his portrait is crafted in such a way that he does not engender the sympathy of the reader. Since his basic activities as a military and political careerist do not differ significantly from the heroes of the work, his depiction helps to illuminate the ethical system Nikephoros played upon in creating his narrative.

Botaneiates was the only Roman to rebel against the Empire out of his own volition. Whereas Bryennios was pushed to rebellion by Michael VII's lack of proper care for the Empire and the insistence of his family and supporters, and John is forced by Roussel, no motivation is given

---

[80] 3.18.17–22.  [81] 3.18.22–24, Gautier, *Histoire*, 245n6.  [82] See chapter 4, p. 52.
[83] As noted by Tinnefeld, "Kategorien der Kaiserkrutik," 151.

for Botaneiates's rebellion. Nikephoros wrote that Botaneiates had long been planning to revolt and decided to declare himself openly when he heard the news about Bryennios's rebellion.[84] Botaneiates abandoned the eastern cities that had supported his rebellion when Michael VII called in the Turks to fight against him. His success in taking Nicaea is attributed entirely to divine Providence in a passage that leaves little room for doubt that Nikephoros the author believed it was an honor Botaneiates did not deserve.[85]

Botaneiates was supported by Turkish allies, including Manuel Komnenos's old friend Chrysoskoulos. Michael VII and his minister Nikephoritzes armed Suleiman the son of Qutlumush against Botaneiates's rebellion. Botaneiates moved westward quickly to evade Suleiman. Suleiman sent troops to harass the passage of Botaneiates's forces but they could not bring on a full battle. Botaneiates sent Chrysoskoulos to negotiate a cessation of fighting with Qutlumush's men.[86]

Nikephoros does not criticize either Michael VII or Botaneiates for appealing to the Turks. Yet it is difficult to imagine that members of his audience would not have blamed Botaneiates's decisions for the worsening of imperial fortunes in Asia. The fight with the Turks for control of Asia Minor was the dominant experience in the lives of Nikephoros and his contemporaries. For all those whose family estates were permanently lost, anything less than complete singleness of mind in opposition of the Seljuk advance may have seemed like dereliction of duty. At no point in his career, either in eastern Anatolia or once he had become emperor, did Botaneiates effectively combat the Turks.

Botaneiates sent secret correspondence to the notables of Constantinople promising gifts and honors in return for help. This is described in terms of secrecy and conspiracy rather than as a reflection of any concern for the Empire on Botaneiates's part.[87] When Bryennios did the same thing he wrote to those in power about what they needed to know. Bryennios's letters are written to persuade rather than incite rebellion.[88] The differences are slight, but the tone of the whole interaction is different. Bryennios sent the promises of gifts in an effort to avoid battle because he was reluctant to fight against his fellow citizens.

Botaneiates's supporters in the senate and clergy met at Hagia Sophia to discuss Botaneiates's rebellion. They agreed to release prisoners and arm the urban population.[89] The vocabulary again is one of conspiracy. Given the value Nikephoros placed on nobility and the common Byzantine

[84] 3.15.1–10.    [85] 3.17. See pp. 116–17.    [86] 3.16.
[87] 3.16.1–5.    [88] 3.10.13–19.    [89] 3.18.7–11.

contempt for *hoi polloi*,[90] the decision to arm the city's population has an air of desperation and rashness to it. Botaneiates's allies in Constantinople armed their servants and slaves and had them threaten to burn down the houses of those in power who did not support Botaneiates.[91] The implication is that only bodily intimidation would bring more people to support Botaneiates's rebellion. This incitement to violence is in contrast to the involuntary and accidental burning of the suburbs of Constantinople by Bryennios's soldiers. Additionally, an army of convicts and lower social orders would be a disparagement to its leader.

The negative portrayal of Botaneiates may have been constructed in part to exonerate Alexios's coup. A tyrant could be justly opposed. For Alexios to be a savior of Rome rather than a usurper, Botaneiates would have to be a tyrant. He would become a natural focus for blame. Botaneiates also serves as a rhetorical foil for Bryennios and John Doukas, pointing up the positive aspects of the unwilling rebels' actions.

Bryennios, Romanos Diogenes, and John Doukas had different political careers and, in all likelihood, they had different personalities and characteristics. Yet a few key traits are common in Nikephoros's portraits of all three. All are portrayed as having fought with courage and honor in losses which were not due to their own errors. The Turks refused to allow Romanos's army to come to grips. They simply retreated out of reach until Romanos's forces were tired and over extended. Romanos and John were both abandoned by the generals commanding their rear guards. All three had mercenary forces switch sides in the course of battle. Romanos and Bryennios suffered ambushes. All exhibited exemplary military skills and were effective in their personal fighting. They were good generals and mighty fighters who lost battles through no fault of their own.

Nikephoros presents Bryennios, Romanos, and John as all having been pushed into rebellion unwillingly. John was proclaimed emperor by the mercenaries who had defeated and captured him. Bryennios was forced into it by Michael VII's suspicions and his brother's prodding. Romanos was already a recognized emperor when he was declared a rebel by his wife and her first husband's family. A reasonable analysis of the actual political situations would indicate that all three men indeed did want to become emperor or remain emperor. Yet Nikephoros makes considerable effort to present John and Bryennios as not wanting to cause civil strife. Loyalty to the Roman Empire and support of that state are presented as great virtues.

---

[90] Paul Magdalino, "Byzantine Snobbery," 58–78.   [91] 3.19.

The classical Roman cultural valuation of personal physical courage, and degradation of military deceit, is central to the success of Nikephoros's rhetoric in making Bryennios, Romanos, and John look like heroes rather than losers. Cultural systems that valued success above all would not support a positive presentation of these men because they all lost. The nostalgic Roman valuation of honor, even above success, provided a cultural framework in which Romanos, Bryennios, and John were heroes in that they were personally courageous and fought with honor. In addition to exonerating them for their failures, the appeal to Roman standards of virtue codes these gentlemen as truly Roman. They are shown to fully participate in the same conception of proper political conduct, and masculinity, as the great military heroes of old Rome.

# CHAPTER 12

# A Roman mother

Through the centuries Byzantine emperors had mothers, wives, and daughters, and these women consistently took on significant political roles when opportunities arose. Imperial women appear more frequently in eleventh- and twelfth-century histories than they did earlier and this has been interpreted as indicative of a greater political role for women, brought on by the 'aristocratization' of Byzantine politics in the Komnenian era.[1] At least some of the appearances of women in eleventh- and twelfth-century histories, however, may be due to the increased use of classical Roman behavioral and historical models on the part of historians.[2] Just as Roman models of virtue animate the portraits of Bryennios, Romanos, and John Doukas, classical paradigms of female behavior are also at play in the characterization of Nikephoros's most prominent female character, Alexios's mother, Anna Dalassene.

Anna Dalassene is a rather ambiguous character in the *Material for History*. Her skillful marriage policy is used to promote the connection between the Komnenos family and imperial rule. She is easily the strongest female character in the history and it seems safe to say she had a powerful impact on her sons' careers. Yet, under careful scrutiny, the episodes in which she appears do not add up to a rounded portrait of her character, or even a consistent description. Nearly every time she appears or is mentioned,

---

[1] Kazhdan and Wharton, *Change*, 99–102; Kazhdan and Constable, *People and Power*, 113; Barbara Hill, *Imperial Women in Byzantium, 1025–1204: Power, Patronage and Ideology* (New York: Longman, 1999), 66–71; Barbara Hill, "Alexios I Komnenos and the Imperial Women," in *Alexios I Komnenos*, ed. Margaret Mullett and Dion Smythe (Belfast Byzantine Enterprises, 1996), 42–48; Paul Lemerle, *Cinq etudes sur le XIe siecle byzantin* (Paris: Centre national de la recherche scientifique, 1977), 297–300; Magdalino, "Innovations in Government," 150–51.

[2] The argument for literary patterning on classical Roman models in no way negates the non-literary evidence for an increased prominence of aristocratic women in the Komnenian era, on which see Jean-Claude Cheynet, "Le rôle des femmes de l'aristocratie d'après les sceaux," in *Mélanges V. Sandrovskaja* (St. Petersberg: 2004); article number 6 in Jean-Claude Cheynet, *La société byzantine : l'apport des sceaux*, Bilans de recherche (Paris: association des amis du Centre d'histoire et civilisation de Byzance, 2008).

Anna's actions or opinions explain the actions of the men with whom she is interacting. In each case Nikephoros is primarily concerned with portraying the character of the men in the story. Some of Anna's scenes reflect positively on her and others less so because her portrayal depends upon her shifting function in the text.

There is no doubt that Anna Dalassene was a highly significant political figure in the eleventh century and a significant presence in her son's government.[3] In the *Alexiad*, Anna Komnene explains that Alexios delegated the civil administration of the Empire to his mother while he was on nearly constant campaign in the opening years of his rule and provides what she says are verbatim quotations from the imperial chrysobull granting her grandmother that authority.[4] Zonaras confirms Anna Dalassene's role in administration.[5] Anna Komnene also describes her grandmother as reforming the morals of the palace. Anna Dalassene's wisdom and virtue were praised in court orations of the late eleventh century.[6] Chrysobulls signed by Anna Dalassene survive in the Athos archives. In some cases she speaks as if she were Alexios and in others she speaks in her own voice on behalf of her son.[7] These documents demonstrate Anna acting with full imperial authority, along the lines described in the *Alexiad*. In fact she is seen overturning decisions made by Alexios regarding the tax burdens of the Docheiariou monastery.[8] Not only was she acting as the primary governor while Alexios was campaigning, but she contravened Alexios's authority when he did take an interest in civil affairs. The independent evidence for Anna's forceful exercise of imperial authority proves that her strong character was not just a literary construct. Yet the reality of her authority should not blind us to the various ways her presentation in Nikephoros's history functions within the narrative logic of the text.

A keen appreciation of classical ideals of female behavior lies behind Nikephoros's odd repetition of a slightly altered dramatic scene that occurs in the history of Michael Psellos. In describing the abdication of Isaac Komnenos in 1057, Psellos has Isaac's wife Katherine plead with him not to

---

[3] Jean-Claude Cheynet and Jean-Francois Vannier, *Études prosopographiques* (Paris: Publications de la Sorbonne, 1986), 95–99; Élisabeth Malamut, "Une femme politique d'exception à la fin du xie siècle: Anne Dalassène," in *Femmes et pouvoirs des femmes à Byzance et en occident (VIe–XIe siècles)*, ed. Stéphane Lebecq, *et al.* (Lille: Centre de Recherche sur l'Histoire de l'Europe du Nord-Ouest, 1999), 103–20.

[4] Komnene 3.6–3.7.        [5] Zonaras 746.1–8.

[6] Margaret Mullett, "The Imperial Vocabulary of Alexios I Komnenos," in *Alexios I Komnenos*, ed. Margaret Mullett and Dion Smythe (Belfast Byzantine Enterprises, 1996), 365.

[7] Malamut, "Une femme politique," 110.

[8] *Actes de Docheiariou*, ed. Nicolas Oikonomides (Paris: P. Lethielleux, 1984), document #2.

give up power. When Isaac abdicates in Nikephoros's history, his brother John's wife, Anna Dalassene, urges John to take power himself. Although different in style and details, the two speeches have enough in common in terms of content and force that scholars have considered them to be the "same speech."[9] This is not a case of misattribution of an actual speech by one of our historians, but of a similar rhetorical response to the challenge of writing about abdication. Something about the circumstance of men giving up power suggested to Psellos and Nikephoros that they should first introduce women into the plot and then have them speak up forcefully. Nikephoros was happy to incorporate large sections of Psellos's history into his own with few changes, so something significant drove him to rework this scene with different characters. The key to the function of the speeches by Katherine and Anna lies in understanding the authors' appreciation of classical Roman social norms.

The speeches by Katherine and Anna are each one of the few instances of direct female speech in Psellos's and Nikephoros's histories. Like their classical predecessors, the historians' decision to quote speech directly rather than describe it was deliberate and purposeful.[10] Direct speech by women was made particularly significant by the continuing appreciation of the ancient Greek injunction for women not to be heard.[11] This normative stance, however contested in practice, became a standard part of classical Roman discourse.[12] The particular speeches made by the Byzantine wives in question were speeches of advice that attempted to persuade. This is significant because Greek and Roman women were considered to be most dangerous when they influenced the actions of men.[13] Late Roman historians regularly told stories of empresses who influenced their husbands when they wanted to criticize those emperors.[14] The cultural ideas that

---

[9] Gautier, *Histoire*, 81n11.

[10] Matthew Fox and Niall Livingstone, "Rhetoric and Historiography," in *A Companion to Greek Rhetoric*, ed. Ian Worthington (Oxford: Blackwell, 2007), 544–59; Anthony Kaldellis, *Procopius of Caesarea*, 29–32.

[11] Thuc. 2.45.2; Winkler, *Constraints*, 5–8; Eva Cantarella, *Pandora's Daughters: The Role and Status of Women in Greek and Roman Antiquity*, trans. Maureen B. Fant (Baltimore: Johns Hopkins University Press, 1987), 38–51.

[12] Clark, "Ideology;" Susan Fischler, "Social Stereotypes and Historical Analysis: The Case of the Imperial Women at Rome," in *Women in Ancient Societies: An Illusion of the Nights*, ed. L. Archer, S. Fischler, and M. Wyke (Houndmills, 1994); A. P. M. H. Lardinois and Laura McClure, *Making Silence Speak: Women's Voices in Greek Literature and Society* (Princeton, NJ: Princeton University Press, 2001).

[13] Elizabeth Fisher, "Theodora and Antonia," in *Women in the Ancient World. The Arethusa Papers*, ed. J. Peradotto and J. P. Sullivan (Albany: State University of New York Press, 1984), 297–98; Alison Keith, *Engendering Rome: Women in Latin Epic* (Cambridge University Press, 2000), 65–100.

[14] Liz James, *Empresses and Power in Early Byzantium* (London: Leicester University Press, 2001), 20.

made this sort of speech-making by women unsettling still underpin the logic of our eleventh- and twelfth-century texts.

In addition to appealing to classical notions of appropriately gendered behavior generally, in the context of wives attempting to convince their husbands to strive vigorously for imperial power, our authors are engaging with Procopius of Caesarea's use of those norms in his famous description of Theodora's speech before Justinian and his counselors during the Nika riots of 532. To properly interpret Psellos and Nikephoros we must attempt to recover a medieval reading of Procopius.

In Procopius's description, Theodora's speech stands out because it is reported as direct speech. This is the only time Theodora speaks in *History of the Wars,* although she is mentioned in passing on a few other occasions.[15] Procopius calls attention to the incongruity of a woman speaking by having Theodora open her speech by apologizing for expressing her opinion.[16] Procopius thus has Theodora appear more modest through her acknowledgment that women ought to be deferential and simultaneously points out just how transgressive she is being.

Beyond the surprise of having a woman speak in a council, the content of Theodora's speech is unexpected. She offers a courageous call to fight rather than flee. This is not a sentiment associated with femininity in classical constructions of gender. Rather, Theodora is being portrayed like a man and her expression of the masculine characteristics of strength and courage serves to point out how much the men are acting like women. The primary function of Theodora's speech is to shame the men around her "into acting manly" by being more masculine than they.[17] After listening to Theodora, the men were "seized by boldness" and began to plot militarily.[18] The result of their new-found valor was an attack on the rioters in the hippodrome in which, Procopius says, 30,000 people died.

In that the immediate function of Theodora's speech is to shame Justinian, Procopius was following a common Late Roman rhetorical strategy. Shaming men was one of the several common uses of the stereotype of "female weakness" for patristic writers.[19] Stories and discussions of women in Late Roman texts have less to do with depicting the lives of women than with using those rhetorical statements to comment on the power of the men who stand in relation to those women.[20] In Theodora's case the

---

[15] Leslie Brubaker, "The Age of Justinian: Gender and Society," in *The Cambridge Companion to the Age of Justinian,* ed. Michael Maas (Cambridge University Press, 2005), 429.
[16] Procop. *De bellis* 1.24.33–34.     [17] Brubaker, "Gender and Society," 430.
[18] Procop. *De bellis* 1.24.38.     [19] Clark, "Ideology," 166.
[20] Cooper, "Insinuations of Womanly Influence," 151.

assertion of masculine courage by a wife serves to cast her husband as weak and effeminate. To avoid this characterization, Justinian and his generals immediately turn to arms.

Yet this merely leads to the larger question of why Justinian needed to be shamed in the first place. Why does Procopius include this scene of gender inversion in his text? Brubaker explains it as a marker of the intensity of the difficulty at that moment:

By depicting men as fearful (the way the Byzantines believed women behaved) and a woman as daring (the way the Byzantines believed a man behaved), Procopius inverted Byzantine gender stereotypes to indicate the gravity of the occasion: the situation was so bad that the natural order was reversed, with men quaking like women and a woman speaking like a man.[21]

I would argue that in addition it is a way of denigrating Justinian. Having Justinian shamed by a woman's boldness is one of several attacks on his manhood evident in the episode. Not only does her daring point out his fearfulness, but he also is caught listening to his wife's advice. Further, Justinian is no victim merely of the private workings of womanly influence, but has so little control over his household that his wife is seen speaking in public.

This degradation based on mishandling of gender roles is supplemented by suggestions that Justinian is in fact a tyrant rather than an emperor.[22] Theodora's speech includes a not-particularly-veiled comparison between Justinian and the infamous ancient tyrant Dionysius of Syracuse in her final line "For as for myself, I approve a certain ancient saying that royalty is a good burial-shroud."[23] The ancient aphorism was not that "royalty," but rather "tyranny," made a good shroud. The well-known story was that when Dionysius faced a dangerous rebellion in 403 BCE, he was persuaded not to flee by a friend who advised that tyranny made a good burial-shroud.[24] Theodora's quotation, even modified, "suggests a comparison" between Justinian and the infamous Dionysius.[25] Both rulers survived the riots by militarily defeating the insurrections. Not all of Procopius's readers would have caught the classical allusion and been able to spot the change

---

[21] Brubaker, "Gender and Society," 430.

[22] Kaldellis argues that Procopius's *Wars* is as critical of Justinian as the *Secret History*: Kaldellis, *Procopius of Caesarea*. The *Buildings* also need not be read as panegyric: Philip Rousseau, "Procopius's *Buildings* and Justinian's Pride," *Byzantion* 68 (1998): 121–30.

[23] Procop. *De bellis* 1.24.37.5–6.

[24] J. A. S. Evans, "The 'Nika' Rebellion and the Empress Theodora," *Byzantion* 54 (1984): 381. Diod. Sic. 14.8.5; Ael. *VH* 4.8.14; Isoc. *Archidamus*, 45.1; Plut. *Cat*, 24.8, *An seni* 783D.

[25] Evans, "'Nika' Rebellion," 382.

in wording, but some certainly did.[26] It would have been clear to them that Procopius portrayed Theodora as prompting Justinian to act like a merciless tyrant.

The very response to the insurrection in itself accuses Justinian of lack of moderation, and mercilessness; two chief characteristics of a tyrant. Procopius records the number of the civilian dead as 30,000. Such a number could not but be seen as an excessive slaughter. Procopius does shield both Justinian and his generals, Belisarius and Mundus, from accusations that they willingly decided to attack civilians. Justinian merely ordered them to go to the hippodrome, and then various obstacles led them to attack the populace rather than the rebel emperor Hypatius. So Procopius's overt meaning is not accusatory and can even be seen as sympathetic to Justinian. The feebleness of the obstacles he describes, however, invite the reader to question whether Belisarius and Justinian were in fact guilty of bloodlust. Belisarius and his army were prevented from attacking Hypatius directly by:

a small door . . . which had been closed and was guarded by the soldiers of Hypatius who were inside . . . Concluding, therefore, that he must go against the populace who had taken their stand in the hippodrome – a vast multitude crowding each other in great disorder – he drew his sword from its sheath and, commanding the others to do likewise, with a shout he advanced upon them at a run.[27]

Procopius goes on to draw implicit contrasts between Belisarius's brave, experienced and armed soldiers and the disorganized populace trying desperately to flee. Once Mundus saw that Belisarius was attacking the populace rather than Hypatius's guards, he too joined in the attack on the people in the hippodrome. The narrative is constructed so that even a slightly penetrating reading suggests that Justinian ordered his generals to attack the populace. The story that Belisarius, soon to become famous as the conqueror of Africa, together with his army, was prevented from arresting Hypatius because a few guards had closed a "small door" is simply not convincing. The common modern reading of the episode holds Justinian responsible for the attack on the rioters.[28]

Largely because of her courageous speech during the Nika riots, Theodora has entered the modern imagination as a heroine.[29] This is a

---

[26] Kaldellis, *Procopius of Caesarea*, 36–38.
[27] Procop. *De bellis* 1.24.49–50, trans. H. B. Dewing (Harvard, 1914).
[28] For example see John Moorhead, *Justinian* (London: Longman, 1994), 47; Timothy E. Gregory, *A History of Byzantium* (Blackwell, 2005), 127; Cyril Mango, ed. *The Oxford History of Byzantium* (Oxford University Press, 2002), 46.
[29] On Theodora's image in the nineteenth and twentieth centuries see Averil Cameron, *Procopius and the Sixth Century* (Berkeley: University of California Press, 1985), 67–70.

case where differences between modern and late antique values and under-standings of appropriate gender behavior lead to the attribution of an entirely different meaning to the text. A society that prizes courage in women would read the story first as about Theodora, and second as a positive story about Theodora. When read with careful attention to what we know about the values and ideals of behavior of the sixth century, it becomes clear that this is a serious misreading. As a result of Theodora's advice, Justinian lost his sense of moderation and ordered an inhumane slaughter. It did keep Justinian in power, but at a price that would make later generations shudder.

Procopius's story of Theodora advising Justinian to fight was well known in the medieval period as an event showing the evils of womanly influence. When the episode appears in Michael Glykas's twelfth-century universal history, the story is that Hagia Sophia was built by Justinian to atone for his great sin. The emperor was ready to flee the riotous city, "but his wife commanded him saying "royalty was a good shroud,"" and then 35,000 people fell in the fighting.[30] In this brief version of the story, the blame falls squarely on an unnamed Theodora. Psellos's *Historia Syntomos* says that Justinian's submissiveness to women was as blasphemous as his doctrinal errors.[31] According to Genesios's history, when Michael I abdicated, his wife Procopia protested, telling him that "royalty was a good shroud."[32] Michael abdicated anyway. This clear allusion to Procopius's Theodora was incor-porated verbatim into John Skylitzes' history in the late eleventh century.[33] Michael I is portrayed as a peaceful man precisely because he did not listen to his wife.[34] However appealing Theodora's story is to modern minds, it seems clear that it was considered a negative episode in the Middle Ages.

---

[30] Note that the number of dead had risen from 30,000 to 35,000 by the twelfth century: Glykas 459.17–456.5.

[31] Psellos, *Historia* 71.87.

[32] Genesios, in *Iosephi Genesii Regum libri quattuor*, ed. I. Thurn and A. Lesmueller-Werner (Berlin: Walter de Gruyter, 1978), 5, book 2.4.

[33] Skylitzes, *Michael* 3.21–22.

[34] A strong cultural distaste for wives who try to influence their husbands explains why the hagiographer of Theodora, the wife of the ninth-century iconoclast emperor Theophilos, chose not to portray her as acting on behalf of icon veneration while her husband was alive. She is revered as a saint for restoring icon veneration after Theophilos died, but as a good wife, according to her *vita*, she made no attempt to chastise her iconoclast husband or otherwise influence his behavior. Indeed she remains entirely silent from the moment of her selection as his bride until after her deposition and monastic retirement. Her hagiographer's choice to portray her as making no efforts on behalf of iconophilia is to be found "in the rich history of imperial invective, where female strength, that is insubordination, comes at the price of male weakness and the ruination of Empire." So deep was the apprehension felt about female empowerment that "Theodora cannot defy her husband's authority without at the same time discrediting herself and the iconophile men with whom she was allied." Vinson, "Gender and Politics," 469–515.

This context of rhetorical use of classical gender ideals and the appreciation of Roman historiography – Procopius in particular – elucidates the function of the speeches by political wives in Psellos's and Nikephoros's histories. Katherine's speech to her husband Isaac Komnenos, at the point of his abdication in favor of Constantine Doukas, is the longest speech by a woman in Psellos's history. Psellos sets the scene by describing Isaac as deathly ill and surrounded by his grieving family. He uses terminology of ancient Greek tragedy for ritual female lamentation: "The empress led the dirge, and the daughter, answering her mother with weeping, bewailed in turn more mournfully."[35] That Katherine is first seen as the leader of the chorus of dirges connects her with an ancient tradition of female mourning that deeply associated women with irrationality and grief.[36] While the women wailed, the men remained calm and Isaac asked to become a monk. Katherine immediately accused Psellos of having encouraged Isaac to retire. Isaac said it was his own idea "but this [woman] (he really said that) pleading like a woman, hinders us from the better counsel, and accuses every one of the proposition rather than me." Katherine responded:

"Yes I do," she said, "and I take upon my neck all your sins, and if you revive, I have what of course I seek and desire; if not, then I will defend you before the judge, even God, for the things that you have done wrong. And may all [your] deeds be blameless for you; yet for you I would gladly be torn asunder by worms, covered by deep darkness and consumed by utter fire! So then do you not pity our solitude? What kind of soul do you have to take yourself away from the palace, and leave me behind to a most sorrowful widowhood, and grievous orphan-hood to your daughter? But these things will not be enough for us, but worse things will appear for us; hands, probably not benevolent, will carry us into distant exile, perhaps they may decide something worse, and a bloodthirsty man will see your dear ones and know no pity. You will live on after your change in habit, or perhaps die with honor, but for us a life will remain, more bitter than death!"[37]

Katherine's pleading is hyperbolic and disordered, jumping quickly from one argument to the next. She is not presented as possessed of refined rhetorical skills but rather as near hysteria. Isaac is presented as disliking both Katherine's advice and her act of advising. He derisively calls her, not

---

[35] Psellos, *Chronographia*, 7.80.13–14.
[36] Margaret Alexiou, *The Ritual Lament in Greek Tradition* (Cambridge University Press, 1974); Hans Van Wees, "A Brief History of Tears: Gender Differentiation in Archaic Greece," in *When Men were Men: Masculinity, Power and Identity in Classical Antiquity*, ed. Lin Foxhall and John Salmon (London: Routledge, 1998), 10–53; James Amelang, "Mourning Becomes Eclectic: Ritual Lament and the problem of continuity," *Past and Present* 187 (2005): 3–32.
[37] Psellos, *Chronographia*, 7.81–83. I am grateful to Elizabeth Fisher for her help in clarifying points of this text.

"my wife," but "this one," *aute*. It is considered rude to use this form of the pronoun to refer to a person while he or she is present in modern Greek. That the usage was considered rude, or at least dismissive, in the eleventh century is suggested by Psellos's aside assuring the reader that these were Isaac's exact words. Isaac then says that she is "pleading like a woman," signaling perhaps that he would rather she not speak and that he will not be taken in by her pleading.[38] He does ignore all of Katherine's pleading and proceeds with his plan to take monastic vows.

When Nikephoros Bryennios describes Isaac Komnenos's abdication, it is a very different story. Nikephoros has Isaac offer the imperial power first to his brother John and only turn to Constantine Doukas when John refuses to become emperor. On this point Nikephoros's history stands in contradiction to the witness of Psellos, Attaleiates, and Skylitzes Continuatus, but is far more in keeping with a vision of the past favorable to the Komnenos dynasty. As in Psellos's story, Isaac falls ill while hunting. Katherine does not appear and there is no discussion of Isaac's decision to retire. Rather the story focuses on his succession. Isaac made a rousing speech to John asking him to take up the difficult burden of imperial rule. John was greatly distressed and "ready to suffer all things rather than to take up the public affairs."[39] His wife on the other hand:

took his reticence very badly and sitting close beside her husband she assailed him with these words: "Why my lord, do you turn the sword toward yourself and the dear ones, neither pitying their youth or caring about us? Do you not know that if someone else takes up the Empire of the Romans, he will hasten to get all your family out of the way thinking thus to secure the matters of Empire more firmly to himself? Why are we brought to naught, casting ourselves and the dear ones to manifest danger and why are we driven from the kingship of the Romans which everyone desires? Why this harmful philosophy and untimely modesty? But if you may not be persuaded by me, hasten most quickly to be persuaded by the counsels of your emperor and brother and take up the affairs." Saying these things and more – for she was a clever one at speaking and doing – since he was not persuaded, she turned to supplications and she presented intercessions with tears and lamentations. But since he was unrelenting and hardened to everything, giving up on persuading him, she was silent, deeply hurt and ashamed on his behalf. Thus he turned away from kingship.[40]

---

[38] Psellos, *Chronographia*, 7.82.3–4.     [39] 1.4.10–20.
[40] 1.4.20–5.6: ἀλλ' ὁ μὲν οὕτως εἶχε προθέσεως, ἡ δ' αὖ ὁμευνέτις αἰσθομένη τῶν λεγομένων βαρέως ἔφερε τὴν παραίτησιν καὶ παρὰ τῷ ἀνδρὶ παρακαθίσασα τοιούτοις ἐχρῆτο παρ' αὐτὸν λόγοις· «ἵνα τί, λέγουσα, κύριέ μου, ξίφος ἕλκεις πρὸς ἑαυτὸν καὶ τὰ φίλτατα, μήτε τὸ τούτων οἰκτείρων ἄωρον μήτε ἡμῶν κηδόμενος; οὐκ οἶσθα ὡς εἴ τις ἐπιλάβηται ἄλλος τῆς Ῥωμαίων ἀρχῆς, ἐκ ποδῶν ποιῆσαι σπεύσειεν ἅπαν τὸ γένος ἡμῶν, οἰόμενος οὕτως

Martial imagery characterizes Anna's opening argumentative "assault." Once the rational, masculine argument fails, she turns to feminine begging and pleading with tears and laments. The term translated as "intercessions" above, *enteuxis,* also means sexual intercourse. The implication is that she went through all the modes of persuasion available to her, of both masculine and feminine forms.

Nikephoros thus abbreviates Psellos's memorable abdication scene for Isaac but recreates it in a new form for Anna Dalassene and John. Anna's speech is similar to Katherine's speech in Psellos, but is not a copy.[41] Since much of book 1 of Nikephoros's history is copied close to verbatim from Psellos's, there must have been specific reasons why he chose to compose a new speech saying essentially the same thing, and especially for switching the speaker from Katherine to Anna. His audience would have known Psellos's history and probably remembered the drama of Katherine's pleading with Isaac. The recurrence of the same basic episode, acted by different characters· is a strong indicator that something in the story was rhetorically necessary. By having Isaac offer the purple to his brother John, Nikephoros has created the same situation of a man turning down power, which seems to call for a speech by a woman asking him to pursue power.

One key difference between the eleventh-century women and Theodora is that they were unsuccessful in persuading their men to act rashly. The women ended up frustrated. Since their advice was ignored and had no effect on politics, why was it so important to record their advice? Why are women's voices heard here after being so consistently silent? The very act of ignoring their wives allowed these men to appear masculine while engaging in actions that were passive and weak; hence essentially feminine. Consider how these men would have looked otherwise. Both Isaac and John would simply rather not be emperor. Isaac is given the excuse of illness, but no one expresses any surprise that he recovered. John was of perfectly good health and possessed of the proper aristocratic training for government service. He is described by Nikephoros as simply not wanting to take up the heavy

---

ἐπ' ἀσφαλοῦς ἡδράσθαι αὐτῷ τὰ τῆς ἀρχῆς; ἵνα τί γοῦν οὕτω μεματαιώμεθα ἑαυτοὺς καὶ τὰ φίλτατα εἰς προῦπτον ἐπιρρίπτοντες κίνδυνον καὶ τὸ πᾶσιν ἱμερτὸν ἀπωθούμεθα τὴν βασιλείαν Ῥωμαίων; τίς ἡ ἐπιβλαβὴς αὕτη φιλοσοφία καὶ ἄκαιρος μετριοφροσύνη; ἀλλ' εἴ τι ἐμοὶ πείθῃ, σπεῦσον ὡς τάχιστα ταῖς συμβουλαῖς πεισθῆναι τοῦ βασιλέως καὶ ἀδελφοῦ καὶ τῶν πραγμάτων ἐπιλαβοῦ». ταῦτα καὶ πλείω τούτων εἰποῦσα – ἦν γὰρ δεινή τις καὶ λέγειν καὶ πράττειν – ἐπειδὴ μὴ ἔπειθε, πρὸς ἱκεσίαν ἐτράπετο καὶ τὰς διὰ δακρύων καὶ στεναγμῶν ἐντεύξεις προσέφερεν· ὡς δ' ἄτεγκτον ἑώρα καὶ πρὸς πᾶν σκληρυνόμενον, ἀπογνοῦσα τοῦ πείθειν ἐσίγα, πολλὰ καθ' ἑαυτὴν ἀλγοῦσα καὶ τούτου καταστυγνάζουσα. οὕτω μὲν οὖν ἐκεῖνος τὴν βασιλείαν ἀπεσκεύαστο.

41  Psellos's speech for Katherine is not simply "reused" as Hill maintains. Hill, *Imperial Women in Byzantium,* 61.

burden of government. Looking only at the course of events one would expect these men to appear cowardly, irresolute, and irresponsible.

The stories of women arguing in favor of political action work to excuse their husbands' inaction by affording them the opportunity to resist womanly influence and exercise self-control and moderation. Whereas Justinian was influenced by a woman who pushed him to immoderate excess, these men refuse to be goaded. Their steadiness in the face of female hysteria gives them the opportunity to appear resolute, calm, strong and in control, when in fact they were cowed by circumstances. They may have been stepping down, but at least they stood up to their wives.

Katherine and Anna's arguments with their husbands differ significantly from Theodora's in that they advocated for their families. They urged their husbands to seek power, not because they personally lusted after power or glory, but because they wanted protectors for their families. Theodora is guilty of an unfeminine concern with political power which renders her masculine and transgressive. In contrast, Katherine and Anna stay fully and safely feminine by embracing the role of the protective Roman mother. Concern for properly raising and caring for children was part of the classical Roman construction of female virtue.[42] Twelfth-century encomia show that two of the central virtues for imperial women were fertility and control of family.[43] Katherine and Anna both argue that their children will be imperiled if their father gives up political power and make the protection of their families their main concern. This change from the Procopian narrative casts Anna and Katherine as far more positive characters. They function to display their husbands' self-control and temperance, but they do so without taking on the negative characteristics of Theodora.

While both Katherine and Anna thus look better than Theodora, Anna receives more favorable treatment yet. Katherine becomes a portrait in female hysteria, through a hyperbolic, unstructured utterance better characterized as a rant than a speech. Nikephoros puts Anna in a better light by first saying that she was clever and competent and then making her speech more coherent. Only when rational arguments failed did she turn to tears and "intercessions." The initial martial vocabulary lets John resist a real assault, but it also gives Anna the complement of being manly enough to mount a real assault.

The depiction of Isaac's abdication was a particularly sensitive topic because the reasons for the abdication are not obvious. Psellos and Nikephoros make the sole cause of Isaac's abdication the illness which

[42] Fischler, "Social stereotypes," 118.    [43] Hill, "The Ideal Komnenian Woman," 8.

he contracted while hunting. It was not uncommon for emperors to take monastic vows on their deathbeds as a means of atoning for the inevitable sins of power. The difficulty here is that Isaac did not die from this illness and no one expressed surprise that he survived. Psellos mentions that there was opposition to Isaac's fiscal discipline. Modern historians emphasize the political damage of the dispute Isaac had had with the patriarch and consider him as having been forced out of office.[44] The orderliness of the transfer of power from Isaac to Constantine Doukas was also anomalous. Doukas did not become emperor by being proclaimed by his troops and leading a dangerous armed rebellion. Rather he was simply given power by Isaac. Other medieval observers were struck that Isaac did not try to give that power to a member of his family, particularly when he had several male kinsmen of the appropriate age to choose from. Attaleiates and Skylitzes Continuatus both make a pointed note that Isaac passed over his brother John, his nephew, and his son-in-law in order to offer imperial power to someone outside of his household.[45] Clearly Isaac's choice to voluntarily bestow imperial power on another family was seen as aberrant.

Either Isaac was unusually peaceable for a medieval general and emperor, or he was so politically unsuccessful that he was effectively deposed. Psellos, as the only man in the room at the time who wrote a history, was able to craft the change in regime as an act of generous abdication rather than forceful deposition. Portraying Isaac as retiring voluntarily and choosing Constantine Doukas was a way for Psellos to bolster the legitimacy of the dynasty he started to serve without insulting the one he used to work for. The image of a strong and resolute Isaac freely selecting Constantine Doukas may have served Psellos's political purposes. Whether Isaac was forced out of power or retired, as Psellos claimed, the end of his political career was an embarrassment to his nephew's regime and hence demanded careful historical treatment. Once Psellos's narrative of peaceful abdication was established, Nikephoros had to deal with the embarrassment raised by Attaleiates's and Skylitzes Continuatus's puzzlement that Isaac had passed over his brother in favor of a man from another family. In needing to rehabilitate John, Nikephoros turned to the same rhetorical strategy that Psellos had used to make Isaac look strong.

---

[44] Ostrogorsky, *History of the Byzantine State*, 341; Michael Angold, *The Byzantine Empire, 1025–1204: A Political History*, 2nd edn. (London: Longman, 1997), 75–77; Michael Angold, "Imperial Renewal and Orthodox Reaction: Byzantium in the Eleventh Century," in *New Constantines: The Rhythm of Imperial Renewal in Byzantium, 4th–13th Centuries*, ed. Paul Magdalino (Aldershot: Ashgate, 1994), 243.

[45] Attaleiates 69; Skylitzes continuatus 108.

Psellos and Nikephoros do not quote Procopius directly or even allude unmistakably to his history. Yet they play upon the same cultural logic that underlies Procopius's skillful manipulation of gender norms. Theodora's story had prominence in the historical consciousness of later generations because Procopius had created a powerful scene of a strong woman goading her weak husband into tyranny. Psellos drew on this cultural memory and these gender norms when he made Isaac look strong by giving him a woman whose tears and arguments he could stoutly resist. Nikephoros chose not to quote Psellos in this instance but rather redeployed the same rhetorical strategy in order to burnish the image of John Komnenos. Both histories include episodes of female pleading because there was a danger of a man looking effeminate. The rhetorical trope of the goading woman became a graceful cover for male weakness and passivity by prompting a display of manly strength in resisting womanly influence.

Anna Dalassene speaks again in Nikephoros's history in the course of the dramatic story of her trial for treason. After the battle of Manzikert when Romanos Diogenes had been released by Alp Arslan and was trying to regain his throne, Anna was accused of writing to Romanos and conspiring with him against Michael VII Doukas. As the mother of Romanos's daughter-in-law, she was closely linked with Romanos and had every reason to wish for him to remain in power and help him by keeping him informed of what was happening in the capital. From a purely political viewpoint, there is every reason to think that Anna did try to help Romanos. The Doukai would not have bothered to get her out of town unless she had a real ability to cause them trouble. Yet Nikephoros's story insists strongly that the charges were entirely false.

Rather than being minimized or swept aside altogether, Anna's trial for treason is given a highly dramatic and rhetorically elaborate portrayal. Nikephoros interrupted Psellos's story line at this point to include Anna's alleged treason. No other source records Anna's trial and exile. The accusations were ultimately attributed to "he who always envies good people."[46] An unnamed Satan is the real agent who "finding and using some bold-mouthed man with a tongue like a serpent" provoked the false charges of treason.[47] Michael acted "wrathfully" without attention to the accuser or the accused.[48] A court was arranged and "the noble, well-born and wise woman was brought to the palace."[49] Michael was too ashamed to preside. Anna herself again speaks forcefully and dramatically:

[46] 1.22.16.     [47] 1.22.17–18.     [48] 1.22.23.     [49] 1.22.24.

Then, the radiant, noble and great-souled lady enters, and suddenly she produces
an icon of the great Judge, which she had hidden under her robe. With dignified
bearing she fixes her gaze on the judges and said "Here is the Judge who stands
between me and you today, before whose gaze carry out no verdicts unworthy of
the Judge who 'knows the secrets of the heart.'"[50]

Nikephoros describes how at first Anna's actions caused the judges to feel
revulsion at the false accuser, but that they quickly rendered the verdict
they knew Michael wanted.[51] Uncharacteristically, Nikephoros uses biblical
imagery in this scene, saying that the false accuser was willing to "sell justice
for an obol," and comparing the trial to that of Caiaphas, the high priest
who tried to gather false witnesses against Jesus.[52] Anna and her children
were exiled to the Prinkipo island in the sea of Marmara, only to be recalled
after Romanos's death.[53]

Why would Anna's actions on behalf of Romanos need to be so strongly
denied in the twelfth century? While Anna comes off about as well as
she could in this story, we still need to explain why Nikephoros included
it. Nikephoros did not include every event in his history and so the stories he does tell are there for a reason. The dramatic story of her pulling
the icon out of her dress was probably a well-known family tale that
Nikephoros's audience would have wanted to hear. In that Nikephoros's
history functioned as a compendium of great family lore, it may have
been natural to include the story about how Anna stood up to the
judges.

Beyond that, the story may speak to some lingering discomfort with
her political power. Anna's cry that Christ is her judge is an appeal of a
disempowered person speaking truth to power. To cling to hope of divine
help is certainly an act of piety, but it is also a manifestation of lack of
temporal resources. In this markedly unreligious text, the sudden intrusion
of Christian imagery highlights the absence of the political and military
resources that form the matrix of action for the rest of the book. By
portraying Anna as a slandered victim clinging to God, Nikephoros denies
the reality of her political authority. There may be some significance to

---

[50] 1.22.27–33. Ps. 44.21: εἴσεισι γοῦν ἡ γενναία καὶ μεγαλόψυχος φαιδρῷ τῷ προσώπῳ καὶ τὴν
εἰκόνα δὲ κρύπτουσα ὑπὸ τὴν χλαμύδα τοῦ πάντων Δικαστοῦ ἐξάγει ταύτην ἀθρόον καὶ
σεμνῷ τῷ σχήματι καὶ τῷ βλέμματι πρὸς τοὺς δικαστὰς ἀτενίσασα, «οὗτος», ἔφη, «δικαστὴς
ἐμοῦ τε καὶ ὑμῶν καθίσταται σήμερον, πρὸς ὃν ἀτενίζοντες ψήφους ἐκφέρετε μὴ ἀναξίας τοῦ
δικαστοῦ τοῦ εἰδότος τὰ κρύφια».
[51] 1.22.43–47: ποία πρόληψις, ὦ ἐμβρόντητοι, εἶπεν ἄν τις πρὸς αὐτοὺς θαρραλέως, ὁπηνίκα ὁ
μὲν κατηγορῶν ἀναιδῶς φθέγγεται, ὁ δὲ φεύγων γενναίως τὰς κατηγορίας ἀποσκευάζεται,
καὶ ὁ μὲν ἀγύρτης ἐστὶ καὶ ὀβολοῦ πιπράσκων τὴν δίκην εἰ δέοι, ὁ δὲ πάσης ὑποψίας ἀνώτερος
καὶ πρὸς αὐτὴν μικροῦ δεῖν ἐρυθριῶν τὴν ἀλήθειαν.
[52] Matthew 26:57–66; John 18:12–23.    [53] 1.22.48–49.

Nikephoros's decision to portray a woman known to have wielded great authority as utterly helpless and victimized.

Anna otherwise appears in her role as mother. Motherhood is not ideologically straightforward in regard to constructions of power relations. Men must have mothers to get born, but in many discourses of male power reproduction is symbolically appropriated as a male action.[54] In classical politics, paternity is what counted for establishing political power.[55] Roman mothers had a far greater role in the education and formation of their sons than ancient Athenian mothers and could expect the deference of their young adult sons.[56] Yet deference to mothers was a matter of a young man's choice rather than obligation, and efforts to break away from maternal tutelage were considered appropriate.[57]

The stories of young Roman men resisting and then dispensing with their mother's advice have helped create our image of strong Roman mothers, but the stories also display the key moments in which the sons turn into men. Conceptions of gender drawn from Galen's medical tradition held boys as being closer in physical temperament to women, girls, and eunuchs. Full maleness came only with adulthood.[58] A Roman boy needed to increase in masculinity to become a properly gendered adult man. So when an adult son acts like a child in deferring to his mother, it is a transgression of gender norms. Outgrowing a mother's advice was part of attaining full masculinity as well as adulthood.

Imperial motherhood is an even more complicated category. On the one hand, the wife of an emperor who is the mother of another can strongly symbolize continuity of stable government by ensuring that the current peace and stability will endure unperturbed into future generations.[59]

---

[54] To cite a simple example, the women involved in the process whereby Arphaxad begat Salah who begat Eber are omitted from the narrative in Genesis 11:13–14.

[55] The principle can be rather strongly stated: "Nowhere in the classical . . . world does birth into social/political manhood, any kind of manhood, from any social sector, erupt from womankind. Boys may have mothers, but (political) men have mentors, sponsors, colleagues and 'friends'." Lin Foxhall, "Introduction," in *When Men were Men: Masculinity, Power and Identity in Classical Antiquity*, ed. Lin Foxhall and John Salmon (London: Routledge, 1998), 7.

[56] Dixon, *The Roman Mother*, 168–209.     [57] Dixon, *The Roman Mother*, 181.

[58] Women, children, and eunuchs were soft and moist whereas men were hard and dry. Kathryn M. Ringrose, *The Perfect Servant*, 54–55; Katharine Ringrose, "Reconfiguring the Prophet Daniel: Gender, Sanctity, and Castration in Byzantium," in *Gender and Difference in the Middle Ages*, ed. Sharon Farmer and Carol Braun Pasternack (Minneapolis: University of Minnesota Press, 2003), 73–85. On Roman male adulthood see McDonnell, *Roman Manliness*, 173–80.

[59] The sudden and widespread popularity of the cults of the deified Livia and Agrippina the Younger in the Greek world has been explained as a response to the desire to emphasize the stability of Roman rule. The cults of the empresses did this by adding the element of fertility and maternal care for household to the imperial pantheon. Susan Fischler, "Imperial Cult: Engendering the Cosmos," in *When Men were Men: Masculinity, Power and Identity in Classical Antiquity*, ed. Lin Foxhall and John Salmon (London: Routledge, 1998), 175.

Images of empresses, with husbands and sons, can also "complete the image of the patriarchal emperor" by allowing him to "display control over his household."[60] The category of imperial mother becomes problematic when the patriarchal husband is missing. Eudokia's decision to marry Romanos Diogenes in 1068 followed well-established traditions of empress regents quickly choosing new husbands. While re-marrying restores the ideal image of a properly ordered imperial household by completing the husband-wife-son package, it creates uncertainty about whether the second husband will support the inheritance rights of the first-husband's children – hence the Doukai attack on Romanos. If the empress regent does not remarry and rules for her son, the uncertainty turns to whether and when the minor will grow to be man enough to take control of the government.

Emperors must be seen as overcoming the tutelage of their mothers in order to attain adulthood and be men. Psellos's *Historia Syntomos* includes a negative portrait of Alexander Severus (222–235), whose chief failing was over-dependence on his mother, Mamaea. Psellos says that while she was pious, she was not fit for imperial rule. That she drew up the army on behalf of Severus is seen as sufficient explanation for Severus's military failure.[61] Despite her sainthood, Psellos considered Irene a bad empress because of her jealousy of her son Constantine VI, for whom she ruled as regent well into his twenties before having him blinded and ruling independently from 797–803.[62] These historical examples were problematic for two reasons: women were in positions of authority and their boys were not men. Mamaea, in mustering troops, was too masculine, but Severus, in giving his mother childlike deference, was effeminate, or at least not masculine enough to be emperor.

Within this cultural system imperial mothers needed to fade into the background when their boys become imperial men. Strong, nurturing imperial mothers are needed to help produce heirs and guide them to adulthood, but their sons cannot be adults, and hence fully masculine, until the women stop mothering them.

Anna Dalassene appears in several scenes in the role of a Roman mother, exercising care for her children.[63] While her actions assimilate her to patterns of appropriate Roman behavior, she also displays the sort of tutelage that Roman boys needed to overcome. Anna rushed from Constantinople to Bithynia when she heard the news that her oldest son, the *kouropalates* Manuel, was near death from illness.[64] She found him staying in a small

---

[60] Fischler, "Imperial Cult," 179.     [61] Psellos, *Historia* 40.     [62] Psellos, *Historia* 91.
[63] Paidas, "Social Gender," 740–44.     [64] 1.12.7–10.

monastery. Manuel immediately embraced her and asked "only to be worthy of a common tomb."[65] When he died, Anna acted with appropriate grief and restraint:

The noble and great-hearted mother completed the required rites for her son and grieved as much as is appropriate for the loss of such a son, a soldier, and general. Recovering her pain a little, she sent the famous Alexios campaigning with the emperor.[66]

Anna's grief at the death of her son recalls Plutarch's Cornelia mourning the death of her sons Tiberius and Gaius Gracchus. Both women were noble and *megalopsuchos* in the face of their sons' death.[67] Anna's restrained grief and immediate decision to send another son to war for the Empire also recall Cornelia's paradigm. Plutarch admires Cornelia's strength in being able to discuss her sons' achievements and deaths without grief or tears.[68] Both women grieve, but not inappropriately, displaying the strength of Roman heroines.

In her stoic calm, Anna is stronger than her son Alexios who was "shedding streams of tears since he was divided between two emotions, compassion for his mother and martial enthusiasm, for he indeed loved both warfare and his mother."[69] Romanos Diogenes himself wept when he saw Alexios and ordered him to return to his mother, saying that it would not be right to leave her without a comforter.[70] Alexios attempted to persuade Romanos to let him stay, but he was unsuccessful and returned to his mother. Anna appears strong and steady in this episode. The emperor's regard for a mourning widow was also noble. Alexios's return to his mother's side was obedient. The episode creates a favorable impression of all three characters, while simultaneously highlighting Alexios's lack of maturity.

The other three instances where Anna enters the narrative are occasions for her to give opinions about Alexios's career or otherwise mother him. Anna advised Alexios to decline the commission to fight Roussel, his first major victory.[71] Alexios ignored his mother's advice and took on the task, which led to his first major success. Alexios here is shown to be a better

---

[65] 1.12.18: . . . μόνον δὲ αἰτησάμενος ταύτην κοινῆς ἄμφω ἀξιωθῆναι ταφῆς.

[66] 1.12.19–24: ἡ δὲ γενναία μήτηρ καὶ μεγαλόψυχος τὴν ὀφειλομένην ὁσίαν ἀποπληρώσασα τῷ υἱῷ καὶ τοσοῦτον πενθήσασα ὅσον εἰκὸς τὴν τοιοῦτον παῖδα ἀποβαλοῦσαν στρατιώτην τε ἅμα καὶ στρατηγόν, βραχύ τι τοῦ πάθους ἑαυτὴν ἀνενεγκοῦσα τὸν κλεινὸν ἐκπέμπει Ἀλέξιον συστρατευσόμενον τῷ βασιλεῖ.

[67] Plut. *C. Gracch.* 40.1.2: Cornelia bore her grief "εὐγενῶς καὶ μεγαλοψύχως." Anna was a "γενναία μήτηρ καὶ μεγαλόψυχος," 1.12.19–20.

[68] *C. Gracch.* 40.3.3–5.    [69] Nikephoros, *Hist.* 1.12.24–26.

[70] 1.22.29–37.    [71] 2.20.1–4.

judge of politics than his mother and able to defy her will. While Alexios thus displays his independence, the inclusion at all in the history of his mother's opinion about what he should do portrays him as beholden to his mother. Other men in Nikephoros's history do not ask their mothers, or fathers, about what jobs they should take.[72]

When Andronikos Doukas asked Alexios to consider marrying his daughter Irene, Alexios responded that he needed to ask his mother.[73] This was an impediment to the union because Anna is said to have always hated Caesar John Doukas and his family.[74] Modern observers have attributed this dislike of the Doukas household to Anna's supposed jealousy over having Constantine Doukas succeed her brother-in-law Isaac as emperor.[75] According to Nikephoros, opposition to the marriage of Alexios and Irene Doukaina came from Emperor Michael and his brother Konstantios as well as from Anna Dalassene. In assessing where the real opposition was, the historiography fastens onto any information about Anna and makes her the prime mover. The text, however, lists her opposition along with that of the reigning emperor. Although Michael was a weak character, his opinion as emperor probably still counted for quite a bit.

The insertion of Anna into the discussion of Alexios's engagement functions to portray him as subject to maternal authority. Alexios is denied the opportunity to exercise proper control over his family and self-determination regarding his choice of wife. Rather he continues to defer to his mother's tutelage.

Anna's mothering of Alexios appears in the midst of a story about his campaign against Basilakes. During that campaign, a eunuch monk stayed with Alexios in his tent. The monk has a role to play in the story of one of Alexios's military ruses. It is specified that Alexios's mother had entrusted the care, *pronoia,* of Alexios to the monk, since he was "skillful and adept."[76] The term *pronoia* indicates oversight as well as care and may imply moral guidance. At this point Alexios was about twenty-one years old and had been commanding armies for over six years. One would think he could choose his own servants and take responsibility for his own personal morality. Although just a remark in passing, this detail presents Alexios as continuing to be under his mother's protection and guidance.

---

[72] Constantine Doukas refused his father's order to fight against Romanos after the battle of Manzikert at a time when his father, Caesar John Doukas, was running the government for Michael VII: 1.23.9–11.

[73] 3.6.28–29.    [74] 3.6.33–34.

[75] Steven Runciman, "The End of Anna Dalassena," 517; Garland, *Byzantine Empresses,* 187.

[76] 4.21.1–4: ἐντὸς δὲ τῆς ἰδίας σκηνῆς τὸν συνόντα αὐτῷ μοναχόν, ἄνδρα ἐκτομίαν, ᾧ τὴν αὐτοῦ πρόνοιαν ἡ μήτηρ ἐπίστευσεν ὡς ἐντρεχεῖ τε καὶ περιδεξίῳ . . .

In these three cases, Alexios is shown as responding in some way to his mother's advice. Alexios ultimately acts independently of his mother in taking up the commission to fight Roussel and choosing to marry Irene. One could not say that Alexios was under the thumb of his mother, but he did consult her. On the surface this behavior is innocuous enough. It is in fact respectful and admirable in a sense. Yet, when considered against a background of classical constructions of imperial motherhood, the ongoing involvement of his mother in his affairs once he had reached adulthood functioned to challenge Alexios's manhood. So long as Alexios was subject to his mother he was not fully a man and certainly not imperial. Anna's tutelage would need to be forcefully overcome in order for Alexios to rule effectively as emperor. In portraying Alexios as subject to Anna's guidance, Nikephoros does *not* portray Alexios as ordering his own household. A proper adult man would take care of his widowed mother rather than the other way around.

The case that Alexios was overly deferential to his mother could be made lightly and easily by Nikephoros because everyone in his audience knew that Anna went on to hold great authority within Alexios's imperial administration. Nikephoros's history does not cover the period in which Alexios granted Anna control over domestic administration, but it plays into a cultural system in which that would be seen as a bad idea. In Zonaras's history Alexios is negatively portrayed as subject to his mother. Zonaras explains that Alexios was unhappy about being emperor "in name only" because his mother ran the government for him. His story is that Alexios was unwilling to remove Anna from authority because he was "in awe of his mother."[77] In Zonaras's story Anna steps down voluntarily because she is able to perceive Alexios's unhappiness. This characterization of Alexios as disempowered and afraid of his mother is highly critical. The effectiveness of medieval rhetoric has certainly contributed to the idea held by more than one notable modern scholar that Alexios was a "weakling before women."[78] Nikephoros's few brief scenes of Anna attempting to direct Alexios's carreer would be enough to remind his audience of Alexios's prolonged adolescence. The same ideal of adult masculinity that allows John Komnenos's strength to be displayed precisely by his refusal to be

---

[77] Zonaras 746.4–7: ἤχθετο μὲν οὖν ὁ βασιλεὺς ὡς ἐν μόνῳ σχεδὸν τῆς βασιλείας ἀπολαύων ὀνόματι, ᾐδεῖτο δὲ τὴν μητέρα καὶ ἀκούσης ἐκείνης ἀφελέσθαι τὴν ἐξουσίαν οὐκ ἤθελεν.

[78] "faible devant les femmes," Lemerle, *Cinq études*, 298; seconded by Magdalino, "Innovations in Government," 150, and Michael Angold, "Alexios I Komnenos," 406, but disputed by Hill, "Alexios I Komnenos and the Imperial Women," 37–54.

guided by Anna in turn means that Alexios's deference to her exposes his lack of full manhood.

When all of Anna's appearances are considered, she emerges as a profoundly polyvalent character, both admirable and celebrated for her strengths and subtly functioning to challenge Alexios's masculinity. In her first appearance, Anna's strong argumentative assault on her husband affords him the opportunity to display his strength in ignoring her. John was man enough to ignore Anna, whose strength is never called into question. The story about Anna's trial shows off her piety and proclaims her courage and *megalopsychia*. Her response to the death of her son Manuel likewise displays inner strength and *megalopsychia*. Anna's characterization is not negative and employs some of the main characteristics of classical Roman motherhood.[79] Her continued involvement in mothering her adult son, however, calls Alexios's manhood into question. Unlike his father, Alexios pays attention to Anna's opinions. The Gracchi ignored their mother's feelings in the pursuit of what was right for Rome. Cornelia is a heroic character even though she had no control over her boys. Those in the audience who regarded Alexios as not exhibiting the proper kind of military virtue were likely to see Anna's continued influence over her son as indicating Alexios's weakness, immaturity, and insufficient masculinity.

---

[79] Dixon, *The Roman Mother*, 168–209.

# CHAPTER 13

# A bold young man

The portraits of the great and noble Roman men that fill Nikephoros's narrative exalt the memory of those individuals. They also stand in implicit contrast to the character of Alexios Komnenos who despite being the ostensible hero of Nikephoros's history, does not share their character or values. Alexios has already entered several of the previous chapters either because his rise to prominence forms the core of the overall plot, or because the characterization of other individuals seems to speak to his character. Now it is time to turn to Nikephoros's depiction of Alexios directly and assess the possible meanings of Nikephoros's remarkably ambiguous portrait. Nikephoros presents material that his audience could use to construct a positive image of Alexios. At the same time he undercuts some of his compliments with paradoxical juxtapositions and alienates Alexios from the most prominent virtues of his heroic characters. A reflective audience could apprehend a negative characterization of Alexios without difficulty.

Nikephoros portrays Alexios differently in books 1 and 2 than in books 3 and 4. There is a shift in rhetorical strategy as the second half of the history becomes far more patent in its criticism of Alexios than the first. In book 1 Alexios is lavishly praised, but shown to be ineffective and foolish. Criticism here takes the form of irony and juxtaposition of dishonorable circumstances and mistakes with hyperbolic praise. In the later parts of book 2 and increasingly in books 3 and 4, as Alexios becomes militarily successful, Nikephoros aligns Alexios with Turks and military tricksters, painting a picture of ruthlessness and dishonorable grasping after any advantage. Alexios's lack of honor is contrasted particularly with Bryennios the Elder's noble conduct in book 4.

Nikephoros's praise of the young Alexios is hyperbolic. Alexios is always given an honorary epithet in his early appearances.[1] He is most often called

---

[1] Seger, *Bryennios*, 32–33.

the *kleinos* Alexios, the famous Alexios.[2] He is also the most wondrous,[3] the beautiful,[4] and the golden.[5] In books 3 and 4 he is sometimes called brave,[6] but he most often is referred to by his military title or simply his name. This change in the use of epithets of praise led Seger to believe that Alexios died after Nikephoros had written the first two books of his history, so that Alexios was praised lavishly while alive and less so after his death.[7] In light of the more clearly negative reading of the later books offered here, the opening books may be taken as similarly, if less overtly, unsympathetic. The change in rhetorical strategy may be due, in part, to Alexios's changing age and political stature. It may also reflect a change in Nikephoros's circumstances of composition or the reception of the earlier books.[8]

Nikephoros's initial description of Alexios is particularly fulsome. When he first introduces Alexios, in the description of John and Anna's children, Nikephoros modifies a rhetorically elaborate description that Psellos wrote about John Doukas. Psellos opens the chapter of his continuation of the *Chronographia* devoted to Caesar John Doukas with the following lavish praise:

What could one say about this man, so as to make words equal with the splendors of his habits and the virtues of his soul? For every kind of need was met in him and he was able to be the most beautiful offering in life and combining two opposite qualities, for being the most sharp in intelligence of all that I have perceived and seen, even so he displayed a most gentle soul comparable to the noiseless flowing of a stream of oil.[9]

The contrast between sharp intelligence and gentleness, as well as the likening of the man's character to a "stream of oil" derives from the initial description of Theaetetus in Plato's dialogue of that name.[10] Nikephoros's

---

[2] 1.12.23; 2.12.10; 2.12.11; 2.25.22; 2.28.9; 2.6.23–24.    [3] 2.8.30.    [4] 2.19.17; 2.28.7.

[5] 2.13.23.    [6] 3.6.36; 4.26.8; 2.9.26; 4.23.5; yet Alexios appears more frequently in books 3–4.

[7] Seger, *Bryennios*, 32–33.

[8] The politics of the presentation of Nikephoros's history will be explored in chapter 14.

[9] Psellos, *Chronographia*, 7 (*Michael*) 16.1–7: τί ἄν τις εἴποι περὶ τοῦ ἀνδρὸς τούτου, ὥστε ἐξισῶσαι τοὺς λόγους ταῖς τῶν ἠθῶν ἀγλαΐαις καὶ ταῖς τῆς ψυχῆς ἀρεταῖς; παντοδαπὸν γὰρ οὗτος χρῆμα καὶ οἷον κάλλιστον τῷ βίῳ ἀνάθημα, καὶ ἐκ δυεῖν τοῖς ἐναντίοιν ξυγκείμενος, ὀξύτατος γὰρ τὴν σύνεσιν ὢν ξυμπάντων ὧν ἐγὼ καὶ ᾔσθημαι καὶ τεθέαμαι, οὕτω πραοτάτην ἐνδείκνυται τὴν ψυχήν, ὡς εἰκάζεσθαι ῥεύματι ἐλαίου ἀψοφητὶ ῥέοντος.

[10] 144a–b5: εὖ γὰρ ἴσθι ὅτι ὧν δὴ πώποτε ἐνέτυχον – καὶ πάνυ πολλοῖς πεπλησίακα – οὐδένα πω ᾐσθόμην οὕτω θαυμαστῶς εὖ πεφυκότα. τὸ γὰρ εὐμαθῆ ὄντα ὡς ἄλλῳ χαλεπὸν πρᾷον αὖ εἶναι διαφερόντως, καὶ ἐπὶ τούτοις ἀνδρεῖον παρ' ὁντινοῦν, ἐγὼ μὲν οὔτ' ἂν ᾠόμην γενέσθαι οὔτε ὁρῶ γιγνόμενον· ἀλλ' οἵ τε ὀξεῖς ὥσπερ οὗτος καὶ ἀγχίνοι καὶ μνήμονες ὡς τὰ πολλὰ καὶ πρὸς τὰς ὀργὰς ὀξύρροποί εἰσι, καὶ ᾄττοντες φέρονται ὥσπερ τὰ ἀνερμάτιστα πλοῖα, καὶ μανικώτεροι ἢ ἀνδρειότεροι φύονται, οἵ τε αὖ ἐμβριθέστεροι νωθροί πως ἀπαντῶσι πρὸς τὰς

initial description of Alexios owes more to Psellos's description of John Doukas than to Plato:

The third in turn Alexios was filled with all graces. For his face was as graceful as one could ever see in another and he was always shining and filled with good sense, and what could one say about him, to be able to make equal with words the splendors of his habits and the virtues of his soul? He had every kind of physical need and chosen adornment and was able to be the most beautiful offering in life by combining two opposite qualities: for he was the most sharp and energetic of all which we have seen, even so he displayed a most gentle soul so that he made himself seem nearly unsusceptible to anger.[11]

Nikephoros's simplifies Psellos's grammar slightly and adds a few more compliments. He omits Plato's oil metaphor while preserving the essential contrast between sharpness and gentleness. Nikephoros's description of Alexios is even more over the top in praise than Psellos's. Regardless of how scholars choose to approach Psellos's original,[12] Nikephoros's passage needs to be seen in the context of the rest of his history, in which the hyperbolic praise stands in contrast to less flattering depictions of Alexios's character.

---

μαθήσεις καὶ λήθης γέμοντες. ὁ δὲ οὕτω λείως τε καὶ ἀπταίστως καὶ ἀνυσίμως ἔρχεται ἐπὶ τὰς μαθήσεις τε καὶ ζητήσεις μετὰ πολλῆς πρᾳότητος, οἷον ἐλαίου ῥεῦμα ἀψοφητὶ ῥέοντος, ὥστε θαυμάσαι τὸ τηλικοῦτον ὄντα οὕτως ταῦτα διαπράττεσθαι.

"I assure you that, among all the young men I have met with – and I have had to do with a good many – I have never found such admirable gifts. The combination of a rare quickness of intelligence with exceptional gentleness and of an incomparably virile spirit with both, is a thing that I should hardly have believed could exist, and I have never seen it before. In general, people who have such keen and ready wits and such good memories as he are also quick-tempered and passionate; they dart about like ships without ballast, and their temperament is rather enthusiastic than strong, whereas the steadier sort are somewhat dull when they come to face study, and they forget everything. But his approach to learning and inquiry, with the perfect quietness of its smooth and sure progress, is like the noiseless flow of a stream of oil. It is wonderful how he achieves all this at his age." Translated by F. M. Cornford, in *Plato: The Collected Dialogues*, ed. E. Hamilton and H. Cairns (Princeton University Press, 1961), 848–49.

[11] 1.6.20–29: ὁ δ᾽ αὖ τρίτος Ἀλέξιος παντοίων ἦν χαρίτων ἀνάπλεως· χάρις γὰρ ἐπήνθει τῷ προσώπῳ ὁποίαν οὔ τις ἐν ἄλλῳ ἐθεάσατο πώποτε καὶ φαιδρὸς ἦν ἀεὶ καὶ ἀγαθωσύνης ἀνάπλεως, καὶ τί ἄν τις εἴποι περὶ τούτου ὡς δυνηθῆναι τοὺς λόγους ἐξισῶσαι ταῖς τῶν ἠθῶν ἀγλαΐαις καὶ ταῖς τῆς ψυχῆς ἀρεταῖς; παντοδαπὸν ἦν χρῆμα φυσικῆς τε καὶ προαιρετικῆς κοσμιότητος καὶ οἷόν τι κάλλιστον τῷ βίῳ ἀνάθημα ἐκ δυοῖν τοῖν ἐναντίοιν συγκείμενον· ὀξύτατος γὰρ ὢν ξυμπάντων ὧν αὐτοὶ τεθεάμεθα καὶ δραστηριώτατος, οὕτω πρᾳοτάτην ἐδείκνυτο τὴν ψυχὴν ὡς μικροῦ δεῖν καὶ ἀκίνητον πρὸς ὀργὴν ἑαυτὸν ἀποφαίνειν.

[12] Some do not consider the last book of the *Chronographia* to be a true continuation of the text, but a politically motivated encomiastic tract: Anthony Kaldellis, *The Argument of Psellos' Chronographia* (Leiden: Brill, 1999), 11; Anthony Kaldellis, "The Corpus of Byzantine Historiography: an Interpretive Essay," in *The Byzantine World*, ed. Paul Stephenson (London: Routledge, 2010), 213. Others have suggested that it ought to be read ironically as a criticism of a disastrous emperor: Krallis, "Attaliates as a Reader of Psellos," 189–90; Jeffrey Walker, "Michael Psellos on Rhetoric: A Translation and Commentary on Psellos' Synopsis of Hermogenes," *Rhetoric Society Quarterly* 31, 1 (2001): 14.

In the stories about Alexios's earliest military campaigns, Alexios appears as a parody of an overly bold, youthful warrior. Nikephoros uses formal martial vocabulary to describe Alexios's actions as a child. He did not "return" to Anna from Diogenes's camp but rather "marched forth breaking quarters."[13] Alexios camped at Caesarea in his first military campaign, under the command of his brother Isaac. Isaac left Alexios to guard the fortress while he gave battle to the approaching Turks. After defeating and capturing Isaac, the Turks attacked the fortress, provoking Alexios into a daring sortie. Alexios bravely charged out and immediately engaged the enemy:

He pushed into the middle of the fighters and first struck his spear against the one coming against him and immediately showed him death. Then, when he was surrounded and arrows were sent against him from everywhere, he was unharmed and he was guarded by the right hand above. But his horse received the most arrows and fell to the ground with his rider.[14]

Those fighting with Alexios dismounted to "struggle nobly" with him and ripped him from danger. Of the fifteen men who went out with Alexios, only five returned safely to camp. The episode is ostensibly laudatory in presenting Alexios as guarded by divine power, but for other characters in Nikephoros's history sustaining wounds in a desperate fight was a mark of having fought hard and well. Notably Andronikos Doukas and Bryennios the Elder received numerous wounds before they were defeated. They stand in pointed contrast to Alexios who emerged entirely unscathed from a battle in which he lost two-thirds of his men.

Back inside the fortification Alexios encouraged the soldiers "so that they would not do something unworthy of the noble character of the Romans."[15] The soldiers are described as responding enthusiastically to Alexios's exhortation and praising him in terms of a savior and an angel:

So long as it was day, they were strong and admiring the nobility of the youth, they applauded and raising their hands as suppliants they called him savior and benefactor, saying "Well done! Oh young man, oh savior, oh helmsman, oh deliverer of the remnants of this Roman army. Well done! Oh angel scarcely having a body! May we delight in your brave exploits and may you be kept for us as our common help for many years!"[16]

---

[13] 1.12.36: καὶ ἄκοντα γὰρ τοῦτον ἐπαναζεῦξαι πρὸς τὴν μητέρα παρεσκεύασεν.

[14] 2.5.10–15.     [15] 2.5.22.

[16] 2.5.23–28: ἕως μὲν οὖν ἡμέρα ἦν, ἐκαρτέρουν καὶ τὸ γενναῖον τοῦ νέου θαυμάζοντες ἐπήνουν καὶ χεῖρας ἱκέτιδας ἀνατείνοντες σωτῆρα καὶ εὐεργέτην ἐκάλουν, "εὖγε," λέγοντες, "ὦ νεανία, ὁ σωτήρ, ὁ κυβερνήτης, ὁ τῆς περισωθείσης τῆσδε Ῥωμαϊκῆς στρατιᾶς ῥύστης, εὖγε ὁ ἀσώματος μικροῦ δεῖν ἐν σώματι· ὀναίμεθά σου τῶν ἀνδραγαθημάτων καὶ τηρηθείης ἡμῖν εἰς χρόνους μακροὺς κοινὸν ὄφελος."

As soon as night fell however, one of the soldiers, "exceptional among them in bravery and experience, named Theodotos," recognized that as soon as it was dark most of the soldiers would run away.[17] This prediction greatly saddened Alexios as "he supposed everyone was as brave as he was."[18] The soldiers did in fact abandon their position while Alexios was having dinner, still wearing his armor.[19]

In this story Nikephoros plays with paradoxical juxtapositions of Alexios's ascribed valor and actual incompetence. While Nikephoros ostensibly praises Alexios lavishly throughout, he tells the story of a disastrously ill-judged engagement, devoid of glory or even purpose. Alexios's poor judgment gained nothing other than the deaths of those trying to keep him out of trouble. His outnumbered attack against the Turks, in which he lost ten out of fifteen men, was reckless and senseless. The soldiers' hymn in praise of Alexios is wildly incongruous after such a drubbing. That Theodotos was mentioned by name and described as exceptional in bravery and experience indicates that his judgment that the men would abandon the fortress ought to be regarded as a sensible military assessment. A good commander would recognize that the situation was untenable. The detail that Alexios dined in his armor (only after fasting all day) at the very moment his forces were abandoning his camp presents a biting contrast between ostensibly laudatory behavior and pitiable outcomes. Generals keep their armor on so that they are always ready to respond to new challenges. Alexios ate in his armor, but failed to respond to the unfolding challenge of a large-scale desertion among his forces.

When he found himself alone at dawn, having been abandoned by nearly all his soldiers, Alexios escaped on a mule. When the mule could go no further Alexios dismounted and marched on, fully armed, into the neighboring mountains.[20] He refused to put down his breastplate and armor, remembering that his father had laughed at a man who had abandoned his arms.[21] The pressure of climbing up the mountain made his nose bleed all night. When he finally arrived at a village, the inhabitants, "seeing the cloak which covered his breastplate sprinkled with gore of blood, naturally moaned and cried."[22] The implication of their moans is that they mistakenly assumed that his blood came from wounds received in battle. They cleaned him up and then handed him a mirror. Alexios claimed that he did not know what to do with it explaining that men and especially soldiers are not accustomed to looking in mirrors because:

[17] 2.6.1–8.   [18] 2.6.4–5.   [19] 2.6.6–8.   [20] 2.6.23–27.   [21] 2.6.27–30.
[22] 2.7.1–3: οἳ καὶ ὁρῶντες αὐτοῦ τὴν ἐπὶ θώρακος χλαῖναν κατάστικτον τῷ λύθρῳ τοῦ αἵματος ἔστενόν τε καὶ ἐδάκρυον ὡς εἰκός.

This is only a pursuit for women, and especially those who are trying to please their husbands. Weapons and a plain and simple life are adornments for military men.[23]

The story of Alexios's escape constitutes more two-edged praise. The acts of climbing a mountain in his armor and disdaining his personal appearance show a strong military character. Yet a good general would work never to be in the position of escaping a fortress alone on a mule. How heroic could Alexios have been when the blood that horrified the villagers had come from his own nose? The claims to exaggerated masculine roughness only point out Alexios's youth. Again this story is not overtly critical of Alexios but there is a disjuncture between the stated laudatory exclamations and the overall result of the contextualized characterization.[24]

Nothing compelled Nikephoros to include these stories of Alexios's first youthful military outing in his history. If making Alexios look good were the real goal of the work, Nikephoros could have omitted the story about how Alexios lost two thirds of his men in battle and then was abandoned by the rest. At least he could have left out the body count. Anna Komnene omitted these stories entirely from her narrative of Alexios's youth. Nikephoros poured on glorifying vocabulary to paint these episodes as heroic exploits, but did not take the truly flattering step of pretending they had never happened.

Another bad situation presented as a heroic adventure is Alexios and Isaac's escape from the dinner party at Dekte, already discussed in chapter 5. On their way back to Constantinople after Alexios had ransomed his older brother Isaac from his Turkish captors, they stopped at their kinsman's house at Dekte near Nikomedeia and were unexpectedly attacked by Turks. They had accepted an invitation from a kinsman to stay with him for dinner, accompanied by a few guards. A raiding party of about 200 Turks was in the area and one of the local farmers, assuming that they must be working for the generals, showed them the way to the party. The Turks quickly surrounded the house and most of those inside were inclined to surrender immediately.[25] Alexios then makes another rousing speech:

For me, men, not to test the enemy, but to abandon yourselves to slavery and certain danger both brings the charge of cowardice and seems completely stupid.

---

[23] 2.7.9–13: "γυναιξὶ γὰρ καὶ τοῦτο μόναις ἐπιτετήδευται μεριμνώσαις ἀρέσκειν τοῖς σφῶν ἀνδράσιν· ἀνδρὶ δὲ στρατιώτῃ κόσμος τὰ ὅπλα καὶ τὸ τῆς διαίτης λιτόν τε καὶ ἄθρυπτον."

[24] Sharp contrasts between image and reality form part of Choniates' irony: Ljubarskij, "Byzantine Irony: The Example of Niketas Choniates," 287–98.

[25] 2.9.

I think this is bad behavior not only for Roman men, but also for women who are noble and wise. Besides suffering now, in the future we will be shut off from human compassion and we will fail to earn *encomia* for ourselves, which are for men who struggle nobly and are worthy of their good-birth . . . Those dying [in battle] are pitied by commoners, praised by the wise, blessed by everyone. Those abandoning themselves to slavery and danger deserve no compassion and are considered most miserable by everyone. But as the saying goes, one must choose between a good life and a good death.[26]

He then continues to explain how they can marshal the household servants into an array that could hold off the Turks long enough for everyone else to break out of the house.[27] The "saying" Alexios quotes is from Sophocles's *Ajax*.[28] While it is entirely possible that the line had become a proverbial expression by the twelfth century, it also fits Nikephoros's purpose as an allusion to its Sophoclean context. Ajax declares that a man of honor must have either a good life or a good death when he is contemplating his suicide in response to his own horrific dishonor. The tragic ignominy of Ajax mocks Alexios's bravura.

Alexios's speech rallied his kinsmen, their guards, and servants and they proceeded according to his plan to fight desperately against their attackers. Alexios and Isaac make it out of the trap alive. Nikephoros includes several scenes of hand-to-hand fighting and battlefield banter. A eunuch of enormous size initially frightens some of the Turks but then needs to be helped out by Alexios. Two Alan mercenaries, charged with protecting Isaac and Alexios, debate on the field whether helping the boys is worthwhile and then go on to fight extremely well for them. Like many of Nikephoros's detailed battle scenes, these recollections make good stories. Together they help make the fight at Dekte a satisfying action sequence.

The story of the fight at Dekte is similar to Alexios's earlier military engagement in the stark juxtaposition of glorifying description with an embarrassing and problematic situation. Yet Alexios emerges as a good fighter and leader. He begins here to display some of the characteristics

---

[26] 2.10.1–13: ἐμοὶ μέν, ὦ ἄνδρες, τὸ μηδόλως ἀποπειρᾶσθαι τῶν πολεμίων, ἀλλὰ σφᾶς αὐτοὺς εἰς δουλείαν προδοῦναι καὶ προῦπτον κίνδυνον πρὸς τὸ δειλίας ἔγκλημα φέρειν καὶ πάσης εὐηθείας δοκεῖ εἶναι μεστόν. οἶμαι γὰρ μὴ ὅτι γε Ῥωμαίους ἄνδρας τῶν εὖ γεγονότων τοῦτο δρᾶσαί ποτε, ἀλλ' οὐδὲ γυναῖκας εὐγενεῖς τε καὶ σώφρονας· πρὸς γὰρ τῷ δεινὰ παθεῖν καὶ τὸν ἔλεον τῶν ἀνθρώπων ἀφ' ἡμῶν ἀποκλείσομεν καὶ τῶν εἰς τὸ μέλλον ἐγκωμίων ἀποτευξόμεθα, ἃ τοῖς γενναίως ἀγωνισαμένοις καὶ ἀξίως τῆς σφῶν εὐγενείας . . . θανόντες ἐλεοῦνται μὲν παρ' ἰδιωτῶν, ἐπαινοῦνται δὲ παρὰ σοφῶν, μακαρίζονται παρὰ πάντων· οἱ δὲ σφᾶς αὐτοὺς προδόντες εἰς δουλείαν ἢ κίνδυνον πάσης συγγνώμης πόρρω τυγχάνουσι, ταλανίζονται δὲ παρὰ πάντων τῆς ἀθλιότητος, ἀλλ' ἢ καλῶς ζῆν ἢ καλῶς τεθνηκέναι δέον σκοπεῖν, τοῦτο δὴ τὸ τοῦ λόγου.
[27] 2.10.13–28.    [28] Soph. *Aj.* 479: ἀλλ' ἢ καλῶς ζῆν ἢ καλῶς τεθνηκέναι τὸν εὐγενῆ χρή.

that will be hallmarks of his character in Nikephoros's subsequent portrait: dogged tenacity and a willingness to do anything to achieve victory. The extreme resolution displayed here becomes a consistent aspect of Alexios's character. After the battle at Dekte, Nikephoros shifts his narrative to present Alexios as a master strategist for whom any way to get a victory was the right way to fight.

As was discussed in chapter 8, Alexios is consistently portrayed as fighting through deception. Alexios's campaign of harassment against Roussel was designed to avoid a pitched battle against the Normans.[29] Alexios was flatly devious when he convinced Tutakh to capture Roussel with the promise of a monetary reward when he had no money to offer.[30] Deception was the essential element when he raised Roussel's ransom by pretending to blind him. Alexios drew up some men into a formal battle line, not to engage in battle, but to chase off a group of Turkish raiders by bluffing.[31] In his efforts to "steal victory" from Nikephoros Bryennios, Alexios became the consummate trickster.[32] Alexios's conduct in the battle is a series of attempted tricks and deceptions, from trying to deceive his own forces about the strength of Bryennios's army to capturing Bryennios's parade horse and lying that Bryennios had fallen. The account of Alexios's fight against Basilakes centers on his ability to trick Basilakes into attacking his camp at night.[33] From the time of his first independent command Alexios is portrayed as a master of deception who fought by whatever means were necessary to achieve his desired outcome. He amassed an impressive list of victories without fighting head-on battles.

The inclination toward devious military tactics is one expression of Alexios's drive to succeed at any cost. In fighting Bryennios, Alexios resolved to win or die fighting, a sentiment he had also expressed before battling out of his kinsman's house at Dekte.[34] This characteristic resolution also manifested itself as simple ruthlessness. In Alexios's speech to the Amaseians he threatens the rebellious citizens that the only benefit they will receive from supporting Roussel will be "slaughters, captivities, maiming and mutilations."[35] These maiming and mutilations are not threatened to come from Roussel or continued Norman rule, but from Roman imperial reprisals to rebellion. Alexios warns the citizens not to disobey because eventually the emperor will maim and mutilate them, alluding to the practice of blinding rebels. He warns that if there is a riot Roussel's supporters will "try to get far away from the action and bring the wrath of the emperor

---

[29] 2.20–24.    [30] 2.21.    [31] 2.27.    [32] 4.5.6–13.    [33] 4.22–24.    [34] 4.7.    [35] 2.23.13–15.

down on you."[36] In a militarily indefensible position, Alexios was trying to frighten people into helping him. The speech is a threatening depiction of imperial power and could be chilling when attributed to a man who had become emperor.

The description of Isaac's suppression of the revolt at Antioch also provides a disturbing depiction of raw imperial power. As *dux* of Antioch, Alexios's brother Isaac Komnenos had to suppress a rebellion against him after he had expelled the Patriarch Aimilianos from the city. When rebels had seized the acropolis of Antioch and plundered the houses of the leading citizens, Isaac called in troops from the surrounding cities. He sent these soldiers into the city where they "barely" put down the rebellion after a "great slaughter."[37]

Alexios's ruthlessness is most openly displayed during the debate at the court of Michael VII about how to respond to the news of Botaneiates's rebellion. John Doukas brought the news to Michael that conspirators in the city were planning to break into the prisons and arm felons and slaves in order to incite a revolution. Michael called for Alexios and asked his advice about what should be done. Alexios argued for an immediate use of military force:

The plan Alexios came up with was very much the best and most advantageous. He said that most of the people in the crowd that had gathered were noncombatants and craftsmen and they would not withstand seeing completely armed men ready for battle. "It is necessary at least to arm the imperial guards who carry axes and to send them with a general against the crowd."[38]

Alexios's hard-nosed advice was too much for Michael:

After listening to this, the ruler turned down this advice, whether suffering from cowardice or an excess of virtue, as if he were already above what would happen to him, I do not know. At least up to a point it was possible to stop the insurrection and put out the fire before the blaze became immense; but he did not want to.[39]

[36] 2.23.22–24.

[37] 2.29.13–16: . . . εἰς πολλὰ γὰρ μέρη τὸ στράτευμα διελὼν ἐκέλευσε ἀπιέναι πρὸς τὰ στενωπὰ καὶ τοὺς ἀπαντῶντας ξυλλαμβάνειν, ὡς μὴ ὁμοῦ γενόμενοι βοηθοῖεν ἀλλήλοις· οὗ γενομένου, συνέβη τῶν Ἀντιοχέων στασιαστῶν φόνον γενέσθαι πολὺν καὶ οὕτω μόλις τὴν στάσιν κατευνασθῆναι·

[38] 3.20.3–8: ὁ δὲ βουλὴν εἰσῆγε μάλα μὲν ἀρίστην, μάλα δὲ λυσιτελεστάτην· ἔφησε γὰρ ὡς τοῦ συναθροισθέντος πλήθους τὸ πλεῖστον ἀπόλεμόν τέ ἐστι καὶ βάναυσον καὶ οὐκ ἂν ὑποσταῖεν καθωπλισμένους ἄνδρας ἰδόντες καὶ πρὸς μάχην ἑτοίμους· "χρὴ γοῦν πελεκηφόρους καθοπλίσαντας βασιλέων φύλακας κατ' ἐκείνων ἐπιπέμπειν σὺν στρατηγῷ."

[39] 3.20.8–12: ὁ δὲ κρατῶν τῶν λεχθέντων ἀκούσας τὴν βουλὴν ἀπεστρέφετο, εἴτε δειλίᾳ συσχεθείς, εἴτε ἀρετῆς ὑπερβολῇ ἀνωτέρω τῶν ξυμπιπτόντων ἤδη τούτῳ παθῶν γενόμενος, οὐκ ἐπίσταμαι. τέως γοῦν ἐνὸν καταλῦσαι τὴν στάσιν καὶ κατασβέσαι τὸ πῦρ πρὸ τοῦ εἰς μεγίστην ἀναφθῆναι φλόγα· ὁ δὲ οὐκ ἠθέλησεν.

Any court debate in the great palace at Constantinople about whether to use military force against riotous civilians necessarily calls to mind the debate in which Theodora urged Justinian to fight created in Procopius's wars. Nikephoros's audience was well aware of the great slaughters that could be wrought when emperors decided to attack civilians in Constantinople.

The scene indicates that if Alexios had been emperor at the time, he would have chosen to use military force against the rioters and retain his grip on power. The strong implication is that when he did become emperor, Alexios was like Justinian, effective but ruthless. Nikephoros says that Michael's government could have been saved if he had taken Alexios's advice, but explains that Michael did not take it, either from cowardice or from an "excess of virtue."[40] If becoming a monk rather than violently suppressing a rebellion was an act of excessive virtue, Alexios's ruthless council may have been a vice.

After Michael VII abdicated, the meekness of his brother Konstantios Doukas serves as a further foil for Alexios's ambition. When Michael VII announced his intention to resign as emperor he told Alexios that he could try to set up his brother Konstantios Doukas as emperor, if he wished. According to Nikephoros, Konstantios declined for two reasons: his youth, and his belief that everything would be fine for him if Botaneiates became emperor.[41] He was concerned with his personal safety and showed no interest in pursuing power for its own sake or for the support of his family.

Konstantios was born after his father had taken up imperial rule as Constantine X in 1059. He appeared on the coins that were issued during his mother's rule with his brother Michael.[42] Botaneiates sent him to campaign against the Turks in the spring of 1079. If he was considered competent to lead armies in 1079 his claim to have been too young to rule in 1078 was certainly open to discussion. He also displayed the willingness to take up his dynastic role as a contender for Empire. While his troops were assembling for the campaign assigned by Botaneiates, Konstantios persuaded some of them to proclaim him emperor.[43] His decision not to try to become emperor in the midst of Botaneiates's coup was most likely based on prudent analysis of his chances of success. When he had command of an army a few months later, he immediately stepped up to the task of raising a rebellion in his own name.

Given that Konstantios's decision at the time of Botaneiates's coup was sound politics, his portrayal by Nikephoros as a passive weakling needs to be

---

[40] 3.20.9.    [41] 3.21.    [42] Polemis, *The Doukai*, 48–49.
[43] Cheynet, *Pouvoir*, 87–88. Attaleiates 307–09; Skylitzes continuatus 185; Zonaras 724, Polemis, *The Doukai*, 52.

explored. In part Konstantios's passivity allows Alexios to remain at center stage. Alexios takes Konstantios to Botaneiates and intercedes on his behalf, as one would for a child. Alexios, himself only twenty-one years old, is put in the role of protector and patron of the *porphyrogennetos*. When they went to meet Botaneiates, Alexios was wise to the situation while Konstantios was naïve: "Both the *porphyrogennetos* Konstantios and Alexios Komnenos arrived before Botaneiates, the one not knowing what would happen to him before he experienced it, the other foreknowing and prognosticating everything before the event."[44] Alexios's foreknowledge took the form of knowing to address Botaneiates as emperor on first meeting him and immediately asking him to care for Konstantios. This move was certainly politically adept but may not have taken an extraordinary degree of insight.

Konstantios's acceptance of the situation also contrasts with Alexios's vehemence and proposed brutality. In part, Konstantios is portrayed as a child in Alexios's tutelage in order to undermine Konstantios's superior dynastic claim to the throne. Alexios does not usurp Konstantios's authority because Konstantios is portrayed as a child in need of protection. Additionally, however, the audience is left with no doubt that if Alexios had been in charge himself, rather than working for two such passive characters as Michael and Konstantios, the riots in the city would have been suppressed, the conspirators arrested, and Botaneiates defeated.

Political determination can be a good trait in a ruler and, in isolation, the instances just discussed in which Alexios displays strong resolution to pursue his political ends can be read as showing strength of character. The portrayal of Alexios as ruthless and wily in the pursuit of his ambitions could be seen as a meditation on effective emperorship. One could argue that these are necessary characteristics for one who would grasp imperial power.

When all the various traits attributed to Alexios throughout the history are considered in combination, however, the overall evaluation of Alexios's character becomes negative. Alexios's effectiveness as a politician is not doubted, and one might make the case that he had some traits necessary in an emperor, but his personal character is unmistakably denigrated. Several different attacks have been made upon Alexios's character. In fighting by deception instead of forthright attacks he does not display Roman honesty or Roman courage but rather mendaciousness and cowardice. In fighting with skirmishing, false retreats and ambushes Alexios's generalship and fighting style also matches that of the Turks, further alienating him from

[44] 3.22.8–10.

Roman military traditions.[45] In fighting like a Turk, Alexios's behavior is aligned with that of the Empire's enemies. Alexios is unflinchingly ruthless and willing to slaughter unarmed people to maintain the emperor's grip on power.[46] He is beholden to his mother in a way that marks him as immature and lacking in true masculinity.[47] In his first military foray Alexios's behavior was destructive and foolish.[48] Any one of these strands of criticism could be dismissed as incidental, but together they reinforce each other and make it difficult to escape the conclusion that overall Nikephoros held a negative view of Alexios's character. Nikephoros appears to have worked to create a portrait of Alexios that denigrates his character as not properly masculine in a classical Roman sense. Alexios may have been very successful, but he was not a virtuous man.

Nikephoros's history is a tragedy. Tragic in that the Roman Empire was dismembered and defeated at the hands of foreign enemies. Tragic in that the Roman generals were consumed with fighting each other while the Empire was being conquered. Tragic in that good men lost despite fighting bravely. Tragic in that Providence determined winners and losers without regard for merit. Perhaps most of all, tragic in that the wrong man became emperor. The criticisms of Alexios outlined in this chapter work in conjunction with the lionization of Bryennios the Elder to make a strong case that Bryennios would have been the better emperor. The political implications of writing such a history will be explored in section three.

---

[45] See above pp. 94–103.    [46] See above pp. 167–69.
[47] See above pp. 154–58.    [48] See above pp. 162–64.

# PART III

# *The* Material for History *in twelfth-century politics and culture*

# CHAPTER 14

# *The* Material for History *and imperial politics of the twelfth century*

Whatever section of the imperial palace Nikephoros found himself in, it was not a proverbial ivory tower of impractical and apolitical academic disengagement. Nikephoros did not compose history out of antiquarian interest. Rather, his work participated in the politics of his era. It is time to ask why Nikephoros would wish to create a history containing the valuations revealed in the previous section and explore what political purposes the history may have served. If the argument that the history sustains a critique of Alexios Komnenos is accepted, then the political context of composition was not straightforward. In criticizing the founder of the reigning dynasty, Nikephoros was undertaking political action through writing history. The nature and intentions of his political action deserve study.

Working out the precise political meanings of the text is complex because we lack firm information about the dating of the moment of composition. In the first chapter of the present book it was argued that the time of composition would be either early, before Alexios's death in 1118, with a highly political meaning, or later, well into the reign of John but before Nikephoros's death in 1137, with a less politically actionable meaning.

The history allows for a politically charged reading. If the text were composed toward the end of Alexios's life, it would be difficult to escape the conclusion that it was written with the intention of gaining support for Nikephoros's bid to succeed Alexios instead of the latter's son John. The lionization of Bryennios the Elder would then be seen as making a case for Nikephoros's succession and the disparaging portrayal of Alexios would call for another line to accede to power. There is no incontrovertible evidence against this dating and it remains a live possibility. On balance, however, it seems less likely than a later dating for reasons that will be explored in detail below.

Writing a critique of the reigning emperor's father could have been a dangerous undertaking, but we need to assess the degree of danger and for whom. Would the author be in jeopardy of suffering from imperial wrath, or would the emperor be in jeopardy of being ousted? It is possible to imagine situations in which the history could engender dire consequences for either John or Nikephoros. One of our few points of certainty regarding the politics of this era however, is that both John and Nikephoros died of natural causes and on reasonably good terms. So to support a dating after Alexios's death, we need to reconstruct a situation in which the critique would have been sufficiently innocuous not to seriously threaten John.

The criticism of Alexios in Nikephoros's history probably should not be regarded as esoteric or covert. If we were to imagine that only a few people at court read or heard the classical Roman histories from which Nikephoros derived his cultural memory of Roman honor, then it would be possible to say that the resulting portrait of Alexios could be seen as bitingly critical by some observers and benign by others, depending on the cultural training and stance of the observers. Only those in Nikephoros's audience who had read enough classical history to have ingested the ancient Roman system of honor could count Alexios's behavior as less honorable than that of Nikephoros Bryennios according to the criteria of Roman military culture. While education levels are notoriously difficult to gauge,[1] it seems highly unlikely that classical Roman history would have been so unfamiliar to people in the Constantinopolitan court of the twelfth century for this strand of criticism to have been hidden in any significant way. Certainly by the middle of the twelfth century the court was extremely well versed in stories from Plutarch and there is significant evidence for increasing interest in Roman history in the eleventh century.[2]

Also, while it is true that some aspects of the critique rely on cultural memories of classical Roman honor, others do not. The strand of criticism that aligns Alexios's behavior with that of the Turks does not depend on classical education. That the criticism of Alexios as a "momma's boy" can be fairly accurately described using twentieth-century American slang speaks to its lack of dependence on one particular cultural context. So even if there were members of the court who had not heard stories of Rome's glory days, which is unlikely, they still are likely to have perceived Nikephoros's history as denigrating Alexios. Finally, gossip can be counted on to have taken the messages to any at the court who had missed them. Therefore

---

[1] Margaret Mullett, "No Drama, No Poetry, No Fiction, No Readership, No Literature," in *A Companion to Byzantium*, ed. Liz James (Oxford: Wiley-Blackwell, 2010), 233–38.

[2] Cresci, "Exempla storici greci," 114–45; Magdalino, "Aspects of Twelfth-Century Byzantine Kaiserkritik," 342–44; Athanasios Markopoulos, "Roman Antiquarianism," 277–97.

we need to reject any scenario that would require John to have remained unaware that Nikephoros's history criticized his father's character.

Yet, while not genuinely esoteric, the denigration of Alexios does remain veiled. At every point the history is ostensibly laudatory. The future emperor is never insulted or degraded in any overt patent statement in the history. This veiling seems to function to render the criticism polite. An open insult to the imperial family presumably would have called for a response, but a negative undertone in an ostensibly laudatory text could be politely ignored. While the history is not cryptic enough to expect the negativity to remain unperceived, by maintaining a positive ostensible meaning, it gave the audience members the option of pretending they did not understand.

The veiling made the criticism of Alexios polite, but not weak. Such figured speech should not be considered as lacking in power. Veiled criticism can be more powerful as well as more tactful than plain speech. Beyond any need for safety, ancient and medieval authors could appreciate the "greater persuasiveness of oblique suggestion."[3] Nikephoros may have chosen to write veiled criticism because such a discourse would provoke more thought and consideration on the part of his audience. A history that engaged the audience in thinking through historical possibilities and variations in character could be expected to have more immediate impact on contemporaneous thought than a patent diatribe. In societies where the overt meaning of court rhetoric is understood by all to conform to the wishes of the emperor, truth is presumed to lie in the covert meaning.

Apparently John Komnenos enjoyed a stable reign with little political unrest once he had taken control.[4] He appears to have ruled well in general and continued to build on the military successes of his father. John presided over a period of continued economic growth and recovery of Roman imperial prestige.[5] If any emperor could tolerate insults with benign indifference, it would be John. The very strength of his position would allow him to tolerate criticism without flinching. The critique of Nikephoros's history also fell upon his father, leaving open the possibility that none of Alexios's character flaws passed on to his son.

Nikephoros's rhetorical strategies also shift over the course of the history and the early books are far less biting in their criticism. The audience

---

[3] Ahl, "Safe Criticism," 185.
[4] Paul Magdalino, "The Empire of the Komnenoi (1118–1204)," in *The Cambridge History of the Byzantine Empire c.500–1492*, ed. Jonathan Shepard (Cambridge University Press, 2008), 629–35.
[5] Angeliki Laiou, "The Byzantine Economy: An Overview," in *The Economic History of Byzantium From the Seventh through the Fifteenth Century*, ed. Angeliki Laiou (Washington, DC: Dumbarton Oaks, 2002), 1150–56.

response to the presentation of the first books may have prompted or allowed for the increasing criticism of Alexios in later books. When the mild irony of the initial presentation did not cause too much trouble, Nikephoros may have felt more free to portray Alexios as ruthless, devious, and un-Roman. In this reading, the later chapters of the book were more critical because the first sections were not badly received.

Significantly, the denigration of Alexios's character, as a man, does not lead inexorably to an argument that he would have been a bad emperor. Nikephoros's history ends before Alexios takes power and we do not see how Nikephoros portrays either the coup with its attendant pillaging or Alexios's actions as emperor. The case made for Bryennios the Elder's rule rests on character. Bryennios is depicted as an ideal Roman general, steady, mature, honest, successful and pious. Alexios is young, dishonest, and ruthless. Alexios is willing and able to fight like a Turk. These contrasting character assessments allow the reader to know which man Nikephoros admired, but they do not need to form an absolute case against Alexios's ability to be an effective emperor.

While Nikephoros's text ultimately should be read as critical of Alexios, Nikephoros also leaves room for one to argue that Alexios was the right person to be emperor because the empire needed a devious and ruthless man at the helm. One could reasonably argue, on the basis of stories provided by Nikephoros, that what was needed in an emperor was an absolutely determined, wily man who would stop at nothing to win. Both ruthlessness and deviousness can have positive valuations when it comes to picking a politician or a general. Never does Nikephoros imply that Alexios was unsuccessful. Alexios is shown as highly capable in the execution of military deceptions. Although Nikephoros's history argues forcefully for honorable conduct as the path to true heroism, it is very likely that at least some people at court would have taken the side that a crafty, ambitious, young man was precisely what the empire needed. The viability of that response to the history is part of the reason why the critique of Alexios was not fundamentally dangerous to John. One can easily make the case that winning in any way is better than losing well, and some courtiers could be counted on to have prized victory over proper action.

Nikephoros's history makes a strong and sustained case for the legitimacy of the Komnenian dynasty. While Alexios's character may be denigrated and that of Bryennios the Elder exalted, no attack is made on John's right to be emperor by dynastic succession. Chapter 6 detailed the dynastic argument that runs throughout the history by which logic John was the rightful ruler of the empire by inheritance. This argument relies on proximity to the ruler and ruling family as a criterion for imperial rule. The existence of this argument for Komnenian legitimacy may have helped the critical portrait of Alexios be less politically threatening. John's status is not disputed. If the history were written before Alexios's death with the purpose of gathering support for Nikephoros's succession, one would expect less attention to the dynastic claims of the Komnenoi. The presentation of John and Isaac as having been adopted into the household of Basil II, one of the empire's most successful generals, represents an attempt to bolster the legitimacy of the Komnenian dynasty. The story of the boys' youthful training again is not necessary for the narrative. A history aiming at overthrowing their dynasty could have skipped this stage of the story, or presented the boys as growing up in the monastery.

The argument for Komnenian dynastic legitimacy may indicate that Nikephoros was not arguing for a revolution, at least at the time he was writing. In that the text may be read as saying that Alexios was of poor character but perhaps necessary, then we need not envision it as a call to arms to oppose Alexios's son. Rather the history can be an elegy lamenting the sad state of the world which needed such men to rule. Nikephoros did not like Alexios and roundly criticized his lack of Romanness, his honor, and his masculinity. Nikephoros however was writing a tragedy in which the good guys did not win. Such a lachrymose history is compatible with supporting the Komnenos dynasty. In this reading we can imagine the history soothing the emotional disappointments of Nikephoros and others sidelined by Komnenian success, without it being much of any threat to John's rule. The reading that Nikephoros did not write this text to rouse people against Alexios and John but rather to reconcile courtiers to the reality that a ruthless politician, like Alexios Komnenos, was exactly the right person for the job, would fit well with a later time of composition.

While the critique of Alexios Komnenos may be the most novel conclusion of the current reading of the text, it should not overshadow the lionization of Bryennios the Elder and John Doukas in the evaluation of the political messages of Nikephoros's history. One set of clear meanings in Nikephoros's history is that John Doukas and Nikephoros Bryennios the Elder were heroes and great men regardless of the misfortunes that beset the empire under their care. The incorporation of significant amounts of material from a history or memoir highly favorable to John Doukas was deliberate and functions, along with the positive description of Bryennios, to laud the families that had lost supreme power with Alexios Komnenos's victory. The Doukas family was vital in the success of Alexios's coup, but Alexios's creation of a new system of titles excluded them from the highest ranks of the new aristocracy.[6] The Doukas family was not granted new lands in the west to replace the territories they had lost in the east. Alexios did reward some supporters who owed more direct loyalty to him, such as Gregory Pakourianos, with grants of western territory from which to maintain noble status.[7] Descendants of the Doukas family at court in the early twelfth century may have had cause to resent their dependence on the goodwill of the man they helped into power. The positive depiction of their imperial ancestors in Nikephoros's history would have stoked their sense of honor. The Bryennioi maintained control over their properties, which were restored after the blinding of Bryennios the Elder in 1078. At the time of the rebellion of a pseudo-Diogenes in 1095, Bryennios still held the command of the defenses of Adrianople.[8] While the Bryennioi maintained a source of wealth and prestige, they certainly had reason to be disappointed in the failure of their bid for imperial power and the success of the man who handed Bryennios the Elder over for blinding.

The exaltation of the memory of John Doukas and Nikephoros Bryennios the Elder therefore is as deeply significant as the denigration of Alexios's character in assessing the political meanings of Nikephoros's history. The noble families of the eleventh century are exalted at the expense of the family that pushed them to the sidelines in the twelfth century. The reality of their marginalization would have been evident by the end of Alexios's reign, but resentments would have lasted at least until Nikephoros's generation had faded. A history which glorified the honor of their ancestors and absolved them of their political and military failures would have been welcome during the reign of Alexios, but would still be valued later and so would also fit with a later time of composition.

Together these considerations led me to see the composition as unfolding over time during the later years of Nikephoros's life in the 1120s and 1130s. The history may have been started early in John's reign and written over a long period of time. This interpretation of the dating aligns with Anna Komnene's description of Nikephoros as continuing to work on his history during the last years of his life. A late composition point also carries a built-in explanation for why the text was never finished in that Nikephoros would have been working on the text when he died.

---

[6] Cheynet, *Pouvoir*, 359–77, 413–16; Magdalino, *Manuel*, 180–209; Frankopan, "Kinship and the Distribution of Power," 3–6.

[7] Gregory Pakourianos, "Typikon of Gregory Pakourianos for the Monastery of the Mother of God Petritzonitissa in Bačkovo," in *Byzantine Monastic Foundation Documents: A Complete Translation of the Surviving Founders' Typika and Testaments*, ed. John Thomas and Angela Constantinides Hero (Washington, DC: Dumbarton Oaks), 507, 24–27; Lemerle, *Cinq études*, 168–86.

[8] 10.3.6; Skoulatos, *Les personnages*, 223.

If the above arguments regarding the political circumstances and dating of the text are accepted, we can with greater confidence explore how this reading of Nikephoros's history affects our understanding of Nikephoros's attempted usurpation upon the death of Alexios. The following assessment is necessarily speculative, but the suppositions are grounded in the foregoing analysis of his history. Given the lionization of his own grandfather and the distaste expressed for Alexios Komnenos in the history he wrote later in life, it appears clear to me that Nikephoros had wanted to become emperor. It also seems likely that he was supported in this ambition by some portion of the imperial court, particularly those other descendants of the Doukai, the Bryennioi, and other grand houses of the eleventh century who found themselves sidelined at the end of Alexios's life. The movement may have been heavily supported by Irene and Anna, but Nikephoros cannot be supposed to have been a passive partner.

For the details and sequence of events during the attempted usurpation we remain dependent on the feeble light shown by Zonaras and Choniates. Significantly, we should remain open to the possibility that Zonaras and Choniates told stories about Nikephoros contesting the accession of John *because* they had read Nikephoros's history and seen how he despised Alexios. As observed in chapter 1, Zonaras and Choniates focus attention on the actions of Irene and Anna as a means of disparaging the passivity of Alexios and Nikephoros. Yet the crux of both stories is that some people wished to have Nikephoros succeed Alexios. One firm result of the present study is that Nikephoros must be seen as an active supporter, and indeed advocate, of his own bid for power.

When Nikephoros's efforts to accede to the throne failed, however, he did not continue the pursuit to the point of murder. Readers of medieval history may become inured to the horrors of ruthless political ambition that led Irene to blind her son Constantine VI, Romanos Lakapenos to castrate his son Basil, John Tzimiskes to murder his uncle Nikephoros, and Andronikos I Komnenos to murder his nephew, to name but a few examples. It is in light of the emotional distance of armchair antiquarianism, if not orientalist delight in the prurience of history, that Nikephoros becomes portrayed as a passive weakling for failing to murder his brother-in-law. Nikephoros was denigrated by Choniates for lacking the backbone needed to follow through with his revolt in 1118. The plan described by Choniates would have required Nikephoros to take his hand to his brother-in-law and either blind or kill him. Without doubt any number of politicians in east Roman history would have done the deed in a heartbeat and then built a church in penance. By portraying Alexios as willing to do anything in the pursuit of victory, Nikephoros implicitly places Alexios in the category of men who, had they been in Nikephoros's shoes, would have killed John and become emperor. Perhaps the most biting bit of the history for John Komnenos may have been the realization that his own father had none of the restraint and graciousness from which he had benefited.

Nikephoros's rehabilitation at court and the freedom with which he criticized his emperor's father is grounded in the experience he and John had when Nikephoros laid down his attempt at power. John could be gracious and forgiving to Nikephoros because John knew that Nikephoros had chosen not to attempt to kill him. John knew that he had nothing to fear from a man for whom the imperial office was not worth murder. This reading of Nikephoros's relationship with John holds regardless of whether Nikephoros dropped the dagger at the last moment (as Choniates would have it) or acquiesced more immediately to John's authority. Had Nikephoros himself been entirely ruthless and wily, like Alexios, he might have been emperor; hence his history valorizes resignation and honor. Nikephoros struggled and lost, but he lost with honor, like the great heroes of his history. Nikephoros may have presented Alexios as less than perfectly honorable in order to congratulate himself on not being the sort of person who would become emperor. If emperors needed cut-throat ambition, then perhaps a gentleman should not aspire to the job.

Here is the key emotional logic behind the valorization of the heroic losers of good character throughout Nikephoros' history: Nikephoros chose to value proper character and stoicism in the face of defeat over success at any cost. Whatever his views as a young man, after the failure of his bid for power, Nikephoros prized good conduct. This stance would have given Nikephoros a share of victory regardless of his political fortunes. He may not have ruled, but he was a good man. In retelling the history of his grandfather he told a story of a man who similarly struggled well and lost with honor. Nikephoros's history stood as testimony to the effort and struggle to maintain nobility of character.

The function of Providence in Nikephoros's history becomes clear when the emotional background of painfully thwarted political ambition is brought to the fore. As was explored in chapter 10, Nikephoros depicts Providence as the ultimate explanation for why the good men do not succeed. If Nikephoros accepted that he was deprived of rule through the workings of fortune, then we can imagine the allure that stories of the other men opposed by Providence had for him. Providence allowed Romanos to be defeated at Manzikert. John Doukas and Bryennios both would have been far better emperors than Michael VII and Botaneiates, but were never able to become emperors. Like them, Nikephoros had the skills to be a good emperor and like them he was denied the opportunity by Providence. They are tragic heroes in that they behave well in situations in which they cannot possibly prevail. Theirs was a good fight even if they lost.

Telling their stories with such sympathy and humanity was probably highly cathartic for Nikephoros as he adjusted to the reality that he would never be emperor. Fortune is a wonderfully useful excuse for the unsuccessful. It robs the successful of merit or sense of deservedness for their achievements and absolves the unsuccessful of any personal responsibility for their failures. Nikephoros's words about the uselessness of human valor and military excellence in the face of divine will are emotionally consistent with honoring his grandfather as the better man who nonetheless did not win the Empire. If it were a matter of divine will for Botaneiates and Komnenos to become emperors, then Bryennios's loss cannot be attributed to his human failings. If John Komnenos had the divine mandate to rule, then the best that Nikephoros could do would be to serve him, regardless of which of them would have had the better character and would seem to make the better emperor. Nikephoros's engagement with Providence may be bad theology, but it makes perfect emotional sense if we understand Nikephoros as reconciling himself to the reality of his political loss.

If we see Nikephoros as a man frustrated in his political ambitions because of his own moral stance, then we can see the history as deeply engaged in court politics, critical, and yet open. In processing the reality of the failure of his political ambitions Nikephoros embraced a value system that placed emphasis on moral character and proper conduct in the face of adversity. Stories of Roman heroism in the face of defeat thus had a strong emotional resonance. Nikephoros's emphasis on proper manhood and virtue reinforced the choices he made as an adult. If proper conduct, including self-restraint and magnanimity, is given primacy, then Nikephoros's own conduct was commendable. Ruthless pursuit of gain and austere ambition are not virtues for a man who chose political quiescence. In denigrating Alexios for excessive ruthlessness, Nikephoros upheld his own conduct of acceptance of political loss.

CHAPTER 15

# Nikephoros and Anna

Nikephoros did not have the last word on the history of Alexios Komnenos. His wife, Anna Komnene, also took up writing and the task of completing the history of Alexios that Nikephoros had left unfinished at his death. Anna's *Alexiad* has rightly been hailed as a masterpiece of Greek literature. Anna's history is one of the most widely read medieval Greek histories.[1] Twentieth-century interests in women and religious warfare have attracted attention to Anna both as a female author and as an eye-witness to the first crusade. Her descriptions of the crusaders are commonly excerpted in textbooks and medieval source compilations, where she stands as a representative voice of Byzantium.

Anna turned to the work of completing her husband's history several years after his death, in a markedly different political context. Writing between 1143 and 1153, Anna was responding, not to the eclipse of the eleventh-century aristocracy, but to the politics of the reign of Manuel (1140–1183) and the second crusade. Anna's history contains veiled criticism, like her husband's, but in her case it is directed against the policies of her nephew Manuel Komnenos.[2] Anna defends Alexios's political choices against what must have been mid twelfth-century criticism of him.[3] Anna's depiction of Alexios exalts him in ways that seem to respond to the trends in imperial panegyrics of the 1130s and 1140s.[4] In addition to defending Alexios in the face of mid twelfth-century critiques and responding to the policies of Manuel, Anna's history responds to the negative portrayal of Alexios crafted by Nikephoros. One conclusion from the present study is that Anna was writing at least in part to counter the image of Alexios in the

---

[1] The Penguin English translation of the *Alexiad* ranked 142,103 in Amazon book sales on October 14, 2010, compared with 428,536 for Michael Psellos's *Chronographia*.
[2] R. D. Thomas, "Anna Comnena's Account of the First Crusade: History and Politics in the Reigns of the Emperors Alexius I and Manuel I Comnenus," *Byzantine and Modern Greek Studies* 15 (1991): 269–312; Stephenson, "Anna Comnena's *Alexiad* as a Source for the Second Crusade?," *Journal of Medieval History* 29, 1 (2003): 41–54.
[3] Magdalino, "The Pen of the Aunt," 25–34.   [4] Magdalino, "The Pen of the Aunt," 23–24.

182

work of her husband. Anna responds to Nikephoros's history not just in a general sense by creating a positive depiction of Alexios, but by arguing against some of the cultural and moral predispositions used by Nikephoros.

Thus far substantive discussion of the relationship between Anna's *Alexiad* and Nikephoros's *Material for History* has centered on assessing the extent to which Anna re-worked Nikephoros's notes rather than creating an original composition. The idea has been presented that Nikephoros's notes provided much of the text of the *Alexiad,* and that Anna should be credited more with editing than writing.[5] This suggestion has not met with acceptance.[6] The present detailed reading of Nikephoros's history contributes arguments in favor of Anna's authorship of the *Alexiad* by suggesting a new understanding of Nikephoros's military descriptions and highlighting some systematic differences in rhetorical strategies employed in the two histories. The study of Nikephoros's history makes it yet more clear that, although Anna and Nikephoros probably had access to many of the same sources, they constructed histories with different purposes, arguments, and styles. Anna's history is not so much a continuation of her husband's as a rebuttal.

One of the central arguments for the theory that Anna edited a history already largely written by her husband is that Anna, as a woman, would not have had access to information about the military campaigns that figure so largely in her narrative.[7] Here the military campaigns described in Nikephoros's history have been discussed in terms of their literary construction and their modeling on classical examples and ethical systems. Nikephoros's descriptions of military action create satisfying historical narratives and speak truth about men's character. Given the moral patterns found in Nikephoros's battle scenes, the possible value of these descriptions for establishing the actual course of the military engagements seems slight. Only rudimentary information about the course of a military engagement was needed to form the background for highly crafted literary constructions that say more about men's virtue than the precise disposition of forces on the field. Undoubtedly Nikephoros knew more than Anna about what

[5] James Howard-Johnston, "Anna Komnene and the Alexiad," in *Alexios I Komnenos*, ed. Margaret Mullett and Dion Smythe (Belfast Byzantine Enterprises, 1996), 232–302.
[6] Ruth Macrides, "The Pen and the Sword: Who wrote the Alexiad?," in *Anna Komnene and her Times*, ed. Thalia Gouma-Peterson (New York: Garland Publishing, 2000), 63–81. Diether Reinsch, "Women's Literature in Byzantium? The Case of Anna Komnene," in *Anna Komnene and her Times*, ed. Thalia Gouma-Peterson (New York: Garland Publishing, 2000), 98–101; Barbara Hill, "Actions Speak Louder than Words: Anna Komnene's Attempted Usurpation," 48–49; Stanković, "Nikephoros Bryennios, Anna Komnene and Konstantios Doukas," 172–74.
[7] Howard-Johnston, "Anna Komnene and the Alexiad," 273–74.

it was like to be in an actual battle, but when he came to write about
them he used tropes from other historical descriptions of battles.[8] The
real sources for Nikephoros's descriptions of military events were textual
rather than field experience. Nikephoros learned how to fight by fighting,
but he learned to write about military engagements by reading. Anna had
equal access to the same models of historiography. The discursive world
of ancient Greek and Roman warfare lived in texts which both men and
women were able to read. Anna's lack of military field experience therefore
would not necessitate that she rely on descriptions of battles and sieges that
had already been written by Nikephoros.

Anna does not continue Nikephoros's story from the moment his history
ends, but rather creates her own narrative about Alexios's youth and early
campaigns. The portion of Anna's story that overlaps with Nikephoros's
shows that Anna used Nikephoros's history, but made significant changes
to his presentation of the material. The choices Anna makes about how to
talk about Alexios in this early section of her history are consistent with
her characterization of him throughout the text.

In comparison to Nikephoros's story, Anna's narrative plays up the
unique virtues of Alexios and enhances his personal agency. When
Nikephoros wishes to emphasize Alexios's extreme youth at the time of
his first military campaign, he likens Alexios to Scipio who campaigned
with his father Aemilius Paulus at an early age:

Alexios then appeared as the great hope of the Romans, later becoming the great
help to the Romans, not yet wearing a full-blooming beard, but displaying military
virtues even before the age at which the Roman historians say Scipio accompanied
Aemilius while campaigning against Perseus of Macedonia.[9]

Anna omitted the story about Alexios's first campaign, which did not go
well.[10] She did, however, preserve the idea of saying Alexios had a young
beard and the Roman comparison. She uses these ideas in her description
of Alexios's first commission as a military commander:

Despite his youth – he had only recently shown evidence of the proverbial "first
beard" – he was even then considered by Roman experts to have attained the
summit of the general's art, through devotion to sheer hard work and constant
vigilance; to them he was another Aemilius, the famous Roman, or a new Scipio,
or a second Carthaginian Hannibal.[11]

---

[8] On the gulf between battle experience and battle descriptions see Woodman, *Rhetoric*, 15–32.
[9] 2.3.14–19.    [10] See pp. 162–64.
[11] Komnene 1.1.3; *Anna Komnene: The Alexiad*, revised translation and notes by Peter Frankopan, (New
York: Penguin, 2009), 10.

Both passages mention some of the same Roman heroes, but to different purposes. Nikephoros's historical allusion serves only to emphasize Alexios's youth, not to say he was as good a general as Aemilius Paulus or his son, let alone Hannibal. Anna's point is precisely that Alexios was as good a general as the famous old Romans. Anna includes Hannibal in the list of generals, perhaps because he was Scipio's most famous adversary. Anna's version replaces Nikephoros's statement that Alexios had a young beard with a Homeric quote to the same effect.[12]

In reading Nikephoros's encomiastic passage, Anna increased the praise of Alexios, added to the literary texture through Homeric quotation, and preserved a more generic version of the allusion to Roman history. Anna changed the context for the placement of the allusion in her history because in Nikephoros's history it opens a narrative sequence that does not reflect well on Alexios. This section of Nikephoros's history juxtaposes hyperbolic praise with Alexios's almost comic ineptitude, as Alexios leads ten out of fifteen men to their death, is abandoned by his remaining forces, escapes alone on a mule, and gets a nosebleed climbing a hill. These are all stories that Anna chose not to include in her version of Alexios's youth. She similarly leaves out the story about the escape of Isaac and Alexios from their kinsman's house at Dekte.

Anna places the comparison between Alexios and the great old generals at the start of her version of Alexios's campaign against Roussel. In this narrative she follows Nikephoros's text, telling the same stories of Alexios's persuasion of Tutakh, the speech made to the riotous citizens at Amaseia, the mock blinding of Roussel and the revelation of the trick to Alexios's cousin Dokeianos.[13] Anna presents versions of the conversations and speeches that are similar in argumentation and sometimes even wording, but she omitted the depiction of Alexios's skirmishing campaign against Roussel's fortresses in which Alexios repeatedly ambushed Roussel's forces while they were foraging. Howard-Johnston laments Anna's choice to cut down on the military details recorded in Nikephoros's version of the story. In response, Reinsch praises Anna for those same decisions maintaining that "she condensed the episode to its essential elements" and that "the military details contribute nothing to the narrative flow and the compelling nature of the episode."[14] In my reading, the military details of Nikephoros's version contribute to a larger sustained argument about Alexios's character, as displayed in his military style. A rejection of that characterization, as

---

[12] Hom. *Il.* 24.348.  [13] Komnene 1.2–1.3; trans. Frankopan, 10–15.
[14] Howard-Johnston, "Anna Komnene and the Alexiad," 284–86; Reinsch, "Women's Literature in Byzantium?," 99–100.

well as considerations of style and length, may have affected Anna's choices in streamlining the narrative.

Anna also omitted the narrative about Michael VII's abdication in which Alexios argued in favor of sending the imperial guards to attack the rioting citizens. She also created a markedly different portrayal of Konstantios Doukas. Where Nikephoros presents Konstantios as a passive and meek foil for Alexios, Anna depicts Konstantios as one of Alexios's aggressive young officers.[15] Anna's version also treats Michael's son Constantine, her betrothed, as a legitimate heir, whereas in Nikephoros's narrative Michael's brother Konstantios is presented as his only possible heir.[16]

Anna magnifies the task set to Alexios in bringing down Bryennios's rebellion by drawing a stirring portrait of Bryennios's aptitude for imperial rule.[17] She follows Nikephoros in depicting Alexios as having drastically inferior forces and deciding to fight indirectly: "Thus Alexios gave up the idea of a bold, open attack and planned a victory by stealth."[18] Anna overtly contrasts Bryennios's military strength with Alexios's cleverness in a clear effort to present these as two equally meritorious modes of fighting.[19] She claims that neither man had an advantage over the other in either experience or bravery, in contrast to Nikephoros's depiction of the mismatch in at least experience.[20] Anna's narrative of the battle follows that of Nikephoros fairly closely, including the descriptions of all the various tricks and stratagems Alexios tried, yet as we shall see she imbues it with a different moral meaning.

In Nikephoros's narrative of the battle, the key to Alexios's victory was the unexpected arrival of a contingent of Turks sent by Botaneiates, who in essence go on to win the battle for him. Here Anna and Nikephoros's stories diverge. Nikephoros has the Turkish officers plan out their attack once they have decided to help Alexios.[21] In her version Anna gives Alexios credit for the plan for the second half of the battle: "Alexios, my father, was responsible for the whole idea."[22] Once this phase of the battle started she reiterates "My father Alexios, who had devised the plan, followed . . ."[23] This contrast points out just how little agency is given to Alexios in Nikephoros's version. Nikephoros attributes both the plan and its successful execution to the Turks. Anna's insistence that the battle plan was her father's own idea appears far less gratuitously doting when read

---

[15] Stanković, "Nikephoros Bryennios, Anna Komnene and Konstantios Doukas," 169–75.
[16] Stanković, "Nikephoros Bryennios, Anna Komnene and Konstantios Doukas," 169–75.
[17] Komnene I.4.3.    [18] Komnene I.4.5.    [19] Komnene I.5.1.
[20] Komnene I.5.1, Nikephoros 4.5.    [21] Nikephoros 4.10.
[22] Komnene I.6.2.    [23] Komnene I.6.3.

against Bryennios's presentation in which Alexios is a nodding bystander while the Turkish chieftains plan their attack.

Anna slightly shortens the description of Bryennios's heroic last stand but adds a paragraph after Bryennios's capture maintaining that Alexios had nothing to do with Bryennios's blinding, a point she repeats later.[24] She then adds a scene in which Alexios invited Bryennios to rest alone with him during the journey back to Constantinople. Alexios fell asleep on the grass unguarded, leaving his sword in Bryennios's reach. When Bryennios thought to kill Alexios, a "divine power from above" calmed him and protected Alexios "like some precious object for a greater destiny."[25] This scene helps Anna establish Alexios as God's chosen ruler and instrument, which becomes one of her key arguments through the course of the *Alexiad*.[26] The scene also contrasts strongly with Nikephoros's depiction of the meeting between Bryennios and Alexios which provides an opportunity for Nikephoros to discourse upon Bryennios's greatness.[27] Nikephoros also invokes Providence, but to the different effect that Alexios would never have been able to win without it.

In the following story about Alexios's defeat of Basilakes's revolt, Anna diverts from Nikephoros's narrative to give a lengthy description of Basilakes's strengths and how his striking physical appearance led people to think he would be a good emperor.[28] She says Alexios prepared to fight Basilakes as "if for a contest against a huge Typhon or a hundred-handed Giant, summoning all his general's art and courageous spirit, he was ready to fight a worthy opponent."[29] The aggrandizement of Basilakes serves to magnify Alexios's skill in taking him down. In the description of the campaign Anna rejoins Nikephoros's narrative and tells the story of the night attack with relish. Anna's version has a clearer narrative thread that side-steps the question of how Alexios knew that Basilakes was going to attack at night by attributing it to a guess.[30] Anna retells the details of the battle exploits following Nikephoros. At the close of the story about Basilakes's revolt, Anna departs from the remainder of Nikephoros's text to tell the story of Robert Guiscard's invasion.

[24] Komnene 1.6.7; 1.6.9.  [25] Komnene 1.6.8.
[26] On Alexios as a religious figure see P. Buckley, "War and Peace in the Alexiad," in *Byzantine Narrative*, ed. J. Burke (Melbourne: 2006), 92–109.
[27] 4.15.  [28] Komnene 1.7.2.
[29] 1.7.3: ὁ δέ γε ἐμὸς πατὴρ ὁ Κομνηνὸς Ἀλέξιος ὡς πρὸς Τυφῶνα μέγαν ἢ ἑκατοντάχειρα Γίγαντα ἀντιπαραταξάμενος καὶ πᾶσαν ἑαυτῷ ἀνεγείρας στρατηγικὴν μηχανὴν καὶ φρόνημα γενναῖον ὡς πρὸς ἀντίπαλον παρεσκεύαστο.
[30] Komnene 1.7.5. See the discussion of Nikephoros's version in chapter 8, p. 101.

Anna's story about her father's youthful campaigns also differs markedly from her husband's in frequently appealing to ancient Greek cultural imagery. Throughout these narratives Anna weaves in references to classical Greek mythology and archaic history. Her one reference to Roman history is the comparison between Alexios and great Roman generals discussed above, which is a modified version of Nikephoros's Roman allusion. Elsewhere many of the divergences from Nikephoros's text are inclusions of Homeric imagery. Bryennios is "like some Ares or a Giant."[31] Basilakes was like a Typhon. Anna quotes Aristophanes to mock Basilakes fumbling in the dark while searching Alexios's tent.[32] In the course of the night battle a sword shattered "like Menelaus's when he fought Alexander" in the *Iliad*.[33] Another combatant had "Ares's spirit."[34] The defeat of Basilakes was Alexios's third Herculean labor "for if you equated this Basilakios with the Erymanthian Boar, and my father Alexios with a modern and most noble Herakles, you would not go wrong."[35]

This brief comparison of Anna and Nikephoros's stories about Alexios's early campaigns reveals Anna as increasing Alexios's personal agency, appealing to archaic Greek, rather than Roman, cultural imagery, yet maintaining the presentation of Alexios as a trickster. These three traits are carried through the rest of her history. The focus of the narrative remains fixed on the deeds of Alexios, which are magnified as great at every possible turn. The *Alexiad* is a tightly focused biography of Alexios, with few other characters of interest. The classical allusions described above stand out clearly as having been added to Nikephoros's narrative structure. Such allusions, as well as a strongly Homeric vocabulary, are used throughout the *Alexiad* and serve to align Anna's history with cultural memories of archaic Greek heroism. The presentation of Alexios as a clever master of strategic deception is also part of his characterization thoughout the *Alexiad*. The Greek cultural imagery, however, works to change the fundamental meaning of that characterization in Anna's text.

Like Nikephoros, Anna depicts her father as a great strategist and master of the military ruse. Anna does not dispute Nikephoros's characterization of Alexios as a trickster but rather amplifies it into a central tenet of her history. Yet the moral assessment she gives to military tricks is entirely different as she strives to invert the negative valuation Nikephoros placed on military deception. In the *Alexiad*, Alexios is a man who wins by guile as often as he can, but that propensity for trickery is held up as virtuous

[31] Komnene 1.5.2.    [32] Komnene 1.8.2, Aristophanes *Clouds*, 192.
[33] Komnene 1.8.4, Homer *Il.* 3.361–63.    [34] Komnene 1.8.6.    [35] Komnene 1.9.6.

behavior. It has long been understood that Anna Komnene presents Alexios like Odysseus, buffeted by constant storms and scraping victories by tricks whenever possible.[36] In light of the current study it appears that Anna was speaking directly to Nikephoros's work when she crafted an Odyssean portrait of her father.

In order to undermine Nikephoros's denigration of military trickery as un-Roman, Anna appeals to a different set of available cultural memories to build a different cultural valuation of trickery. Anna's choice of archaic Greek cultural imagery is more than stylistic. In contrast to Roman military morality, the ancient Greek system placed a more even valuation on the dichotomy between Achillean straight-up fighting and Odyssean strategizing. For classical era Greeks the debate between bravery and brains was personified as a conflict between Achilles and Odysseus, between:

chivalrous, face-to-face confrontation, open battle, and use of force (Achilles ethos), as opposed to trickery, deceit, indirect means, and avoidance of pitched battle except in circumstances where the use of force is advantageous (Odysseus ethos).[37]

Anna plays on such a direct contrast between boldness and cleverness, creating an overt dichotomy between Bryennios's military might and Alexios's shrewdness that presents these as equally meritorious yet contrasting styles of fighting:

Certainly they were both handsome and brave, in skill and physical strength equally balanced as on a scale ... Bryennios, confident in his soldiers, relied on his own knowledge and the good discipline of his army, whereas on the other side Alexios had modest hopes, so far as his own forces were concerned, but in reply put his trust in the strength of his own ingenuity and in his art as a general.[38]

When Anna explicitly contrasts Bryennios's might with Alexios's wiliness, she was appealing to the morally neutral Greek dichotomy in opposition to the Roman denigration of trickery upheld by Nikephoros.

---

[36] Emily Albu, "Bohemond and the Rooster: Byzantines, Normans, and the Artful Ruse," in *Anne Komnene and Her Times*, ed. Thalia Gouma-Peterson (New York: Garland Publishing, 2000), 157–68; Macrides, "The Pen and the Sword," 68–70; Quandahl and Jarratt emphasize Anna's portrayal of Alexios as a rhetorician: Quandahl and Jarratt, "Rhetorical Historiographer," 326–27.

[37] Wheeler, "Battle: Land Battles," 188.

[38] 1.5.1: τὼ μὲν γὰρ ἄνδρε τούτω καὶ ἄμφω ἤστην καλὼ καὶ γενναίω καὶ τά γε εἰς χεῖρας καὶ πεῖραν ἴσοι ὥσπερ ἐπὶ τρυτάνης ἱστάμενοι· ὁρᾶν δὲ ἡμᾶς χρεών, ὅπου τὰ τῆς τύχης ἐπέβρισεν. ὁ μὲν γὰρ Βρυέννιος μετὰ τοῦ θαρρεῖν ταῖς δυνάμεσι καὶ τὴν πεῖραν προύβάλλετο καὶ τὴν εὐταξίαν τῆς παρατάξεως· ὁ δ᾽ Ἀλέξιος ἐκ τοῦ ἑτέρου ὀλίγας μὲν ἐλπίδας καὶ πάνυ ἀφελεῖς εἶχεν ὅσον ἐπὶ τῷ στρατεύματι, ἀντιπρούβάλλετο δὲ τὴν ἀπὸ τῆς τέχνης ἰσχὺν καὶ τὰς στρατηγικὰς μηχανάς.

In the Roman reading of Greek culture, the conflict is not between styles or modes of fighting, but between an honorable form of direct combat and cowardly indirect fighting. Odysseus became a villain.[39] Cultural memories of this Roman moral framework animate Nikephoros's history. Nikephoros's deployment of a Roman denigration of military trickery remains implicit in his alignment of great men with Roman modes of fighting and of Turks, Scythians, and Alexios with military deceit. To change this moral framework and recall memories of the older Greek valuation of both might and cleverness, Anna needed to make a strong case for the superiority of military deception. Her case for this position is made consistently throughout her history in congratulating Alexios for his successful deceptions. The constant barrage of allusions to Homeric and mythological heroes also functions to bring memories of ancient Greek constructions of heroism to the forefront of the audience's consciousness. All the Homeric allusions remind the audience that clever men like Odysseus, and Alexios, were also heroic.

In addition to congratulating Alexios on the success of his ruses, and weaving a strongly archaic Greek textual fabric, Anna offers an explicit argument in favor of the use of deception over straight-up fighting:

The general should not invariably seek victory, in my opinion, by drawing the sword; there are times when he should be prepared to use finesse, if the opportunity appears and events allow it, and so achieve a complete triumph. As we know full well, a general's supreme task is to win, not merely by force of arms, but also by relying on treaties, and there is another way – sometimes, in the right circumstances, an enemy can be defeated by fraud.[40]

Anna goes on to describe Alexios's efforts to sow discord among Bohemond's camp in the second Norman invasion by writing friendly letters to certain key supporters of Bohemond, in the hope that Bohemond would suspect them of attempted treachery. Anna's defense of fraudulent fighting can be seen as a direct response to those who would criticize Alexios as more ready to deceive than to fight. She returns to the theme in book 15 as her history nears its close:

---

[39] W. B. Stanford, *The Ulysses Theme* (Ann Arbor Paperbacks, 1968), 128–74; Piero Boitani, *The Shadow of Ulysses: Figures of a Myth* (Oxford: Clarendon Press, 1994).

[40] Komnene 13.4.3: δεῖ γάρ, οἶμαι, τὸν στρατηγὸν οὐκ ἀεὶ διὰ ξιφουλκίας τὴν νίκην ἑαυτῷ σπεύδειν περιποιεῖσθαι, ἀλλὰ καὶ πρὸς πανουργίαν ἔστιν οὗ εὐτρεπίζεσθαι, ἐπὰν ὁ καιρὸς καὶ τὰ συμπίπτοντα τοῦτο διδόασι, τὴν νίκην ἑαυτῷ πάντοσε περιποιούμενον. καὶ τοῦτο γὰρ στρατηγῶν ἰδιαίτατον, ὅσαπερ ἴσμεν, μὴ μετὰ ξιφῶν καὶ μάχης μόνον, ἀλλὰ καὶ πρὸς σπονδὰς τρεπομένων· καὶ ἄλλως ἔστιν οὗ ῥαδιουργοῦντα τὸν ἐχθρὸν καταγωνίζεσθαι, ὁπηνίκα καὶ τοιούτου καιρὸς παρῇ.

The prime virtue of a general is the ability to win a victory without incurring danger – as Homer says, it is by skill that one charioteer beats another. Even the famous Cadmean proverb censures a victory fraught with danger. As far as I am concerned, it has always seemed best to devise some crafty strategic maneuver in the course of battle, if one's own army cannot match the enemy's strength.[41]

From this argument based on an ancient proverb, Homer and logic, Anna turns to an appeal to historical precedents:

Anyone can find examples of this in the pages of history. There is no one method of achieving victory, nor one form of it, but from ancient times up to the present, success has been won in different ways. Victory always means the same thing, but the means by which generals attain it are varied and of intricate patterns. It appears that some of the renowned generals of old overcame their adversaries by sheer strength, whereas others prevailed on many occasions by making good use of some advantage of a different kind.[42]

Although she does not give any specific examples, Anna is concerned to show that fighting by craft is not only sensible but sanctioned by historical precedents.

Anna's Hellenizing history brought to the fore cultural memory of archaic Greek masculinity, in which men wept and fought each other any way they could.[43] By choosing to embed an archaic Greek valuation in her Homeric epic history, Anna may have responded far more directly to her husband's Roman history than we have appreciated. Her apology for Alexios has many aspects, but at least the line of argument valorizing Alexios's tricks and clever stratagems may be a response to the undertone of accusation in her husband's history. In valorizing the defeated, Nikephoros makes a strong case that, in terms of moral value, all victories are not the same. He would not agree with Anna that "victory always means the same

[41] Komnene 15.3.2: καὶ πρώτη ἐστὶν ἀρετῶν ἡ στρατηγῶν σοφία κτᾶσθαι νίκην ἀκίνδυνον· τέχνη δ' ἡνίοχος περιγίνεται ἡνιόχοιο, φησὶν Ὅμηρος. τὸ γὰρ μετὰ κινδύνου νικᾶν καὶ ἡ Καδμόθεν παροιμία διαφαυλίζει. ἐμοὶ δὲ ἄριστον νενόμισται καὶ τὸ ἐν αὐτῇ τῇ μάχῃ μηχανᾶσθαί τι πανοῦργον καὶ στρατηγικόν, ὁπηνίκα μὴ ἀπόχρη τὸ στράτευμα πρὸς τὴν τῶν ἐναντίων ἰσχύν·

[42] καθὼς ἐστιν ἐκ τῆς ἱστορίας ἀναλέγεσθαι τῷ βουλομένῳ, ὡς οὐκ ἄρα μονότροπος ἡ νίκη οὐδὲ μονοειδής, ἀλλὰ διαφόροις κόποις πάλαι μέχρι τοῦ δεῦρο κατορθουμένη, ὥστε τὴν μὲν νίκην μίαν εἶναι, τοὺς δὲ τρόπους, δι' ὧν αὕτη τοῖς στρατηγοῖς περιγίνεται, διαφόρους τε καὶ ποικίλους τὴν φύσιν. τινὲς γὰρ τῶν πάλαι ὑμνουμένων στρατηγῶν αὐτῇ ἰσχύϊ τῷδε τρόπῳ τοὺς ἐναντίους νικήσαντες φαίνονται· ἄλλῳ δὲ ἄλλοι πολλάκις χρησάμενοι τὴν νικῶσαν εἶχον.

[43] On Homeric heroes crying see Van Wees, "A Brief History of Tears," 10–53. Alexios's tears should also be examined in light of Byzantine theology of penance. See Symeon the New Theologian, *Discourse 4.* trans. C. J. de Catanzaro *Symeon the New Theologian: The Discourses* (Paulist Press, 1980), 70–89.

thing." That Anna must work so hard to make her case strongly indicates the power of Nikephoros's moralizing view of politics.

In her emphasis on ancient Greek cultural patterns, Anna may have been running against the common patterns of her society. Anna's argument that military trickery is valorous is overt and belabored. She argues strenuously to make the point that it is good for generals to try to win by fraud. This heavy-handed approach is perhaps gauged to argue against her husband's history, but also may have been necessary because his view was far more common. In appealing to cultural memories of classical Roman history Nikephoros was square in the center of Komnenian culture, as we understand it. His alignment of positive noble behavior with Roman straight-on agonistic combat and ignoble un-Roman behavior with military deception is implicit in the stories that he tells and requires the audience to share a cultural memory of classical Roman military values. Nikephoros's case could be implicit because his audience did in fact share a cultural memory of classical Roman military values. Anna needed to remind her audience openly that "victory always means the same thing" and that the job of the general is to "avoid danger" and if possible "win by fraud" because those beliefs were perhaps less commonly held by her contemporaries.

The Homeric appreciation of military deception is one of several ways that Anna aligned her *Alexiad* with Greek, rather than Roman, cultural norms. The *Alexiad* is commonly seen as part of a conscious re-engagement with "Hellenism" undertaken by late twelfth- and thirteenth-century intellectuals who had no self-doubt about their primary identity as Romans.[44] The intellectual resurgence of Hellenism of the later twelfth century needs to be seen in the context of a pervasive and influential identification with classical Roman culture, heritage, and morals. Roman self-identification was the fundamental bedrock of identity in the medieval Roman Empire. Self-perception as "Hellenes" was adopted by some members of the intellectual elite of the thirteenth century, in partial response to the conquest of the Empire in the fourth crusade. Once the Empire had fallen, some Romans began to look beyond their political allegiance to the Empire and started the process of constructing meaningful cultural memories of their ancient Greek ancestors, which supplemented predominant Roman identities.[45] Yet this Hellenism was at all times a limited phenomenon, and in the middle of the twelfth century, at one of the high points of Roman imperial power, this future process could not have been foreseen. Anna's

---

[44] Kaldellis, *Hellenism*, 225–316; Beaton, "Antique Nation?" 76–95.
[45] Kaldellis, *Hellenism*, 368–88; Hellenic identity plays a minor role in the complex medieval identities adduced by Page, *Being Byzantine*.

affinities for ancient Greek culture need not be seen as a forerunner of the later Hellenism, and in this light they are all the more unusual.

It is possible then that the portrait in the *Alexiad*, commonly taken by scholars as paradigmatic of Byzantine culture, was in fact consciously speaking against the grain of that culture. Anna's portrait of Alexios has had profound impact on scholarly assessments of Byzantine culture as she is commonly presented as the voice of Byzantium. Certain strong negative associations of deviousness and unmanliness that western scholars have had with Byzantine culture may be traced in part to traditional misreading of the *Alexiad*. The image of tricky and devious Greeks, still haunting some western scholarship on the crusades, derives on the one hand from cultural continuities of the same Roman distaste of trickery used by Nikephoros, but also from reading Anna's history – in relative isolation – and taking it as normative for her culture. Anna's portrayal of Alexios has been extremely influential in formulating a conception of Byzantine culture as positively disposed to political and military deception. Non-specialist readers often do not like Anna's Alexios because he is devious and he cries, both characteristics that may be traced to Anna's efforts to present him as an archaic Greek hero. If Anna's valorization of trickery was inspired by the desire to counter her husband's Roman critique of Alexios, then it may be fair to question whether it reflected common attitudes among her contemporaries at all.

Anna's strenuous efforts to defend military trickery as valorous behavior provide a fairly strong indication that twelfth-century audiences perceived the presentation of Alexios as a trickster in Nikephoros's history as derogatory. The freedom Anna and Nikephoros had to give their histories different meanings through appeal to different constructions of cultural memory is striking. How these presentations of history worked to inform the behavior and the culture of their contemporaries form the subject of the following chapter.

# CHAPTER 16

# Roman ideals and twelfth-century Constantinopolitan culture

While they may have had a lovely marriage (for all we know), Anna and Nikephoros disagreed about and with history. Their dueling histories contested the memory of Alexios Komnenos and they carried out this dispute largely through appeals to different layers of their own ancient history. They do not seem to have disagreed substantively about what Alexios did, or even that he was the sort of man who would rather find a way around a problem than confront it. They wrote histories that portrayed Alexios's character in more or less the same way, but placed opposite values on that character by deploying different sets of cultural imagery throughout their histories.

The striking latitude Nikephoros and Anna had for constructing opposing literary value systems through appeal to different aspects of their cultural heritage may be unsettling to visions of medieval cultural history as passing through fairly uniform and slowly shifting intellectual fashions. Instinctively historians have taken the value systems presented in the twelfth-century histories as reflecting the cultural values of the authors. Anna's choice to place herself in her history and maintain an overt authorial presence throughout the text gives the appearance that it would be safe to read her history as reflecting her own values. Nikephoros maintains a lower profile in his history, but both authors give the impression that the history is composed as an honest mirror of personal values. If literary identity simply mirrors personal identity in these cases, we then have a Roman-Hellene inter-cultural marriage. Anna and Nikephoros's freedom to construct cultural systems of value in their histories by rummaging through the great grab-bag of history written in Greek pushes us to ask how their constructions of value map onto their contemporaneous culture.

Understanding historians as participants in the active creation of cultural memory can help bring Anna and Nikephoros back from the brink of mere literary construction and allow us to appreciate how their varying appeals to ancient history function to inform their culture as well as the histories they wrote. A more traditional approach might see Nikephoros's emphasis on Roman culture as part of an early twelfth-century "revival" of Roman culture and Anna's text as part of a later "revival" of Hellenism. Interpreting interactions with the distant past as episodes of re-birth or revival creates several problems however. Only what has died or decayed can be re-born or revived. So each identification of a renaissance, however laudatory in intent, necessarily brings with it an accusation of decay or decline. Traditional narratives of Byzantine history, which note points of "renaissance" or "revival" in the ninth, tenth, twelfth, fourteenth and fifteenth[1] centuries depict this culture as in a nearly constant state of waxing and waning vitality or decay, birth or death. Several of the alternating times of "decay" have been identified by scholars of the Orthodox tradition as valorized periods of theological or hagiographic florescence.[2] While the scholars involved in charting these renaissances would likely see themselves as vigorously combating Edward Gibbon's famous dictum that "the empire of the East subsisted for a period of 1058 years in a state of premature and perpetual decay,"[3] their use of a somatic metaphor of new birth (from death) and revival (from decay) may rather reinforce the impression of Byzantium as a culture with health problems.

In discourses of renaissance, agency is often attributed to the stimulating ancient materials rather than to the medieval or modern artists and writers. Art historians have turned against "renaissance" as a category for understanding the classicism of Byzantine art, in part reacting against the scholarship which, in ascribing agency to the stimulant of ancient tradition and passivity to its medieval recipients, curtailed the investigation into medieval artists' motivations and attitudes.[4] Ascribing agency to the past allows a reified antiquity or heroic-age Christianity to stalk later generations like so many ghosts. In modern literary imagination Byzantium is precisely a culture haunted by the past.

It is rather the medieval authors and artists who, in creating their own culture and responding to the continuous evolution of their own society, reevaluate their appraisals of the past and choose differing moments in the

[1] Treadgold, *Renaissances before the Renaissance*; Kurt Weitzmann, *The Joshua Roll: A Work of the Macedonian Renaissance* (Princeton University Press, 1948); John Hanson, "The Rise and Fall of the Macedonian Renaissance," in *A Companion to Byzantium*, ed. Liz James (Oxford: Wiley-Blackwell, 2010), 338–50; Rice, *The Twelfth Century Renaissance in Byzantine Art*; Runciman, *The Last Byzantine Renaissance*.
[2] The eighth-century "dark age" produced the theology of John of Damascus. The mystical theology of Symeon the New theologian was produced in the early eleventh century, before Psellos "revived" philosophy.
[3] Edward Gibbon, *History of the Decline and Fall of the Roman Empire*, 1788, chapter 32.
[4] Hanson, "The Rise and Fall of the Macedonian Renaissance," 347.

past as meaningful. This was powerfully the case in the original "Renaissance," when a particular vision of the past became deeply constructive for contemporaneous culture. Writing history is one aspect of an active remembering that, while often cloaked as dispassionate truth about things that happened long ago, participates in creating the historian's own culture. The changes perceived by scholars charting "revivals" are shifts in culture initiated by the medieval participants. Cultural and social changes cause alternations in what was considered precious and worthy out of the whole totality of past material. Changes in medieval society led particular moments or monuments from the past to be prized, despised, or forgotten.

This phenomenon of continually shifting valuations of the past may be understood as a reflection of changes in cultural memory.[5] Societies have memories and conceptions about what in the past is formative for their culture. Personally communicated memories shared from grandparents to children form immediate connective memory.[6] Regarding the more distant past, literate societies such as that of medieval Constantinople had the option of several different conceptions. Each generation alters its cultural memory in response to the challenges and particular social and political situations it faces. Some elements of cultural memory – that we are Romans – that we celebrate the memorial of Christ in the Eucharist – persist fairly stably for centuries while other aspects of cultural memory change significantly from one generation to the next.

Historians, along with other creators of cultural products, play key roles in nudging the cultural memory of their society in one direction or another. Authors and artists may select moments or ideas from the past as having a particular significance and put them before the public eye, naturally presented in the guise of the creators' cultural interpretations. This need not be seen as consciously manipulative on the part of the authors who participate in the ongoing construction of their communities' culture. Plenty of authors and artists, however, were perfectly aware of their desire to convince their contemporaries to prize one era and the temper of its

[5] Within the field of memory theory, I find the formulations of Jan Assmann most apt for understanding medieval societies: J. Assmann, *Religion and Cultural Memory*; J. Assmann, "Collective Memory and Cultural Identity," *New German Critique*, no. 65 (1995); J. Assmann, "Communicative and Cultural Memory," 109–18; J. Assmann, *Das kulturelle Gedächtnis: Schrift, Erinnerung und politische Identität in frühen Hochkulturen* (Munich: C.H. Beck, 1992). Valuable guides to the field are Whitehead, *Memory*; Elizabeth A. Castelli, *Martyrdom and Memory: Early Christian Culture Making* (New York: Columbia University Press, 2004), 11–32. Other key texts include : Gerd Althoff, Johannes Fried, and Patrick J. Geary, *Medieval Concepts of the Past*; Geary, *Phantoms of Remembrance*; Connerton, *How Societies Remember*; Maurice Halbwachs, *On Collective Memory*, trans. Lewis A. Coser (University of Chicago Press, 1992).

[6] J. Assmann, "Communicative and Cultural Memory," 109–25.

culture over others and hence exhort their contemporaries to behave in one way or another. In using memories of different eras in the past to grade the characters in their histories Nikephoros and Anna were fighting about what aspects of the past had value and ought to be at the forefront of contemporaneous cultural memory. They were contending about how their societies ought to remember the distant past, which is inextricably connected to how their societies ought to behave in the present.

Stark social change can spark moments of intensity in the practice of memory and concern with proper memorialization. Points of social upheaval are often connected with large-scale contention about how the past should be remembered and what in the past had value.[7] The establishment of the Principate elicited intensive efforts to memorialize the Roman Republic and contention over what import this aspect of the Roman past had for the present.[8] The reign of Alexios Komnenos marked significant changes in medieval Roman political culture, territorial basis, and systems of government. It was a period of social transformation in which the old aristocracy lost the foundation for their wealth and Alexios effectively created a new aristocracy out of his own family. The advent of the crusading movement brought radical upheavals to the politics of the eastern Mediterranean. An era of such social and political change would call for a conversation about the past. It is no surprise, therefore, that Irene asked for a history. Nikephoros responded to the call to make sense of the tumultuous present by grounding his morality in a remembrance of past heroes.

Nikephoros had a lot of potential heroes to choose from. The choices one generation makes to either passively forget or actively erase memories can act as a filter that removes traces by which those events or material could be later re-membered.[9] Cultures engaged in smashing statues in anti-pagan fervor prevented those objects from playing roles as memorials of antiquity for later cultures. Cultures disinterested in classical Roman history allowed portions of Cassius Dio to perish that twelfth-century Constantinopolitans would have cherished. Yet despite the numerous filters of other generations' choices, twelfth-century Constantinopolitans had access to a wide array of material with which to interact in the creation of constitutive cultural

---

[7] Connerton, *How Societies Remember*, 6–7.

[8] Alain Gowing, *Empire and Memory: The Representation of the Roman Republic in Imperial Culture* (Cambridge University Press, 2005).

[9] Patrick J. Geary, "Land, Language and Memory in Europe 700–1100," *Transactions of the Royal Historical Society* 9 (1999); Geary, *Phantoms of Remembrance*; Aleida Assmann, "Canon and Archive," in *A Companion to Cultural Memory Studies*, ed. Astrid Erll and Ansgar Nünning (Berlin: De Gruyter, 2010), 97–108.

memory. Nikephoros's choice to construct his identity as a Roman was active, purposeful, and not inevitable. Stories of Christian martyrs, or Alexander the Great, or of Hebrew prophets, for example, were available but apparently had no interest or emotional resonance for him.[10]

Nikephoros's understanding of Roman history was not what is taught in our contemporary classics departments. The authors Nikephoros read now can be seen as Greeks engaged, to varying degrees, in dealing with Roman ascendancy and memorializing pre-Imperial Roman history.[11] Polybius was concerned with explaining the causes of the Roman imperium and how a Greek could confront the reality of that power with honor.[12] Dionysius harmonized Greek myths of Latin settlement with indigenous Latin ones to create a story in which the Greeks had not lost to the Romans because the Romans were themselves descendants of the Greek Trojans. Dio's detailed treatment of the late Republic points forward to the Principate and works to explain the rise of Octavian.[13] Plutarch participates in the discussion of Roman ascendancy by writing biography that measured ancient Greek and more recent Roman men by a common yardstick.[14] It is easy for us to see these writers as Greeks endeavoring to come to terms with Roman rule or explaining Rome to Greeks. They are responding, in different ways, to the reality of Roman imperium in the eastern Mediterranean.

Yet thirteen centuries after the Roman conquest of Greece, Nikephoros would not only think of himself as Roman, but read Polybius as if Polybius had been a Roman. Nikephoros does not seem to have any awareness that the Greek historians he read had any conception of themselves as non-Romans. Nikephoros would not have picked up any sense that the Greek historians of Rome were negotiating realities of Roman power because that historical struggle had no meaning for him. Rather he read the Greek historians of Rome as Romans telling their own history. Remembering is a matter of selecting what from the past gives meaning to the present. What cannot be recognized as fitting somehow into the formation of one's culture is easily overlooked. The explanations for the rise of Roman power in Polybius and Dionysius would be read in twelfth-century Constantinople

---

[10] On the use of martyrs to create community see Castelli, *Martyrdom and Memory.*

[11] The literature on Greek historiography of Rome is ample. John Marincola, *A Companion to Greek and Roman historiography* (Malden: Blackwell, 2007); Andrew Feldherr, *The Cambridge Companion to the Roman Historians* (Cambridge University Press, 2009).

[12] Eckstein, *Moral Vision*; Craige Brian Champion, *Cultural Politics in Polybius's Histories*, vol. 41 (Berkeley: University of California Press, 2004).

[13] Alain Gowing, *The Triumviral Narratives of Appian and Cassius Dio* (Ann Arbor: The University of Michigan Press, 1992), 35.

[14] Smith, "The Construction of the Past," 431.

as reasons "why we won" rather than "why they won." In so far as reading is a dialogue between text and reader,[15] Nikephoros's reading completed the meaning of the ancient histories in a manner consonant with his own world.

Temporal differences among ancient historians also seem to have been compressed to create Nikephoros's highly generalized view of antiquity. While modern scholars would consider Procopius to be of a markedly different era than Polybius, it seems that Nikephoros would have thought of them both as ancient historians, or as historians of the empire's great old days. Procopius succeeded in writing a highly classicizing history. We have no reason to think that Nikephoros could begin to fathom the western European division of the world into separate ancient and medieval categories, a division that fundamentally denied the reality of his Roman Empire. It would be natural for Nikephoros to think of Procopius as one of the great old historians of the Roman Empire.

Procopius's classicism goes far beyond style. The moral commentary implicit in Procopius's narrative calls on what he perceived to be traditional morality. As was seen in chapter 12, his portrayal of Justinian and Theodora transgressing their gender norms draws on a generalized sense of ancient gender normativity. The functioning of this same sense of normativity is necessary to complete the meaning of the scenes of ranting women in Psellos's and Nikephoros's histories. Dionysius and Polybius similarly talked about *ancient* Roman morals. In different ways they appeal to ancient morality, perhaps in contrast to the degradations of their present. The historicity of these "ancient values" was not a matter of particular concern for any of the authors under discussion.

The vision of purely frontal, self-sacrificial, agonistic Roman combat drawn in chapter 8 is easily recognized as having far more to do with Roman self-presentation and imperial-era nostalgia for the great old days than with any real era of Roman history. Once victorious, the Romans missed the opportunity for real glory Hannibal presented. This imperial-era memory of old Roman sacrificial honor created a packaged Roman past that transports seamlessly into the twelfth century where it could provide the emotional logic behind Nikephoros's noble losers. The belief that Romans prized properly agonistic contests and fought with a self-sacrificial code of military honor, or had done so in their great old days, remained apparent to those who read the Greek historians of Rome, even at a distance of twelve centuries.

---

[15] M. M. Bakhtin, *The Dialogic Imagination: Four Essays*, trans. Michael Holquist (Austin: University of Texas Press, 2004).

The upshot of this is that Nikephoros did not need to create his own understanding of old Roman values from his reading. The authors he read were already thinking about ancient Roman culture and participating in the process of memorializing the ancient Roman Empire. The contest over the memory of the Roman republic was one of the key cultural events of the early empire.[16] A discourse about the values of the Romans in the good old days was already created and active long before the twelfth century. Nikephoros's participation in an established, generalized discourse about Roman honor explains why his appeal to Roman values seems so clear even though his unambiguous references to specific ancient texts are not voluminous.

Nikephoros's reading and writing of history allowed him to remember the past in a way that gave meaning and direction to his present. The production of a history was one step in the ongoing process of creating cultural memory.[17] How far Nikephoros's effort at remembering was shared by his society depends on the circulation of his work and on the receptivity of his audience to his vision. Nikephoros's history would speak to a far smaller audience than, say, Theodosios's erection of the obelisk in the hippodrome. Yet, within the limited circle of the Constantinopolitan court for which he wrote, he had the opportunity to be highly influential. Enough other authors and artists of twelfth-century Constantinople engaged creatively with remnants of classical culture for us to be certain that Nikephoros was not alone in finding elements of the classical past culturally constitutive.[18] The continued interest in Roman history after Nikephoros's history was written indicates that at least some people found his encouragement of Roman paradigms appealing.[19]

---

[16] Gowing, *Empire and Memory.*

[17] On medieval Roman practice of memory in general see Amy Papalexandrou, "Memory Culture in Byzantium," in *A Companion to Byzantium*, ed. Liz James (Malden: Wiley-Blackwell, 2010), 108–22.

[18] From new "ancient" novels to commentaries on Pindar, engagement in classical material is pervasive in various genres of Greek writing of the second half of the twelfth century. A few examples and discussions include: Roilos, *Aphoteroglossia*; Beaton, *The Medieval Greek Romance*; Nilsson, "Discovering Literariness in the Past"; Ingela Nilsson, *Erotic Pathos, Rhetorical Pleasure: Narrative Technique and Mimesis in Eumathios Makrembolites' "Hysmine & Hysminias"* (Uppsala: Acta Universitatis Upsaliensis, 2001); Andrew Stone, "On Hermogenes' Features of Style and Other Factors Affecting Style in the Panegyrics of Eustathios of Thessaloniki," *Rhetorica* 19 (2001); Athanasios Kambylis, ed. *Eustathius of Thessalonica : Prooimion zum Pindarkommentar* (Göttingen: Vandenhoeck & Ruprecht, 1991); *Eustathius of Thessalonica : Commentarii ad Homeri Iliadem et Odysseam*, ed. Gottfried Stallbaum (Hildesheim: G. Olms, 1960); Roderick Saxey, "The Homeric Metamorphoses of Andronikos I Komnenos," in *Niketas Choniates*, ed. Alicia Simpson and Stephanos Efthymiadis (Geneva: La Pomme d'Or, 2009).

[19] Zonaras had strong interests in Roman history. Macrides and Magdalino, "Fourth Kingdom," 127–31.

The role of Nikephoros's history as a source of entertainment and con-
genial diversion should not be forgotten. The story of Michael Doukas's
escape from Roussel's fortress in the night is told with great affection.
Roussel allowed Andronikos Doukas to return to Constantinople for his
wounds to be treated and took Andronikos's two young sons as hostages
in exchange for their father's release.[20] Through the efforts of his tutor,
the elder boy, Michael Doukas, was able to escape from Roussel's fortress
and get to Nicomedia. This adventure of deception, escape, and flight is
told in elaborate detail and with considerable excitement even though the
event has little historical importance. The story changes the level of detail
in Nikephoros's narrative, but its inclusion was justified by the excitement
of the story and the likely presence of the adult Michael and his family
in the audience for the history's performance. This episode serves as a
reminder that Nikephoros's history was a vehicle for telling and enjoying
family stories.

Yet, even as a repository of family lore, the history helped sustain and
codify family and community memory, which in turn contributed to the
cohesiveness and group-identity within the community. For the young
people in the initial audience, most of whom would have counted several
of the antagonists of Nikephoros's history as common grandparents, the
stories in the history were stories of their own origins. Cultural memory provides narratives of community creation that bond communities
together.[21] Memories of community inception and descent, whether from
Paul or Aeneas, help create cohesion in communities. For the new Constantinopolitan court community taking form in the early twelfth century,
practices of remembering the wars of their ancestors contributed to the
formation of their own communal identity.

The history was an effort by Nikephoros to coax his community into
remembering the recent past in the way he believed was appropriate. It
was his effort to craft the cultural memory of his generation. Additionally,
the history can be seen as an effort to inform and instruct the behavior of
Nikephoros's contemporaries. The function of cultural memory to inform
behavior was well understood in antiquity. Nikephoros was participating
in a tradition of studying history in order to form character. Roman orators
were trained in remembering the Roman past so that they would be able to
call up people and events of the past as *exempla*. The use of *exempla* "lay at
the center of Roman thinking about ethics and morality."[22] Plutarch's lives

---

[20] 2.16.8–9.  [21] J. Assmann, *Religion and Cultural Memory*, 5–16.
[22] Gowing, *Empire and Memory*, 16.

used the experiences of past men as training exercises in moral judgment.[23] Other historians were equally forthright in claiming that moral education was one of the key benefits of history.

In Nikephoros's history, political and military affairs similarly become an arena for the formation and display of character and virtue. The character of the men is put on display in the stories about how they responded to the military challenges they faced. Nikephoros describes not just what happened in the past, but who was of good or poor character and the quality of his behavior. In judging previous generations according to a standard of classical Roman behavior, Nikephoros implicitly exhorts his contemporaries to meet that same standard. This is a text with a clear purpose to shape the morals of its audience.

The virtues extolled in Nikephoros's history include a strong loyalty to the Roman Empire and willingness to fight courageously and risk death in the defense of that Empire. The true heroes of the history fight with an open straightforward aggression that Nikephoros implicitly exhorts his audience to emulate. The heroes are physically active and personally brave. Concern for the well-being of one's family and the use of family networks in the service of the Empire are also portrayed as aspects of virtuous behavior. Deep religious devotion is not presented as a necessary characteristic although performance of traditional pious practices is presented as entirely appropriate. This set of virtues is not exclusive to classical Roman culture, but does correspond remarkably well to certain central tenets of Roman honor. In composing a history in which the heroic characters acted like the grand old Romans, Nikephoros was making a case that his contemporaries ought to act like those Romans.

The hortatory moralizing aspects of Nikephoros's work make his eschewal of Christian theological stances all the more interesting. Orthodoxy is not under attack, but de-emphasized in Nikephoros's portrayal of his general's piety. It is a significant cultural shift that saints' lives must compete with Plutarch's lives as models of behavior in twelfth-century Constantinople. That Nikephoros was interested in Plutarch is not evidence that other people did not continue reading hagiography with interest. But it is evidence that hagiography had serious competition. The twelfth century does not appear to have been a great era for the composition of hagiography and scholars have speculated about the decline of the genre.[24] Classical Roman historiography and Christian hagiography are both explicit in their

---

[23] Christopher Pelling, *Literary Texts and the Greek Historian* (London: Routledge, 2000), 46–47.

[24] Paul Magdalino, "The Byzantine Holy Man in the Twelfth Century," in *The Byzantine Saint*, ed. Sergei Hackel (London: Fellowship of St. Alban and St. Sergius, 1981), 51–62.

didactic nature. Both genres aspire to give readers models of action and lessons in good and bad conduct. The challenge Polybius and Plutarch presented to writers and readers of hagiography was therefore direct and forceful. It is not merely a matter of a new kind of literature competing for attention at court, but of a new didactic hortatory literature teaching a different morality.

Whatever meanings Nikephoros intended to put into his text, he was not in control of what meanings his audience took away from it. While the history appears to speak eloquently to Nikephoros's own frustrated ambition and sense of righteousness in resignation, the younger members of his audience may not have cared about the demise of the Bryennioi with anything like that same intensity. Audiences cannot be expected to have a uniform reaction to a performance.[25] It would have been possible for someone to listen to the history and conclude that since the Turks were winning, Alexios was entirely right to fight like a Turk. We perhaps should presume that Nikephoros's audience came to a variety of opinions through discussing and musing privately on his narrative.

The particular political challenges of the Empire in the early twelfth century may have made classical Roman history especially satisfying. The Roman orientation helped Nikephoros tell a heroic tale about a bad political decade of imperial history. In its ability to valorize a noble defeat, a Roman cultural valuation may have been preferable to a Homeric or classical Greek one, in which losers were simply losers regardless of their conduct. Additionally, those who fought against the Veii, Gauls, and Carthaginians displayed their virtue and earned eternal fame by sacrificing themselves for a Rome that, however beleaguered in the hour of their deaths, went on to conquer the world. The invocation of their noble struggles in the narration of the defeats of the eleventh century may have helped to calm fears and inspire hopes that eternal Rome would emerge from its current troubles. Recalling the traditional valorization of the noble defeat was an apt way of approaching the narration of the disastrous late eleventh century for the generation whose task it was to restore Roman glory.

---

[25] See the useful discussion of Pelling, *Literary Texts and the Greek Historian*, 246–53.

# Conclusions

The great heroes of Nikephoros Bryennios's history are men who maintained their honor even in moments of defeat. The present reading of his history suggests that Nikephoros himself was a man who struggled to maintain his honor in the face of his political loss and subordination. The narrative Nikephoros constructed of eleventh-century history valorized a particular conception of masculinity that allowed Nikephoros, his grandfather, and several other eleventh-century generals to be great men despite their lack of victory. Nikephoros developed a vision of ideal masculinity displayed in personal honor, honesty, fair contests, self-control, maturity and moderation. Elements of this ideal can be found in any number of cultures. All however can be seen as part of a generalized conception of ancient Roman adult masculinity. I submit that Nikephoros found the sense of honor he encountered in his readings in Roman history highly appealing and strove to use that ideal of masculinity to write an evaluative history of the eleventh century that would exhort his contemporaries to emulate the great old Romans while honoring the memory of Bryennios the Elder, John Doukas, and Romanos Diogenes.

The victorious Alexios is not denied his merits in Nikephoros's history. Alexios was deeply aggressive and tenacious in his search for victory and, facing difficult circumstances, he displayed ingenuity in devising ways to scrape out advantages. Victory tastes sweeter than defeat, and many doubtless savored Alexios's ability to win without any regard for how well he conformed to Nikephoros's conception of honorable masculinity. Nevertheless, when Nikephoros made his telling of the past an opportunity to grade men's character according to his conception of honor, Alexios came up lacking.

Nikephoros should be seen as an active participant in a faction that wanted him to become emperor. While he accepted the failure of his bid for power, his presentation in twentieth-century historiography as a weakling is due to the continued power of the gendered rhetoric used by later medieval historians to denigrate his masculinity. The politics of his history are strongly in favor of his own house and family, in opposition to the legacy of Alexios Komnenos. John Komnenos may not have found this history politically threatening, but he could not have thought that Nikephoros did not believe in the virtue of his own claim on the throne.

Looking beyond these particularities of the case at hand, there are a few further conclusions to be drawn from the present study. If there are any scholars remaining who doubt the utility of gender studies, or regard the field as a tool of women's history, this study may change their minds. Taking gender as a key category of analysis has led not only to insights into twelfth-century culture, but to changes in the narrative of male political history. Warfare is a testing ground of masculinity. It should not be surprising therefore that consideration of a medieval author's sense of appropriate gender would lead to better understanding of his military narrative. Understanding why the medieval writers described battles and campaigns in the ways that they did will help in the task of evaluating their evidence and figuring out what happened. Military historians of the medieval era can achieve better results when they become gender historians.

The key conclusion for any classicists who may read this book is that the division of ancient and medieval Greek texts into different academic fields is unhelpful. We all have much to gain by paying more attention to each other's work. The boundaries separating the medieval and classical halves of the Roman Empire have nothing to do with the intellectual contexts of those fields. Byzantinists may miss a great deal in their narrative sources when they fail to expect deep engagement with the classical past. Classicists who ignore Greek written after the third century are missing not only great texts, but great texts that comment in marvelous ways on the material and cultures they study. In using ancient Roman history to help him grapple with his present, Nikephoros Bryennios was a classicist. Read him as a kindred spirit.

For medievalists the lesson, hardly novel but perhaps powerfully articulated here, is that the Greek and Latin worlds were both using the classical Roman Empire as a cultural touchstone and model. Nikephoros Bryennios's history offers serious competition to western claims to imperial revival. We have known about the contestation over the Roman political and cultural heritage for a long time, but the immediacy of Nikephoros's intellectual and cultural kinship with the classical Empire may provoke some rethinking of the topic. The increasing militarization of Byzantine culture in the twelfth century has been well established, but not necessarily connected with Byzantine efforts to emphasize their Roman heritage. In orienting our perception of that militarization toward memories of classical Roman virtue, and away from possible western influence, the current study deepens our understanding of the role of classical Roman history in twelfth-century culture.

The citations to Nikephoros Bryennios's history in this book are to the book, chapter and line numbers as they appear in the *Thesaurus Linguae Gracae* (*TLG*). The *TLG* uses Gautier's edition of the text, but changed his line numbers so that the whole of each chapter is numbered consecutively. In the printed version of Gautier's edition the line numbering starts anew on each page. For the ease of those readers with access to the printed edition, the following chart indicates what textual content is on each page of the print version. The left-hand column lists the page number of the printed text and the right-hand column lists the content, with the *TLG* line numbers, that can be found on that page.

| Gautier edition: page number | TLG: book, section, line |
| --- | --- |
| 55 | p. (preface) 4.1 – p. 5.3 |
| 57 | p. 5.4 – p. 5.27 |
| 59 | p. 5.27 – p. 6.23 |
| 61 | p. 6.24 – p. 7.28 |
| 63 | p. 7.29 – p. 8.13 |
| 65 | p. 8.14 – p. 8.30 |
| 67 | p. 8.31 – p. 9.22 |
| 69 | p. 9.23 – p. 10.25 |
| 71 | p. 10.26 – p. 11.10 |
| 73 | p. 11.11 – p. 11.21 |
| 75 | 1.1.1 – 1.1.22 |
| 77 | 1.1.23 – 1.2.16 |
| 79 | 1.2.17 – 1.3.19 |
| 81 | 1.4.1 – 1.4.27 |
| 83 | 1.4.28 – 1.5.21 |
| 85 | 1.5.22 – 1.6.13 |
| 87 | 1.6.14 – 1.6.38 |
| 89 | 1.7.1 – 1.7.25 |
| 91 | 1.7.26 – 1.7.48 |
| 93 | 1.8.1 – 1.9.2 |

(*cont.*)

| Gautier edition: page number | TLG: book, section, line |
| --- | --- |
| 95 | 1.9.3 – 1.9.33 |
| 97 | 1.10.1 – 1.10.26 |
| 99 | 1.10.27 – 1.10.52 |
| 101 | 1.11.1 – 1.11.26 |
| 103 | 1.11.27 – 1.12.18 |
| 105 | 1.12.19 – 1.13.7 |
| 107 | 1.13.8 – 1.14.2 |
| 109 | 1.14.3 – 1.14.26 |
| 111 | 1.14.27 – 1.15.10 |
| 113 | 1.15.11 – 1.16.8 |
| 115 | 1.16.9 – 1.17.6 |
| 117 | 1.17.7 – 1.17.31 |
| 119 | 1.17.32 – 1.18.21 |
| 121 | 1.18.22 – 19.20 |
| 123 | 1.19.21 – 1.20.20 |
| 125 | 1.20.21 – 1.21.11 |
| 127 | 1.21.12 – 1.21.40 |
| 129 | 1.21.41 – 1.22.23 |
| 131 | 1.22.24 – 1.23.4 |
| 133 | 1.23.5 – 1.24.7 |
| 135 | 1.24.8 – 1.24.42 |
| 137 | 1.24.43 – 1.25.12 |
| 139 | 1.25.13 – 1.25.33 |
| 141 | 1.25.34 – 1.25.37 |
| 143 | 2.1.1 – 2.1.19 |
| 145 | 2.1.20 – 2.3.6 |
| 147 | 2.3.7 – 2.4.2 |
| 149 | 2.4.3 – 2.5.8 |
| 151 | 2.5.9 – 2.6.6 |
| 153 | 2.6.7 – 2.6.34 |
| 155 | 2.7.1 – 2.8.9 |
| 157 | 2.8.10 – 2.9.4 |
| 159 | 2.9.5 – 2.10.8 |
| 161 | 2.10.9 – 2.11.11 |
| 163 | 2.11.12 – 2.12.21 |
| 165 | 2.12.22 – 2.13.22 |
| 167 | 2.13.23 – 2.14.23 |
| 169 | 2.14.24 – 2.14.48 |
| 171 | 2.14.49 – 2.15.29 |
| 173 | 2.15.30 – 2.16.28 |
| 175 | 2.16.29 – 2.16.62 |
| 177 | 2.17.1 – 2.17.23 |
| 179 | 2.17.24 – 2.18.13 |
| 181 | 2.18.14 – 2.18.35 |
| 183 | 2.19.1 – 2.19.20 |

| Gautier edition: page number | TLG: book, section, line |
| --- | --- |
| 185 | 2.20.1 – 2.20.30 |
| 187 | 2.21.1 – 2.21.28 |
| 189 | 2.21.29 – 2.22.25 |
| 191 | 2.22.26 – 2.23.26 |
| 193 | 2.23.27 – 2.24.27 |
| 195 | 2.24.28 – 2.25.17 |
| 197 | 2.25.18 – 2.26.16 |
| 199 | 2.26.17 – 2.27.16 |
| 201 | 2.27.17 – 2.28.14 |
| 203 | 2.28.15 – 2.28.40 |
| 205 | 2.28.41 – 2.29.15 |
| 207 | 2.29.16 – 2.29.29 |
| 209 | 3.1.1 – 3.1.22 |
| 211 | 3.1.23 – 3.2.14 |
| 213 | 3.2.15 – 3.3.14 |
| 215 | 3.3.15 – 3.4.11 |
| 217 | 3.4.12 – 3.5.6 |
| 219 | 3.5.7 – 3.6.10 |
| 221 | 3.6.11 – 3.6.36 |
| 223 | 3.6.37 – 3.7.10 |
| 225 | 3.7.11 – 3.8.17 |
| 227 | 3.8.18 – 3.9.7 |
| 229 | 3.9.8 – 3.9.37 |
| 231 | 3.9.38 – 3.10.17 |
| 233 | 3.10.18 – 3.12.7 |
| 235 | 3.12.8 – 3.13.19 |
| 237 | 3.14.1 – 3.15.3 |
| 239 | 3.15.4 – 3.16.9 |
| 241 | 3.16.10 – 3.16.35 |
| 243 | 3.17.1 – 3.18.9 |
| 245 | 3.18.10 – 3.19.14 |
| 247 | 3.19.15 – 3.21.5 |
| 249 | 3.21.6 – 3.22.8 |
| 251 | 3.22.9 – 3.24.2 |
| 253 | 3.24.3 – 3.25.14 |
| 255 | 3.25.15 – 3.26.9 |
| 257 | 4.1.1 – 4.1.20 |
| 259 | 4.1.21 – 4.2.15 |
| 261 | 4.2.16 – 4.2.38 |
| 263 | 4.2.39 – 4.3.25 |
| 265 | 4.3.26 – 4.4.21 |
| 267 | 4.4.22 – 4.5.14 |
| 269 | 4.6.1 – 4.7.4 |
| 271 | 4.7.5 – 4.8.15 |
| 273 | 4.8.16 – 4.9.20 |

(*cont.*)

| Gautier edition: page number | TLG: book, section, line |
| --- | --- |
| 275 | 4.9.21 – 4.11.4 |
| 277 | 4.11.5 – 4.12.24 |
| 279 | 4.13.1 – 4.14.4 |
| 281 | 4.14.5 – 4.16.4 |
| 283 | 4.16.5 – 4.17.10 |
| 285 | 4.18.1 – 4.18.20 |
| 287 | 4.18.21 – 4.20.6 |
| 289 | 4.20.7 – 4.22.9 |
| 291 | 4.22.10 – 4.24.6 |
| 293 | 4.24.7 – 4.26.3 |
| 295 | 4.26.4 – 4.27.7 |
| 297 | 4.27.8 – 4.28.17 |
| 299 | 4.29.1 – 4.30.15 |
| 301 | 4.31.1 – 4.31.24 |
| 303 | 4.32.1 – 4.33.15 |
| 305 | 4.33.16 – 4.35.11 |
| 307 | 4.36.1 – 4.37.16 |
| 309 | 4.37.17 – 4.39.6 |
| 311 | 4.39.7 – 4.40.10 |

APPENDIX 2

# *Vocabulary of virtue*

Each time Nikephoros introduces a new character into his narrative story, he offers a few words of identification. These introductory assessments provide a window onto Nikephoros's typology of human virtue.

Nikephoros frequently describes characters as noble, *gennaios*, or having *gennaiotita*. While etymologically *gennaios* has to do with genetics, Nikephoros's usage seems to have more to do with bravery and proper action than affinities of blood. In Nikephoros's usage it seems that *gennaios* ought to be translated as "brave."[1] Women could also be described as *gennaia*. Alexios's mother Anna Dalassene is brave and magnanimous.[2] She is later well born, brave, and wise.[3] Bryennios exhorted his troops not to do something "base and unworthy of the nobility of the Romans" when they are surrounded by a Turkish ambush.[4] Romanos Diogenes signed agreements with Alp Arslan that were not unworthy of the Romans because he would rather die than betray his nobility.[5] Fighting is often done nobly.[6] Constantine Doukas is successful against Diogenes because his attack was "more noble."[7]

This noble bravery is best when it is personal and physical. Nikephoros's interest in personal bravery is seen in his fondness for the phrase "brave of hand," *ten cheira gennaios*, meaning "brave," in his introductions; usually in conjunction with another character trait.[8] Alexios Charon was "a man hearty and sensible and brave of hand and daring in spirit."[9] Constantine Doukas was "a man both brave of hand and quick in intelligence and admirable."[10] Basilakes was "robust and brave of hand, but very bold and

---

[1] 1.12.19; 1.22.28; 1.24.48; 2.1.14; 2.5.29; 2.12.16; 2.12.18; 2.13.9; 2.15.28; 2.15.30; 2.16.9; 2.16.48; 2.16.51; 2.17.6 etc.
[2] 1.12.19–20.  [3] 1.22.24.  [4] 1.15.13–17.  [5] 1.19.11–13.
[6] 1.11.11; 1.21.22; 2.5.4; 2.5.17; 2.10.7; 2.12.31.  [7] 1.21.23.
[8] It is used alone for Constantine Diogenes, 1.6.15.
[9] 1.2.10–11: ἀνδρὸς φρενήρους καὶ νουνεχοῦς καὶ τὴν χεῖρα γενναίου καὶ τὴν ψυχὴν θαρσαλέου.
[10] 1.21.12–13: ἀνδρὶ καὶ τὴν χεῖρα γενναίῳ καὶ τὴν σύνεσιν ὀξεῖ τε καὶ θαυμασίῳ.

hard to restrain in attacks."[11] Chatatourios was "deep in understanding, brave of hand."[12] Theodotos was "brave of hand and surpassing others in experience."[13] George Palaiologos was "experienced and brave of hand and opinion."[14] The phrase indicates that bravery is defined by Nikephoros, not as a moral or intellectual strength, but as a willingness to endure bodily danger.

The characteristic of being brave/noble, *gennaios*, is frequently paired with the act of struggling or contending in battle. In fact, whenever characters struggle they do it bravely. Nikephoros Bryennios struggled "heroically" and "brilliantly."[15] Otherwise struggling is always done "nobly."[16]

The standard ancient Greek term for brave, *agathos*, is used rarely in these character introductions. Basilakes is a man "brave with respect to war."[17] More often *agathos* seems to have its later meaning of good rather than brave. It is used in non-military contexts. Symeon the *hegoumenos* of Xenophon monastery of Mt. Athos was a "good and moderate man, shining with ascetic success."[18] Nikephoros Bryennios was described as a "man good in appearance and most clever at speaking" in a context where he has chosen explicitly to dress as an emperor rather than to wear arms.[19] John Komnenos was such a good governor that everyone experienced his "kalokagathia."[20]

Another common classical term for bravery, *andreia*, literally "manliness," is conspicuously absent. Nikephoros included a line from Skylitzes which described Saracen generals as having *andreia*.[21] Alexios Charon got his name from his *andreia*, since whenever he fought he sent men to meet Charon.[22] Nikephoros Botaneiates ran away from a battle that was going badly, even though many people attested that he was "manly," with the implication that running away from a battle was unmanly.[23] Manly goodness, *andragathia*, is attributed twice to Alexios Komnenos and also to the great old Roman emperors Nikephoros Phokas, John I, and Basil II, whose very reputation kept the Turks at bay.[24] In a book with a great many brave deeds, however, the paucity of references to *andreia* indicates that bravery

---

[11] 1.14.3–4.    [12] 1.21.32.    [13] 2.6.1–2.
[14] 4.36.2. The same metaphor is also used of Nikephoros Bryennios, 4.15.4; and Alexios Komnenos, 4.26.14.
[15] 1.15.24; 4.12.16.
[16] γενναίως ἀγωνίσασθαι: 2.12.31; 2.5.4; 2.5.17; 1.11.11; 2.29.22; 2.10.7; 4.38.8; 1.21.22; 4.8.11.
[17] ἀγαθὸς τὰ πολεμικά, 3.4.21.
[18] 4.27.4–5: ἀνὴρ ἀγαθός τε καὶ κόσμιος, ἀσκητικοῖς διαλάμπων κατορθώμασιν·
[19] 4.2.32–33.    [20] 1.3.14.    [21] 1.8.4.    [22] 1.2.12–13.
[23] *andreios*, 2.15.4.    [24] 2.5.27; 4.26.15; 1.10.6.

was not particularly linked with manliness.[25] This is especially interesting because *andreia* was one of the cardinal virtues of an emperor.[26] Rather, the emphasis on *gennaios* implies a tight connection between lineage, standards of behavior, and bravery.

Only Nikephoros Bryennios is called heroic. He received numerous wounds in his heroic struggle against the Turks.[27] He also had a heroic soul.[28] Nikephoros Bryennios "rose as a sun among stars" amid his generals who were noble and experienced.[29]

There are several ways of describing intelligence. The old-fashioned virtue of being *sophron* is rare.[30] Thoughtfulness, *phrontis*, has implications of care and worry.[31] Intelligence, *sunesis*, is linked with leadership and planning.[32] Plans are frequently described as either *sunetos* or not *sunetos*.[33] Women, such as Andronikos Doukas's wife, could excel in intelligence.[34] The virtue of being clever, *deinos*, is almost always linked with military action and specifically strategy.[35] Occasionally it refers to a less-specific intelligence.[36] The virtue of being sensible and discreet, *nouneches*, is attributed to some civilian characters.[37] When in the introduction to the history Nikephoros says that Alexios united good sense, *nounechia*, with courage, *andreia*, it implies that Alexios united civilian and military virtues.[38]

---

[25] In contrast see Joseph Roisman, *The Rhetoric of Manhood: Masculinity in the Attic Orators* (Berkeley: University of California, 2005), 106–13.

[26] D. A. Russell and N. G. Wilson, eds., *Menander Rhetor* (Oxford: Clarendon Press, 1979), 77–95.

[27] 1.15.24.    [28] 4.15.5.    [29] 4.5.10.    [30] 2.10.5; 2.7.14.

[31] Bryennios's victorious soldiers were not concerned: 4.10.10; Michael was persuaded not to be concerned with his uncle John: 2.2.2; Isaac Komnenos was concerned with his succession: 1.4.7; Michael was extremely concerned when John and Constantine Doukas were captured by Roussel: 2.17.3; Michael wrestled with a myriad concerns as various enemies attacked the Empire: 3.1.21.

[32] Nikephoritzes's plan to get rid of John Doukas was "not intelligent, but base and knavish:" 2.14.14–15. One of the Alan mercenaries thought that the plan to help out Alexios in his outnumbered fight was "not intelligent but rather bold:" 2.12.26–27; Alexios's plan to fake Roussel's blinding was "extremely intelligent and humane:" 2.24.3; 4.4.3.

[33] 2.12.26; 2.16.21; 2.21.5; 3.16.19.    [34] 3.6.11.

[35] Joseph Tarchaneiotes is a man clever at stratagems and military planning: 1.14.11–12; Botaneiates said that Bryennios's father was a man clever at strategy: 4.3.2; Men are clever in the midst of re-organizing a phalanx: 4.11.9; Alexios brought down one of the most clever of Roman generals, Basilakes: 4.28.6.

[36] 4.15.10–11; Nikephoros Bryennios was clever regarding the perception of the future: 3.2.9; and also a most clever man to speak with: 4.2.33; Stravoromanos, one of Botaneiates's envoys to Bryennios, was a clever and energetic man: 4.2.19. Only once does it have the pejorative sense of "terrible," when referring to those who accused Anna Dalassena of treason: 1.22.39.

[37] The tutor of Michael Doukas who engineers his escape from Roussel is a most discreet eunuch: 2.16.31; 2.16.55. Constantine Choirosphaktes, one of Botaneiates envoys to Bryennios, was a "discreet and learned man:" 4.2.17; Nikephoros Melissenos was a "discreet and marvelous man:" 1.6.11. Alexios Charon was also called a "hearty and sensible man:" 1.2.10.

[38] P. 11.6.

Another largely civilian virtue is that of being active and efficacious, *drasterios*. Nikephoritzes, Michael's despised minister, was "a skillful and efficacious man, adorned in word and experience of many things, but not of profound wisdom and able to stir up more problems than Pericles ever made for Greece."[39] Aimilianos, who plotted for Botaneiates, was a "both knavish and efficacious man."[40] Botaneiates's envoy to Bryennios, Stauroromanos, was a "clever and efficacious man."[41] Nikephoros Bryennios is called "a noble and efficacious and active man" by one of his political opponents.[42] Given this list *drasterios* seems to have been something of a back-handed compliment.[43]

Nobility of birth, *eugeneia*, makes some appearances. Those designated as well born include Isaac and John Komnenos, Constantine Diogenes, Anna Dalassene, Nikephoros Melissenos, Argyros, and Alexios Komnenos.[44] Characters within the work appeal to *eugeneia* in persuading each other to fight. Alexios appeals to his companions' sense of good birth in trying to persuade them to fight the Turks at Dekte, and the mercenary Chaskares says he would be ashamed if the well-born men (Isaac and Alexios) came to harm in his presence.[45] Nikephoros Botaneiates is introduced as one of the "most well-born" men in the east.[46] He proves however to be a negative character in the drama. Good breeding is then not uppermost among the characteristics Nikephoros uses to describe characters he presents positively. Good birth is an element of nobility, but it is not as significant as others.

Virtue, *arete*, seems to describe good character in a general sense.[47] In former days the Turks did not dare attack the Roman Empire because they believed the virtue of emperors Nikephoros Phokas, John Tzimiskes, and Basil was still preserved among the Romans.[48] Romanos ought to have listened to the men who had their own virtue, *oikeia arete*, instead of to flatterers before the battle of Manzikert.[49] It is not strictly a military virtue, as Isaac and John Komnenos were sent to live in the Stoudios monastery as children so that they could learn virtue in imitation of the best men.[50] *Arete* can be pacifist in nature, as when Michael rejected Alexios's advice to forcefully suppress the rebellion in Constantinople against him, "either from cowardice or an excess of virtue."[51]

[39] 2.1.17–20.    [40] 3.18.12.    [41] 4.2.19.    [42] 3.2.21.
[43] The possible negative connotation is not universal. For positive efficacy see 1.11.24; 4.1.5.
[44] 1.1.14; 1.6.15; 1.22.24; 4.31.2; 4.26.15.    [45] 2.10.8; 2.12.24–25.    [46] 3.15.2.
[47] There are many proofs of John Komnenos's virtue, his rejection of kingship chief among them: 1.3.17–18; Nikephoros Bryennios was filled with virtues beyond others: 3.2.6.
[48] 1.10.4–9.    [49] 1.13.19–21.    [50] 1.1.24.    [51] 3.20.9.

The tendency to have some virtues apply to civilians and a largely different set for military men in itself emphasizes Nikephoros's concern with military virtue. Overall the most important characteristic for a military man was to be noble/brave, *gennaios*. The true nature of nobility for Nikephoros can best be appreciated when these ascribed characteristics are measured against actions.

# Bibliography

## SOURCES

*Actes de Docheiariou*, ed. Nicolas Oikonomides. Paris: P. Lethielleux, 1984.

*Anonymi Auctoris Chronicon ad A.C. 1234 Pertinens*, ed. Albert Abouna. Louvain: Corpus Scriptorum Christianorum Orientalium, 1974.

Attaleiates, Michael. *Miguel Ataliates: Historia*, ed. I Pérez Martín, Madrid: Consejo Superior de Investigaciones Científicas, 2002. References are to the page numbers of the more readily available Bonn edition (*Michaelis Attaliotae Historia*, ed. Immanuel Bekker, Bonn: Webber, 1853). The Bonn edition page numbers are noted in the margins of the Madrid edition.

Bryennios, Nikephoros. *Nicéphore Bryennios Histoire; introduction, texte, traduction et notes*, ed. and trans. Paul Gautier, Bruxelles: Byzantion, 1975.

Choniates, Niketas. *Nicetae Choniatae Historia*, ed. Jan Louis van Dieten. Berlin and New York: Walter de Gruyter, 1975.

Constantine Porphyrogenitus. "de Sententiis." In *Excerpta historica iussu Imp. Constantini Porphyrogeniti confecta*, ed. Ursulus Philippus Boissevain. Berlin: Weidman, 1903.

Elias. *Eliae in Porphyrii isagogen et Aristotelis categorias commentaria*, ed. A. Busse. Berlin: Reimer, 1900.

Eustathios of Thessaloniki. In *Eustathii Thessalonicensis opera minora (magnam partem inedita)*, ed. Peter Wirth. Berlin: De Gruyter, 1999.

    *Commentarii ad Homeri Iliadem et Odysseam*, ed. Gottfried Stallbaum. Hildesheim: G. Olms, 1960.

Evagrius Scholasticus. In *The Ecclesiastical History of Evagrius with the scholia*, ed. J. Bidez and L. Parmentier. London: Methune, 1898. Reprint, 1979.

Genesios. In *Iosephi Genesii Regum libri quattuor*, ed. I. Thurn and A. Lesmueller-Werner. Berlin: Walter de Gruyter, 1978.

Glykas, Michael. *Michaelis Glycae annales*, ed. Immanuel Bekker, Bonn: Weber, 1836.

John of Damascus. "Capita philosophica." In *Die Schriften des Johannes von Damaskos*, ed. P. B. Kotter. Berlin: De Gruyter, 1969.

Komnene, Anna. *Annae Comnenae Alexias*, ed. Diether R. Reinsch and Athanasios Kambylis, Berlin and New York: Walter de Gruyter, 2001.

*Anna Komnene: The Alexiad*, revised translation and notes by Peter Frankopan, New York: Penguin, 2009.

Leo of Synada. *The Correspondence of Leo, Metropolitan of Synada and Syncellus*, ed. Martha Pollard Vinson, Washington, DC: Dumbarton Oaks, 1985.

Leo the Deacon. *The History of Leo the Deacon : Byzantine Military Expansion in the Tenth Century*. Translated by Alice-Mary Talbot and Denis Sullivan. Washington, DC: Dumbarton Oaks, 2005.

Pakourianos, Gregory. "Typikon of Gregory Pakourianos for the Monastery of the Mother of God Petritzonitissa in Bačkovo." In *Byzantine Monastic Foundation Documents: A Complete Translation of the Surviving Founders' Typika and Testaments*, ed. John Thomas and Angela Constantinides Hero, 507–63. Washington, DC: Dumbarton Oaks, 2000.

Porphyry. *Porphyrii isagoge et in Aristotelis categorias commentarium*, ed. A. Busse. Berlin: Reimer, 1887.

Psellos, Michael. *Chronographia,* in *Chronographie; ou, Histoire d'un siècle de Byzance (976–1077)*, ed. Émile Renauld. Paris: Société d'édition "Les Belles lettres", 1926–1928. References are to the book, paragraph, and line numbers found in the manuscript. The paragraph numbering sometimes starts fresh within a book. The *TLG* has divided the text into sections based on continuous paragraph numbering. Book 6 therefore has paragraphs 1–203 under "6" and then paragraphs 1–21 under "6-Theod." Book 7 is divided into "7," "7 Const.," "7 Eud. Rom," and "7 Mich."

*De operatione daemonum*, ed. Jean François Boissonade, Nuremberg, 1838. Reprint Amsterdam: A. M. Hakkert, 1964.

*Michaelis Pselli Historia Syntomos*, ed. W. J. Aerts, Berlin and New York: Walter de Gruyter, 1990. References are to the paragraph and line numbers of Aerts' edition. The line numbers do not relate to the paragraph numbers.

*Michaelis Pselli philosophica minora*, ed. John M. Duffy. Leipzig: Teubner, 1992.

*Scripta minora*, ed. E. Kurtz and F. Drexl. Milan: Società editrice "Vita e pensiero," 1936–41.

Skylitzes Continuatus. *He synecheia tes chronographias tou Ioannou Skylitse: Ioannes Skylitzes continuatus*, ed. Eudoxos Tsolakes. Thessalonike: Hetaireia Makedonikon Spoudon Hidryma Meleton Chersonesou tou Haimou, 1968.

Skylitzes, John. Ioannis Skylitzae Synopsis historiarum, ed. Ioannes Thurn, *Corpus fontium historiae byzantinae* 5, Berlin and New York: Walter de Gruyter, 1973.

Symeon the New Theologian. In *Symeon the New Theologian: The Discourses*, ed. C. J. De Catanzaro. Mahwah, NJ: Paulist Press, 1980.

Theophanes continuatus. In *Theophanes continuatus, Ioannes Caminiata, Symeon Magister, Georgius Monachus continuatus*, ed. Immanuel Bekker. Bonn: Weber, 1838.

Tornikes, George. *Georges et Dèmètrios Tornikès. Lettres et discours*, ed. Jean Darrouzès. Paris: Éditions du Centre national de la recherche scientifique, 1970.

Zonaras, John, *Annales,* in *Ioannis Zonarae epitomae historiarum libri xviii*, ed. M. Pinder and T. Büttner-Wobst, 3 vols., *Corpus scriptorum historiae byzantinae*

44–46, Bonn: Weber, 1841–97. Citations are to the page and line numbers of the third volume of Büttner-Wobst's edition, which covers books 13–18 of Zonaras's history.

## SECONDARY WORKS

Ahl, F. "The Art of Safe Criticism in Greece and Rome." *American Journal of Philology* 105, 2 (1984): 174–208.

Ahrweiler, Hélène. "Choma-Aggelokastron." *Revue des études byzantines* 24 (1966): 278–83.

"Recherches sur l'administration de l'empire byzantin aux IX–XI siècles." *Bulletin de Correspondance hellénique* 84 (1966): 1–111.

Ahrweiler, Hélène, and Angeliki E. Laiou. *Studies on the Internal Diaspora of the Byzantine Empire.* Washington, DC: Dumbarton Oaks, 1998.

Albu, Emily. "Bohemond and the Rooster: Byzantines, Normans, and the Artful Ruse." In *Anna Komnene and Her Times*, ed. Thalia Gouma-Peterson, 157–68. New York: Garland Publishing, 2000.

Alexiou, Margaret. *The Ritual Lament in Greek Tradition.* Cambridge University Press, 1974.

Althoff, Gerd, Johannes Fried, and Patrick J. Geary. *Medieval Concepts of the Past: Ritual, Memory, Historiography.* Washington, DC: Cambridge University Press, 2002.

Amelang, James. "Mourning Becomes Eclectic: Ritual Lament and the Problem of Continuity." *Past and Present* 187 (2005): 3–32.

Anderson, Benedict. *Imagined Communities: Reflections on the Origin and Spread of Nationalism.* Rev. edn. London: Verso, 1991.

Angold, Michael. "Imperial Renewal and Orthodox Reaction: Byzantium in the Eleventh Century." In *New Constantines: The Rhythm of Imperial Renewal in Byzantium, 4th–13th Centuries*, ed. Paul Magdalino, 231–46. Aldershot: Ashgate, 1994.

*Church and Society in Byzantium under the Comneni, 1081–1261.* Cambridge University Press, 1995.

"Alexios I Komnenos: An Afterword." In *Alexios I Komnenos*, ed. Margaret Mullett and Dion Smythe, 398–417. Belfast: Belfast Byzantine Enterprises, 1996.

*The Byzantine Empire, 1025–1204: A Political History.* 2nd edn. London: Longman, 1997.

Angold, Michael, and Michael Whitby. "Historiography." In *The Oxford Handbook of Byzantine Studies*, ed. Elizabeth Jeffreys John Haldon and Robin Cormack, 838–52. Oxford University Press, 2008.

Assmann, Aleida. "Canon and Archive." In *A Companion to Cultural Memory Studies*, ed. Astrid Erll and Ansgar Nünning, 97–108. Berlin: De Gruyter, 2010.

Assmann, Jan. *Das kulturelle Gedächtnis: Schrift, Erinnerung und politische Identität in frühen Hochkulturen.* Munich: C.H. Beck, 1992.

"Collective Memory and Cultural Identity." *New German Critique* no. 65 (1995): 125.

*Religion and Cultural Memory: Ten Studies.* Trans. Rodney Livingstone. Stanford University Press, 2006.

"Communicative and Cultural Memory." In *A Companion to Cultural Memory Studies,* ed. Astrid Erll and Ansgar Nünning, 109–18. Berlin: De Gruyter, 2010.

Bakhtin, M. M. *The Dialogic Imagination: Four Essays.* Trans. Michael Holquist. Austin: University of Texas Press, 2004.

Barber, Charles. "Homo Byzantinus?" In *Women, Men and Eunuchs: Gender in Byzantium,* ed. Liz James, 185–99. London: Routledge, 1997.

Barton, Carlin A. *Roman Honor: The Fire in the Bones.* Berkeley: University of California Press, 2001.

Baun, Jane. "Discussing Mary's Humanity in Medieval Byzantium." *Studies in Church History* 39 (2004): 63–72.

*Tales from Another Byzantium: Celestial Journey and Local Community in the Medieval Greek Apocrypha.* Cambridge University Press, 2007.

Beard, Mary. *The Roman Triumph.* Cambridge: Belknap Press, 2007.

Beard, Mary, John A. North, and S. R. F. Price. *Religions of Rome.* 2 vols. Cambridge University Press, 1998.

Beaton, Roderick. "Byzantine Historiography and Modern Greek Oral Poetry: The Case of Rapsomatis." *Byzantine and Modern Greek Studies* 10 (1986): 41–50.

"Cappadocians at Court: Digenes and Timarion." In *Alexios I Komnenos,* ed. Margaret Mullett and Dion Smythe, 329–38. Belfast: Belfast Byzantine Enterprises, 1996.

*The Medieval Greek Romance.* 2nd edn. London: Routledge, 1996.

"Antique Nation? 'Hellenes' on the Eve of Greek Independence and in Twelfth-Century Byzantium." *Byzantine and Modern Greek Studies* 31, 1 (2007): 76–95.

Beck, Hans-Georg. "Die byzantinische 'Mönchschronik'." In *Ideen und Realitäten in Byzanz,* 188–97. London, 1972.

"Hieronymus Wolf." In *Ideen und Realitäten in Byzanz,* 169–93. London, 1972.

Belke, Klaus. "Communications: Roads and Bridges." In *The Oxford Handbook of Byzantine Studies,* ed. Elizabeth Jeffreys, John Haldon, and Robin Cormack, 295–308. Oxford University Press, 2008.

Boitani, Piero. *The Shadow of Ulysses: Figures of a Myth.* Oxford: Clarendon Press, 1994.

Bonnell, Victoria E., Lynn Avery Hunt, and Richard Biernacki. *Beyond the Cultural Turn: New Directions in the Study of Society and Culture.* Studies on the History of Society and Culture, 34. Berkeley, CA: University of California Press, 1999.

Bourbouhakis, Emmanuel C. "'Political' Personae: The Poem from Prison of Michael Glykas: Byzantine Literature between Fact and Fiction." *Byzantine and Modern Greek Studies* 31, 1 (2007): 53–75.

Browning, Robert. "An Unpublished Funeral Oration on Anna Comnena." *Proceedings of the Cambridge Philological Society* 8 (1962): 1–12.

Brubaker, Leslie. "The Age of Justinian: Gender and Society." In *The Cambridge Companion to the Age of Justinian*, ed. Michael Maas, 427–47. Cambridge University Press, 2005.

Buckley, P. "War and Peace in the Alexiad." In *Byzantine Narrative*, ed. J. Burke, 92–109. Melbourne: Australian Association for Byzantine Studies, 2006.

Cameron, Averil. *Procopius and the Sixth Century*. Berkeley, CA: University of California Press, 1985.

"Byzantium and the Limits of Orthodoxy." *Proceedings of the British Academy* 154 (2007): 129–52.

Campbell, J. *Honour, Family and Patronage: A Study of Institutions and Moral Values in a Greek Mountain Community*. Oxford University Press, 1964.

Cantarella, Eva. *Pandora's Daughters: The Role and Status of Women in Greek and Roman Antiquity*. Trans. Maureen B. Fant. Baltimore: Johns Hopkins University Press, 1987.

Carile, Antonio. "Il problema della identificazione del cesare Niceforo Briennio." *Aevum* 38 (1964): 74–83.

"Il cesare Niceforo Briennio." *Aevum* 42 (1968): 429–54.

"La Hyli historias del cesare Niceforo Briennio." *Aevum* 43, 1–2 (1969): 56–87.

Cary, Ernest. "Introduction." In *Cassius Dio's Roman History*. Cambridge, MA: Harvard University Press, 1914.

Castelli, Elizabeth A. *Martyrdom and Memory: Early Christian Culture Making*. New York: Columbia University Press, 2004.

Champion, Craige Brian. *Cultural Politics in Polybius's Histories*. Vol. 41. Berkeley: University of California Press, 2004.

Chaplin, Jane D. *Livy's Exemplary History*. Oxford University Press, 2000.

Cheynet, Jean-Claude. "Mantzikert, un désastre militaire?" *Byzantion* 50, no. 2 (1980): 412–38.

*Pouvoir et contestations à Byzance (963–1210)*. Paris: Publications de la Sorbonne, 1990.

"La politique militaire byzantine de Basile II á Alexis Comnene." *Zbornik Radova Vizantološkog Instituta* 30 (1991): 61–73.

"Le rôle des femmes de l'aristocratie d'après les sceaux." In *Mélanges V. Sandrovskaja*, 30–39. St. Petersberg: The Hermitage Museum, 2004.

*La société byzantine: l'apport des sceaux*, Bilans de recherche. Paris: Association des amis du Centre d'histoire et civilisation de Byzance, 2008.

Cheynet, Jean-Claude, and Jean-Francois Vannier. *Études prosopographiques*. Paris: Publications de la Sorbonne, 1986.

Chrysos, Evangelos. "Romans and Foreigners." In *Fifty Years of Prosopography: The Later Roman Empire, Byzantium and Beyond*, ed. Averil Cameron, 119–36. Oxford University Press, 2003.

Clark, Elizabeth. "Ideology, History, and the Construction of 'Woman' in Late Ancient Christianity." *Journal of Early Christian Studies* 2 (1994): 155–84.

"The Lady Vanishes: Dilemmas of a Feminist Historian after the 'Linguistic Turn'." *Church History* 67 (1998): 1–31.

Clarke, Graeme, ed. *Reading the Past in Late Antiquity*. Rushcutters Bay: Australian National University Press, 1990.

Conley, Thomas. "Byzantine Teaching on Figures and Tropes: An Introduction." *Rhetorica* 4 (1986): 335–74.

Connerton, Paul. *How Societies Remember*. Cambridge University Press, 1989.

Cooper, Kate. "Insinuations of Womanly Influence: An Aspect of the Christianisation of the Roman Aristocracy." *Journal of Roman Studies* 82 (1992): 150–64.

Cresci, Lia Raffaella. "Appunti per una tipologia del ΤΥΡΑΝΝΟΣ." *Byzantion* 60 (1990): 90–129.

"Categorie autobiografiche in storici bizantini." In *Categorie concettuali e linguistiche della storiografia bizantina*, ed. Ugo Crisiculo and Riccardo Maisano, 125–47. Naples: Associazione Italiana di Studi bizantini, 2000.

"Procopio al confine tra due tradizioni storiografiche." *Rivista di filologia e di istruzione classica* 129, 1 (2001): 61–77.

"Exempla storici greci negli encomi e nella storiografia bizantini del XII secolo." *Rhetorica: A Journal of the History of Rhetoric* 22, 2 (2004): 115–45.

"Ποικιλία nei proemi storiografici bizantini." *Byzantion* 72, 2 (2004): 330–47.

"Storiografia drammatica dall'antichità a Bisanzio: elementi di continuità e discontinuità." *Rivista di filologia e di istruzione classica* 133, 3 (2005): 257–82.

Croke, Brian. "Uncovering Byzantium's Historiographical Audience." In *History as Literature in Byzantium*, ed. Ruth Macrides, 25–54. Aldershot: Ashgate, 2010.

Curta, Florin. *Southeastern Europe in the Middle Ages 500–1250*. Cambridge University Press, 2006.

Dagron, Gilbert. "Le christianisme dans la ville byzantine." *Dumbarton Oaks Papers* 31 (1977): 1–25.

*La romanité chrétienne en Orient: héritages et mutations*. London: Variorum Reprints, 1984.

"La règle et l'exception. Analyse de la notion d'économie." In *Religiöse Devianz. Untersuchungen zu sozialen, rechtlichen und theologischen Reaktionen auf religiöse Abweichung im westlichen und östlichen Mittelalter*, ed. Dieter Simon, 1–18. Frankfurt: Klostermann, 1990.

*Emperor and Priest: The Imperial Office in Byzantium*. Cambridge University Press, 2003.

Dagron, Gilbert, and Haralambie Mihaescu, eds. *Le traité sur la guérilla (De velitatione) de l'empereur Nicéphore Phocas (963–969)*. Paris: Éditions du Centre national de la recherche scientifique, 1986.

Darrouzes, Jean. *George et Demetrios Tornikes. Lettres et discours*. Paris: Editions du centre national de la recherche scientifique, 1970.

Davis, Jason. *Rome's Religious History: Livy, Tacitus and Ammianus on their Gods*. Cambridge University Press, 2004.

Dennis, George T. *Three Byzantine Military Treatises*, Dumbarton Oaks texts 9. Washington, DC: Dumbarton Oaks, 1985.

Dixon, Suzanne. "A Family Business: Women's Role in Patronage and Politics at Rome, 80–44 BC." *Classica et Medievalia* 34 (1983): 91–112.

"The Marriage Alliance in the Roman Elite." *Journal of Family History* 10 (1985): 353–78.

"Polybius on Roman Women and Property." *American Journal of Philology* 106 (1985): 147–70.

*The Roman Mother.* London: Croom Helm, 1988.

Eckstein, A. M. *Moral Vision in the Histories of Polybius.* Berkeley: University of California Press, 1995.

Epstein, Julia, and Kristina Straub. *Body Guards: The Cultural Politics of Gender Ambiguity.* New York: Routledge, 1991.

Evans, J. A. S. "The 'Nika' Rebellion and the Empress Theodora." *Byzantion* 54 (1984): 381–83.

Failler, Albert. "Le texte de l'histoire de Nicéphore Bryennios à la lumière d'un nouveau fragment." *Revue des études byzantines* 47 (1989): 239–50.

Feldherr, Andrew. *The Cambridge Companion to the Roman Historians.* Cambridge University Press, 2009.

Fischler, Susan. "Social Stereotypes and Historical Analysis: The Case of the Imperial Women at Rome." In *Women in Ancient Societies: An Illusion of the Nights*, ed. L. Archer, S. Fischler, and M. Wyke, 115–33. New York: Routledge, 1994.

"Imperial Cult: Engendering the Cosmos." In *When Men were Men: Masculinity, Power and Identity in Classical Antiquity*, ed. Lin Foxhall and John Salmon, 165–83. London: Routledge, 1998.

Fisher, Elizabeth. "Theodora and Antonia." In *Women in the Ancient World. The Arethusa Papers*, ed. J. Peradoto and J. P. Sullivan, 287–313. Albany: State University of New York Press, 1984.

Flusin, Bernard, ed. and trans. *Jean Skylitzès, Empereurs de Constantinople.* Annotated by Jean-Claude Cheynet. Paris: Lethielleux, 2003.

Fox, Matthew. *Roman Historical Myths: The Regal Period in Augustan Literature.* Oxford: Clarendon Press, 1996.

Fox, Matthew, and Niall Livingstone. "Rhetoric and Historiography." In *A Companion to Greek Rhetoric*, ed. Ian Worthington, 542–61. Oxford: Blackwell, 2007.

Foxhall, Lin, and J. B. Salmon. *When Men were Men: Masculinity, Power and Identity in Classical Antiquity.* London: Routledge, 1998.

*Thinking Men: Masculinity and its Self-Representation in the Classical Tradition.* London: Routledge, 1998.

Frankfurter, David. "Traditional Cult." In *A Companion to the Roman Empire*, ed. David S. Potter, 543–65. Oxford: Blackwell, 2006.

Frankopan, Peter. "Challenges to Imperial Authority in Byzantium: Revolts on Crete and Cyprus at the End of the 11th Century." *Byzantion* 74, 2 (2004): 382–402.

"Kinship and the Distribution of Power in Komnenian Byzantium." *English Historical Review* 122, 495 (2007): 1–34.

Gabba, Emilio. *Dionysius and the History of Archaic Rome* Berkeley, CA: University of California Press, 1991.

Garland, Lynda. *Byzantine Empresses: Women and Power in Byzantium AD 527–1204*. London: Routledge, 1999.

Garland, Lynda, and Stephen Rapp. "Mary 'of Alania': Woman and Empress Between Two Worlds." In *Byzantine Women: Varieties of Experience 800–1200*, ed. Lynda Garland, 91–123. Aldershot: Ashgate, 2006.

Gautier, Paul, ed. *Nicéphore Bryennios Histoire; introduction, texte, traduction et notes*. Brussels: Byzantion, 1975.

Geary, Patrick J. *Phantoms of Remembrance: Memory and Oblivion at the End of the First Millennium*. Princeton University Press, 1994.

"Land, Language and Memory in Europe 700–1100." *Transactions of the Royal Historical Society* 9 (1999): 169–84.

Gibbon, Edward. *History of the Decline and Fall of the Roman Empire*, 1788.

Goldhill, Simon. *Being Greek under Rome: Cultural Identity, the Second Sophistic, and the Development of Empire*. Cambridge University Press, 2001.

*The Invention of Prose*, New Surveys in the Classics No. 32. Oxford University Press, 2002.

Gowing, Alain. *The Triumviral Narratives of Appian and Cassius Dio*. Ann Arbor: The University of Michigan Press, 1992.

*Empire and Memory: The Representation of the Roman Republic in Imperial Culture*. Cambridge University Press, 2005.

Gregory, Timothy E. *A History of Byzantium*. Oxford: Blackwell, 2005.

Grigoriadis, Iordanis. "A Study of the Prooimion of Zonaras' Chronicle in Relation to Other 12th-Century Prooimia." *Byzantinische Zeitschrift* 91, 2 (1998): 327–44.

Gruen, Erich S. *The Last Generation of the Roman Republic*. Berkeley, CA: University of California Press, 1974.

Halbwachs, Maurice. *La topographie légendaire des évangiles en Terre Sainte : étude de mémoire collective*. Paris: Presses universitaires de France, 1941.

*On Collective Memory*. Trans. Lewis A. Coser. University of Chicago Press, 1992.

Haldon, John. *The Byzantine Wars*. Stroud: Tempus, 2001.

ed. *The Social History of Byzantium*. Chichester: Wiley-Blackwell, 2009.

Halperin, David M. "Why is Diotima a Woman?" In *One Hundred Years of Homosexuality and Other Essays on Greek Love*, 113–51. London: Routledge, 1990.

Hamilton, Edith, and Huntington Cairns, eds. *Plato: The Collected Dialogues*. Princeton University Press, 1961.

Hanson, John. "The Rise and Fall of the Macedonian Renaissance." In *A Companion to Byzantium*, ed. Liz James, 338–50. Oxford: Wiley-Blackwell, 2010.

Harris, Jonathan. *Byzantium and the Crusades*. London: Hambledon and London, 2003.

Henderson, Jeffrey. *The Maculate Muse: Obscene Language in Attic Comedy*. Oxford University Press, 1991.

Hill, Barbara. "Alexios I Komnenos and the Imperial Women." In *Alexios I Komnenos*, ed. Margaret Mullett and Dion Smythe, 37–54. Belfast Byzantine Enterprises, 1996.

"The Ideal Komnenian Woman." *Byzantinische Forschungen* 23 (1996): 7–18.

*Imperial Women in Byzantium, 1025–1204: Power, Patronage and Ideology.* New York: Longman, 1999.

"Actions Speak Louder than Words: Anna Komnene's Attempted Usurpation." In *Anna Komnene and Her Times*, ed. Thalia Gouma-Peterson, 45–62. New York: Garland Publishing, 2000.

Hillenbrand, Carole. *Turkish Myth and Muslim Symbol: The Battle of Manzikert.* Edinburgh University Press, 2007.

Hinterberger, Martin. "O phthonos, anthropine adunamia kai kineteria duname." In *To Vyzantio hōrimo gia allages : epiloges, euaisthēsies kai tropoi ekphrasēs apo ton hendekato ston dekato pempto aiōna*, ed. Christina Angelidē, 299–312. Athens: Institouto Vyzantinōn Ereunōn, 2004.

"Envy and Nemesis in the *Vita Basili* and Leo the Deacon: Literary Mimesis or Something More?" In *History as Literature in Byzantium*, ed. Ruth Macrides, 187–203. Farnham: Ashgate, 2010.

"Emotions in Byzantium." In *A Companion to Byzantium*, ed. Liz James, 121–34. Malden: Wiley-Blackwell, 2010.

"*Phthonos* als treibende Kraft in Prodromos, Manasses und Bryennios." *Medioevo Greco* 11, 1 (2011): 1–24.

Holmes, Catherine. "The Rhetorical Structures of Skylitzes' Synopsis Historion." In *Rhetoric in Byzantium*, ed. Elizabeth Jeffreys, 187–200. Aldershot: Ashgate, 2003.

*Basil II and the Governance of Empire (976–1025).* Oxford University Press, 2005.

"Political-Historical Survey: C 800–1204." In *The Oxford Handbook of Byzantine Studies*, ed. Elizabeth Jeffreys, John Haldon, and Robin Cormack, 249–63. Oxford University Press, 2008.

Holmes, Catherine, and Judith Waring. *Literacy, Education and Manuscript Transmission in Byzantium and Beyond.* Leiden: Brill, 2002.

Hornblower, Simon. "Warfare in Ancient Literature: The Paradox of War." In *The Cambridge History of Greek and Roman Warfare*, ed. Philip A. G. Sabin, Hans van Wees, and Michael Whitby, 22–53. Cambridge University Press, 2007.

Howard-Johnston, James. "Anna Komnene and the Alexiad." In *Alexios I Komnenos*, ed. Margaret Mullett and Dion Smythe, 232–302. Belfast Byzantine Enterprises, 1996.

Hunger, Herbert. *Schreiben und Lesen in Byzanz: die byzantinische Buchkultur.* Munich: C.H. Beck, 1989.

Hussey, J. M. *Church and Learning in the Byzantine Empire, 867–1185.* London: Oxford University Press, 1937.

James, Liz. *Empresses and Power in Early Byzantium.* London: Leicester University Press, 2001.

Jeffreys, Elizabeth. "Nikephoros Bryennios Reconsidered." In *The Empire in Crisis (?) Byzantium in the Eleventh Century*, 201–14. Athens: Institouto Vyzantinon Ereunon, 2003.

*Rhetoric in Byzantium.* Aldershot: Ashgate, 2003.

Jeffreys, Elizabeth, John Haldon, and Robin Cormack, eds. *Oxford Handbook of Byzantine Studies.* Oxford University Press, 2008.

Kaegi, Walter. *Some Thoughts on Byzantine Military Strategy.* Brookline: The Hellenic Studies Lecture, 1983.

Kaldellis, Anthony. *The Argument of Psellos' Chronographia.* Leiden: Brill, 1999.

*Procopius of Caesarea: Tyranny, History, and Philosophy at the End of Antiquity.* Philadelphia: University of Pennsylvania Press, 2004.

ed. *Mothers and Sons, Fathers and Daughters: The Byzantine Family of Michael Psellos.* Notre Dame: University of Notre Dame Press, 2006.

*Hellenism in Byzantium: The Transformations of Greek Identity and the Reception of the Classical Tradition.* Cambridge University Press, 2007.

"Historicism in Byzantine Thought and Literature." *Dumbarton Oaks Papers* 61 (2007): 1–24.

"A Byzantine Argument for the Equivalence of All Religions: Michael Attaleiates on Ancient and Modern Romans." *International Journal of the Classical Tradition* 14, 1/2 (2008): 1–22.

"Paradox, Reversal and the Meaning of History." In *Niketas Choniates: A Historian and a Writer*, ed. Alicia Simpson and Stephanos Efthymiadis, 75–100. Geneva: La Pomme d'Or, 2009.

"Procopius' *Persian War*: a Thematic and Literary Analysis." In *History as Literature in Byzantium*, ed. Ruth Macrides, 253–74. Farnham: Ashgate, 2010.

"The Corpus of Byzantine Historiography: An Interpretive Essay." In *The Byzantine World*, ed. Paul Stephenson, 211–22. London: Routledge, 2010.

Kambylis, Athanasios, ed. *Eustathius of Thessalonica: Prooimion zum Pindarkommentar.* Göttingen: Vandenhoeck & Ruprecht, 1991.

Kaplan, Michel. "L'église byzantine des vie–xie siècles: terres et paysans." In *Church and People in Byzantium*, ed. Rosemary Morris, 109–23. Birmingham: Centre for Byzantine Ottoman and Modern Greek Studies, 1990.

Kazhdan, Alexander. "Aristocracy and the Imperial Ideal." In *The Byzantine Aristocracy, ix–xiii Centuries*, ed. Michael Angold, 43–57. Oxford: British Archaeological Reports, 1984.

ed. *The Oxford Dictionary of Byzantium.* New York: Oxford University Press, 1991.

"State, Feudal and Private Economy in Byzantium." *Dumbarton Oaks Papers* 47 (1993): 83–100.

Kazhdan, Alexander, and Giles Constable. *People and Power in Byzantium: An Introduction to Modern Byzantine Studies.* Washington, DC: Dumbarton Oaks, 1982.

Kazhdan, Alexander, and Simon Franklin. *Studies on Byzantine Literature of the Eleventh and Twelfth Centuries.* Cambridge University Press, 1984.

Kazhdan, Alexander, and Annabel Jane Wharton. *Change in Byzantine Culture in the Eleventh and Twelfth Centuries*. Berkeley, CA: University of California Press, 1985.

Keith, Alison. *Engendering Rome: Women in Latin Epic*. Cambridge University Press, 2000.

Kolbaba, Tia M. *The Byzantine Lists: Errors of the Latins*. Illinois Medieval Studies. Urbana: University of Illinois Press, 2000.

Kowaleski, Maryanne, and Mary C. Erler. "A New Economy of Power Relations: Female Agency in the Middle Ages." In *Gendering the Master Narrative: Women and Power in the Middle Ages*, ed. Mary C. Erler and Maryanne Kowaleski, 1–16. Ithaca: Cornell University Press, 2003.

Krallis, Dimitri. "Attaliates as a Reader of Psellos." In *Reading Michael Psellos*, ed. Charles Barber and David Jenkins, 167–91. Leiden: Brill, 2006.

  "History as Politics in Eleventh-Century Byzantium." Ph.D. Dissertation, University of Michigan, 2006.

Kraus, Christina S. "Forging a National Identity: Prose Literature Down to the Time of Augustus." In *Literature in the Greek and Roman Worlds*, ed. Oliver Taplin, 311–35. Oxford University Press, 2000.

Krueger, Derek, ed. *Byzantine Christianity*. Minneapolis: Fortress Press, 2006.

Kuefler Mathew. *The Manly Eunuch: Masculinity, Gender Ambiguity, and Christian Ideology in Late Antiquity*. University of Chicago Press, 2001.

Kustas, George L. *Studies in Byzantine Rhetoric*. Thessaloniki: Patriarchikon Hidryma Paterikon, 1973.

Laiou, Angeliki. *Mariage, Amour et Parenté à Byzance aux XIe–XIIIe siècles*. Paris: De Boccard, 1992.

  "Imperial Marriages and Their Critics in the Eleventh Century: The Case of Skylitzes." *Dumbarton Oaks Papers* 46 (1992): 165–76.

  "Law, Justice, and the Byzantine Historians: Ninth to Twelfth Centuries." In *Law and Society in Byzantium: Ninth-Twelfth Centuries*, ed. Angeliki Laiou and Dieter Simon, 151–86. Washington, DC: Dumbarton Oaks, 1994.

  "The Byzantine Economy: An Overview." In *The Economic History of Byzantium From the Seventh through the Fifteenth Century*, ed. Angeliki Laiou, 1145–64. Washington, DC: Dumbarton Oaks, 2002.

Laiou, Angeliki, and Cécile Morrisson. *The Byzantine Economy*. Cambridge University Press, 2007.

Lardinois, A. P. M. H., and Laura McClure. *Making Silence Speak: Women's Voices in Greek Literature and Society*. Princeton University Press, 2001.

Lemerle, Paul. *Cinq études sur le XIe siècle byzantin*. Paris: Centre national de la recherche scientifique, 1977.

Lendon, J. E. *Empire of Honour: The Art of Government in the Roman World*. Oxford University Press, 1997.

  *Soldiers & Ghosts: A History of Battle in Classical Antiquity*. New Haven: Yale University Press, 2005.

"War and Society." In *The Cambridge History of Greek and Roman Warfare*, ed. Philip A. G. Sabin, Hans Van Wees, and Michael Whitby, 498–516. Cambridge University Press, 2007.

Liddell, Henry George, Robert Scott, Henry Stuart Jones, and Roderick McKenzie. *A Greek–English Lexicon*. Rev. edn. Oxford: Clarendon Press, 1968.

Ljubarskij, Jakov. "New Trends in the Study of Byzantine Historiography." *Dumbarton Oaks Papers* 47 (1993): 131–38.

"Nikephoros Phokas in Byzantine Historical Writings. Trace of the Secular Biography in Byzantium." *Byzantinoslavica* 54, 2 (1993): 245–53.

"Byzantine Irony: The Example of Niketas Choniates." In *In To Byzantio Orimo Gia Allages: Epiloges, Euaisthesies Kai Tropoi Ekphrases Apo Ton Endakato Ston Dekaton Pempto Aiona*, ed. Christine Angelidi, 287–98. Athens: Institute for Byzantine Research, 2004.

"Byzantine Irony – the Case of Michael Psellos." In *Vyzantio kratos kai koinōnia: mnēmē Nikou Oikonomidē*, ed. A. Avramea, A. Laiou, and E. Chrysos, 349–60. Athens: Institouto Vyzantinōn Ereunōn, Ethniko Hidryma Ereunōn 2003.

Macleod, Colin. *Collected Essays*. Oxford: Clarendon Press, 1983.

Macrides, Ruth. "Kinship by Arrangement: The Case of Adoption," *Dumbarton Oaks Papers* 44 (1990): 109–18.

"The Pen and the Sword: Who Wrote the Alexiad?" In *Anna Komnene and her Times*, ed. Thalia Gouma-Peterson, 63–81. New York: Garland Publishing, 2000.

Macrides, Ruth, and Paul Magdalino. "The Fourth Kingdom and the Rhetoric of Hellenism." In *The Perception of the Past in Twelfth-Century Europe*, ed. Paul Magdalino, 117–56. London: The Hambledon Press, 1992.

Magdalino, Paul. "The Byzantine Holy Man in the Twelfth Century." In *The Byzantine Saint*, ed. Sergei Hackel, 51–66. London: Fellowship of St. Alban and St. Sergius, 1981.

"Aspects of Twelfth-Century Byzantine Kaiserkritik." *Speculum* 58, 2 (1983): 326–46.

"Byzantine Snobbery." In *The Byzantine Aristocracy, IX to XIII Centuries*, ed. Michael Angold, 58–78. Oxford: British Archaeological Reports, 1984.

"Honour among Romaioi: The Framework of Social Values in the World of Diogenes Akrites and Kekaumenos." *Byzantine and Modern Greek Studies* 13 (1989): 183–218.

"Hellenism and Nationalism in Byzantium." In *Tradition and Transformation in Byzantium*, 1–29. Aldershot: Ashgate, 1992.

*The Empire of Manuel I Komnenos, 1143–1180*. Cambridge University Press, 1993.

"Justice and Finance in the Byzantine State, Ninth to Twelfth Centuries." In *Law and Society in Byzantium, Ninth–Twelfth Centuries*, ed. Angeliki Laiou and Dieter Simon, 93–116. Washington, DC: Dumbarton Oaks, 1994.

"Innovations in Government." In *Alexios I Komnenos*, ed. Margaret Mullett and Dion Smythe, 146–66. Belfast Byzantine Enterprises, 1996.

"The Pen of the Aunt: Echoes of the Mid-Twelfth Century in the Alexiad." In *Anna Komnene and her times*, ed. Thalia Gouma-Peterson. New York: Garland, 2000.

"Medieval Constantinople." In *Studies on the History and Topography of Byzantine Constantinople*, I–III. Aldershot: Ashgate, 2007.

"The Empire of the Komnenoi (1118–1204)." In *The Cambridge History of the Byzantine Empire c.500–1492*, ed. Jonathan Shepard, 627–63. Cambridge University Press, 2008.

Malamut, Élisabeth. "Une femme politique d'exception à la fin du XIe siècle: Anne Dalassène." In *Femmes et pouvoirs des femmes à Byzance et en occident (VIe–XIe siècles)*, ed. Stéphane Lebecq, Alain Dierkens, Régine Le Jan, and Jean-Marie Sansterre, 103–20. Lille: Centre de Recherche sur l'Histoire de l'Europe du Nord-Ouest, 1999.

*Alexis Ier Comnène*. Paris: Ellipses, 2007.

Mango, Cyril, ed. *The Oxford History of Byzantium*. Oxford University Press, 2002.

Marincola, John. *Greek Historians*. Greece & Rome, New Surveys in the Classics, no. 31. Oxford University Press, 2001.

*A Companion to Greek and Roman Historiography*. Malden: Blackwell, 2007.

Markopoulos, Athanasios. "Byzantine History Writing at the End of the First Millennium." In *Byzantium in the Year 1000*, ed. Paul Magdalino, 183–97. Leiden: Brill, 2003.

"Roman Antiquarianism: Aspects of the Roman Past in the Middle Byzantine Period (9th–11th Centuries)." In *Proceedings of the 21st International Congress of Byzantine Studies*, ed. Elizabeth Jeffreys and F. Haarer, 277–97. Aldershot: Ashgate, 2006.

McCormick, Michael. *Eternal Victory: Triumphal Rulership in Late Antiquity, Byzantium, and the Early Medieval West*. Cambridge University Press, 1986.

McDonnell, Myles Anthony. *Roman Manliness: Virtus and the Roman Republic*. Cambridge University Press, 2006.

McNamara, Jo Ann. "Women and Power Through the Family Revisited." In *Gendering the Master Narrative: Women and Power in the Middle Ages*, ed. Mary C. Erler and Maryanne Kowaleski, 17–30. Ithaca: Cornell University Press, 2003.

Mellor, Ronald. *The Roman Historians*. London: Routledge, 1999.

Meyendorff, John. *Byzantine Theology: Historical Trends and Doctrinal Themes*. 1st edn. New York: Fordham University Press, 1974.

Millar, Fergus. *A Study of Cassius Dio*. Oxford: Clarendon Press, 1964.

Momigliano, Arnaldo. *Essays in Ancient and Modern Historiography*. 1st paperback edn. Middletown, CT: Wesleyan University Press, 1982.

Moore, J. M. *The Manuscript Tradition of Polybius*. Cambridge University Press, 1965.

Moore, Paul. *Iter Psellianum: A Detailed Listing of Manuscript Sources for all Works Attributed to Michael Psellos, Including a Comprehensive Bibliography*. Toronto: Pontifical Institute of Mediaeval Studies, 2005.

Moorhead, John. *Justinian.* London: Longman, 1994.

Moravcsik, Gyula. ed. *De administrando imperio. Constantine VII Porphyrogenitus.* Washington, DC: Dumbarton Oaks, 1967.

Morris, Rosemary. *Monks and Laymen in Byzantium, 843–1118.* Cambridge University Press, 1995.

Morrisson, Cécile. "Byzantine Money: Its Production and Circulation." In *The Economic History of Byzantium from the Seventh through the Fifteenth Century,* ed. Angeliki Laiou, 909–66. Washington, DC: Dumbarton Oaks, 2002.

Mullett, Margaret. "Aristocracy and Patronage in the Literary Circles of Comnenian Constantinople." In *The Byzantine Aristocracy: IX–XIII Centuries,* ed. Michael Angold, 173–201. Oxford: British Archeological Reports, 1984.

"Alexios I Komnenos and Imperial Renewal." In *New Constantines: The Rhythm of Imperial Renewal in Byzantium, 4th–13th Centuries,* ed. Paul Magdalino, 259–67. Aldershot: Ashgate, 1994.

"The Imperial Vocabulary of Alexios I Komnenos." In *Alexios I Komnenos,* ed. Margaret Mullett and Dion Smythe, 359–97. Belfast Byzantine Enterprises, 1996.

"Novelisation in Byzantium: Narrative After the Revival of Fiction." In *Byzantine Narrative: Papers in Honour of Roger Scott,* ed. J. Burke, *et al.,* 1–28. Melbourne: Australian Association for Byzantine Studies, 2006.

"No Drama, No Poetry, No Fiction, No Readership, No Literature." In *A Companion to Byzantium,* ed. Liz James, 227–38. Oxford: Wiley-Blackwell, 2010.

Mullett, Margaret, and Roger Scott, eds. *Byzantium and the Classical Tradition.* Birmingham: Centre for Byzantine Studies University of Birmingham, 1981.

Mullett, Margaret, and Dion Smythe, eds. *Alexios I Komnenos.* Belfast Byzantine Enterprises, 1996.

Neville, Leonora. *Authority in Byzantine Provincial Society, 950–1100.* Cambridge University Press, 2004.

"A History of the Caesar John Doukas in Nikephoros Bryennios' *Material for History.*" *Byzantine and Modern Greek Studies* 32, 2 (2008): 168–88.

"Strong Women and their Husbands in Byzantine Historiography." In *The Byzantine World,* ed. Paul Stephenson, 72–82. London: Routledge, 2010.

Nilsson, Ingela. *Erotic Pathos, Rhetorical Pleasure: Narrative Technique and Mimesis in Eumathios Makrembolites' "Hysmine & Hysminias."* Uppsala: Acta Universitatis Upsaliensis, 2001.

"Narrating Images in Byzantine Literature: The Ekphraseis of Konstantinos Manasses." *Jahrbuch der Österreichischen Byzantinistik* 55 (2005): 121–46.

"Discovering Literariness in the Past: Literature vs. History in the *Synopsis Chronike* of Konstantinos Manasses." In *L'écriture de la mémoire: la littérarité de l'historiographie,* ed. Paolo Odorico Panagiotis, A. Agapitos, and Martin Hinterberger, 15–31. Paris: Centre d'études byzantines, néo-helléniques et sud-est européennes, 2006.

"To Narrate the Events of the Past: On Byzantine Historians and Historians on Byzantium." In *Byzantine Narrative*, ed. John Burke, 47–58. Melbourne: Australian Association for Byzantine Studies, 2006.

North, Helen. *Sophrosyne: Self-Knowledge and Restraint in Classical Antiquity.* Ithaca: Cornell University Press, 1966.

North, John. "The Religion of Rome from Monarchy to Principate." In *Companion to Historiography*, ed. Michael Bentley, 57–68. London: Routledge, 1997.

*Roman Religion.* Oxford University Press, 2000.

"Rome." In *Ancient Religions*, ed. Sarah Iles Johnston, 225–32. Cambridge: Belknap, 2007.

Odorico, Paolo, and Panagiotis A. Agapitos, eds. *Pour une "nouvelle" histoire de la littérature byzantine : problèmes, méthodes, approches, propositions.* Paris: Centre d'études byzantines, néo-helléniques et sud-est européennes, 2002.

Ostrogorsky, George. *Pour l'histoire de la féodalité byzantine.* Trans. Henri Grégoire. Brussels: Éditions de l'Institut de philologie et d'histoire orientales et slaves, 1954.

*History of the Byzantine State.* New Brunswick: Rutgers University Press, 1969.

"Observations on the Aristocracy in Byzantium." *Dumbarton Oaks Papers* 25 (1971): 1–32.

Page, Gill. *Being Byzantine: Greek Identity before the Ottomans.* Cambridge University Press, 2008.

Paidas, Constantine D. S. "Issues of Social Gender in Nikephoros Bryennios' *Yle Istorion.*" *Byzantinische Zeitschrift* 101, 2 (2008): 737–49.

Papalexandrou, Amy. "Memory Culture in Byzantium." In *A Companion to Byzantium*, ed. Liz James, 108–22. Malden: Wiley-Blackwell, 2010.

Pazdernik, Charles. "Procopius and Thucydides on the Labors of War: Belisarius and Brasidas in the Field." *Transactions of the American Philological Association* 130 (2000): 149–87.

"Xenophon's *Hellenica* in Procopius' *Wars:* Pharnabazus and Belisarius." *Greek Roman and Byzantine Studies* 46, 2 (2006): 175–206.

Peachin, Michael. "Rome the Superpower: 96–235." In *A Companion to the Roman Empire*, ed. David Potter, 126–73. London: Blackwell, 2006.

Pelling, Christopher. *Literary Texts and the Greek Historian.* London: Routledge, 2000.

Peradotto, John, and J.P. Sullivan, eds. *Women in the Ancient World: The Arethusa Papers.* Albany: State University of New York Press, 1984.

Pernot, Laurent. *Rhetoric in Antiquity.* Trans. W. E. Higgins. Washington, DC: The Catholic University of America Press, 2005.

Polemis, Demetrios I. *The Doukai: A Contribution to Byzantine Prosopography.* London: Athlone, 1968.

Pownall, Frances. *Lessons from the Past: The Moral use of History in Fourth-Century Prose.* Ann Arbor: University of Michigan Press, 2004.

Quandahl, Ellen, and Susan C. Jarratt. "'To Recall Him . . . Will be a Subject of Lamentation': Anna Comnena as Rhetorical Historiographer." *Rhetorica* 26, 3 (2008): 301–35.

Rapp, Claudia. "Ritual Brotherhood in Byzantium." *Traditio* 52 (1997): 285–326.

Reinsch, Diether Roderich. "Der Historiker Nikephoros Bryennios, Enkel und nicht Sohn des Usurpators." *Byzantinische Zeitschrift* 83 (1990): 423–24.

"Women's Literature in Byzantium? The case of Anna Komnene." In *Anna Komnene and Her Times*, ed. Thalia Gouma-Peterson, 83–105. New York: Garland Publishing, 2000.

"O Nikephoros Vryennios – Enas Makedonas syngrapheas." In 2. *Diethnes Symposio Vyzantinē Makedonia, dikaio, theologia, philologia*, 169–78. Thessaloniki: Hetaireia Makedonikōn Spoudōn, 2003.

Reynolds, L. D., and Nigel Guy Wilson. *Scribes and Scholars: A Guide to the Transmission of Greek and Latin Literature*. 3rd edn. Oxford: Clarendon Press, 1991.

Rice, David Talbot. *The Twelfth Century Renaissance in Byzantine Art*. University of Hull Publications, 1965.

Rich, J. W. "Dio on Augustus." In *History as Text: The Writing of Ancient History*, ed. Averil Cameron, 86–110. Chapel Hill: The University of North Carolina Press, 1989.

Ringrose, Kathryn M. *The Perfect Servant: Eunuchs and the Social Construction of Gender in Byzantium*. University of Chicago Press, 2003.

"Reconfiguring the Prophet Daniel: Gender, Sanctity, and Castration in Byzantium." In *Gender and Difference in the Middle Ages*, ed. Sharon Farmer and Carol Braun Pasternack, 73–106. Minneapolis: University of Minnesota Press, 2003.

Roilos, Panagiotis. "The Sacred and the Profane: Re-enacting Ritual in the Medieval Greek Novel." In *Greek Ritual Poetics*, ed. Dimitrios Yatromanolakis and Panagiotis Roilos, 210–26. Cambridge, MA: Harvard University Press, 2004.

*Aphoteroglossia: A Poetics of the Twelfth-Century Medieval Greek Novel*. Washington, DC: Center for Hellenic Studies, 2005.

Roisman, Joseph. *The Rhetoric of Manhood: Masculinity in the Attic Orators*. Berkeley: University of California, 2005.

Rosenqvist, Jan Olof. *Die byzantinische Literatur : vom 6. Jahrhundert bis zum Fall Konstantinopels 1453*. Berlin: Walter de Gruyter, 2007.

Roth, Johnathan P. "War." In *The Cambridge History of Greek and Roman Warfare*, ed. Philip A. G. Sabin, Hans van Wees, and Michael Whitby, 368–98. Cambridge University Press, 2007.

Rousseau, Philip. "Procopius's *Buildings* and Justinian's Pride." *Byzantion* 68 (1998): 121–30.

Runciman, Steven. "The End of Anna Dalassena." *Annuaire de l'institute de philologie et d'histoire orientales et slaves* 9 (1949): 517–24.

*The Last Byzantine Renaissance*. University Press, 1970.

Russell, D. A., and Nigel Guy Wilson, eds. *Menander Rhetor*. Oxford: Clarendon Press, 1979.

Sabin, Philip A. G. "Battle: Land Battles." In *The Cambridge History of Greek and Roman Warfare*, ed. Philip A. G. Sabin, Hans van Wees, and Michael Whitby, 399–433. Cambridge University Press, 2007.

Saller, Richard. "Roman Kinship: Structure and Sentiment." In *The Roman Family in Italy: Status, Sentiment, Space*, ed. Beryl Rawson and Paul Weaver, 7–34. Oxford: Clarendon Press, 1997.

Santosuosso, Antonio. *Storming the Heavens: Soldiers, Emperors, and Civilians in the Roman Empire*. Boulder: Westview, 2001.

Saxey, Roderick. "The Homeric Metamorphoses of Andronikos I Komnenos." In *Niketas Choniates*, ed. Alicia Simpson and Stephanos Efthymiadis, 121–44. Geneva: La Pomme d'Or, 2009.

Scheid, John. *An Introduction to Roman Religion*. Trans. Janet Lloyd. Bloomington: Indiana University Press, 2003.

"Augustus and Roman Religion: Continuity, Conservatism, and Innovation." In *The Cambridge Companion to the Ages of Augustus*, ed. Karl Galinsky, 175–96. Cambridge University Press, 2005.

Schenkeveld, Dirk M. "Prose Usages of Ἀκούειν 'To Read'." *The Classical Quarterly* 42, 1 (1992): 129–41.

Scott, Roger. "The Classical Tradition in Byzantine Historiography." In *Byzantium and the Classical Tradition*, ed. Margaret Mullett and Roger Scott, 61–74. Birmingham: Centre for Byzantine Ottoman and Modern Greek Studies, 1981.

Seger, Johannes. *Nikephoros Bryennios: Eine philologische-historische Untersuchung*, Byzantinische historiker des zehnten und elften Jahrhunderts 1. Munich: Verlag der J. Lindauerschen Buchhandlung, 1888.

Shepard, Jonathan. "Byzantium's Last Sicilian Expedition: Scylitzes' Testimony." *Rivista di studi bizantini e neoellenici* 14–16, no. 24–26 (1977–79): 149–59.

"A Suspected Source of Scylitzes' *Synopsis Historion*: The Great Catacalon Cecaumenus," *Byzantine and Modern Greek Studies*, 16 (1992): 171–81.

"The Uses of the Franks in Eleventh-Century Byzantium." *Anglo-Norman Studies* 15 (1993): 275–305.

ed. *The Cambridge History of the Byzantine Empire, c. 500–1492*. Cambridge University Press, 2008.

Shuckburgh, Evelyn S. trans., *The Histories of Polybius*, with a new introduction by F. W. Walbank. Bloomington: Indiana University Press, 1962.

Simpson, Alicia. "Studies on the Composition of Niketas Choniates' *Historia*." Ph.D. Dissertation, King's College London, 2004.

"Before and After 1204: The Versions of Niketas Choniates' "Historia"." *Dumbarton Oaks Papers* 60 (2006): 189–22.

Skoulatos, Basile. *Les personnages byzantins de l'Alexiade: analyse prosopographique et synthèse*. Louvain: Bureau du recueil College Erasme, 1980.

Smith, Rowland. "The Construction of the Past in the Roman Empire." In *A Companion to the Roman Empire*, ed. David S. Potter, 411–38. Oxford: Blackwell, 2006.

Smythe, Dion. "Alexios I and the Heretics: The Account of Anna Komnene's *Alexiad*." In *Alexios I Komnenos*, ed. Margaret Mullett and Dion Smyth, 232–59. Belfast Byzantine Enterprises, 1996.

ed. *Strangers to Themselves: the Byzantine Outsider*. Aldershot: Ashgate, 2000.

"Gender." In *Palgrave Advances in Byzantine History*, ed. Jonathan Harris, 157–65. New York: Palgrave, 2005.

"Middle Byzantine Family Values and Anna Komnene's *Alexiad*." In *Byzantine Women: Varieties of Experience 800–1200*, ed. Lynda Garland, 125–39. Aldershot: Ashgate, 2006.

Stanford, W. B. *The Ulysses Theme*. Ann Arbor: Ann Arbor Paperbacks, 1968.

Stanković, Vlada "Nikephoros Bryennios, Anna Komnene and Konstantios Doukas: A Story about different Perspectives." *Byzantinische Zeitschrift* 100, 1 (2007): 169–75.

Stephenson, Paul. "Byzantine Policy Towards Paristrion in the Mid-eleventh Century: Another Interpretation." *Byzantine and Modern Greek Studies* 23 (1999): 43–63.

*Byzantium's Balkan Frontier: a Political Study of the Northern Balkans, 900–1204*. Cambridge University Press, 2000.

"Conceptions of Otherness After 1018." In *Strangers to Themselves: The Byzantine Outsider*, ed. Dion Smythe, 245–57. Aldershot: Ashgate, 2000.

"Anna Comnena's *Alexiad* as a Source for the Second Crusade?" *Journal of Medieval History* 29, 1 (2003): 41–54.

Stone, Andrew. "On Hermogenes' Features of Style and Other Factors Affecting Style in the Panegyrics of Eustathios of Thessaloniki." *Rhetorica* 19 (2001): 307–39.

Sullivan, J. P. *Literature and Politics in the Age of Nero*. Ithaca: Cornell University Press, 1985.

Talbot, Alice-Mary and Denis Sullivan, *The History of Leo the Deacon: Byzantine Military Expansion in the Tenth Century*. Washington, DC: Dumbarton Oaks, 2005.

Thomas, R. D. "Anna Comnena's Account of the First Crusade: History and Politics in the Reigns of the Emperors Alexius I and Manuel I Comnenus." *Byzantine and Modern Greek Studies* 15 (1991): 269–312.

Tinnefeld, Franz Hermann. *Kategorien der Kaiserkritik in der byzantinischen Historiographie*. Munich: W. Fink, 1971.

Tougher, Shaun. *The Reign of Leo VI (886–912): Politics and People*. Leiden: Brill, 1997.

Treadgold, Warren. "Byzantium, the Reluctant Warrior." In *Noble Ideals and Bloody Realities: Warfare in the Middle Ages*, ed. Niall Christie and Maya Yazigi, 209–34. Leiden: Brill, 2006.

Treadgold, Warren T. *Renaissances before the Renaissance: Cultural Revivals of Late Antiquity and the Middle Ages*. Stanford University Press, 1984.

Treggiari, Susan. "Women in the Time of Augustus." In *The Cambridge Companion to the Age of Augustus*, ed. Karl Galinsky, 130–50. Cambridge University Press, 2005.

Turner, David. "The Empire Strikes Back: An Alternative "History" of Europe; An Upper House Seminar presented at the British School of Classical Studies in Athens." 1995–6.

Ungern-Sternberg, Jürgen von. "The Crisis of the Republic." In *The Cambridge Companion to the Roman Republic*, ed. Harriet I. Flower, 89–112. Cambridge University Press, 2004.

Van Wees, Hans. "A Brief History of Tears: Gender Differentiation in Archaic Greece." In *When Men were Men: Masculinity, Power and Identity in Classical Antiquity*, ed. Lin Foxhall and John Salmon, 10–53. London: Routledge, 1998.

Vinson, Martha. "Gender and Politics in the Post-Iconoclastic Period: The *Lives* of Antony the Younger, the Empress Theodora, and the Patriarch Ignatios." *Byzantion* 68 (1998): 469–515.

Viscuso, Patrick. "Theodore Balsamon's Canonical Images of Women." *Greek, Roman, and Byzantine Studies* 45 (2005): 317–26.

Vitz, Evelyn, Birge, Nancy Freeman Regalado, and Marilyn Lawrence. *Performing Medieval Narrative*. Cambridge: D.S. Brewer, 2005.

Vryonis, Speros Jr. "Byzantine Civilization: A World Civilization." In *Byzantium: A World Civilization*, ed. Angeliki Laiou and Henry Maguire, 19–35. Washington, DC: Dumbarton Oaks, 1992.

Wagener, A. Pelzer. "Aiming Weapons at the Face-A Sign of Valor." *Classical Philology* 24, 3 (1929): 297–99.

Walbank, F. W. *A Historical Commentary on Polybius*. 3 vols. Oxford: Clarendon Press, 1967.

*Polybius*. Berkeley: University of California Press, 1972.

*Selected Papers: Studies in Greek and Roman History and Historiography*. Cambridge University Press, 1985.

Walker, Jeffrey. "Michael Psellos on Rhetoric: A Translation and Commentary on Psellos' Synopsis of Hermogenes." *Rhetoric Society Quarterly* 31, 1 (2001): 5–49.

"'These Things I Have Not Betrayed: Michael Psellos' Encomium of His Mother as a Defense of Rhetoric." *Rhetorica* 22 (2004): 49–101.

Warrior, Valerie M. *Roman Religion*. Cambridge University Press, 2006.

Weitzmann, Kurt. *The Joshua Roll: A Work of the Macedonian Renaissance*. Princeton University Press, 1948.

Wheeldon, M. J. "'True Stories': The Reception of Historiography in Antiquity." In *History as Text: The Writing of Ancient History*, ed. Averil Cameron, 33–63. Chapel Hill: The University of North Carolina Press, 1989.

Wheeler, Everett L. *Stratagem and the Vocabulary of Military Trickery*. Leiden: E.J. Brill, 1988.

"Battle: Land Battles." In *The Cambridge History of Greek and Roman Warfare*, ed. Philip A. G. Sabin, Hans van Wees, and Michael Whitby, 186–222. Cambridge University Press, 2007.

White, Hayden V. *Tropics of Discourse: Essays in Cultural Criticism*. Baltimore: Johns Hopkins University Press, 1978.

Whitehead, Anne. *Memory*. London: Routledge, 2009.

Wilson, Nigel G. *Scholars of Byzantium*. Baltimore: Johns Hopkins University Press, 1983.

Winkler, John J. *The Constraints of Desire: The Anthropology of Sex and Gender in Ancient Greece*. New York: Routledge, 1990.

Winsbury, Rex. *The Roman Book: Books, Publishing and Performance in Classical Rome*. London: Duckworth, 2009.

Woodhull, Margaret L. "Matronly Patrons in the Early Roman Empire: The Case of Salvia Postuma." In *Women's Influence on Classical Civilization*, ed. Fiona McHardy and Eireann Marschal, 75–91. London: Routledge, 2004.

Woodman, A. J. *Rhetoric in Classical Historiography: Four Studies*. Portland: Areopagitica Press, 1988.

# Index

32076007R00142

Made in the USA
Lexington, KY
27 February 2019